The Other Irish

The Other Irish

The Scots-Irish Rascals that made America

Karen McCarthy

STERLING

New York

STERLING
New York

An Imprint of Sterling Publishing
387 Park Avenue South
New York, NY 10016

© 2011 by Karen McCarthy
Designed by Rachel Maloney

ISBN 978-1-4027-7828-5 (hardcover)
ISBN 978-1-4027-9098-0 (epub)

Library of Congress Cataloging-in-Publication Data

McCarthy, Karen (Karen Frances)
 The other Irish : The Scots-Irish rascals that made America / Karen McCarthy.
    p. cm.
 Includes bibliographical references and index.
 ISBN 978-1-4027-7828-5 (alk. paper)
 1. Scots-Irish--United States--History. 2. Scots-Irish--United States--Biography.
 3. United States--Civilization--Scots-Irish influences. I. Title.
 E184.S4M19 2011
 305.891'63073--dc22

2011005368

Distributed in Canada by Sterling Publishing
^{c}/o Canadian Manda Group, 165 Dufferin Street
Toronto, Ontario, Canada M6K 3H6
Distributed in the United Kingdom by GMC Distribution Services
Castle Place, 166 High Street, Lewes, East Sussex, England BN7 1XU
Distributed in Australia by Capricorn Link (Australia) Pty. Ltd.
P.O. Box 704, Windsor, NSW 2756, Australia

For information about custom editions, special sales, and premium and corporate purchases, please contact Sterling Special Sales at 800-805-5489 or specialsales@sterlingpublishing.com.

Manufactured in the United States of America

2 4 6 8 10 9 7 5 3 1

www.sterlingpublishing.com

Le Adrian, mo ghrá, mo solas, mo chuid den tsaol

CONTENTS

"*Every Irishman—and that means anyone with one drop of Irish blood—sooner or later makes a pilgrimage to the home of his ancestors. I have just made such a pilgrimage. I am half Irish, the rest of my blood being watered down with German and Massachusetts English. But Irish blood doesn't water down very well; the strain must be very strong.*"

—John Steinbeck in
America and Americans and Selected Nonfiction, 2003

PREFACE

They've had a litany of names. In Ireland they're called Ulster-Scots, Ulstermen, Northerners, Ulster Protestants, Presbyterians, Unionists. In America they were called Irish until the mid-1800s, when the Catholic Irish arrived. Given the animosity between the two peoples, those who traveled from the north of Ireland changed their name to Scotch-Irish to distinguish themselves from their old foes. When it became widely known that Scotch was a whiskey, they became Scots-Irish.

They are a race of people whose genome is part Irish, part Pictish, with strains of as many as nine other ancient European tribes. After the fall of the Roman Empire they were known simply as Scottish, but when some families moved to Ireland during the Plantation of Ulster in the early 1600s, their history and experience in Ireland shaped their character in a manner different from those who stayed in Scotland. In the hostile landscape of northern Ireland they developed a new sense of independence, fortitude, stern work ethic, and an early system of democracy.

After more than a hundred years living in the province of Ulster in the north of Ireland, these Ulster-Scots or Irish Presbyterians began immigrating to America in the early 1700s. They settled the frontier, intermarried with other migrants, imbued the national character with their own nature and values, and, arguably, became the most patriotic of all Americans. They provided American icons like Davy Crockett, literary giants from Mark Twain to Stephen King, American warriors from Sam Houston to George Patton. They invented NASCAR—the biggest spectator sport in America—and provided more than twenty presidents.

An estimated 250,000 traveled the ocean to the New World, and some scholars include an additional 150,000 that landed in the early nineteenth century. By 2008 an estimated 36.3 million Americans reported "Irish" ancestry; another 3.5 million people identified themselves more specifically with "Scots-Irish" ancestry. In the South, one can't swing a muskrat without hitting a Scots-Irishman, but outside the South they are little known. While "Irish" became synonymous with Irish Catholic, these "Scots-Irish" remained proud, independent-minded, self-reliant Presbyterians.

Call them what you will— they are the little-lauded *Other* Irish.

CHAPTER 1

INVASION OF THE OTHER IRISH

— two years after "The '15"

No sooner had the brigantine *Friends' Goodwill* left the port of Larne in northern Ireland for Boston in 1717, than she sailed into winds shrieking out of the north. Gray clouds covered the sky and turned the ocean to blackness. Hundreds of passengers heaved as the ship rocked and waves crashed onto the deck. A low rumble of thunder was followed by a tremendous flash of lightning. The wind tore at the topsails; the mainsails ripped apart even as the sailors scrambled to lower them. A deluge fell from the sky. All hands grabbed buckets and spent five hours frantically bailing the ship out.

"Chests, barrels, boxes, trunks, kettles, pots, pans and in fact every moveable article were tossed about in all directions," one migrant wrote of his voyage. "This and the darkness that prevailed caused such a scene . . . men women and children call for relief and cry most earnestly for God to send them help. . . . Not a single passenger on board but conceived they had only a few minutes to spend this side of eternity."[1]

Another wind change and the ship was bombarded by waves that rose to half-mast. This majestic ship that set sail with a sense of adventure and big hopes for a new life, was left destitute, her passengers and crew exhausted, vulnerable, and limping across the ocean.

Only a few weeks earlier, five ships had readied to sail from Ireland's northern harbors. It had been an exciting week of preparation for hundreds of families who packed up and took their leave of what was said to be one of the loveliest districts in Ireland. Their tiny hamlet was gently lapped by the silvery waves along the Atlantic shoreline. Little whitewashed cottages dotted the rolling mountains. Inside there was only a simple bed, a few iron pots, a basket of potatoes, and some peat for the fire that cooked their food and kept them warm through harsh winters. Smoke curls from the gable-end chimneys drifted away as the little party trekked along the soft forest pathway and gentle slopes on their long journey to the port of Larne.

A few miles south in Belfast Harbour, hundreds were heading for the brigantine *Robert* behind the Reverend James McGregor who led his flock from their little parish in County Derry. They owed him eighty pounds at the time he embarked in 1717, but he gave up the idea of getting it back and looked instead to a grand, new life in Massachusetts. Besides, America offered a much needed fresh start for McGregor. He had been admonished by the Synod of Ulster for drinking too much. But since he willingly admitted that "less might have serv'd," his flock tolerated his failing by virtue of his honesty.

They passed the five-hundred-year-old Carrickfergus Castle that had protected the northern coast of Ireland from barbarian attack and the Houston and Jackson cottages that stood in its shadow.

Belfast Harbour was packed with people and their possessions when the Derry pioneers arrived. There was barely enough room to squeeze onto the pier for people who were singing, preaching, yelling, laughing, and clattering from all directions. Sailors added to the chaos, shouting orders as they scampered up rope ladders, hoisted the sails, loaded the decks, and made ready to depart.

Children in their Sunday best chased each other around the wagons and pallets. Street merchants sold their wares to whomever might have a shilling to spare. Friends and families cried and hugged and waved goodbye for the last time. There was never such a majestic sight as two brigantines docked in the harbor, wooden decks creaking, their massive sails unfurling, ready to catch the brisk Irish wind that would drive them across the ocean. Adventurers clambered aboard. Robust farmers, tradesmen, weavers, hardy women, and lively children dragged their supplies up the gangway and climbed below deck into steerage, where they were packed in like rats.

McGregor stood on a mount to address his flock.

"If thy presence go not with me, carry us not up hence," he quoted from Exodus.

"We must say farewell to friends, relations, and our native land so that we may withdraw from the communion of idolaters and have the opportunity of worshipping God according to the dictates of conscience and the rules of his inspired word."[2]

Port of Larne.
The Scenery and Antiquities of Ireland, *by J. Stirling Coyne, illustrated by W.H. Bartlett (London: George Virtue, ca. 1840). Image provided by Kitty Liebreich, www.kittyprint.com.*

A bargain was made between the captain and those passengers who couldn't afford the fare: the migrant agreed to be auctioned off as an unpaid, indentured servant when they landed. The captain got his cut of the sale, and after about four years in the service of some wealthy American, the migrant would be sent on their way with a cow, a coin, and maybe a piece of land. It seemed as good a way as any to get to the New World.

Transporting indentured servants was a lucrative business that attracted a new menace to the pier. Rural youths who dreamt of sailing away on a galleon one day were lured aboard for a tour of the ship, then knocked out or drugged, remaining unconscious until they were long out of port, and would later find themselves up for sale on the other side of the Atlantic.

For those who retired to the local tavern to wet their whistles, there was another culprit at large—the British navy. Many men gulped down a mug of ale only to catch sight of a shilling at the bottom. It was an old British navy trick that legally bound the customer to the navy on the grounds that he had "accepted" the King's shilling. Without a chance to take their leave of family or friends, they were off to a stinking, poorly ventilated, overcrowded, bug-infested ship, upon which no sane man would volunteer to serve.

In both harbors sailors cast off the lines and weighed anchor. The Irish wind set them off on their grand adventure into the wild unknown, where they believed their character, resilience, and fortitude, forged from decades in the wild countryside, would keep them in good stead.

In Larne the *Friends' Goodwill* sailed with Captain Goodwin at the helm. In Belfast the *Robert* set sail under Captain Ferguson, with McGregor, his flock, and a family of Armstrongs on board. John Armstrong was a respectable local tradesman, but he had little money and hadn't secured employment in advance. He would need to convince a court in Boston that he and his family were self-sustaining.

With grand dreams, thousands of these Presbyterians watched the pier shrink away, unaware they were now confined to ships of misery and death.

From the time she left port, *Friends' Goodwill* faced violent storms and constant headwinds. She made such little progress that the six-week trip stretched into months. Food supplies ran out, and passengers began to starve; they fished for sharks but ate anything they caught.

A menace probably more dangerous that the storm was calm seas. With no wind or rain, the creaking boat was dead in the water. Days of dry heat exhausted water supplies, leaving the adventurers parched and weak. One old lady passed away from starvation and thirst. Her body was unceremoniously tossed overboard to the consternation of her grandchildren.

Five months of storms and dead seas left them wretched, emaciated, and hobbling across the sea. Finally they were driven to desperate measures—someone would have to be eaten if any of them were to survive. As they drew lots, Captain Goodwin pleaded with them to wait; he was sure they'd spot land any day now. Fortunately he was right; they docked in Boston Harbor in mid-September; with one passenger missing from the manifest.

The *Robert* made the crossing as scheduled and had already docked, but many passengers were sickly after spending weeks below decks in dim, cramped, filthy quarters overrun with rats and cockroaches.

These were the lucky ones. On most voyages, conditions were so harsh that the initial terror of the rough seas was replaced with fear of death from disease and starvation. One ship set sail with 146 passengers, six of whom died and were eaten. Pirates appeared from nowhere; they wrecked the mast with cannonballs, boarded the ships, kidnapped and looted at will, then left the disabled galleon adrift on the seas.

"It is indeed very amazing that after all the risques and dangers that people have run," a 1729 report wrote of the exodus, "and the many misfortunes they have fallen under in those attempts, some having perished at sea, some robb'd by pirates, many of them cheated and abused by the villainy of masters of ships [they are] still running in greater numbers of ever."[3]

Five thousand Presbyterians migrated from Ireland in the first wave. By the end of the 1700s an estimated quarter of a million had "run," leaving many to wonder, what was so bad in Ireland that they willingly sailed into treacherous storms, pirates, disease, and cannibalism?

The Irish Raiders

Dal Riada

Since the time of the Roman Empire, a Gaelic tribe called the Dal Riata had wandered around Ireland—or Scotia as the Romans called it in those days—before settling in County Antrim on the far northeastern coast of the island. Before long, their restless nature pushed them across the twelve-mile stretch that separated "Scotia" from the land that was then called Alba at the north end of Britain.

Alba was overrun by marauding tribes. It was dominated by a warlike race called the Picts that had been tormenting the Romans for a few hundred years. In AD 122, the Roman Emperor Hadrian was compelled to build a wall ten feet wide and fifteen feet high, guarded by thousands of sentries to keep the Picts out of his empire. When the Irish arrived, both tribes burst across the dyke and unleashed general mayhem on the Roman province of Britain.

Hadrian's Wall marked the furthermost point of the Roman Empire. The Romans never invaded Ireland or meddled with its tribes. By then the barbaric practices of the Irish clans were legendary—though probably mythic. At the inauguration of one Irish king called The O'Donnell, a horse was killed and boiled in a pot. The O'Donnell drank the broth and ate the horsemeat after tearing it from the bones with his bare hands. He tossed the leftovers to his clansmen, who feasted hungrily while he took a bath in the cauldron.

By AD 500 the ungovernable Dal Riata raiders had gained supremacy over the Picts. No sooner had they renamed the land Scotia Minor to connect it to the motherland of Ireland, than the Picts began to viciously fight back. A massive army of Dal Riata tribesmen arrived from Ireland, massacred the Picts, and elected themselves the absolute kings of the land.

Over the next three hundred years, Scotia Minor dropped the suffix and became known simply as Scotia. The tradition of paying tribute or taxes to the motherland gradually lapsed, and Scotia started to drift away from its status as an Irish colony. One last Pict rebellion in AD 834 became the catalyst for the final rupture with Ireland. The Dal Riata king Kenneth MacAlpin stood almost seven feet tall with long, thick, dark hair, massive shoulders, and biceps measuring more than a foot around. In a merciless rage, he led his army on a rampage of vengeance, plundering, burning and rebellious Pict's town to the ground, and killing everyone in his path. Having laid waste to Pictland, MacAlpin made a lasting peace with the remaining Picts. He married a Pictish princess, starting a tradition of intermarriage that led to the gradual fusion of the Irish and Pictish tribes. The result was another Gaelic race, but this one was distinctly Scottish.

The Scottish Disintegration

David the First of Scotland wasn't the warrior type that warranted favor or respect from the Scots. As a child, he was exiled to England after his uncle usurped the Scottish throne. He grew up in the English court, where he had the Gaelic spirit knocked out of him, or as one nobleman put it, "[he had] rubbed off all tarnish of Scottish barbarity through being polished by intercourse and friendship with us."[4]

Much had changed in the two hundred years since Kenneth MacAlpin's death.

Scotland had been under constant siege from the Vikings from Scandinavia and the Britons and the Normans from France, and by 1093 it had fallen into a complete state of disarray. With the support of the English army, David returned from England, waged ten years of war against his nephew, and finally took the throne.

Perceived as a collaborator, King David was not popular with a race of people who demanded their leaders earn their allegiance. With his long thin nose, narrow face, droopy eyes, and spurious ways, he was accepted as king by virtue of an English ultimatum—make him your king or face war with England.

David needed to make friends closer to home. To that end, he implemented a scheme that reorganized the Christian Church and political structure of Scotland. It had lasting and disastrous consequences.

He made an ally of the French military by introducing a feudal system and making the French overlords of the arable land. The next thousand years, tracts were leased to the peasants in exchange for a commitment to farm the land and provide forty days of annual military service to the landlord, or *laird*. With the support of the lairds, David's crown was secure. The system, however, crippled Scotland's economy for a millennium by creating an impenetrable, immovable class system that tied the peasant to the land and left him at the landlord's mercy.

While the Scots grew increasingly impoverished: In England David was known as a pious king, a reformer, a benefactor to the Church, and a civilizing influence on his people.

"The whole barbarity of that nation was softened," wrote one English abbot, "as if forgetting their natural fierceness they submitted their necks to the laws which the royal gentleness dictated."[5]

The stability David brought to his realm was built on the backs of the peasant. By strapping them to the land, he created a large and powerless underclass. He gave land to the Church to build monasteries, but few preached to the people. Admittedly, the Scottish population was scattered across a lawless and untraversable country. A priest took his life in his hands just leaving the monastic walls, and the Church was not prepared to provide any security to serve the spiritual needs of their violent flock.

To make matters worse for the peasant, nobles shifted land leases around at will. They would put families off the land and give it to another farmer if he could pay higher rent. This discouraged farmers from making improvements to their land or bonding with the land at all. The result was a kingdom of overcrowded stone hovels with holes stuffed with heather to keep the wind and rain out. There was no floor except for the muddy land on which the house was built, and there was no chimney, so the shack was invariably filled with smoke. Cattle were brought inside at night, and this served to attract vermin and disease. The bubonic plague that wiped out about a hundred million people in the 1300s was still found in Scotland in the 1600s.

The 1500s saw Scotland degenerate into one of the poorest and most backward countries in Europe. The best land was in the Scottish lowlands along the border with England, but wars with the English were constant.

While the lowlanders fought the English to the south, highlanders raided from the north. Fights between the peasants were endless, as subsistence-level farmers stole livestock from other farms to survive. Houses were often burnt down for retribution.

The lairds became a law unto themselves. They paid no taxes, so the king had to live by his own means, unable to finance a standing army or penal system. The lairds ruled over their own lands like subkingdoms. A clannish system of loyalty emerged in which the laird was responsible only to himself and the tenants who farmed his land.

Thus wars were exacerbated by the lack of walls separating one farm from the next. When cattle wandered off, the laird was required to retrieve them. Often they returned with more cattle than went missing to begin with, so fighting between the lairds became customary, justifiable, and usually violent. The peasant's livelihood depended on his laird's courage, not on his title. In Scotland, justice was meted out by vigilante nobles who were described by one Scottish writer as "a selfish, ferocious, unprincipled set of hyenas." High praise indeed, for these were the qualities tenants needed to survive and the only merits to which they were loyal.

As Europe in the Middle Ages developed a merchant class, the Scottish remained stuck in the feudal system of the Dark Ages. While Europe built cities, Scottish towns remained filthy mud holes. Life was an endless drudge of farming bad land, beating your neighbor to a pulp, drinking whiskey till you passed out, and dancing to the harp and bagpipe at every opportunity. The annual event for the latter occurred once a year during the "lifting," a period after winter when the cattle had become so weak that they couldn't get on their legs to get out to pasture. All the neighbors rallied to help carry the cattle into the fields, stand them up, and let them totter about.

Eventually ecclesiastical opulence fell into disrepute. Avaricious and unchaste priests left their flock to languish on the outer reaches of Christianity. There was no moral censor. Any money that was donated to the Church went to religious houses, cathedrals, and universities, not to schools or parish churches. Bishops were aristocrats who bought their divine positions, and monks lazed around in grand comfort.

From time to time invaders arrived to break the monotony, but since the tenants were required to serve only forty days a year in military service to the laird, he would just go home in the middle of a battle if his time was up. Even their commitment to fighting was waning. It was a miserable, pointless, slothful life that encouraged neither enterprise, ambition, or self-respect.

The Beggar's Summons

No one saw the mysterious figures creeping around the shadows of Scotland's friaries or heard the tap-tap of little hammers fixing notices to their oak doors, but when the Scots woke up on a freezing January morning in 1559, they found the catalyst that would change their lives forever fluttering in the bitter wind from friary doors.

"The blind, crooked, lame, widows, orphans," the notice warned, "and all other poor visited by the hand of God as may not work, to the flocks of all friars within this realm, we wish restitution of wrongs past and reformation in times coming."[6]

It was called the Beggar's Summons, and it sparked a powder keg of anger and discontent from Scotland's decrepit tenants, who had been crushed under the weight of nobles and clergy for centuries. Two days of rioting erupted: priests were struck by stones, relics were destroyed, stained glass windows and statues were smashed, and altars were ransacked. Two hundred years' worth of neglect, idolatry, abuse, and corruption was unleashed in a fury.

The nobles quickly recognized the fundamental shift in Scottish society. The peasants, by virtue of their anger and numbers, had become more dangerous than the Crown. The nobles needed someone to placate the fervor on the filthy, vermin-infested streets before an all-out rebellion cost them their lands. They recalled from exile the only man they believed could save them—one of the "ruffians of the reformation."

John Knox had struggled to bring the true faith to Scotland long before the mysterious Beggar's Summons appeared. A serious, sturdy youth with thick, dark hair and resolute eyes, he grew up in the early 1500s on a small farm on the banks of the River Tyne in the decrepit Scottish countryside. At fifteen he decided to join the priesthood and set off across the barren wasteland, past dilapidated churches destroyed by centuries of barbarism and papal abandon. It was the first time the youth witnessed the travesty of history, the abuses of power, and the despair that gripped his nation.

While studying, Knox met teachers that returned from Germany fired

up by the vision of a young theology professor there. Martin Luther had hammered what became known as the Ninety-Five Theses to the door of a church in Wittenberg, Germany, to protest what he considered clerical abuses, particularly by the Church's practice of selling forgiveness for one's sins. His theses became the catalyst for a Protestant Reformation that ripped through Europe.

Two of Knox's teachers went to Germany to meet Luther but unfortunately found on their return to Scotland that a prominent Scottish cardinal had ordered them to be burned at the stake. One was burned on such a blustery day that the executioner had to re-light the fire so many times, it took six hours for the poor wretch to die.

Outraged by the executions, their Scottish supporters captured the

George F. Folingsby, The Relief of Derry, *July 1689. On stone by N. Sarony and Paul Marny. Published by James Magill, Donegall Place, August 1861.* Derry City Council, Heritage and Museum Service, *reprinted with permission.*

cardinal in his home at St. Andrew's Castle, murdered him, and hung his body from a window. Knowing they would share his fate if they were captured, the rebels appealed to Protestant England for rescue. For the next four months the band of beleaguered conspirators waited for help inside the ancient castle that towered over the North Sea. They formed the first Protestant congregation in Scotland and invited Knox to serve as the garrison's preacher.

Finally, their hopes were raised when they saw ships sail up the coast— their new Protestant cousins from England must be sailing to their rescue. But as the ships drew closer, the colors fluttering over the flagship were not those of Protestant England, but of the Catholic kingdom of France. French soldiers disembarked, positioned their cannons, and at four o'clock in the morning began a devastating artillery bombardment that eventually brought the fortress walls crashing to the ground. All the Protestants inside were captured and condemned to enslavement aboard French galleys.

Knox had always been a sturdy man, but a life chained to oars in cramped lower decks where he was flogged mercilessly was more than any man could endure. The prisoners were given water and a biscuit daily, fed vegetable soup three times a week, and forced to participate in Catholic Mass. No matter how sick, weak, or demoralized they became, or how many beatings they had to suffer, they defiantly pulled their shirts up over their ears so they wouldn't have to listen to Catholic idolatry.

Knox's faith that God would deliver them from bondage never wavered. His conviction was a tonic that strengthened resolve of his half-starved, lacerated fellow Protestants who had lost all hope of making it off the ship alive. Nineteen months later he was set free. Whether because he was part of a prisoner exchange negotiated by an English duke, or because his skeletal body was so ravaged by sickness and starvation that he was useless to the French captain, no one knew. Knox, however, believed a power had intervened so he would survive. His body was broken, but his ordeal had strengthened his spirit—he was determined to fight to bring the true faith to Scotland.

By the time he got home, the Scottish nobles had already rejected the Pope and the Vatican. They banned Mass and condemned all doctrines contrary to Protestantism. They called their own particular brand of the new religion Presbyterianism; it was a polity that involved the election of elders instead of the appointment of bishops, as was the hierarchical tradition of the English or Anglican Church. They declared their Kirk, or Church, the established religion of Scotland. They formed a covenant and pledged to defend it against Catholic superstition and idolatry. This covenant became the basis for the reconstruction of a nation.

Knox introduced the harsh dogma known as Calvinist theology. Calvinism declared an individual's soul was predestined by God to go to heaven or hell regardless of any good or charitable works performed by the individual. Man played no role in his own salvation, God was omnipotent, and salvation was determined by His grace alone.

This theology disappeared two centuries later in the environment of the New World, where individual responsibility and self-reliance were essential to survival. A society that put more power in the hands of the individual also demanded the power to determine his own salvation. In the mid-1500s, however, it was likely Knox's dogmatic approach was the recipe Scotland needed to pull it from lawlessness and depravity and curb the abusive excesses of the aristocrats.

Knox was misogynistic and contemptuous of the nobility. He tore through Scotland with such a force that even its queen was driven to tears when he condemned her choice of husband. He eradicated traditional forms of entertainment like May Day, carnivals, gambling, and theatrical performances. Except for hymns, there was no dancing or music on the sabbath. The Kirk became the moral censor that meted out punishments to fornicators and drunkards. Within a single generation, Scotland was transformed from a land of heathens to one of puritans.

Despite the Presbyterian austerity introduced by Knox, the people loved him. The Kirk provided a clergy that was dedicated to leading exemplary lives. It provided religious instruction, education, and helped the poor and sick. The people were roused out of their lethargy by fiery sermons. The common man got to choose his own ministers and the elders that represented him at the annual General Assembly. The local presbyteries acted like town councils where anyone could voice their opinions and concerns. For the first time, in a remote European outpost where few travelers ventured and no cultures intermingled, peasants discovered they had a right to be heard, and that fostered a sense of dignity that resulted in moral, educated, and civilized behavior.

Much of their leisure time was spent in the insatiable thirst to hear the word of God. They gathered at Holy Fairs to hear preachers speak for hours and days on end. They were excited into a spiritual frenzy unlike anything they had ever known in the drudgery of their former half-life existence.

"At first you find a great number of men and women lying upon the grass . . . some with their faces toward heaven, others with their faces turned downwards . . ." wrote one man about a Holy Fair. "In another place . . . you will find some weeping and others laughing . . . the parson is sweating, bawling, jumping and beating the desk."[7]

Knox delivered fiery sermons into his sixties. Then on November 24, 1572, as his wife read from Paul's First Letter to the Corinthians, the trailblazer of the true faith that defeated popery in Scotland quietly passed away. Knox had made a great many enemies at court by promoting his radical views that political power was not divinely endowed to kings but was ordained by God and vested in the people. His was the first vision of popular sovereignty to exist in Europe. It would be almost two hundred more years before his fledgling notion that a government of, by, and for the people would be adopted in the New World.[8]

Five years before his death, Knox preached at the young King James's coronation when he ascended to the Scottish throne. He had known the pin-sized head and spindly legs of the effeminate heir since his birth, and watched him grow with the populist ideals of the Kirk. Knox had high hopes that James would be a great monarch who truly recognized the authority of the people.

When Knox died, however, the implacable feudal system was still in place, and the peasant was still at the mercy of the nobleman. Instead of realizing Knox's hopes, James threw off the trappings of populist idealism and reasserted his position as the country's absolute monarch, subject to no earthly authority, deriving his sovereignty directly from God. He even asserted royal authority over the Kirk, but he couldn't take away the dignity the Scots developed during Knox years, or the sense of national identity that became synonymous with Presbyterianism. This remained a unifying force as they migrated during the centuries to come.

The Plantation of Ulster

James's reign ushered in a whole new standard of bloody wars, treachery, betrayal, genocide, and regicide to the history of Ireland, Scotland, and England. As heir and king to the English and Scottish kingdoms, he contrived a plot to accomplish what neither the Roman Empire nor any of his predecessors could do—subdue Scotland and conquer Ireland.

England's refusal to stay out of Ireland was draining the royal exchequer. For all the civilizing influence the Protestant Reformation had on Scotland, it, like everything else, never traversed the Irish Sea. So while the Scots were becoming moral, educated religious zealots, their ancestral Irish cousins remained ungovernable lapsed Catholics, with an avaricious, fornicating clergy. They were still a tribal culture, poor and illiterate, and they hated the English.

Powerful chieftains had crushed every military invasion of Ireland. James's predecessor, Elizabeth I, sent thousands of English "planters" to Ireland to form a colony in an effort to drive the Irish from their land by sheer force of numbers. Unfortunately, each wave of planters was either killed or intermarried and became more Irish than the Irish themselves. It caused the monarchs such distress that Elizabeth I was said to be haunted till the day she died because her army—the best army in Europe—had not been able to subdue her great Irish adversaries.

James adopted a different strategy. With a little bit of luck and a lot of trickery, James managed to capture the most powerful Irish chieftain from the north, when he unwittingly came to the rescue of a little tribe being menaced by the English in the south of Ireland. The chieftain escaped to Europe under the auspices of raising an army, but he never returned. The Irish were left without an effective leader.

James seized the northern lands of the exiled chieftain and drove his people from their homes. With the land vacated, James needed planters to move in quickly. The English weren't particularly eager to move to Ireland, besides which they never proved to be effective planters. James turned to a hardier stock—he granted Irish lands in the northern province of Ulster to Scottish lords who in turn parceled tracts out to Scottish lowlanders. These people had been fighting almost continuously for a thousand years—if anyone could contend with the Irish, it was the Scots.

As an incentive to brave the Irish threat, the lords released the Scots from the shackles of the feudal system and gave them thirty-one-year leases in Ireland with the choice of what to farm. This was an opportunity for which they would happily confront any number of dispossessed Irish. Eight thousand Scottish peasants took their meager possessions, and the zealotry of their reformed religion, and set sail back across the twelve-mile stretch of sea that separated Scotland from Ireland.

Long land leases motivated the Ulster settlers to improve their holdings. They drained bogs and planted crops. They built stone houses and formed small communities where they could meet and trade and share agricultural techniques. They kept flocks of sheep and built up woolen and linen industries that allowed a merchant class to emerge. A man could improve his social standing by virtue of hard work and self-reliance. He could choose his ministers and elders and have a say in local affairs. The populist experiment may have failed in Scotland, but it was taking root in Ireland.

They built churches and spent a full day every month listening to impassioned sermons that roused them to such fervor one witness said he had "seen them myself stricken and swoon with the Word-yea, a dozen one day carried out of doors as dead, so marvelous was the power of God, smiting their hearts for sin, condemning and killing."⁹

A thousand years earlier their Dal Riata ancestors left Ireland as ungovernable, semi-heathen, feisty, fun-loving Gaels, now a new tribe returned seasoned by war, reformed by religion, and economically enterprising. Unfortunetly since there was no longer any kinship with the Irish whom they dispossessed, their idyllic Ulster colony inevitably became a nightmare.

The evicted Irish lived by plunder. Lurking in the thick woodlands and the foggy inlets of the cragged Irish coastline, they launched sudden murderous assault on the Presbyterians, burning houses and destroying crops, then retreated into the fog and thick forests. When the attack was over, the Presbyterians came out of hiding and rebuilt. No sooner were they on their feet than the cycle would begin again. The last days of James's life were plagued by arthritis, gout, and fainting fits, and he finally died of dysentery without seeing his colonial experiment succeed.

James was succeeded by his imprudent son Charles, who immediately demanded increased taxation and the installation of an Anglican hierarchy in all Protestant churches—including the Presbyterian's. When he tried to dismiss parliament, the politicians decided to oust him with an army of "godly, honest men" led by the most maniacal savage England ever produced.

Oliver Cromwell was born into an ordinary town in a remote part of the English countryside. A beady-eyed member of the minor gentry, he was an unexceptional child with unremarkable academic ability. In his early twenties he had some sort of spiritual awakening, after which he devoted his life to uncompromising religious beliefs.

He was elected to parliament in 1628, where he became a vocal opponent of King Charles and the hierarchy of bishops that the monarchy imposed on the Church. When the government promoted him to the position of Lieutenant General of the army, Cromwell became even more outspoken. He thundered against a list of offenses committed by the beleaguered king. When he declared regicide to be the will of God, the government had Charles beheaded. Cromwell stepped into the highest office—Lord Protector of the Realm.

While the English were skirmishing amongst themselves, the Irish had begun a decade-long violent uprising to recover their land in the north. By the spring of 1642 the rebellion had spread through the whole of Ireland.

Reports of widespread massacres spread rapidly through England and Scotland as the Presbyterians fled the country.

Once Cromwell's control over England was secure, he led his massive army into Ireland with a ferocity that would put Sherman's march to shame. He crushed the Catholic uprising and all Presbyterian Royalist sympathizers who didn't support Cromwell or the execution of the king. The Catholics fought to the death, suffering half a million casualties in the process. but many Protestants gave up in the face of the terror that rained down on them. The Catholic survivors were subjected to a draconian penal system. They were entirely dispossessed of their lands. Their religious liberty was repudiated and their right to education denied. The Presbyterians in the north were largely spared, but the tribal tradition of Ireland was forever destroyed.

Cromwell returned to London where he was offered the Crown. As an anti-Royalist he was compelled to refuse but attended his inauguration as Lord Protector of the Realm in the full royal regalia of purple velvet, ermine, and a golden scepter. He allowed people to call him "your highness" and moved into the king's palace. Soon after, he decided to impose direct military rule over England, Scotland, and Ireland, rather than govern through an assembly of the people. England had replaced a king with a dictator.

When Cromwell finally died of malaria in 1658, a violent storm wracked England all through the night. It was said to be the devil coming to carry away his soul. Once he was gone, parliament, which was mired in political crisis and fed up with civil war, decided to return to the devil they knew. They extended an invitation to Charles II to come home and restore the monarchy. Although Charles II was Protestant, parliament didn't know he had made a pact with his Catholic grandfather, Louis XIV of France, to convert to Catholicism in exchange for France's military and political support—the repercussions of that wrinkle weren't far off. Meanwhile, Cromwell's body was exhumed from its royal resting place, and the corpse was dragged through the streets and hung from the gallows. His head was put on a spike and left on display for twenty years. One day it disappeared, to where no one knew, but most agreed it probably blew away in the wind.

Not the appearance of power, but the reality

A Short but Peaceful Interlude

As the late 1600s advanced, the English focused on their own business and let the Presbyterians in the north of Ireland get on with rebuilding their farms and industries. An enterprising farmer was allowed to sell or rent his land to make a little profit and extend his wealth and productivity. This liberty was never granted to his ancestors in Scotland. Opportunity to advance one's social position encouraged the Ulsterman to become more ingenious, think independently, and work hard. Different circumstances and terrain fostered an Ulster character unlike that of the Scottish ancestors.

Farmers grew flax to spin linen and reared sheep for wool. They turned their small agricultural economy into a more urbanized, industrial, and expansive society. They increased agricultural efficiency, which allowed them trade with foreign countries. Mills, hamlets, and churches popped up in the desolate, wet, and windy north of Ireland.

They continued to choose their own elders and have a say in local government. King James I's vision for a prosperous colony was in effect a democratic experiment where small government presence, religious liberty, fair trade, and hard work rewarded the common man with economic prosperity, morality, and dignity.

Unfortunately it wasn't to last.

The War of Two Kings

When Charles II died, his brother James II became king. James II was a rough-looking man with puffy eyes that made him look like a simpleton. Without his overgrown blond wig and his royal finery, he could have passed for a tradesman in the vermin-infested London streets. He was a staunch Catholic, the first Catholic monarch in over a hundred years, and he was also an unguarded ogler and keeper of a harem. Needless to say, he didn't inspire much respect from his subjects.

In battle he was admired as one who gallantly charged into the fray. Like his father, the beheaded Charles I, he believed in the absolute power of the monarchy, so was destined to make the same mistakes. No sooner was he crowned in 1685 than he instituted sweeping reforms to ensure his own security, including the replacement of Protestant military commanders with loyal Catholics. An alarmed Protestant parliament began surreptitiously looking for a credible replacement.

William of Orange was a particularly ugly-looking man with a thin, hooked nose and a high forehead protruding from a massive black wig. His mother had little interest in him, so he was reared by tutors who filled his head with the notion that he was predestined to become an instrument of Divine Providence. He married James's daughter Mary, hoping he would succeed the English throne, although he showed little interest in his queen and spent most of his time in the company of handsome men.

He fought numerous wars against the Catholic monarchs in Europe and was widely regarded as the champion of the Protestant faith, so as heir to the Crown of the Netherlands and son-in-law to the King of England, the English parliament promptly invited him over to usurp their Crown.

William arrived in England at the head of fifteen thousand men. The disgruntled army of James II deserted to the Williamites. The unfortunate James fled to France, where he continued to issue orders to his viceroy in Ireland to rid the country of Protestant garrisons, while he focused on raising an army to invade England and wrest his crown back from William.

The English newspapers covered the events of the year 1689 daily. News of the "war of the two kings" quickly spread across Europe, gaining an almost mythic status. It was an aristocrats' war, but it was fought and won by the common man, who had little in the way of defense except resilience, stubbornness, dignity, and national pride.

The Siege of Derry

The first Protestant garrison ordered to be relieved was that of the ancient walled city of Derry. Derry, a little city on a hill, had been a monastic center since the sixth century. By the seventeenth century it was an enclosed merchant city on about thirty-three acres, surrounded by walls that reached twenty-six feet high and up to thirty feet wide. The only entrances were four heavy, oak gates, all of which were guarded by large cannons. The city stood in sharp contrast to the lush, green-forested hills that rolled down from its walls to the winding River Foyle. Strategically located at the very tip of the island overlooking the North Atlantic, there were few places in the world as beautiful, abundant, or peaceful as the fortified city of Derry in 1688.

Two thousand people lived in the city when the Protestant garrison was ordered to leave. They were to be relieved in a few days by a Catholic regiment called the Redshanks. Unfortunetly, the Protestant garrison marched out days before their replacements arrived, leaving the residents confused, undefended, and at the mercy of the menacing Irish Catholics who they believed would rise up and massacre them at any moment.

The Redshanks were only a few miles away when word of an approaching army spread through the countryside. Terrified farming families poured into the city. The population swelled from two thousand to thirty thousand, only seventy-five hundred of whom were able-bodied men.

The anxious citizens were crammed into the streets when a booming voice sounded the alarm from the city walls—a force of a thousand well-equipped soldiers were marching toward Ferry Quay Gate. The town leaders had no idea what to do and no idea what was happening. Officially it was only an order to change guard, but news that King James had been deposed had reached them from London.

The thunderous sound of the approaching army echoed all over the city. Town leaders were still fretting over a course of action when thirteen young boys, who were apprenticed to various tradesmen in the city, grabbed the keys to the Ferry Quay gate, ran out, and slammed it shut. It was treason. They had prevented a change in the king's garrison. Nevertheless, men joined the apprentice boys on the wall and trained what few muskets they had on the soldiers below. The army halted and waited for further orders.

The Redshanks believed if King James showed up at the walls of Derry, his presence would induce the defenders to surrender. James landed with a force of eight thousand men, to join the seven thousand under the command of his viceroy. It was a formidable force for a tiny city populated by only a few thousand citizen-soldiers.

In April 1689, James's army stood cold, wet, and mired in mud from the deluge of an Irish spring. James rode up to the walls to call for surrender. The defenders opened fire and killed some of James's men—it was an act of war. The message they sent resounded loud and clear: "No Surrender."

James instructed his army to bomb them out or starve them out and rode back to Dublin. The Redshanks built a massive boom (wooden barricade) across the winding River Foyle to the north so no relief ships could reach the city. They set up batteries, stocked with hundreds of mortars ready to fire an unrelenting barrage onto the overcrowded streets. The greatest weapon in their arsenal was the simplest one—the ability to starve out the defenders.

Inside men organized themselves into militias. Several men from the Crockett family helped drag cannons to the highest parts of the walls. A twelve-year-old boy called James McGregor who would later lead a flock to the New World stood by Bishop's Quay Gate, musket in hand, nervous but ready for the battle cry. Others braved the fields outside to fell trees and prevent the Redshanks from scaling the walls. Few of those men made it back alive.

When the order came to attack, the Redshanks unleashed a merciless barrage. Their mortars couldn't breach the city walls, but they could wreak disaster on the people who were crammed into the streets inside.

The city was not equipped to manage a crowd this big. It couldn't provide shelter from the ravages of the Irish weather or provide protection from the pounding cannonade. Conditions deteriorated rapidly. People dug holes in the ground to make crawl spaces for shelter. When the food ran out they were reduced to what one historian called "walking shadowy skeletons." They ate anything they could find. A rat was a shilling, a mouse six pence, a quarter of a fattened dog was five shillings and six pence—dogs that had been fattened on the decaying corpses of the dead.[10]

As the people of Derry dug in, word spread across Europe that the little garrison was standing firm in the face of "treachery, cowardice and timidity within the walls and an infuriated foe without."[11]

Women and children with sunken eyes and shrinking stomachs watched the people around them get blown to pieces by mortars. On the walls, gunners fired back with all cannons, sending out their one and only message, "No Surrender." Months passed. Thousands of emaciated corpses were piled up along the streets. The defenders fired every piece of metal at their disposal; they ate every rat they could catch. They prayed that at any moment relief would arrive. Finally the McGregor boy spotted something fluttering over the tall trees on the other side of the River Foyle. After a few minutes he fired a round to alert the citizens inside—the topsails from a fleet of King William's small ships were visible over the trees. King Billy had come to their aid.

Raspy cheers erupted, and tears poured from their listless eyes, but no sooner had McGregor sounded the relief, than he realized the little ships couldn't breach the boom.

For another month they endured starvation and bombardment. Then one morning they were awoken by the sound of a cannon fire coming from the north. Three of William's frigates were on the river firing on James's forces. While war raged between the armies of the two kings, William's soldiers worked for three days to smash the boom. Finally they crashed through. By sheer force of will the Presbyterians dragged their skeletal bodies onto their feet to witness the long-awaited relief of Derry.

For one hundred and five days they endured the most horrific conditions. But they had stood firm and now were watching the Redshanks retire from the field. Their determination to keep fighting with all they could muster and their willingness to starve rather than capitulate made the defenders of Derry legends throughout Europe. A few thousand citizens with muskets and cannons had beaten one of the most formidable armies on the continent.

Two words were seared into the collective unconscious of every generation of Scots-Irishman that came after them. It became the maxim by which they lived their lives in Ireland and in the New World. Whenever and wherever they were attacked, they marched out to meet the enemy with the same words as the defenders of Derry.

"No Surrender."

Allure of the New World

"Our ancestors reduced this kingdom to the obedience of England," wrote Jonathan Swift, author and dean of St. Patrick's Cathedral in Dublin in the 1700s, "for which we have been rewarded with a worse climate, the privilege of being governed by laws to which we do not consent, a ruinous trade, a house of peers without jurisdiction."[12]

Swift's outrage was shared by Ireland's Northern Residents. The reward for their hard work and industry, for remaining loyal to William of Orange, for defending their plantation against Irish Catholic rebellions was religious persecution and taxation without representation.

The success of the Scots-Irish democratic experiment alarmed the English parliament. The Ulster colony had, after all, been established almost a hundred years earlier to benefit the Crown, not the Scots who were sent there. Now it had gone awry, as English cloth manufacturers were in competition with the woolen industry in the north of Ireland. The Ulstermen were getting rich at the expense of the English.

In a devastating blow to Ulster's economy, parliament passed a law restricting the sale of wool products to all countries except the British market. The British then resold them in the rest of the empire.

The resilient group refocused their efforts into linen production, but, in the early 1700s, six years of drought ruined crops, including the flax they needed to make linen.

Crop shortages also caused the price of food to soar. With no income, they had to eat the seed they needed for the following year. Things were going from bad to worse.

In 1702, the formidable King William died when he fell off his horse after it tripped over a molehill. His successor believed the interests of the realm were best served by all its people worshipping in the hierarchical Anglican tradition of the monarchy. Bishops were to be appointed not elected. This ran contrary to the fundaments of the Kirk that had existed since the time of John Knox. Those who refused to conform were turned out of the pulpits and forced into exile, leaving Ireland without any religious leadership. If a minister remained, he couldn't teach; the marriages he performed were illegal; the dead couldn't be buried without a minister of the Anglican Church presiding. To make matters worse, they had to pay a religious tax to the monarch's church.

Over the next decade, many of the long land leases that had remained stable for generations came up for renewal. Landlords began ratcheting up the rents and auctioning farms off to the highest bidder. Families were forced off the land they had cultivated for decades. With economic, religious, and land restrictions that threatened their livelihood, they had no choice but to emigrate.

"Whoever travels through this country . . . would hardly think himself in a land where either law, religion, or common humanity was professed . . ." wrote Jonathan Swift about the country at large. "[People] every day dying and rotting by cold and famine and filth and vermin."[13]

The cumulative result of all these setbacks was a mass exodus of Presbyterians beginning in 1717. They were enticed to the New World by wealthy Americans in search of servants with the promise of cheap land and freedom to practice their religion. Soon the assailed, poverty-stricken people were selling what possessions they owned or committing themselves to seven years of indentured servitude in exchange for a ship's passage. They marched with their democratic experiment, individual spirit, and unwavering courage toward the ports of Belfast and Larne.

As the sailors weighed anchor, cast off the lines, and watched the blustery winds fill the sails, the cragged Irish coastline disappeared. It was the only home they had ever known, and it was a heart-breaking farewell. They turned westward to the New World where they expected a hearty welcome from their fellow Protestants and Quakers.

It was thirty years since Reverend James McGregor saw a ship as majestic as the *Robert* sail down the River Foyle to bring relief to Derry. Growing up is be a man of the cloth, he saw his flock subjected to religious oppression, economic hardship, and war, yet he also saw this make them tougher and more enterprising. McGregor had hoped for a good life in Ireland; now he hoped for a better life in Boston. Unfortunately, Boston didn't feel the same way about them.

There Are More Irish Than People Here

When the ships finally limped into Boston Harbor in 1718, the authorities wouldn't allow anyone to disembark without medical clearance for fear they'd spread disease through the city. When they were finally cleared, they had to wait until the indentured servants were sold. It seemed like they'd never escape the ship's miserable filth.

When they eventually stumbled down the gangway onto the concrete pier of their new home, they were tired, poor, huddled masses yearning to breathe free. Unfortunately the warm welcome they expected from their fellow Protestants turned out to be contempt for their illiteracy and filthiness. Their children, people said, looked as if they hadn't been washed since the day they were born, and the rest of them were boisterous, headstrong, and a bit too fond of the drink.

At that time, Boston was busy building batteries, paving streets, employing teachers, and building churches. In short, they were setting the city up as a paragon of civility in the New World. They raised taxes to take care of the poor, but poverty became such a problem that they couldn't absorb, nor did they want, the poor, hungry Irishmen.

When John Armstrong and his family crawled off the boat, he and Captain Ferguson were promptly hauled up in court. Armstrong couldn't convince the authorities that he could support his family. Ferguson pleaded that the children were indentured servants, but to no avail. The court ordered him to cart the "Armstrong wife and two youngest Children out of the Province or indemnify the town." Ferguson also had to pay one hundred pounds as a surety that they wouldn't come back.

Armstrong got back on the *Robert* along with McGregor and about three hundred more of the unwelcome rascals and sailed north to Casco Bay. Colonial Governor Samuel Shut granted them tracts of land there, but failed to tell them that the winters were brutal and that the Indians were particularly violent and had decimated every previous attempt to settle the area. They spent a cold, miserable winter in temporary shelters, tormented by Indian raids.

Eventually Armstrong and a few others wrote to the governor for help. They got a few bushels of wheat.

By the spring, McGregor and many of the colonists started looking for a more hospitable place to settle. To the northwest they found fertile land full of trees and fruit and wandering brooks where they could grow barley, potatoes, and beans. They named it Londonderry in honor of the defenders. Reverend McGregor stood under a large oak tree looking out over his flock and, in a commanding voice, told them their wanderings were over. They had reached a "great rock in a weary land," and now it was time for courage, prayer, and steadfastness in the midst of strange people and lurking dangers.[14]

Back in Boston the feeling of resentment had become so intense that in 1729 it was reported, "A mob arose to prevent ye landing of Irish."[15] As word of these hostilities made its way back to Ireland, new settlers sailed up the Delaware River into Pennsylvania to a colony formed by a Quaker pacifist named William Penn. It was managed by another man from the north of Ireland called James Logan, who had arrived in 1699 from County Armagh only a few miles from where the first settlers sailed. A statesman and scholar, he had a soft, kindly face under his enormous wig. His penchant for science and fur trading had made him a very wealthy man.

Logan didn't agree with Penn's pacifism and fretted that the colony had no militia. He solved his problem by extending an invitation to his countrymen.

"At the time we were apprehensive from the Northern Indians. . . . I therefore thought it might be prudent to plant a settlement of such men as those who formerly had so bravely defended Londonderry and Inniskillen as a frontier in case of any disturbance," he wrote in 1720. "These people . . . will also, I expect, be a leading example to others."[16]

Logan miscalculated. By the time his fellow countrymen arrived, the best land around Philadelphia had been bought by Quakers, Germans, and English. The Scots-Irish moved south and west, where they settled on land without bothering to secure legal rights. By the time officials caught up to them they had usually cultivated the land, declared a sort of squatter's right, and refused to move. As far as they were concerned, if no settlers were already on the land then it was just going to waste. That was sinful, as sinful as the ground rent that they refused to pay. They set an example for the indentured servants, who were given enough coinage to buy some land when their term of service expired. It now seemed like a waste of money if they could get away with squatting instead.

"A settlement of five families from the North of Ireland gives me more trouble than fifty of any other people,"[17] Logan lamented ten years later.

Officials tried to dispossess the squatters by burning down their cabins, but as soon as they left, farmhouses would be rebuilt and the land cultivated anew. When officials went out to survey lands that had been granted to someone else, they found them already appropriated by the Scots-Irish and so ferociously defended, no one had the wherewithal to challenge them.

As the new arrivals laid claim to Indian lands, the Pennsylvanian authorities scrambled to negotiate deals to avoid a breach of peace. But the settlers kept swarming in. One official complained that there were now "more Irish than people" in the colony.

"It looks as if Ireland is to send all its inhabitants hither," fretted Logan. "Last week not less than six ships arrived, and every day, two or three arrive also. . . . It is strange that they crowd where they are not wanted."[18]

The sylvan melting pot of Pennsylvania was soon in an uproar. The colony stopped issuing land to the Scots-Irish settlers completely, but since they couldn't run them off the land they'd already taken, officials made very liberal offers if they would remove themselves.

The governors of Virginia and North Carolina stepped in with invitations to settle on a seven-hundred-mile stretch of land in the Shenandoah Valley. It wasn't motivated by benevolence—the eastern seaboard needed an Indian buffer. However, the valley was potentially an unhampered Scots-Irish tract. If they accepted the governors' offer they would have to move beyond the scope of the colonial authority's ability to provide courts, sheriffs, schools, or churches. They would have to live in a lawless hinterland beyond the reach of civilization where menacing Indians roamed at will.

It was an easy choice.

If there was ever a race bred to tame the frontier, it was King Billy's boys, who were already heading south along wild rivers and through perilous valleys into the unexplored wilderness.

CHAPTER 2

THREE FRONTIERSMEN AND THEIR GUNS

avid Crockett and his old hunting buddy "Indian Joe" Hudson had just crossed the Tennessee state line on their way to the Rockies for two weeks of hunting when they heard a heated debate on talk radio. Presidential hopeful Senator Barack Obama had just shown up in a small town in southwest Virginia promising that if elected he would not to take their shotguns, rifles, or handguns away. The issue seemed so important to the senator's campaign that he climbed into the Appalachians with his sleeves rolled up, looking like your average guy, trying to convince a den of Second Amendment diehards that he respected their right to bear arms.

The two old Tennessean boys, who were hauling a truckload of camping gear, dry ice, rifles, and ammunition for a week's hunting in the Rockies knew the presidential nominee needed to chip off part of the Southern vote to win the White House, and he couldn't do that if Southerners thought he was going to confiscate their guns. Every election year it was the same old thing, and they never could quite figure out what all the fuss was about.

"People down here are attached to their guns because they've grown up close to the earth," said Crockett, the six-and-a-half-foot-tall descendent of an American legend, who strode around his truck with a Stetson and a Weatherby 300. "They know that food doesn't grow shrink-wrapped on trees."[1]

Indian Joe nodded. Joe isn't a real Indian; he got that nickname because he can track as good as any Indian Crockett ever met. He's a sturdy hunter of Scots-Irish Presbyterian stock, sixty-eight, but "in the woods or on the water he is twenty-eight," Crockett boasted. Indian Joe fought a fair few forest fires with the combined federal agency firefighting team in his day. The two men were neighbors and hunting buddies for years.

Elk hunting in the mountain woods of northwest Wyoming. (New York : Underwood & Underwood, ca. 1904.) Courtesy of the Library of Congress.

When they got to the campsite in western Montana, Crockett's old friend, A.J. Smith, an eighty-year-old retired factory worker from Chattanooga, was sitting in front of the cook stove eating bacon and beans out of a battered old black pot. A.J. is a tough, wiry mountain man and has been hunting his whole life.

Crockett unloaded his truck. The sun was setting over the Rockies, and he could see snow glistening on the mountain peaks. It was still cool, but the sky was clear and the ground was dry. They passed around bottles of Tennessee Sour Mash, "Jack Daniels and George Dickel" that they bring on hunts for medicinal purposes like "hurt feelings" and "bad luck," and of course, to celebrate "good luck."

Before dawn the next day, they drank coffee that could strip paint, took their water, rifles, and ammunition, and saddled up. They weren't an hour into the steep dirt trails of the forest when A.J.'s horse bucked him off the side of the mountain. The horse stumbled and rolled over him; Crockett and Indian Joe could hear his ribs cracking from ten feet away. They hoisted him out and carried him back to base camp, where they tried to figure out how to get him back to civilization. A.J. let out a roar—he might be eighty years old with busted ribs, but he wasn't going down the mountain. He made them tape up his ribs with masking tape, then climbed back onto his horse and disappeared into the hills.

"He's just a tough old Tennessee boy," Crockett laughed. "A regular hillbilly."

Three days of lonesome wandering later, Crockett was standing on the top of a ridge. The sky was so clear he could see across the entire expanse of Montana almost to Long's Peak in Colorado. There was still snow on the tops of the mountains, but it was starting to warm up in the valleys. He inhaled that innate sense of freedom he got from being alone in the wild. That's when they heard that old familiar rattle. He was looking around for the snake when he realized he was standing on it. He jumped back, fired his rifle. Joe suddenly appeared out of nowhere, and he started firing. They were both shooting but their rifles were sighted to shoot long distances so they kept missing and the snake kept striking and rattling. Finally Joe hit it.

"Are you bit?" Joe asked.

"I don't know." Crockett answered.

"Take your clothes off, and let's see if you are bit," Joe suggested.

Crockett, still a little ruffled started taking his jacket off.

"I don't think he bit you in the chest! Take your pants off," Joe laughed.

The fangs hadn't pierced the thick leather of his boots. They were both still laughing when Joe wandered off one way and Crockett the other to resume their search for the ever-elusive elk.

The week was almost up when Crockett was pushing through the thick woods late one afternoon and heard an elk bugle off in the distance. He bugled back, crouched down in the undergrowth, aimed his scope, and waited until the animal appeared between the trees. Crockett fired, bolted another shell, and fired again. The massive elk hit the ground like an elephant. Crockett climbed out of the undergrowth just in time to see it slide down the mountain. He dropped his pack and ran after it, grabbed hold of it to try to turn him over to stop the slide, but the animal was so big the two of them ended up careening down the mountain like a toboggan until they slammed into a tree.

"I had to crawl back up the mountain and get my pack and my rifle, which I had left up there," he said. "I opened up my pack and got out my winch, a pulley, and a rope, and I tied him to a tree so he couldn't roll down anymore. And I started working on him."

There was only one way to get that elk off the mountain and that was to work him into five pieces. Crockett got out his axe and worked away till nightfall. As it grew dark he realized he'd lost his bearings after sliding so far down the mountain. He'd no idea where the camp was and even if he found it, he didn't know if he'd be able to find his way back with the winched-up elk, and he wasn't leaving that elk.

"I had a little radio, but the batteries were low and I couldn't find any fresh ones. There I was, sitting up there in the dark with no batteries, no flashlight, so I started shooting every now and then. Shooting in case anyone would hear."

After nearly ten hours of sitting in the dark with the two legs of an upside-down elk tied to a tree, Crocket heard a gunshot in the distance. He fired another round. He heard another shot. Someone had come looking for him.

"I saw the flashlights, and then I was shooting. Shooting back and forth. Lo and behold, A.J. Smith was coming through the woods at four in the morning on foot. Here he is with busted ribs."

Between them they got the elk "dressed" and hauled it down the mountain where they packed it into ice chests that would preserve the meat for the twenty-six-hour drive home. There was always great excitement when they got back. Family and neighbors visited for the afternoon and divided the meat up so everyone got to eat good elk, venison, and sometimes a piece of grouse. Nothing went to waste.

"Southern people are closer to realizing that water is not a gift," Crockett said as his family and friends fired up the grill for an afternoon of Southern socializing. "You go find it, you find the spring. It is work to find game, clean it, and provide food. It is work to take care of the horses and mules. People on farms understand that. They know there is a cause and effect to everything they do."

Out there in rural Tennessee, and throughout the rest of the South, there's a simplicity in their commitment to the right to bear arms. Land is an integral part of their psyche, and guns are an integral part of living close to the land; but how did the land and its defense become so inextricably woven into and peculiar to their DNA?

Forging the Frontier

If ever there was a family bred for the American frontier it was the Crocketts. From the time of the Siege of Derry, when they bombarded a huge army, to the time they sailed out of the little port of Larne with nothing but passion, courage, independence, and sense of adventure, the Crockett family were the archetypical Scots-Irish pioneers. It seemed appropriate that John Crockett, father of America's legendary frontiersman, came screaming into the world in the midst of a murderous squall during their transatlantic crossing, and that Grandfather David Crockett was part of the first available convoy of the great unwashed and unwanted Other Irish on the perilous overland journey to the uncharted edges of the frontier.

When the exhausted trailblazers, with their rickety little wagons and scrawny packhorses, finally stumbled into the Shenandoah Valley, the half-starved days of sickness, storms, pirates, hostile Indians, and wild beasts were quickly forgotten. Their bare feet were raw from walking, and their clothes torn and ragged from pushing through the thicket, but they ran onto the lush green grass of the valley, waded in the rushing brooks, and stared in awe at pine-covered mountains. In every direction there was game to hunt and fertile land covered in fruit and flowers beyond their imagination.

"I believe I saw more peaches and apples rotting on the ground than would sink the British fleet," squealed a delighted woman.[2]

Men unpacked the wagons and built fires and shelter for the night. Others went out to hunt for food. That night they sat down to venison, turkey, and wild honey and got the first good night's rest they'd had in months. The next morning men started hewing trees and hauling up the deeply rooted stumps to clear the land for planting.

Timber was used to build rustic cabins for shelter. They had one door and no windows, so the light and air could only get in through the doorway. They filled the crannies between the logs with clay and poked little rifle holes so they could shoot any hostile marauders. Within months, little cabins dotted the hillsides; streams of smoke drifted up from their chimneys and disappeared into the clear valley air. Livestock grazed peacefully. Indian corn and potatoes started taking root in the freshly tilled soil.

Women got busy spinning breeches and shirts designed for the practicalities of their new lives. They shaped simple moccasins and coats made out of deer and bearskins. This rapid transformation in appearance quickly set them apart from the wigs and buckles and frilly shirts of New England. Almost immediately the frontier revitalized the hunter-warrior encoding in their bloodline.

"The bosom of this dress," said one visitor, "served as a wallet to hold a chunk of break, cakes, jerk, dow for wiping the barrel of the rifle." [3]

In a belt around their waist, they wore the most essential accoutrements; a tomahawk and a scalping knife for hunting and self-defense. No one could go about without muskets and knives in case of an Indian raid or bear attack. Skill with a rifle and knife was essential to survival, and a good marksman had great status in his community.

"The inhabitants of this country, in common with all the backwoods people," wrote one backwoods traveler, "are wonderfully expert in the use of it, thinking it a bad shot if they miss the very head of a squirrel." [4]

Hunting and tracking—skills necessary for survival—became competitive pastimes.

Soon out-shooting, out-bragging, and showing off became integral to frontier culture and a wholly noble pastime. Unfortunately it confused neighboring settlements that thought they were under Indian attack. Maryland passed a law stating "no man to discharge three guns within the space of a quarter hour . . . except to give or answer alarm." Virginia prohibited shooting "any guns at drinkeing (marriages and funerals onely excepted)." [5]

Their wild, adventurous nature was amplified the further west they moved in search of better land and greener pastures. With constant movement and the arrival of new migrants who had to push beyond existing settlements in the south and west for available land, class distinctions blurred; the old order fell away, and a new order that emphasized individualism, adventure, self-reliance, and personal achievement came into existence. Respect was earned by physical accomplishments, not literacy or education or gentility. It was the basis for a distinctly American character.

They built schools and churches as they had done in Ireland, but it was more symbolic on the frontier since rarely were there any preachers available to minister to them. Deprived of a pastor for moral censorship, or even a village to generate gossip that would keep their behavior in check, there was no one to dampen their *joie de vivre* or stop their remarkable descent into debauched, drunken merrymaking.

On the frontier there was always someone dying and someone getting married, and someone who could adapt their Irish family recipe for making whiskey out of potatoes into making it out of corn. Weddings were a day-long affair that started with all the men of the settlement racing for a bottle of whiskey, which when drunk, was followed by the ceremony, then a raucous serenade on pots and pans that followed the couple all the way to the bedding.

"Attended a marriage," one bewildered reverend wrote in 1772. "It was a scene of wild and confused merriment . . . They are much addicted to drinking parties, gambling, horseracing and fighting."[6]

The whole community stopped work to take part in funeral services. Processions up to a half a mile long often followed the body to the grave.

"When death entered their community . . . the people gathered at the house of mourning, and . . . observed a custom which they had brought with them from Ireland called the 'wake' or watching with the dead," recounted one traveler. "The scriptures would be read . . . but ere long, according to established usage the glass, with its exhilarating beverage, must circulate freely, so that, before the dawn, the joke and the laugh, if not scenes more boisterous, would break in upon the slumbers of the dead."[7]

A few settlements managed to find a minister, but invariably it didn't help as he tended to take to the drink himself. Nevertheless a drunken Presbyterian minister was better than an Anglican one and his concept of a holy hierarchy. When one Anglican missionary tried to preach in the Carolina mountains, the settlers started a dogfight outside his church, let his horse loose, stole his keys, and got his congregation drunk.

Settlers continued to pour down the Great Wagon Road and into the Shenandoah Valley, bringing their inherent sense of industry and mischief. Living beyond the reach of any presbytery or colonial jurisdiction meant they could pursue their high-spirited mayhem with an even greater commitment.

The Crocketts and the Chickamauga

In the late 1700s Grandfather Crockett decided North Carolina was overcrowded and it was time to take his wife and three grown sons, John, James, and Joseph, further inland to the more fertile lands of the Watauga settlement in what is now Tennessee. At that time it was a no-man's-land founded on the boundary between Virginia and North Carolina. It was the most dangerous journey the Crocketts had yet undertaken.

As settlers moved further westward, the land became so thinly populated it was beyond the scope of any colonial authority to provide sheriffs, courthouses, or any semblance of order and governance. Most states assigned the responsibility of self-defense to the individual. Virginia outlawed traveling without an armed party; it armed anyone too poor to arm themselves and fined anyone found with a shoddy gun. Even travelers passing through would be fined a shilling if they were found without "their guns fixed and a quantity of powder and shot with them."[8] In South Carolina and Georgia church wardens were required to check that each man coming to church was armed for the purpose of "better security of this Province."

On the frontier, men had a duty, not just a right to bear arms. Everyone traveled on horseback with pistols and swords. John Elder, a Presbyterian minister and a native of County Antrim, carried his rifle up the winding stairs into the pulpit, where he kept it close at hand. The men in his congregation stacked theirs under guard inside the church door.

Vigilantism became the only form of justice available in a land so lawless that men were murdered, women raped, homes burned, people tortured, and eyes gouged out for the simple failure to repay a debt.

"Delinquents of the worst species have been shot," one traveler reported after seeing forty men ride out to mete out some frontier justice. "After which their heads have been stuck on poles, to deter others from following their example."[9]

When vigilantism took on the semblance of mob rule, settlers agreed some sort of local governance had to be established. Leaders were elected based on qualities of personal courage, a strong Protestant work ethic, and an independent spirit. The Crockett patriarch was such a man.

Grandfather Crockett helped form the Watauga Association to establish local government and a well-regulated militia. Two of the first men to volunteer were John and Joseph Crockett, but everyone was required to be armed and ready to serve. It was a simple association created by a group of uneducated Scots-Irish who created and extended the rights and privileges of self-government to all its citizens. It was lauded as the first free and independent community on the continent. Unfortunately, they soon discovered the land they thought was under Virginian jurisdiction was in fact owned by the Indian and therefore outside the scope of any colonial treaty.

"He settled there under dangerous circumstances, both to himself and his family," grandson Davy Crockett understated later, "as the country was full of Indians, who were at that time very troublesome."[10]

The Indians started sending small raiding parties to surprise settlers in their fields, scalp them, and run off. They'd sneak through the woods ambushing a lone field worker, then dumping the mutilated body somewhere conspicuous to let the community know they were being watched.

"He skulks in ravines, behind rocks and trees," read an account. "He creeps out in the night and sets fire to houses and barns, he shoots down from behind a fence, the ploughman in his furrow; he scalps the women at the spring, and the children by the roadside, with their little hands full of berries."[11]

News of atrocities poured in. One group of settlers was ambushed at a funeral where the Indians even opened the coffin and scalped the dead woman. A Virginian father and his sons were captured; the twelve-year-old was tied to a tree and burned alive in front of his father and brother.

The Scots-Irish settlers were described as fun-loving, kindly people who would give someone the shirt off their backs, but they were also known for shooting anyone who meant them harm. The Indian menace nurtured their capacity to endure and inflict appalling horrors. They fought the Chickamauga Indian–style—as they were butchered, tortured, and scalped, so they butchered, tortured, and scalped in return. Frontier terror mutated into a thirst for vengeance. In the Paxton township of Pennsylvania, it was rumored that the peaceful Conestoga tribe was collaborating with hostile Indians. A group of men killed six of them, then went on to find twenty more in a Quaker workhouse and massacred them all, including children.

Tensions were about to explode in 1776 when Grandfather Crockett and his two sons petitioned North Carolina and Virginia to annex their little settlement and negotiate a land treaty to end hostilities. The following year, North Carolina reached agreement with the Cherokee on a boundary between the settlers and Indians. Grandfather Crockett had found a way to protect his kinsmen. Unfortunately, before the treaty even went into effect, it was violated by new speculators who stumbled onto Cherokee lands.

A mixed group of renegade Indians calling themselves "Chickamauga" went on a murderous rampage through the settlements, swearing to turn the land into a "dark and bloody ground." John Crockett was out patrolling on militia duty when they crept up on the Watauga settlement and killed everyone inside. Ten people were slaughtered before they smashed into the Crockett house, where Grandfather Crockett and his son Joseph fired on their attackers in a desperate effort to save the family.

"My grandfather and grandmother Crockett were both murdered, in their own house," Davy Crockett wrote later. "At the same time, the Indians wounded Joseph Crockett, a brother to my father, by a ball, which broke his arm."[12]

The man who tried so hard to make peace between the two peoples was dead. John Crockett had to live out his life knowing he had failed to save his family. Turning to alcohol, he drifted out of the settlement with nothing but a bag of debts and a terrible head for business. He tried land speculation and lost his farm. He moved again, bought a mill beside a stream that overflowed and swept it away. Eventually he bought a tavern near Jonesborough, on the lawless road to Knoxville, where his ability to write his name qualified him for the underpaid job as local magistrate.

One day a brash, twenty-three-year-old, on his way to Tennessee to seek his fortune, strolled into his courthouse and requested a license to practice law. No one knew they had granted a license to the man who would redefine the American nation, to the man with whom the life of John Crockett's son would be inexorably bound.

Andrew Jackson

Andrew Jackson Sr. walked out of his cottage, across the thick green grass on a little plot of land that passed for a garden, and looked out over the lapping shores of Belfast Lough. A mile or two down the coast, the garrison in Carrickfergus Castle was still watching over the industrious Presbyterian farmers, desperately trying to make ends meet despite the trade restrictions the English imposed. Jackson Sr. was only twenty-seven but already he was a respected member of the small community—his cottage a veritable palace, with two bedrooms and a parlor for special occasions.

It was fifty years since the Reverend James McGregor and his flock gamboled along the shoreline on their way to the harbor. Since then hundreds of letters had been sent home telling of the glorious land and abundant opportunities waiting in the New World.

Jackson Sr. quietly turned back inside. His wife Elizabeth, a feisty woman of Presbyterian stock, knew by his expression that he had made up his mind.

Over the next few weeks, they sold their land lease and cottage, packed up their belongings, and bought tickets on the next brigantine sailing for Charleston. From there they joined family along the Catawba River on the border with North Carolina in a settlement called Waxhaw. The Other Irish had been settling there in 1751 after the Waxhaw tribe died off from small pox and war. Unlike the Crocketts, the Jacksons could settle into a fairly tranquil and productive existence.

Within two years Jackson Sr. had built a simple but comfortable cottage and cleared enough land to support his growing family and garner a large degree of respectability in the community. Then, one day while he was chopping wood, he just dropped dead, leaving his pregnant wife Elizabeth and his two sons virtually destitute.

Andrew Jackson Jr. was born a fatherless child in the spring of 1767 in the little family cabin in the isolated Carolina backcountry. Perhaps it was the absence of paternal discipline, or a congenital sense of rebelliousness, but Jackson felt very comfortable growing up around rough people who liked to race horses, cockfight, drink heavily, and fight for their personal honor. He was the quintessential Scots-Irish frontier boy. He swore, chewed tobacco, drank whiskey, was willful and reckless, and was generally the wildest, most uncontrollable kid in the village. He was also intensely competitive: under no circumstances would he be defeated.

"I could throw him three times out of four," said an old schoolmate, "but he would never stay throwed."[13]

The neighbors said he was destined to fight his way through life, but Elizabeth had more ambition for her youngest son. She scraped enough money together to send him to school, but he was neither studious nor teachable and received, it was said, only as much education as he couldn't avoid. Then in 1780 at the age of thirteen, his high-spirited childhood abruptly ended, when the Revolutionary War finally reached Waxhaw, and the British wreaked devastation on the little settlement before it had a chance to mobilize its militia and make a stand.

"Men hunted each other like beasts of prey," Jackson recalled. "The savages were outdone in cruelties to the living and indignities on the dead."[14]

After the massacre the thirteen-year-old Jackson joined a local regiment as a courier. He was captured and taken prisoner by a British officer who demanded he polish his boots. When the teenager refused, the officer slashed his head with a sword. It was a deep gash that left him scarred for life. His two older brothers fought with the patriots and died;

his mother contracted yellow fever tending to the sick and died. All he got back were her clothes. He was never able to find her grave.

In one year, the sandy-haired, high-spirited frontier boy was a scarred orphan with a bitter hatred of the British and anyone to whom they were allied. He never forgot the atrocities at Waxhaw or the barbarism to which he believed all men were capable. He went back to frontier life where he still appeared to be a "roaring, rollicking, game-cocking, card-playing, mischievous fellow," but a darkness developed in Jackson. For the rest of his life any man who crossed him would endure cruel and excessive punishments. He would never suffer at the hand of another again.

During a short stint in Charleston, he squandered his little inheritance on extravagances like a fine horse and saddlery, expensive pistols, a gold watch, and fancy clothes. He also took an interest in the law, and after an apprenticeship, he was admitted to the North Carolina bar in 1787 at the age of twenty. During his first case in a little town called Salisbury, he confounded the judge, defendant, and gallery alike when he challenged the prosecuting lawyer to a duel.

His code of frontier justice was better suited to an even wilder and less regulated society. The following year he set off across the Alleghenies into the territory that would later become Tennessee, where he heard there were plenty of opportunities for ambitious men with courage enough to brave the anarchy that raged along the road to Nashville.

"There is no one here but carries arms under his clothes," warned a traveling French nobleman. "At the slightest quarrel, knife or pistol comes to hand. These things happen continually; it is a semi-barbarous state of society."[15]

Jackson saddled up his stallion, took a law book or two, ammunition, tobacco, liquor, a blanket, and three pistols and joined a little party waiting for an armed escort to take them through the Alleghenies. It didn't matter that it was a party of crack-shots, the backcountry road was overrun with villains and hostile Indians. They'd need all the help they could get.

After some hairy moments and bumps on the road, the armed party arrived in the settlement to find it had grown into a veritable metropolis of about two hundred people and a lawyer. This bode well for Jackson, who looked the part of a frontier lawman with "a tall, lank, un-couth-looking personage . . . with long locks of hair hanging over his face."[16]

He took rooms in the lodging house of the Widow Donelson where he promptly fell in love with her daughter, Rachel, a pretty, vivacious woman, known for her intelligence, wit, and ability to hold her own in any conversation. Rachel was unhappily married, and when her ex-husband told her their divorce was final, Rachel and Jackson married. Unfortunately the ex-husband lied, Rachel was a bigamist, and although the situation was rectified, Jackson embarked on a lifetime of fighting to defend her honor.

Colonial law was at odds with frontier law on the subject of dueling. A tradition had been established during British rule that any person threatened by violence had a legal duty to retreat from the scene; failure to do so made the homicide victim culpable in his own murder. However, in Tennessee the law deemed an honorable man had the right and duty to seek vengeance. This gave rise to regular gunfights and sometimes to vigilantism. It branded the American psyche with the notion that facing off, not running off, is the standard of self-defense and the measure of the man.

Jackson certainly measured up; he fought fifteen duels on Rachel's behalf. One damp, spring morning he faced off against an expert marksman, Charles Dickenson. An argument that started over a horse led to the marksman insulting Rachel. Dickenson fired first, seriously wounding Jackson in the chest, but Jackson fired the fatal bullet.

"If he had shot me in through the brain," he said resolutely. "I should have still killed him."

Jackson publicly caned one man, stabbed another, and generally clocked up an impressive list of quarrels, threats, fights, and other violent outbursts.

"Yes, I had a fight with Jackson," a senator admitted late in life; "a fellow was hardly in the fashion then who hadn't."[17]

Far from landing him in a frontier jailhouse—had such a thing even existed—Jackson's feisty ways qualified him to practice frontier law better than anything he'd learned in a book. With his bad grammar and a lamentable education, he rode the circuit between settlements to keep order in a turbulent society. Every year he crossed miles of wilderness and rocky roads; he swam rapids, dodged Indians, and slept in the outdoors with one hand on his rifle.

Before long his record of facing down and apprehending hardened criminals made him a legend in Tennessee. In 1802, he was appointed major general of the Tennessee militia, the men he called the "hardy sons of the West." He hoped one day to lead them into battle against a worthy foe. He had to wait ten years, but when that enemy appeared, it tore through Alabama with a ferocity that even he had never before encountered.

In 1812 Civil War broke out within the Creek nation. A faction called the Red Sticks wanted to stop the expanding settlements and return to a traditional way of life. They were inspired by Shawnee Chief Tecumseh who organized a league of Indian tribes trained by the British to fight the Americans with the battle cry "War now! War always! War on the living! War on the dead!"

In the fall of 1813 the Red Sticks brutally slaughtered over five hundred whites, half-breeds, and Creeks in a stockade owned by Samuel Mims in Alabama.

As the Red Sticks continued to rampage across the frontier, the Tennessee governor ordered Major-General Jackson to call up his militia of twenty-five hundred men. Two of the militiamen descended from families that had lived within seventy miles of the Jackson cottage in northern Ireland. The triumvirate of Scots-Irishmen shared an ancient history and a frontier upbringing that produced a distinct class of rugged warrior. One was a twenty-six-year-old sharpshooter from Tennessee called Davy Crockett; the other was a nineteen-year-old frontiersman from Virginia called Sam Houston.

Davy Crockett

Davy Crockett, "King of the Wild Frontier," was the stuff of legend. They said as a baby he drank wild buffaloes' milk, and as a boy he could kill a hundred bears in one season and put a rifle ball through the moon. He personified the Scots-Irish sense of humor and incomparable gift for regaling the neighbors with tall tales and exaggerated exploits. He not only made himself a legend, he brought a sense of myth and romance to a barbaric existence in the wilderness.

He was the quintessential Scots-Irish by bloodline and situation. His father, having no knack for business, kept his family in all the grandeur of a one-room, windowless, wood hut that hadn't a decent piece of furniture but had strategically bored rifle-holes for defense. John Crockett carried the scars from the massacre at Watauga. It was into these humble origins that Davy was born in 1786 with no choice but to become a self-made man.

When Davy was twelve years old, his father rented him out to a Virginia cattle driver to help pay off some debts. The accidental cowboy found himself herding cattle across four hundred miles of frontier. When his time was done, the child walked seven miles in a snowstorm and hitched a ride with a wagon train that was going close to his home.

It wasn't long before he heard his father was out looking for him with a "two year old hickory" for playing truant from school; Crockett took off running. When he returned two years later, neighbors said he was "about six feet high . . . broad shouldered, stood erect, was a man of great physical strength, of fine appearance, his cheeks mantled with a rosy hue, eyes vivacious and in form he had no superior."[18]

He was also a crack-shot who won the first prize of a side of beef at every shooting match in the county. He was a popular young man, full of mischief, bravado, and exhibitionism, although this didn't help him when he fell in love with a Quaker girl.

Whyever, she rejected her wayward suitor, he believed it was because he was uneducated, so he took himself back to school. Six months later he decided he'd learned about as much as he would ever need to know and left. He had a knife, a musket, and about as much education as anyone else on the frontier. He didn't have the other two items essential for survival in the ungovernable Tennessee territory: a tract of land and a wife.

A few years later he met an Irish girl called Polly Finley who had a "good wheel" and great talent as a weaver, but his prospective mother-in-law would have nothing to do with a half-educated rascal. The standoff between two stubborn Presbyterians began when Crockett rode up to the Finley home with an extra horse and invited Polly to elope. Word spread quickly, and everyone raced to the Finleys' cabin to watch the drama. Mrs. Finley wouldn't let Polly out of the house; Crockett wouldn't go away. Eventually, Mr. Finley, mortified by the spectacle, persuaded Crockett to get off the horse and get married in the house. A minister was called and a type of Other Irish wedding ensued.

"The champion of the race who returned first with the bottle, gave a toast, drank to the bridegroom's health and having passed round the bottle the whole party proceeded to salute by the firing of muskets from the houses they passed and answering these salutes with pistols," read one account of these frontier nuptials. "The minister commenced the marriage service with prayer. . . . The ceremony being concluded the whole company sat down to the entertainment . . . the room was cleared for the dance and other amusements."[19]

He was nineteen when the couple started their married life with two cows that his mother gave him, a fifteen-dollar credit at the local store that a friend gave him, and a lease on a small tract of land for him to farm. He was twenty-one when he discovered he was a hunter not a gatherer. The only thing he abhorred more than farming was having to pay rent on the land for the privilege. Before long he packed up his wife and two sons and went across the mountains where he could roam around as a hunter and trapper.

Out there in the untouched mountains and isolated valleys, he relied solely on himself and his own efforts. There was no government and no lawman. If danger lurked he defended his homestead. There were no stores to buy food. If his family was hungry he went out with his rifle and came back with a bear—until the winter when he ran out of gunpowder. Without his musket his family could neither be fed nor protected—he would have to cross the Tennessee River and trek six miles south to his brother-in-law.

He set off in four inches of snow with his rifle, tomahawk, and knife. Crossing the river on submerged logs, he fell in up to his chin and only kept his rifle dry by carrying it over his head. By the time he staggered into his brother-in-law's house, he was half dead with hypothermia. It took him two days to recuperate, during which time he ate his in-laws out of their venison, then took off with the keg of gunpowder. The river was now coated with ice. Unfortunately it wasn't thick enough to walk on, as he discovered halfway across when he plunged through. He had to leave his rifle on the far bank, wade across with powder over his head, and then go back for his rifle. Afterward he wondered, "how much a body could suffer and not die."

While he was out in the wilderness, the local village fell into a state of complete lawlessness. Settlers decided it was time to form a local government and a penal system and offered the job of chief magistrate to the only literate marksman they knew. The Crocketts were lured out of their stark isolation and rejoined the community.

"We lived in the backwoods and didn't profess to know much and no doubt used many wrong words. But we met and appointed magistrates and constables to keep order," Crockett wrote. "We didn't fix any laws for them though; for we supposed they would know law enough whoever they might be; and so we left it to themselves to fix the laws."[20]

Crockett took to fixing his own laws with the alacrity of an exhibitionist, with a fertile imagination and flair for the dramatic. When debtors were dragged up before him for trial, he threatened to have them executed to "scare the debt out of them." He sent hog thieves outside for a whipping. He became popular in the community as an honest, respectable, pleasant, unexpectedly good-humored magistrate.

The attack on Fort Mims in the summer of 1813 put an end to Crockett's colorful existence in the relentless mayhem of the frontier. He signed up for ninety days' service with the Tennessee militia and was sent with a group of other woodsmen on a scouting expedition deep into Creek territory. They learned that a large Creek war party was on its way to the main Tennessee force under Jackson. Crockett and his men set off on a sixty-five-mile trek to warn the general. He was also about to meet another kinsman from the craggy shores of Carrickfergus, a young ensign who had taken up arms and was already on the march in response to Jackson's call for vengeance.

Sam Houston

When the Houstons first left their patch of land in the northeast corner of Ireland and sailed to Virginia in 1735, they were probably the only settlers whose nerves weren't set on edge by the strange noises emanating from the surrounding woodlands. The Houstons' little farm stood in the shadow of the centuries-old Ballyboley Forest. Trees bowed over dirt paths and undergrowth twined thickly so that no sunlight could penetrate; shrieking, loud flapping, and moaning were regularly heard. Strangers who unwittingly wandered along its dark paths disappeared into the "otherworld" and were never seen again.

The Houstons were a hardy Presbyterian family with a staunch Protestant work ethic who had settled in a remote corner of Virginia at a crossroads about seven miles east of Lexington. They arrived, unpacked, cleared fields, and built a home. Sixty years later, when Sam Houston was born, the sleepy Virginia backwoods hadn't changed. There was a limitless expanse of land to farm as long as they had manpower and tools. As soon as the children were old enough, they were sent out into the fields to plow and harvest. If they had time to play, then they had time to do extra chores. During the winter, they would get a month or two of schooling to learn some rudimentary reading and arithmetic. It was a scholarly career that lasted all of six months. Despite his lack of childhood fun and education, Sam had a keen imagination and read whatever he could find, particularly accounts of the Trojan wars and exploits of Achilles in the *Iliad*.

Houston Sr. was a tall, powerful man and said to be as brave as a lion. He was a hardworking farmer and a responsible father, but his real love was soldiering. He was a rifleman during the Revolutionary War and stayed in the militia after the fighting ended, only to die "in the harness" during annual training when Sam was only thirteen. The Widow Houston, a feisty woman of Scots-Irish stock, tied her possessions onto a packhorse, took a shotgun and eight children, and set off on foot for the cheap fertile land about eight miles from the Tennessee River where they cleared forest land and started over.

Houston was like his father. His slightly cheeky grin hinted at his adventurous streak, and his drowsy eyelids gave the impression he was either deep in thought or keeping some mischievous secret. He was far more interested in tracking, hunting, and foraging in the backwoods than in tilling the land. Across the Tennessee River he could see the little wigwams of an Indian settlement. He watched the men go hunting, the children running with all the freedom and adventure that he wanted.

By the time he was fifteen, his brothers had grown tired of his forays into the backwoods while they did all the work. A huge argument broke out when the four older boys ganged up on the young Houston and packed him off to a job in the local country store. Not long after, Houston disappeared. The Widow Houston sent her sons out to find her baby boy. They spotted him across the river with the Cherokees, roaming in and out of wigwams, dressed up like a warrior with moccasins and a bow and arrow. He had a new name, "The Raven," given to him by his newly adopted father, Chief Oolooteka.

The Houston boys crossed the river to bring their annoying little brother home, but they couldn't get him out of Chief Oolooteka's wigwam. He said he preferred measuring deer tracks to tape and the wild liberty of the Red Men better than the tyranny of his own brothers. Eventually they gave up and left him there, convinced he'd either end up an Indian chief or die in a madhouse.

Like Crockett, Houston cherished freedom and independence. He loved how roaming the land fostered man's independent nature. For the next three years, Houston lived with the Cherokee, returning home only if he needed some clothes, which his mother dutifully spun, or to buy items from the store he'd earlier abandoned. He brought trinkets and treasures from across the river, but trading didn't pay his bill. Eventually he ran up a debt of a hundred dollars, and the store owner told him it was time to pay up. A hundred dollars was a considerable sum of money to a nineteen-year-old with no income.

A few days later he rowed back across the Tennessee River and announced he was opening a one-room schoolhouse. The news took everyone by surprise especially since there were no schools in Tennessee and the aspiring teenage schoolmaster barely had six months of schooling himself, but Houston had spent hours poring over dog-eared copies of classic literature in his wigwam and developed complete faith in his ability to teach.

A handful of children showed up on the first day and so he got to work.

Gradually a few more trickled in, and before the year was out, his class was full, the children were learning, and his debt was paid off.

A year later his teaching days came to an end when a unit of the regular army arrived on a recruiting mission in full regalia with banners and bugles and lured the starry-eyed teenager away to new adventures. Because he was underage, his mother had to give permission. She not only helped him enlist; she sent him off with his father's rifle.

"Here, my son, take this musket and never disgrace it," she told him. "For remember, I had rather all my sons should fill one honorable grave than that one of them should turn his back to save his life."[21]

Houston rode away in his tailored navy blue uniform. Within a few weeks he made third lieutenant. When the attack on Fort Mims happened, he was ordered to join General Jackson's forces. The three men from the northeast corner of Ireland were about to meet, appropriately, in battle.

The Creek War

The winter march of the twenty-five hundred changed the landscape of the frontier. Small tribes scattered in the shadow of Jackson's army, which built roads as it advanced to attract settlers to take the lands abandoned by the Indians. But as the weeks progressed, supplies ran short and starvation, sickness, and freezing weather plagued the army. Jackson was relentless—driven by force of will, a thirst for vengeance, and his conviction that there was a redcoat behind every Indian attack.

With the army faltering from hunger, Crockett went out to hunt for food and sent a stampede of hogs into the cavalry camp. The men grabbed their rifles and opened fire on all the pigs and a stray cow that had tagged along. They ate well for a week. By November they came upon a Red Stick village called Tallushatchee. Jackson surrounded the town, and, when the warriors ran out to attack the Tennessee militia, his men opened fire in all directions, killing anything that moved.

When the massacre of Tallushatchee was over, they found charcoaled bodies lying in the ashes of a cabin that caught fire. A half-burned boy was still alive, silently watching, refusing to beg for help. Dogs feasted on the mangled bodies of their masters. Even for soldiers, it was a revolting scene.

"We shot them like dogs," Crockett said with shame.[22]

HOUSTON PIERCED WITH AN ARROW.

Houston pierced with an arrow. Courtesy of Texas State Library and Archives Commission.

A baby was found in his dead mother's arms and was brought to Jackson. In some momentary fit of compassion for the young orphan, he sent him back to Rachel to be adopted. It didn't matter that he'd been orphaned on Jackson's orders, as far as the general was concerned, the slaughter of Tallushatchee was atonement for Fort Mims.

Jackson fell back to Fort Strother in December to wait for reinforcements. Eight hundred Cherokee warriors rode into camp under the leadership of Chief Junaluska to join the fight on the side of the Americans. In February, Houston arrived with a unit of infantrymen.

Crockett was sent to join a regiment hunting for Creeks who'd escaped into the Florida swamps. While they were scouting, some Indian fighters from his unit befriended two Creeks who were out hunting. The Indian fighters with Crockett's unit murdered and beheaded them, and in some bizarre sort of ritual, took turns striking the severed heads with their war clubs. Crockett was losing the stomach for the campaign.

Back in Alabama, the Red Sticks spent the winter fortifying themselves on a small wooded peninsula on the Tallapoosa River. To the back of them was the wide twisting river; to the front they built an impenetrable log barricade. Meanwhile Jackson's army was training hard for the vicious battle ahead. In March, they mobilized and descended on the fortified peninsula where Jackson realized the enemy would be almost impossible to dislodge.

"This bend which resembles in its curvature that of a horse-shoe, includes, I conjecture, eighty or a hundred acres. The River immediately around it, is deep, & somewhat upwards of a hundred yards wide," he wrote with respect. "As a situation for defense it was selected with judgment, & improved with great industry and art."[23]

March 27 began with the roaring of a two-hour-long artillery barrage that did little damage to the Red Stick fortification. They needed to storm the barricade, but an assault would be suicide. Jackson's ally, Chief Junaluska, and a dozen Cherokee warriors devised another strategy—they swam to where the Red Stick canoes were moored and maneuvered them to the opposite bank, thus destroying the Creek escape plan and providing Jackson with a diversion. A frontal bayonet attack was ordered. Even with the Cherokee diversion, a hail of arrows rained down on the Tennesseans, pushing them back and inflicting massive casualties. Suddenly the twenty-one-year-old Houston appeared at the top of the barricade. Encouraged by his success, the other soldiers scaled the walls and swarmed over the Creeks in a vicious hand-to-hand battle.

Suddenly an arrow struck Houston in his thigh. He called for a lieutenant to pull it out. Lying on the blood-splattered muddy ground, surrounded by the yells of soldiers, the screams of the dying, and the crack of gunshots, the officer tried twice to wrench out the deeply lodged arrow.

"Try again," Houston shouted at him, "and if you fail this time, I will smite you to the earth."[24]

The lieutenant took firm hold of the arrow and ripped it from Houston's leg. With blood pumping from the wound, Houston had to leave the field to have it bound. It was then Jackson saw Creeks escaping across the river and called for volunteers to storm the ravine. Houston, his wound dressed, jumped to his feet and called his men to action. He plunged forward at the head of his unit, taking two bullets in the arm.

The battle raged for five hours. Hundreds of Creeks were bayoneted; others were shot as they tried to swim across the river. When the firing stopped, the butchered bodies of nine hundred Red Stick warriors were strewn on the ground or floating on the river. Soldiers desecrated the war-painted bodies of two prophets by cutting strips from their skin to make harnesses. Others took a body count by cutting the noses off the dead.

Jackson went on to burn sixty Creek villages and kill thousands of villagers with such ferocity that within a month the Creek Nation was in ruins and forced to surrender.

"I am in your power . . . my people are all gone," the Creek Chief Red Eagle told Jackson. "I can do no more but weep over the misfortunes of my nation."[25]

Thirty-five other tribes who feared Jackson's march of terror signed the Treaty of Fort Jackson and ceded twenty million acres of prime fertile land to the Americans. The Creek War was over, but the destructive effect of the treaty would not be fully felt by the Indians for another twenty years.

The Backwoodsmen Go to Congress

Jackson came home to find himself the most popular man in Tennessee. He was given the commission of major general in the army of the United States—the highest army rank in the country. He next clocked up two terms in Congress, a seat in the Senate, and six years on the Tennessee State Supreme Court. By 1824 he was preparing a presidential campaign.

Crockett went back to his farm predicting Jackson would "shine conspicuous." He became involved in local affairs and won a seat in the state legislature as an honest frontiersman who knew very little about government and had never read a newspaper or seen a public document.

Houston was appointed a United States agent to the Cherokees. In full Cherokee regalia, he represented them in Washington when treaties were breached, land payments were not made, or reservation boundaries not respected. He took Jackson's place as major general of the Tennessee militia, and in 1823 at thirty years of age, he won a seat in Congress as another rough-hewn man of the people.

The three ill-educated descendents from the north of Ireland, reared on the lawless frontier, born into households of meager means, and baptized in war, were becoming the most powerful men in Washington.

Jackson and Crockett quickly discovered they were politically at odds when Crockett proposed that all Tennessee lands be given directly to the people or to the squatters living on them. Jackson opposed him, siding with those who maintained the land should be sold and the money used to build schools. Crockett claimed that was a wasted effort since his constituents weren't likely to go to school anyway. Jackson proposed increased tariffs and a standing army. Crockett opposed both, but the final rupture came in 1830 when Jackson introduced the Indian Removal Act, proposing all Indians be moved to lands west of the Mississippi, peacefully and by negotiation, but forcibly if necessary.

Since the defeat of the Creeks in 1814, many Indians had given up their traditional way of life and settled into farming. They opened shops and mills and formed local associations for governance much like the settlers. They built paved roads and inns for travelers. They kept livestock, raised cotton, tobacco, wheat, and potatoes, and traded their products in New Orleans. Many had gardens and apple orchards, but Jackson would not consider coexistence. He argued a clash of civilizations was inevitable and the weaker—in this case the Indians—would perish in the face of land-hungry settlers. Behind his benevolence, one of his underlying motives was security. Tribes tended to ally themselves with European nations. The only way to keep America safe from foreign powers was to remove the Indians from American soil east of the Mississippi.

"This country once settled, our fortification of defense in their lower country completed, all Europe will cease to look at it with an eye to conquest," he reasoned.[26]

There was also the simple issue of land availability. As the rapidly growing United States expanded into the lower South, settlers started squatting on lands belonging to the Indian nations. More land was needed to grow cotton, and speculators pressured the government to acquire these territories for white expansion.

Debate raged in Washington for months. One senator said the bill would "bring a foul and lasting stain upon the good fait, humanity and character of the nation."[27] Nevertheless, the Indian Removal Act finally passed by a margin of five votes. Crockett lost his land-hungry constituents' support by opposing the bill on moral grounds.

"I would rather be politically dead than hypocritically immortalized," he declared.[28]

Four years earlier, Houston had left Congress to become governor of Tennessee but when his wife of a week left him and ran back home, he resigned in embarrassment citing his "questionable authority to serve."[29] Crockett came to the governor's office on his last day inquiring about his plans. The tall, broken thirty-five-year-old man who had been a gallant and devoted soldier could think of only one place to go: back to the Cherokee family of his childhood, to the same people he had removed to Arkansas. He slipped back into Cherokee ways. He grew his hair long and dressed in traditional Cherokee garb. He married a Cherokee-American woman, and they opened a trading post on the Neosho River near Fort Gibson. He started to drink heavily, and soon the "Raven" was known as the "Big Drunk."

Houston helped Oolooteka and his Cherokee family divest their lands and move west to Arkansas. Sixteen thousand other Cherokee refused to leave, so the federal government sent in seven thousand troops to round up families at bayonet point. They were not allowed time to gather their belongings, and as they left, whites looted their homes. They were forced into stockades that had been built by the Georgia militia, where the food and filth was so appalling that almost a thousand Cherokee died before they even began their march west along the Trail of Tears.

Contractors had been paid sixty-five dollars to provide food and hay for their horses but provided nothing. Warriors fanned out to hunt for game to feed the starving people, but a summer drought and harsh winter took the lives of almost three thousand Cherokee en route. By the time they reached the Mississippi River in December, it was filled with ice floes—barges sank and people drowned as they tried to cross.

"There was a general air of ruin and destruction in this sight, something which gave the impression of a final farewell, with no going back; one couldn't witness without a heavy heart," wrote French nobleman Alexis de Tocqueville, who witnessed the plight. "I must confess it is an odd coincidence that we should . . . witness the expulsion or perhaps the dissolution of one of the last vestiges of one of the oldest American nations."

By the time it was done, Jackson had removed forty-six thousand Indians from their land and opened up twenty-five million acres of land to speculators and settlers.

Crockett went back to Tennessee to run for reelection, but lost to his Jackson-backed opponent—a peg-legged lawyer called Adam Huntsman—by 252 votes.

"When . . . I returned home, I found the storm had raised against me sure enough; and it was echoed from side to side, and from end to end of my district, that I had turned against Jackson," he wrote. "This was considered the unpardonable sin. I was hunted down like a wild varment."[30]

With his political career in ruins, Crockett threw a barn dance and invited everyone from miles around. The party went on all night with people drinking and dancing and enjoying themselves. Some guests stayed several days and went out hunting and sporting with their host. Then Crockett was gone.

"He wore that same veritable coonskin cap and hunting shirt, bearing upon his shoulder his ever faithful rifle," said a friend who watched him ride away. "No other equipment save his shot-pouch and powder horn."[31]

Crockett went in search of virgin territory where he could live in peace with his family. He wanted to return to the days when Tennessee was the edge of civilization, free from government and political intrigue. He sought a place where honesty was still admired and men were free. He searched for a wild land, full of hardy, self-determined, self-reliant Scots-Irish settlers just like himself.

"If they want to vote for a one-legged Jackson man," he said after he located his new home, "they can go to hell and I'm going to Texas."[32]

The New Frontier

When Crockett crossed the Red River Valley in 1835, all he could see were game, woodlands, and wilderness stretching beyond the horizon, just like the American frontier had been a hundred years before. There was no government protection or interference—it was just man and nature, along with a lot of hostile Comanche, pirates, and criminals.

"Mounted on a favorite horse, armed with the trusty rifle, and accompanied by their dogs, they can explore their way through the woods by the sun and the bark of the trees," one traveler recorded. "Clad in their usual homely dress, an otter skin cunningly folded and sewed is the depository of tobacco, ammunition, and means for kindling a fire; a wallet slung behind the saddle contains sustenance for man and horse."[33]

This Mexican territory was rich in minerals, fertile but uncultivated. People hunted for food, cowboys rounded up wild horses, and trappers hunted for skins and furs to sell in Louisiana. It was also dirt poor. For three hundred years it had been under Spanish rule, but shortly before Crockett's arrival the Mexicans ran the Spanish back to Europe and declared their own independence. Not that it made much difference to Texas—it was as neglected under Mexican rule as it had been under Spanish.

The inevitable result of poverty and neglect was complete lawlessness. Gangs robbed traders on the roads, and pirates robbed those on the sea. These new settlers took the initiative to form their own assembly and militia and take control of the situation themselves, much as they had always done. Soon thousands of high-spirited, adventurous Americans were swarming into Texas and fanning out across the land.

"They add a reckless hardihood, a restless Spirit of Adventure, resources and confidence in themselves, keen perception, coolness, contempt of other men, usages, and Laws, and of Death, equal to the Wild Indian," an English general wrote home.[34]

The Mexican government was alarmed by what it perceived to be an American plot to annex the region, but it was initially too mired in its own political struggles to deal with Texas.

Houston knew it wouldn't last. Two years earlier he had sobered up from his three-year whiskey binge, left the charred remains of his political career, his Cherokee wife Tiana, and crossed the Red River to follow Crockett into what they believed was the "land of promise." No one really knew the reason for his sudden transformation. Some said he was planning a harebrained invasion to wrestle Texas away from Mexico for Jackson. It's speculated the president asked him to hunt down some Indian fugitives in Texas and to negotiate treaties with the Comanche along the border.

As soon as Houston arrived, he discovered that after a series of coups, rebellions, and executions, General Antonio Lopez de Santa Anna of the Mexican army had taken control of Mexico, dissolved congress, and abandoned the constitution. It didn't bode well for Texas.

"Mexico is involved in civil war," Houston wrote to Jackson in 1833. "The Federal Constitution has never been in operation. The Government is essentially despotic, and must be so for years to come . . . the people of Texas are determined to form a state government."[35]

Santa Anna was an educated, handsome man from a respected Spanish Colonial family, known for his bravery in battle, his gambling, womanizing, and tendency to switch loyalties as self-interest dictated. Convinced that Jackson was plotting a coup, Santa Anna made the mistake of issuing orders that always seemed to provoke a Scots-Irish rebellion: he increased taxes, demanded crops be grown for the benefit of Mexico, and ordered the disarmament of the Texas militia. These hardy men of the South never had and never would surrender to such terms that would leave them unarmed and helpless in the face of a despotic government. They poured into the ranks of volunteer citizen-soldiers under Houston's command. Crockett joined the Volunteer Auxiliary Corp.

In 1833 Mexico took steps to collect taxes. It was met with a minor rebellion. Two years later Santa Anna sent a hundred soldiers into the town of Gonzales to take back a cannon but eighteen settlers ran the Mexicans off.

The Texans established their own provisional government and tasked Houston to build and train a regular army. He circulated posters to entice Americans to join the cause: "Volunteers from the United States will . . . receive liberal bounties of land . . . come with a good rifle and come soon. . . . Liberty or death! Down with the usurper.[36]

The Mexican secretary of war ridiculed his efforts to build an army out of the undisciplined mountainmen of Kentucky and Missouri. Brimming with arrogance Santa Anna began an overly confident march on Antonio de Bexar in the dead of winter. His soldiers died of hypothermia or dysentery in the bitter cold. Comanche raiding parties picked off the sick and weak, but his force remained a formidable sight to isolated settlers that scattered as the Mexicans advanced burning their homes and crops. The call went out—all Texans were to report to a lightly fortified walled Franciscan mission in San Antonio called the Alamo, where they would take a stand.

The Alamo

The Texan infantry rushed to reinforce the fortress against the Mexican menace. The ranking officer was a dashing twenty-six-year-old Colonel William Travis from South Carolina. With his shock of red hair and piercing blue eyes, he could be seen directing the frantic activity all over the fort. He had only a hundred and fifty men to defend the Alamo against fourteen hundred of Santa Anna's soldiers. Travis was told 630 army regulars were on their way, so the Alamo defenders dragged in ninety bushels of corn and drove in thirty head of cattle from the surrounding countryside to withstand a long siege until relief arrived. Women and children took refuge inside the church. Men positioned cannons on the walls, loaded their guns, sharpened their knives, and readied for war.

On the night of February 8, 1836, nerves were rattled when a thundering of horses was heard outside. Twelve men led by a familiar rough-hewn figure in a coonskin hat and deer skin coat approached the mission.

"Colonel, here I am," Crockett told Travis. "Assign us to a position and I with my Tennessee boys will try to defend it."

The expert marksmen were assigned to the position where they expected the heaviest assault. By February 22 the steady rumble of the Mexican army was heard across the Texas plains. That night a solitary figure sat off in a corner. The low drone of a bagpipe broke the anxious silence. A young piper, John McGregor, began to play a rousing melody on the instrument that had a long and proud association with battle. Crockett joined in on the fiddle, and between them they broke the heavy tension and drowned out Santa Anna's thunder.

"[Crockett] made everybody laugh and forget their worries," a Texan said later.[37]

The last time a Crockett and a McGregor found themselves in battle together was at the Siege of Derry in 1688, when the twelve-year-old

James McGregor kept lookout for reinforcements and the Crockett men positioned cannons for a counterattack. But the Alamo was not Derry with thirty-foot wide, towering brick walls and cannons capable of unleashing a merciless bombardment. It was a small fort designed to withstand an attack from native Indians.

An ear-splitting boom broke the predawn hours the next morning. As Santa Anna unleashed nine-pound cannons and two howitzers in a relentless bombardment, the defenders ran to their posts. It was worse than they imagined. The Alamo defenders mustered everything they had that day, but they needed reinforcements. The next day, with Houston's army nowhere to be seen, Travis sent out a dispatch.

"Fellow citizens & compatriots—I am besieged, by a thousand or more of the Mexicans under Santa Anna—I have sustained a continual Bombardment & cannonade for 24 hours & have not lost a man . . . I shall never surrender or retreat. Then, I call on you in the name of Liberty, of patriotism & everything dear to the American character, to come to our aid, with all dispatch—If this call is neglected, I am determined to sustain myself as long as possible & die like a soldier . . . Victory or Death."[38]

Twenty-two men from a nearby town snuck through the enemy lines armed with their own rifles to reinforce their compatriots. They saw the full strength of the enemy as they slipped past. They knew the desperate state the defenders were in, but as true patriots, they still showed up for the fight. A few days later, hearing three hundred infantrymen were coming, Crockett and two volunteers rode out to lead them to the fort. No one knew the regiment had run into transportation difficulties seventy miles away at Gonzales and turned back. Crockett found fifty men, remnants of different units who had refused to retreat with the rest of the army and pushed on in the darkness in search of the Alamo. Fifty-three men rode back to the mission to take a stand. No more help was coming—two hundred men were left to face a heavily armed foe of fourteen hundred.

At five a.m. on day 12 of the siege, a panicked captain ran into Travis's quarters.

"Colonel Travis, the Mexicans are coming," he yelled.

Crockett was already up firing on the enemy. Travis ran to the north wall when his garrison started taking heavy fire.

"Come on boys the Mexicans are upon us, and we'll give them hell," he yelled.[39]

Santa Anna called for the final and most deadly assault on the Alamo. Mexican soldiers charged the battered walls from four directions. In a storm of gunfire, with artillery shelling them on all sides, the defenders twice fought back the Mexicans' assault. Santa Anna called in his reserve battalion, which swarmed over the walls into the fortress. Travis was shot dead as he plunged into the fray.

The Texans fired an eighteen-pound cannon from the south wall and two twelve-pound cannons from the chapel. They bored holes in the chapel walls and trained their rifles on the enemy invaders. Crockett "went to every exposed point and personally directed the fighting," a survivor said.[40]

The north wall fell, leaving a gaping hole for the enemy to pour through. The gunners on the south wall swung their cannon around and started firing, but this left them vulnerable to the rear. Within minutes the Mexicans scaled the wall behind them and shot them to death. The men on the twelve-pound cannons fired their last ball, grabbed their rifles, and charged into bloody close combat—outnumbered ten to one.

Crockett and the Tennesseans were the last men seen alive fighting with knives, overwhelmed on all sides by Mexican soldiers.

By six-thirty in the morning the battle for the Alamo was over; the Mexican flag was raised over the fortress. Over two hundred lifeless bodies covered the bloody ground below. Mexican soldiers bayoneted any man they found alive. Crockett and six other men were captured and brought before Santa Anna. He ordered their execution.

Crockett was run through with a bayonet then shot. He fell to the ground to die beside his hardy Tennesseans. The coonskin hat beside his head was the only evidence that there lay an American legend.

"[They] died moaning, but without humiliating themselves to their executioners," a Mexican soldier wrote.[41]

Houston was at Washington-on-the-Brazos, where delegates from across the colony had gathered to draw up a declaration of independence. When he got Travis's dispatch, he slipped away to Gonzales to rendezvous with four hundred soldiers who were waiting for orders. It was then he learned the Alamo had already fallen.

For the next six weeks as Houston retreated with his small, untrained army, hundreds of volunteers from all over Texas tracked him down and swelled his ranks. They had two six-pound cannons, scrap iron for ammunition, their own rifles, no tents, no food, and no military training, but they didn't care if they were outmanned or outgunned, they refused to retreat.

"We must act now, and with great promptness. The country must be saved," he decided. "I held no councils of war. If I err, the blame is mine."[42]

On April 20, Santa Anna's army made camp in a sort of cul-de-sac at the junction of Buffalo Bayou and the San Jacinto River. Houston's army was less than a mile away.

At three-thirty in the afternoon, during the Mexican siesta, Houston's army formed battle lines. They wheeled their two cannons into position and charged, yelling "Remember the Alamo!" Caught off guard, the Mexicans scattered, commanders roared orders, and men fired one haphazard volley before the Texans were upon them. Santa Anna fled his tent, jumped on a horse, and galloped into the marshlands. The Texans shot, stabbed, and beat every Mexican they could find. The battle lasted eighteen minutes.

Santa Anna was found in the bushes and dragged out to sign a treaty. The Mexicans conceded the colony, and Houston, the poor Scots-Irishman who ran away from home to be a Cherokee, became the first president of the new Republic of Texas.

Legacy

As night fell in eastern Tennessee and the big gathering at the Crockett homestead started to disperse, David Crockett finished unpacking the truck, cleaned his guns, and locked everything away in the hunting lodge. It had been a good hunt followed by a lively gathering of friends and family. It was a week during which he could flex those traits that had become fundamental to the American identity: self-reliance, self-determination, and a love of freedom.

Two hundred years after his family had blazed new trails and fought for freedom in America with the same zeal with which they fired cannons from the walls of Derry, the latest David Crockett left his pickup truck on the land and drove his eco-friendly car to his city job as Director of the Office of Sustainability in Tennessee. He works on water issues, climate change, and wildlife conservation initiatives, exemplifying the same passion for the land as his legendary ancestor, revamped for twenty-first century issues. But to him the land is more than the environment; it is synonymous with the founding ideals of the nation.

"Americans feel it is their God-given right to be free," he said. "You know there will probably never be a time that you have to take up arms to defend your rights as they did in times past. But there is something in the DNA of Americans, particularly Southerners, that says, 'I know that will never happen, but I damn well know that if it did, we would have the right to determine our destiny as we always have.'"[43]

CHAPTER 3

THEM THAT BELIEVE

"There is death in these boxes."

Pastors bellowed those six little words for generations before Jimmy Morrow took to the pulpit in his small, secluded church in the Appalachian wilderness. Tall, thin, with intense dark eyes, the fifty-five-year-old Morrow paced back and forth like a pendulum, delivering his sermon with the vocal rhythm of an auctioneer, repeating biblical verse after verse, lulling his congregation into an hypnotic ecstasy.

"I am the first and I am the last and beside me there is no God," went his recitative sermon. "I am Alpha and Omega, the beginning and the ending, saith the Lord, which is, and which was, and which is to come, the Almighty."[1]

Shouts of "Hallelujah" and "Amen" erupted from the pews. Worshippers burst into song; others swayed with their arms raised to heaven, moved by the Holy Ghost. Morrow extemporaneously chanted passages from Isaiah, Exodus, Philippians, Revelation, and the New Testament Gospel of Mark on which these folk based their faith:

"And these signs shall follow them that believe; In my name shall they cast out devils; they shall speak with new tongues; They shall take up serpents; and if they drink any deadly thing, it shall not hurt them; they shall lay hands on the sick, and they shall recover."

Soon Morrow too felt the "anointing," that joyous sensation that the Holy Ghost was moving inside, giving him the power to take up the serpents. No one ever went into that box without first feeling God move in a convincing way; "hypocriting" was certain death. Morrow lifted the lid and thrust his hands into a tangled pit of venomous rattlesnakes—the ancient symbol of evil—to prove himself God's obedient soldier waging war against the devil. He held a writhing snake aloft while those in the pews danced, shouted, and sang with outstretched arms; others fell to their

Pastor Jimmy Morrow. The Edwina Church of God in Jesus Christ's Name, 2000.
Courtesy of Pastor Morrow.

knees with their head bowed in prayer. Morrow's incantations continued while he held death high, knowing that Mark only said he would take up serpents, not that he wouldn't be bitten. Over the years, he had learned that lesson the hard way.

Morrow was a hyperactive kid with a mop of wild dark hair known as "Little Rowdy." One morning when he was six years old, he awoke with a strange compulsion to go outside and pray. He left the homestead and wandered off into a field not too far from Morgan's Gap, Tennessee, where his ancestors had been praising Jesus and handling snakes in outdoor services since they arrived from northern Ireland in the early 1700s. All alone out there on the crest of the mountains, he knelt down and repented.

"When I prayed and I repented of my sins, God showed me in a vision that I would preach to millions to people," he said with conviction.[2]

Given the remote, sparsely populated terrain in which his family had lived for generations without running water or electricity, it was hard to imagine that Morrow could ever reach millions. Instead of the rules and refrains of the Episcopalians and Congregationalists in the East, they were beyond civilization, fighting for survival against wild beasts and mysterious threats. The terrain spawned a unique belief system that blended cultural traditions with the need for a daily direct encounter with God who assured them they were not perilously alone. Little else was important, certainly not education; preachers only needed to be called by God, to preach, few had seen the inside of a school, and fewer seemed to know what the word *seminary* even meant. All that mattered was the literal word of God; the result was supernatural encounters and an emotional outpouring from people striving to have complete faith in His will and to be freed from the fear of death.

According to mountain lore, snake handling originated in Jerusalem in the first century AD, then swept across Europe and then on to the New World, where it continued to mean victory over death. There was no single originator of serpent handling; families arrived with the tradition from the Old World and passed it down through generations. Historians had different theories for the origin of the ritual, but the Appalachian worshipper who only read the King James Bible neither knew nor cared for their opinion.

The word of God was all Morrow knew. He'd seen preachers taking up serpents since he was two years old sitting on his mother's knee. If they weren't at church they were at a house meeting, if they weren't at a house meeting they were praying alone. This was life in Appalachia among dirt poor, hardworking people, whose only respite was found in a swim in a creek, a love of storytelling, and the joy of the Lord.

Morrow's face lights up when he tells tales about the old days—like the time their dog got drunk on moonshine, or the time a tornado demolished their barn before it "hit the house and throwed it up" off its foundations. It took them a whole day to find their mule that escaped off into the mountains. There was the night his wife Pam was born. Doc Smith, who was also the local sheriff, was on his way up the mountain to catch a criminal when he heard Pam's mother had gone into labor. He dropped in to deliver the baby, then went on up the mountain, caught his man, and hauled him down to the jailhouse.

The Morrows had a farm on top of the mountain, accessible only by a small trail cut into the cliff face or by wading across the creek in the summer when the water was low. "Little Rowdy" and his six siblings got up every morning, ran to the henhouse to gather eggs for breakfast, then went out to hoe corn and tobacco, milk cows, slop the hogs, and feed the cows and ponies. At night he'd go coon hunting with his father. Somewhere in there he got some sleep and a few hours of schooling. Weekends were dedicated to church—even a hyperactive kid like Morrow didn't miss a Sunday service.

Shortly after that day the young Morrow repented in the field, two mysterious preachers came to their house and told his mother he needed to be baptized. They took him off to a temple, baptized him in a pool with a few other children, and took him back home. He never saw them again, and he never felt the same way again.

"I was the happiest I've ever been in my life," he said. "I knowed the Lord was preparing me to preach. I knowed that God had something for me to do."[3]

He had a rather inglorious beginning in the service of the Lord, cleaning the little wooden church and taking up prayer requests. Finally, in his early teens in the middle of his uncle's service in the small Tennessee mountain Church of Jesus Christ, he heard the Lord telling him to preach. When he reached the pulpit he felt like a bucket of warm water had been poured over him, removing any apprehension he had about speaking to the congregation without a prepared sermon. Somehow he knew "the spirit of truth" would come and he'd know exactly what to say. Not that he took up serpents that day, or any day during the next seven years. He spent years growing as a preacher before waking up one morning with the visceral feeling that he had been anointed by God and was ready.

"I weren't in no Church, I handled my first serpents out in the wild," he said. "I just prayed and asked the Lord for some snakes."[4] He went back into the mountains, found three copperheads, picked them up, and put them in a box. He took them to Sunday services for the next five years before setting them free, but not before being bitten twice. The first bite to the hand felt like "the worst toothache imaginable." The second was a strike to the chest that mysteriously turned out to be painless. Once bitten, only Jesus could do the curing, so the congregation gathered round the injured worshipper and did the praying.

When Morrow recovered from the strike to his chest, he went straight back to church to do it all again. There was no pain that could compare to the unspeakable joy called the anointing, or the victory, that came from taking up serpents knowing that he was on God's side, fighting against the devil and winning. There were legions of devils in those boxes, and the Lord had given him power over them.

After he began to take up serpents, Morrow became more and more immersed in the supernatural manifestations of the Holy Ghost, until one day he spontaneously began speaking in tongues—the unknown tongue that meant he was speaking directly to God, just as the disciples had done when they were filled with the Holy Ghost in the Bible.

During some sermons he reported visions of blue vapor and streaks of fire after which hundreds of people were compelled to pile up to the altar, falling down "slain by the Spirit," begging to be saved.

"Been times where people stayed all night," Morrow remembered. "Singing, shouting, praying, getting slain till the roosters were crowing."[5]

Morrow's church is one of many serpent-handling churches in Appalachia that descended from a long line of God's fearless soldiers. They are fiercely independent and heartily proud of being "God's peculiar people." Yet they are of the Other Irish bloodline that was once considered dour and scripturally obsessed in the Old World.

So why, in the New World, did this "godly hysteria" emerge?

Planting the Presbyterians

"The most serious evil of the colonies was the number and force of the influences which were impelling large classes to violence and anarchy," lamented one eighteenth century writer, "and the breaking down among them of the salutary respect for authority which lies at the root of all greatness."[6]

When they came swarming across the sea, embittered by religious bigotry of the Anglican Church of England and the economic repression imposed by the English government, the Scots-Irish plunged into the great, untamed frontier to settle in isolated backcountry communities where they were alone in an almost supernatural terrain that yielded mysterious phenomena and unknown terrors. They usually built a little church, but frontier populations were so scattered that rarely was a pastor available to preach. With no moral guidance, there was a steady descent into moral laxity. They took to making and drinking moonshine, dancing, and singing. One visitor witnessed people traveling for fifty miles or more through hostile terrain to gamble on cockfights and horse races or engage in brutal fights in which "the gouging out of each other's eyes was considered allowable according the rules governing such matches."[7]

The further they moved from civilization, the more boisterous, ungovernable, and immoral they became. New immigrants had to move farther west and south to find unoccupied land. Many of them moved because they lacked the money to buy land, so they squatted on public territory instead. If they cleared the land, planted corn, and built a cabin, they could then legally sell their improvements, take what little money they made, and repeat the pattern somewhere else—usually deeper into hostile Indian country—until they had saved up enough money to buy their own property.

The further south and west they went, the further they were from the Presbyterian Church that had begun to take root in the east decades before they arrived. In 1676, a brown-haired, blue-eyed, determined young student from County Donegal in northern Ireland responded to the call of an Anglican colonel in Maryland for a missionary. Despite being an ordained Presbyterian minister, the twenty-four-year-old Francis Makemie left northern Ireland and set up a presbytery in a cabin in Maryland, and another in Philadelphia. The old colonel had unwittingly opened the door to the prototypical rebellious Presbyterian and marked the beginning of the end for English colonial rule in the American colonies.

While preaching Presbyterian doctrine without a license in the Anglican town of New York, Makemie was arrested by the worst governor the British ever imposed on America. Lord Cornbury was widely considered a "degenerate and pervert," sunk in corruption, who plundered the treasury and spent half of his time dressed in women's clothes. Nonetheless he had the authority to confine Makemie to jail, where he languished for six weeks before three of the colony's most famous lawyers came to his defense. Suddenly the case of the errant preacher became a high-profile defense of religious tolerance, and his eventual acquittal was considered a watershed for religious freedom in America. Makemie was dubbed the father of American Presbyterianism. Queen Elizabeth I recalled the decadent Lord Cornbury to England.

Unfortunately the swarm of immigrants swamped Makemie's fledgling church. With moral degeneracy and stories of debauched revelry emanating from the frontier, new presbyteries were needed to bring the heathens back to Christ, but there simply weren't enough preachers. The

Presbyterian Church required its preachers to be educated, yet there was no educational institution in the colonies. Ministers trained in the old world needed to be willing to leave Europe and settle on the frontier—which they weren't. Someone needed to educate men already in America and dispatch them to desolate places. Another Other Irish pioneer finally took up the challenge of Makemie's work and led the Presbyterian charge into the West.

The Log College

"Religion lay as it were, a-dying and ready to expire it's last breath of live in this part of the visible church,"[8] wrote one minister about the state of affairs on the frontier.

Certainly the frontiersmen who were accustomed to "braining bears and battling Indians"[9] preferred no religion to the lackluster sermons that brimmed with dour theology that wandering ministers served up on rare occasions. As the old theological order languished, a new order full of great color and excitement was needed if these lost souls were to be led back to a Christian life. Into the void stepped the "Log College" group, happy to deliver rousing, dramatic rhetoric that better served the times and terrain.

The Log College was the brainchild of William Tennent, an Anglican turned Presbyterian zealot, born in Ulster in 1673, shortly after Makemie left for America. With his white ruffled collar and restrictive black garb, it appeared he'd be more at home in the halls of Roman ecclesiastical authority than on America's wild frontier. Yet the edge of civilization is where this soldier of God found himself in the early 1700s after he fled the religious intolerance perpetrated by the English Anglicans in Ireland. He set sail for America with his wife, four young sons, and a few paltry possessions in 1716.

His first inauspicious assault to win souls from the devil began when he was admitted to the Synod of Philadelphia and given a parish in New York for a meager seventeen pounds a year. Travelers who took advantage of his homely hospitality on the well-worn road between New York and Philadelphia, on which he lived, left him barely able to support his family; fortunately his powerful cousin, James Logan, was William Penn's agent in Pennsylvania. Logan saved his kinsman from destitution with a fifty-acre tract at Neshaminy Creek in 1728. Logan hoped this would "encourage him to prosecute his views, and make his residence near us permanent."

William and his firebrand son Gilbert set about building a simple log cabin to educate young men for the ministry that he ran almost single-handedly. It was disparagingly known as the "Log College," but William proved to be such a successful teacher that his derided little school was soon dispatching the vanguard of a religious revival. The Log College graduates went out imbued with his zeal for the Lord and his distrust for rationalists who stressed theology over heartfelt conversion.

One of the first in the Southern charge was Charles Beatty, a classically educated student from County Antrim in northern Ireland. He arrived a destitute youngster and turned to peddling to earn a living. One day as he peddled his wares along Neshaminy Creek he happened upon the Log College and, recognizing it to be an institute of learning, cockily offered to sell William his trinkets in Latin. William sold him on the ministry instead. In 1755 he was sent out as chaplain to Benjamin Franklin's five hundred men who were building forts to defend settlers in Pennsylvania close to Indian country. The savagery of Indian country failed to bring the soldiers closer to God; Beatty complained to Franklin that few of them attended his prayers.

"When they were enlisted they were promised, besides pay and provisions, a gill of rum a day, which was punctually served out to them, half in the morning and the other half in the evening, and I observed they were punctual in attending to receive it," Franklin recalled. "Mr. Beatty, it is perhaps below the dignity of your profession to act as a steward of the rum; but if you were only to distribute it out after prayers, you would have them all about you."[10]

So Beatty started measuring out the liquor. From then on his sermons were "generally and punctually attended."

Many settlements were too small and too poor to support a full-time minister. William needed to find a new approach to frontier ministry. He found the solution in hardy young ministers who willingly went out on horseback armed with the Bible and a rifle. They galloped from one settlement to another, holding services in bars and in open fields. One preacher traversed the mountains with an armed escort, wandering from place to place preaching wherever and to whomever would listen. He found homeless groups of settlers fleeing the Indians, and lost settlements deep in Indian country where men had never seen a shirt or heard a sermon.

Circuit rider.
Alfred Waud, Harper's Weekly, *October 12, 1867.*

The frontier was a no-man's-land beyond the reaches of civilization, colonial law, or military protection. Preachers, too, were chased by Indians; almost all went into pulpit carrying a rifle while the congregation stacked theirs at the entrance to the church. Out in Kentucky, the Reverend John McMillan escorted an inexperienced circuit rider to a meeting. When they stopped at an inn en route, McMillan ordered two glasses of whiskey and proposed a blessing. The new preacher closed his eyes and gave a blessing that was so long, McMillan reached out and drank both glasses.

"My brother," McMillan explained when the new preacher saw the empty glasses. "On the frontier you must watch as well as pray."[11]

And so, having traded their black suits for leather and packed their lives into saddlebags, these circuit riders impressed the frontier heathens with their fearlessness and commitment. Rowdy settlers turned out in droves to worship in field meetings. They were roused by this new dynamic evangelism and galvanized to the Lord's service by William's most controversial protégé—his own son Gilbert Tennent.

Son of Thunder

"I beseech you as a messenger of the great God, that ye awake," Gilbert Tennent thundered to mesmerized listeners, his face red with intensity, fists shaking in the air. "I beseech you as a messenger of the great God, as on my bended knees, by the groans, tears, and wounds of Christ that ye would Awake. Yea, I charge you all by the curses of the law, and blessings of the gospels, that ye would Awake."[12]

Awaken they did. Multitudes ran to the altar to fall down begging for baptism by the Holy Spirit, repenting of their wayward ways and begging for salvation.

Three times a day he delivered the fire and brimstone of His word, thundering from the altar to sound the trumpet of God's judgment and the terrors of the Lord. He became a firebrand for a frenzied religious revival throughout the colonies. To add to his powerful voice he adopted a sort of John the Baptist religious eccentricity by growing his hair long and wearing an overcoat bound with a leathern girdle when in the pulpit.

Thousands turned out to hear him brandish the terrors of God and the threat of hell for those who did not repent before the final judgment. He howled about sin, retribution, and repentance; he boldly summoned his hearers to repentance and newness of life. This fervor swept the colonies eliciting an enthusiastic reception from the heathen settlers and rousing them to a more vital interest in religion.

The power of his preaching ignited America's first Great Awakening.

Tennent was a teenager when he embarked with his father on the perilous voyage across the ocean and tumbled down into Pennsylvania with the rest of the Scots-Irish. He was old enough to see how British religious intolerance adversely affected the Presbyterians at home, how they couldn't be baptized, or married, or buried without an English Anglican minister's approval. He saw how personal, political, and religious freedoms were inextricable. He saw how the Anglican insistence on ecclesiastical hierarchy repressed the common man's freedom to worship as he saw fit. He saw his grandfather clandestinely preach Presbyterian doctrine to poor farmers in open-air gatherings at night. Tennent would never acquiesce to surreptitious preaching. He railed defiantly from God's side, he crusaded with his father's beliefs that personal piety superseded theology, that the importance of being called to preach far outranked doctrinal study.

"He was one of the most conspicuous ministers of his day," wrote one historian. "Ardent in his zeal, forcible in his reasoning, and bold and passionate in his addresses to the conscience and the heart."[13]

His zealotry also made him one of the most controversial figures of the Log College's group of itinerant preachers, but it wasn't due entirely to his father's teachings, or the influence of reforming evangelists he encountered in the northeast. It was a life-threatening illness that drew Tennent into the business of saving souls. In 1728 at the age of twenty-five he became dangerously ill and was suddenly confronted with his own mortality and the realities of eternity.

"I was exceedingly grieved I had done so little for God," he lamented. "I therefore prayed to God that He would be pleased to give me one/half year more. I was determined to promote His kingdom with all my might."[14]

Promote God's kingdom he did. Dubbed the "Son of Thunder," his rousing style of terror and hope spread quickly to other itinerant evangelists. Soon somber presbyteries were criticizing it as highfalutin, incoherent, and hysterical. They were more concerned that ministers should be men of good character and education who conformed to the decrees of the Church, and less concerned about whether a man had been called by God to preach. They wanted the revivalists to submit to discipline and acknowledge the error of their ways.

Tennent would not acquiesce. He was committed to reviving the colony's spiritual life by emphasizing heartfelt conversion and pious action over theology and ecclesiastical politics. Besides, no hardy frontiersman would travel across miles for refrains and restrictions, and Tennent understood this new world. The synod forbade itinerant preachers from interloping into existing presbyteries. The Log College group ignored the ruling. Then the synod declared that a certificate of satisfactory scholarship was needed from them before anyone could be licensed to preach—a move that restricted William Tennent's ability to ordain the ministers he worked so hard to teach. Suddenly there seemed little difference between the restrictive presbyteries and the Anglicans.

Gilbert Tennent responded in 1739 with what was considered "one of the most severely abusive sermons that was ever penned." He portrayed those preachers he called "The Uncoverted Ministry" as proud, bigoted hypocrites.

"Ye serpents, ye generation of vipers," he admonished, quoting the Gospel of Matthew. "How can ye escape the damnation of hell?"

He brought hell to bear on the Presbyterian Church. Their ranks ruptured into the pro-revival, emotional type Presbyterians called the "New Side" and the established order known as the "Old Side." Fiery New-Side evangelists traversed the colonies preaching in simple language that salvation was possible to all who chose to repent and believe in Jesus Christ. In Pennsylvania ten thousand people, hungry for salvation, gathered at a single outdoor service, and all across the colonies fields were filled with rhetorical fireworks and spontaneous hymn singing.

"You may hear screaming, singing, laughing, praying, all at once; and, in other parts, they fall into visions, trances, convulsions," reported one Bostonian at a revival. "When they come out of their trances, they commonly tell a senseless story of Heaven and Hell, and what they saw there."[15]

The supernatural element that had appealed to the Scots-Irish Presbyterians in the remote mountain terrain since Jimmy Morrow's ancestors arrived was sparked again by an intense fervor that provided an outlet for the pressure of an often terrifying mountain life. With God on their side, they weren't alone in the wilderness. Tennent's message put more emphasis on a personal relationship with God than on any intermediary—be it a saint or minister. He stressed that the individual is responsible for his own salvation, that it had not been preordained by an arbitrary God. It was an anti-authoritarian and anti-Calvinistic message.

Calvinism, the theological tradition that emerged in sixteenth-century Europe, to which the Scottish and Irish Presbyterians had ascribed, was an Old World notion that certain people, called the "Elect," were chosen by God to be saved and everyone else was damned. No amount of personal effort or pious living could change this outcome. However, it held that work was the will of God, and while men were not to lust after wealth, they were to reinvest the profits of their labor into further ventures. Using profits to help others rise from a lesser level of subsistence violated God's will, since they weren't earning through their own labor. It was impossible to know who was a member of the Elect—but it was assumed that vagabonds and lazy people were damned, but hardworking, successful people were most likely one of the chosen. This work ethic, that infused hard work with divine dignity, became fundamental to Protestant thinking and to the American work ethic.

For the first settlers, transforming the wilderness was an opportunity to prove they were the chosen people, but as generations passed without education or theological teachings, the concept of the Elect as a spiritual doctrine was forgotten. As families survived the hostile frontier and prospered, they believed that success and salvation could be achieved through individual effort. It was a fundamental rupture in Protestant thinking and the beginnings of a distinct American style of Christianity that was infused with self-reliance, personal responsibility, and "godly hysteria."

Yet for all the souls they saved, the Presbyterians were still hampered by the education requirement needed to become a minister. While Tennent laid more importance on the need to be called by God over theological acrobatics, he still advocated the need for ministerial education. Many more "Log Colleges" popped up on the frontier, mimicking the original, but the speed at which ministers were educated was vastly outpaced by the speed of migrating settlers. Tennent watched Baptist churches that subscribed to no educational requirement deploy preachers like an intractable army.

Since the mid-1600s a pair of Englishmen had been preaching the Baptist doctrine in a couple of little churches in New England. They advocated adult baptism because an infant can't make the choice to follow Jesus; they believed in the virgin birth, that Jesus died for our sins, that salvation was achieved through faith alone, and that there would be a Second Coming of Christ. They believed the power of Christianity is supernatural; the gospel depends not on human learning but on divine power. For them, no amount of theological education could make up for the lack of a call from God. This held a powerful appeal for the poor, scattered, and uneducated and even more so to those immersed in the mysticism of frontier folk culture seeking an emotional release from the pressures of frontier living.

As the Presbyterian-led revivals swept through the South, a pair of uneducated Baptist farmer-preachers left New England for the Virginia–North Carolina border. They began to "raise up" other farmer-preachers and evangelize throughout the region. Any Baptist who was moved by the spirit could just start preaching to a group of like-minded Christians. Many preachers were illiterate but could recite the Bible and speak about important subjects such as life and death or heaven and hell like unhindered zealots.

"Multitudes, some roaring on the ground, some wringing their hands, some in ecstasies, some praying, some weeping," read an account of one gathering. "Others so outrageously cursing and swearing that it was thought they were really possessed of the devil."[16]

Those spontaneously surfacing Baptist preachers didn't bother with licenses since they didn't believe the colonial government had any authority over their church. They were persecuted and arrested for unlawful assemblies. Mobs sometimes broke up their meetings, and preachers were often beaten or pelted with cow dung.

Meanwhile another kind of evangelical was entering the frontier fray.

In the early 1700s in England, a small band of ministers tried to reform the Anglican Church by advocating a return to the gospel, stressing that salvation relies on willful repentance, not on God's arbitrary election. They became known as Methodists, and they proselytized with sermons delivered by dynamic circuit riders who galloped abroad to administer to the poor, riding thousands of miles each year to save souls.

Even the New-Side Presbyterians couldn't compete with the Methodist and Baptist ministers all over the South. Twenty years before his death, Tennent took charge of the Second Presbyterian Church in Philadelphia. From there he watched his converts—in the absence of enough Presbyterian ministers—fall into the ranks of the Baptist and Methodist zealots that drenched the South. As the years passed, Tennent became more troubled by the rupture he'd caused in the Presbyterian ranks in 1739. He began to posit the idea of a reunion, and by 1758 the old and new factions of the Presbyterian Church were reunited, albeit dominated by the evangelism of the New-Side zealots.

While William and Gilbert Tennent, two humble Presbyterians from the north of Ireland, championed the Great Awakening in America to imbue the poor with hope, confidence, and dignity, the larger Presbyterian Church had been feuding with the colonial government who wanted to appoint an Anglican bishop to the colonies. The Presbyterian Church was forced to become politically active to defend their hard-earned religious liberties. As far as they were concerned, an Angelical bishop meant ecclesiastical tyranny; if parliament could appoint bishops, they could forbid marriages and funerals and establish taxes just as they had in northern Ireland.

Tennent didn't live to see the full effect of the Great Awakening he sparked, which taught that all men are equal in the eyes of the Lord. The Presbyterians unleashed a religious revival that seeped into the souls of men and forged a political and revolutionary spirit—if they were responsible for their own salvation, then why not their own government?

"The Revolution was effected before the War commenced," said President John Adams later. "The Revolution was in the minds and hearts of the people; a change in their religious sentiments of their duties and obligations. This radical change in the principles, opinions, sentiments, and affections of the people, was the real American Revolution."[17]

Westward March

The years after the Revolutionary War were filled with a rising sense of national pride. Religion gave rise to patriot unity and allowed disparate territories to rise up as one nation against the world's mightiest empire.

The late 1700s were marked by a massive migration from the eastern seaboard into the newly opened Allegheny Mountains. The entire nation seemed to be moving, searching for new opportunities with their newfound optimism. By 1820, it is estimated that eight hundred thousand left the Northeast in the westward migration. Within a single generation, eleven new states were admitted to the union. The nation effectively doubled in size.

Churches again found themselves straining to administer to new settlements in Kentucky, Tennessee, and Ohio. Travelers returned from the frontier with reports that people were acting "like freed prisoners . . . they can fight against God without fearing man."[18] Moonshine was again being served at social gatherings: log rolling, corn husking, and house raisings along the whiskey-sodden new frontier.

As the Scots-Irish Presbyterians settled farthest west, two Presbyterian missions were established, staffed with itinerant ministers who visited the very edge of civilization searching for their flock. They sought out existing Presbyterians for ministry, but it would be ten more years before they had the resources to search for new converts.

Meanwhile the Baptists sent out their fearless farmer-preachers with a simple doctrine. The Methodists dispatched circuit riders that traveled to remote settlements and found isolated families. They rode across hundreds of miles each month, administered sacraments, married, baptized, and buried the dead. They preached in the churches of other denominations, in schoolhouses, courthouses, and private houses and often in the open air. They were so committed to saving souls, the saying emerged that if the weather was bad, the only people who'd be out in it were cows and Methodist ministers.

Despite the threefold effort by the major denominations, people were still falling by the wayside. In this much larger, more terrifying new frontier, an entirely new way of reaching lost souls was needed. A Scots-Irish Presbyterian who galloped to the head of the westward procession stumbled upon the solution.

Salvation at Rogues Harbor

At seven years old the young James McGready had never forgotten his prayers; as a teenager he never swore, got drunk, or broke the Sabbath; so pious was he out on the family's North Carolina settlement, that the boy's uncle whisked him off to Pennsylvania to study theology. If McGready had any doubts about his vocation, they were eliminated early when a bout of small pox brought him face to face with the prospect of eternity and frightened him so much that he repented and accepted Jesus Christ as his savior the following week.

In 1788 at the age of thirty, he was ordained a Presbyterian preacher and took off for his old haunt in North Carolina to set about saving souls. Like Tennent, he was physically strong with a voice like thunder, but unlike his predecessor, he was remarkably plain in his dress and manners. His devotion and oratorical prowess convinced those that met him that he was very near to God. Unfortunately, the North Carolinians couldn't have been further from God. Sixty or so years had passed since the Great Awakening, and frontier society had slipped into a moral, religious, feisty, and drunken decline.

McGready set about laboring with "wonted zeal, and often with great success." He converted a handful of lost souls, but he made a lot of enemies among the sinners at whose burials he refused to officiate if alcohol was served and among the clergy against whose "formality and deadness" he railed. Finally he got a letter written in blood telling him to leave the country if he valued his life. He pulled up stakes and headed for Kentucky.

Out there on the edges of civilization, he took charge of three congregations—Gaspar River, Red River, and Muddy River, collectively known as "Rogues Harbor." It was populated by desperados and other degenerates who had, unsurprisingly, little or no interest in religion. McGready devoted all his energy into ministering to their spiritual condition, and a year later his Herculean effort paid off with the inauspicious conversion of one woman.

Having saved one soul, he was encouraged to hold a service at the Gaspar River Meeting House. The wayward congregation mysteriously became absorbed in religion and ignored all their work and obligations for an entire week to ponder the notion of their salvation. Soon they were seeing heaven and believing that McGready was in such close communion with God that he could perform miracles—like the time he averted an oncoming storm by muttering to heaven. Moments later the clouds parted and the sky cleared. After that, there was nothing for the heathens to do but to repent.

"[He would] so array hell and its horrors before the wicked, that they would tremble and quake, imagining a lake of fire and brimstone yawning to overwhelm them," said a preacher. "And the wrath of God thrusting them down the horrible abyss."[19]

McGready's legendary sermons and supernatural incidences spread across the frontier. Knowing the heathens had little to do by way of socializing except to fight, drink, or pray, he launched a religious service that was the high point of the frontier's social calendar. He invited two Presbyterians and a Methodist along to extend the services. They preached to the point of exhaustion, whereupon the Methodist, unable to restrain himself to the standards of Presbyterian order, began to twist his way around the log benches "shouting and exhorting with energy and ecstasy."

With that display of uninhibited zealotry, the dam broke. The floor was instantly covered with terrified sinners falling down and screaming to heaven for mercy. Even children cried out for redemption.

"What shall we do to be saved?" the sinners begged to know.

"I have no religion, I am going to hell," a woman screamed.

"We are all going to hell together, we will all be damned," a man cried.[20]

By the end of the marathon service, despite all the drama and chaos, only ten people were saved, but McGready had learned a lesson—he decided to depart from Presbyterian reserve and throw his subsequent sermons into a storm of emotionalism.

It was the beginning of the Second Great Awakening.

Word spread through the settlements about the sermons at "Rogues Harbor." Pioneers started arriving from every direction, some making a hundred-mile, week-long trip to be baptized by the Spirit. They came in wagons, on horseback, and on foot, with tents, bread, and meat to last days. Their motives were both to socialize and to see if they could be converted by divine influence. No sooner were the wagons parked and the tents pitched along Red River than they were thrown into a maelstrom of intense emotions, groaning and writhing in guilt, despair, terror, hope, and the joy of salvation. Sermons went on day and night through storms and blistering heat. Finally after four days and four nights, the camp meeting broke up and they all went home.

Kentucky's revival fire spread rapidly throughout the South. The fervor appealed to whites, free blacks, and slaves. At Cane Ridge, Kentucky, one of McGready's protégés held a camp meeting with twenty thousand people in attendance, more than even the Son of Thunder could muster. Seven ministers preached day and night to thousands who hung on every word. At one point three hundred people were simultaneously testifying and shouting "Amen" and "Hallelujah." The noise became tumultuous: the slain were groaning, preachers were shouting, children were crying, people were singing, horses were stampeding. Worshippers eagerly shared their experiences with others in a stream of endless chatter. Someone said it sounded like the "roar of Niagara." The campfires kept burning through rain and thunder, and the preachers kept working: some climbed up trees for pulpits; one tied an umbrella to a pole and held it over his head while he spoke so people knew where to cluster. It was even said cloven tongues sat on the preachers.

Cane Ridge was America's Pentecost.

Inspired by the success of his camp meetings, McGready set up his own presbytery. The Kentucky Synod were horrified that he was ordaining illiterate men for what they called a bizarre form of undisciplined religious barbarism dominated by emotional intensity. They closed down his presbytery and started preparing heresy charges. McGready responded by breaking away and forming his own synod with the simple doctrine: anyone can repent and be saved. It was warmly received by the hardy frontiersmen who wanted to be stirred, not bored to death by theology.

As McGready's physical strength waned in his final years, his sermons lacked the alacrity of his early tirades. In 1816, he delivered an impressive sermon at a Cumberland Presbyterian camp meeting about the "The character, history, and end of the fool." He praised God to find that the holy fire still filled his soul as it had done during the Second Great Awakening sixteen years earlier. Two months later at the age of fifty-four he died, but the tradition of experiencing the presence of God and the frenzied joy of salvation long outlived him. As the revivals swept through Appalachia, they absorbed folk traditions from the terrain.

A hundred years after McGready's death, the amalgam of the supernatural folk beliefs and religious emotionalism came down from the mountain as something even more outrageous and unorthodox. This new tradition of worship included speaking in tongues, possession by the Spirit, curing the sick, casting out devils, and the ultimate ritual of God's true soldier—the taking up of serpents. It was called Pentecostalism—an umbrella term for isolated Christian groups that experienced supernatural phenomena. Pentecostal services began with spontaneous singing, dancing, clapping, and falling into trances as they felt the Spirit move in them. Once they achieved this state of being anointed they could experience the "burst of joy" that came from handling snakes. In that moment, they won victory over the devil and felt that God was reaching down to touch them. That joy kept them coming back even if they were bitten. Some were in pain, hemorrhaging, suffocating, or experiencing temporary blindness and unconsciousness, but the congregation prayed on until they either recovered or died—in which case they were just "going home." But not even pain or death could take away the ecstasy of being on God's side.

A hundred years earlier, French traveler and historian Alexis de Tocqueville prophetically observed, "there is no country in the whole world in which the Christian religion retains a greater influence over the souls of men than in America."[21] The twentieth century would prove him right.

The Fundamental Problem with Monkeys

It was "the fantastic cross between a circus and a holy war," wrote the *New York Times* in 1925 about one of the most sensational court cases of twentieth-century America. That year in Tennessee, years of tension led to a face-off between science and religious dogma.

For years, Darwinism had been plowing through the foundations of Christian belief and making its way into public school curriculums. In response, the Bible Institute of Los Angeles responded by publishing twelve pamphlets called *The Fundamentals: A Testimony To The Truth*. This was the birth of the modern fundamentalist movement that advocated a strict return to fundamental Christian principles like the infallibility of the Bible, the virgin birth, the atonement, the resurrection, and the Second Coming of Christ. They were opposed to almost all other religions, as well as modernity and evolution. They later added drinking, gambling, dancing, movies, singing (except hymns), homosexuality, and anything else they considered ungodly.

In 1921, they became politically active and introduced thirty-seven anti-evolution bills into twenty state legislatures. In 1925 they successfully lobbied Tennessee state legislatures to stop the teaching of evolution in schools. However, they underestimated the problem with monkeys.

No sooner had the Tennessee legislative votes been cast than the American Civil Liberties Union announced it would financially support anyone challenging the new law. A couple of entrepreneurs in Dayton, Tennessee, figured this had all the makings of a publicity coup that would be a boon for business in their little town of eighteen hundred people. They found a twenty-five-year-old local schoolteacher, John Scopes, who was willing to teach evolution in class. Scopes's friend and co-conspirator reported him to the authorities, and then they all stepped back to watch the mayhem erupt.

Those faithful to the fundamental principles of Christianity mobilized behind the most famous trial of the era. The prosecutor was a devout Presbyterian of Scots-Irish stock, widely known and hugely popular as a three-time candidate for the White House and former Secretary of State under Woodrow Wilson. He was a peace advocate, prohibitionist, anti-Darwinist, and champion of the common man, which earned him the title "The Great Commoner." William Jennings Bryan voiced his convictions with a deep commanding voice that made him one of the most popular speakers in American history. Coincidentally he had been baptized at fourteen during a revival at Reverend James McGready's Cumberland Presbyterian Church.

The famous trial lawyer, Clarence Darrow from Ohio—a free-thinking agnostic whose father was an abolitionist and whose mother was an early supporter of female suffrage, led the defense team. Darrow volunteered his services when he heard the fundamentalists had secured Bryan to prosecute.

The trial was the first in American history to be broadcast live by radio into millions of homes across the nation. Two hundred reporters camped outside the courthouse to get on-the-scene coverage. H. L. Mencken, the celebrity journalist from the *Baltimore Sun*, showed up to give the coverage some of its most colorful if not hyperbolic titles, including the "Monkey Trial," the "infidel Scopes," and accounts of "the theological bilge" of the local "yaps" and "yokels." Thousands of miles of telegraph wires were hung to send coverage out daily; small planes stood by daily to fly film from a specially built airstrip. The case took over the front page of the *New York Times* for days. Every day a thousand people squeezed into a courthouse built for three hundred so that catching a breath of air in the blistering July heat was almost impossible. Trained chimpanzees performed on the courthouse lawn.

Across the nation, there was a bitter debate between Americans who wanted change and those who wanted conformity, moral purity, and order. Bryan was staunchly opposed to Darwinism not just because it undermined the teaching of the Bible, but because he believed the concept of survival of the fittest caused hatred and conflict. He was convinced it would degrade the foundations of morality and blamed the Great War on Darwinian preponderance in Germany.

"Word that the great Bryan was to speak made the courthouse a magnet," reported the *Chicago Tribune* on the first day of the trial. "And long before the time set for the afternoon session of the Scopes trial the crowds filled the courtroom."

Policemen fanned the room to try to keep the air circulating. Scopes himself could hardly squeeze through the three thousand people clamoring outside or the thousand packed inside. The afternoon of opening statements unleashed a fury that continued unabated for the next two weeks.

Bryan began with an hour-long assault against teaching evolution.

"This is that book!" he declared, brandishing a copy of Hunter's *Civic Biology*. "There is the book they were teaching your children that man was a mammal and so indistinguishable among the mammals that they leave him there with 3,499 other mammals. Including elephants!"[22]

The audience listened to every word.

"The Christian believes man came from above, but the evolutionist believes he must have come from below," Bryan thundered to loud applause. He later added spryly that the book was also trying to teach people they had come "Not even from American monkeys, but from old world monkeys."[23]

The presiding judge, John T. Raulston, a conservative Christian who started each day's court proceedings with a prayer, allowed the defense to call only one scientific expert to testify about evolution. State leaders pressured him keep the trial brief and the State free of ridicule. With their experts dismissed, Dudley Malone, a divorce lawyer from Darrow's team took to the floor to present little more than rhetoric.

"We feel we stand with science," he declared. "We feel we stand with intelligence. We feel we stand with fundamental freedom in America. We are not afraid."[24]

Cheers erupted as the crowd leapt to their feet to give Malone a standing ovation. A policeman pounded a table so hard with his nightstick it split in two. When another officer rushed forward to help him quiet the crowd, he yelled, "I'm not trying to restore order. Hell, I'm cheering." Dayton buzzed late into the night over the day's proceedings. The *New York Times* headlines called it "the greatest debate on science and religion in recent years."[25]

On the sixth day of the trial, the defense ran out of witnesses, so Darrow called Bryan to the stand as an expert—albeit hostile—on the

Bible. The infuriated defense team demanded to know the legal reason for Bryan's questioning, which they deemed served only one purpose, and that was to ridicule those who believe in the Bible. Darrow made no secret that he believed them to be "ignoramuses" who believed in a "fool religion." For two hours he flung questions at Bryan, such as, where did Cain get his wife? and did the fish drown during the great flood?

"I believe in creation as there told," Bryan affirmed, speaking for Christians across the country. "And if I am not able to explain it I will accept it."[26]

Bryan was ready and willing, he said, to protect the word of God against the great atheists. Crowds cheered in support of his defiance. Outside loudspeakers pumped the tension-filled inquisition to three thousand people—twice the population of the entire town—who were packed onto the courthouse lawn. They waited to hear the great Bryan face down a firing squad in defense of the Bible, to hear his assurances that man was made in God's image, and to know that Jesus died on the cross for their salvation.

Eventually the judge had enough of the bickering and the overcrowded, suffocating court and adjourned for the day. Thousands of excited people milled around outside the courthouse. Telegraphs were typed up; radio news piped out updates to the country; little planes zoomed off with newsreels to editing bays. By and large they mocked Bryan's literal interpretation of the Bible and undermined the fundamentalist cause.

The next day Judge Raulston announced that he considered Bryan's whole testimony irrelevant and expunged it from the record. With no more experts or witnesses, Darrow requested a return of guilty that would allow him to appeal to the Tennessee Supreme Court. After a nine-minute deliberation the jury found Scopes guilty, and he was fined a hundred dollars.

Darrow lost his appeal in the state Supreme Court and the anti-evolution law remained in effect for forty more years.

Technically the trial was a victory for the fundamentalists. In reality, the fundamentalist hero was ridiculed, the fundamentalists themselves caustically satirized by Mencken as backward hillbillies, full of "degraded nonsense which country preachers are ramming and hammering into yokel skulls."[27] Darwin's theories continued to be taught, and the need to separate theology from general education became even more firmly entrenched in the minds of Americans. Gradually prayer and other religious activities were abolished from public schools. The fundamentalists may have won, but victory was hollow and its price was mortification.

Bryan stayed in Dayton for two more days rewriting his closing arguments into a fiery speech with which he planned to launch a nationwide anti-evolutionary tour. He prepared to refute the theory of evolution with four arguments: first it contradicted creationism, second the survival-of-the-fittest destroyed both faith in God and love of others, third the study of evolution was a distraction from socially useful pursuits, and fourth it undermined efforts to reform society.

On July 26, 1925, five days after the Scopes verdict was returned, and three days into his grueling tour, Bryan died in his sleep from diabetes and fatigue.

"If I should die tomorrow," he told a journalist a few days earlier, "I believe that on the basis of the accomplishments of the last few weeks I could truthfully say, well done."[28]

Onward Christian Soldiers

Bryan's death created a leadership void that no other fundamentalist leader could fill. Christianity ruptured between those who wanted to adjust to the new intellectual climate and those who insisted that the old ways of their faith must be preserved. A modernist and not necessarily literal reading of the Bible offered a sort of theistic solution in which evolution happened under God's guiding hand. Fundamentalists, however, refused to compromise. They wanted one nation under God, not a morally bankrupt society. Forced by their denial of the science of life's origins, they retreated from mainstream society to establish their own education institutions.

Fundamentalists weren't the only Christians suffering because of the Monkey Trial. The Pentecostals, considered by many to be an hysterical, fringe movement, moved toward the mainstream, shedding their supernatural elements like speaking in tongues and handling serpents and encounters with the Holy Ghost in favor of social values, education, and the direct—but more reserved—encounter with God. The serpent handlers retreated to the remote mountains from whence they came.

Presbyterians, Methodists, and Baptists stripped God of supernatural works in an attempt to adapt to the more secular atmosphere of the twentieth century. Instead of growing their shift towards the mainstream threw them into a freefall, losing thousands of members each week. As the courts reduced the role of religion in state affairs, a marked decline in America's morality began. There was a widespread tendency to consider religious people as enemies of freedom and label them pejoratively as fundamentalist.

Religion had been a powerful force in shaping American culture and values. The country was populated by those seeking religious tolerance; its independence was won when its religious freedoms were threatened. Religion underpinned American life. Moreover it was shaped by the frontier experience, which gave a Southern flavor to American Christianity, a flavor that equated religious duty with patriotism and stressed the importance of God's presence in daily life. In the twentieth century, the disconnected landscape of sprawling suburbs and exurbs were comparable to the scattered frontier settlements of the 1700s. Americans were no longer braining bears and fighting Indians, but they had their own stresses: two world wars, economic depressions, unemployment, and personal despair. Yet they were deprived of miracles, their omnipotent God, and the sense of community that came with church membership.

As America morally declined, they watched the family disintegrate before an onslaught of illegitimacy, illiteracy, unemployment, juvenile delinquency, crime, and poverty. The sixties brought big business, industrialization, and urban alienation. The seventies brought a Supreme Court decision to legalize abortion that led to over a million terminations being performed annually. The Welfare Reform Act of 1996 seemed to push the country toward socialism—an anathema to the Calvinist work ethic on which the country had been founded. Rap music emerged advocating violence against white people. Between 1960 and 1990, there was a 560-percent increase in violent crime, 200-percent rise in divorce, and 400-percent rise in illegitimate births. Minors were the fastest growing segment of the criminal population. Meanwhile, welfare spending went up 630 percent.

Religious conservatives resurfaced with a fury to counteract the assault on American morality. To them Christianity, red-blooded Americanism, and patriotism were synonymous—it was their religious and patriotic duty to rescue America from this degeneration. They adopted a more combative, warlike vocabulary, sending out God's soldiers to rescue a country morally adrift. They crusaded with a pro-prayer, pro-family package that advocated unrestricted private enterprise and advocated a superior national defense.

They opposed abortion, pornography, homosexuality, and evolution. In less than ten years seventy-two thousand protestors were arrested for picketing abortion clinics; extremists firebombed over a hundred clinics and killed a number of doctors. The statistics showed a drop of two hundred thousand abortions per year in the mid-1990s. Force, it seemed, produced results.

Then, they found a new forum.

It was a simple argument. If you're a fundamentalist and you have kids and a TV and 90 percent of programming offends you, throwing out the TV isn't enough; you have to control the content to which they have access. There was only one way to go—use the tools of modernity against modernity. Mass communication replaced mass frontier gatherings. A modest, well-groomed, corporate executive image that appealed to mainstream America replaced the leather jerkins, bedrolls, and rifles. With televangelism, the decline in American Protestantism was slowed and then reversed.

Now they needed to address the issue of leadership.

First into the fray was a dashing man with a youthful appearance and engaging spirit, who was able to appeal to the middle-of-the-road and the ultra-conservatives. A Southern Baptist from Charlotte, North Carolina, and graduate of the fundamentalist college Bob Jones University, the Reverend Billy Graham contrasted the disintegration of the United States with the Garden of Eden, where there were "no union dues, no labor leaders, no snakes, no disease." He railed against weak politicians, liberals, labor organizations, and foreign-aid programs. He believed Satan masterminded communism, and only a great religious revival could purge America of the termites eating it from within. It was an age-old message equating Christianity with patriotism dressed up in a new format.

Despite being the spiritual adviser to twelve United States presidents and reaching an audience of 2.2 billion, Graham did not advocate religious involvement in the political arena, and when his warlike rhetoric subsided in the 1980s in favor of reconciliation with Russia and China, he was all but raised to heretical status in the eyes of most fundamentalists.

In 1966 the son of a conservative Virginian senator stepped into the spotlight with the launch of a nationally syndicated TV program called *The 700 Club*. Originally a music and preaching format, it became the flagship news talk show of the Christian Broadcasting Network, airing weekly to twelve million viewers. In a 1992 fund-raising letter, it's founder, Marion Gordon Robertson, who went by the nickname "Pat" because he thought Marion was too effeminate, described feminism as a "socialist, anti-family political movement that encourages women to leave their husbands, kill their children, practice witchcraft, destroy capitalism, and become lesbians." [29] In 1988 he made an unsuccessful bid to win the Republican Party presidential nomination, losing to Vice President George H. W. Bush.

Other televangelists were more scandalous. Pat Crouch and his wife, Janice, who founded the California-based Trinity Broadcasting Network, told viewers that if they didn't donate they could spend eternity in the flames of hell—then bought a five-million-dollar home. Crouch was later accused of trying to lure a man into a gay sexual tryst. Jim and Tammy Baker founded Praise the Lord television before Jim admitted he had slept with a Playboy model and used the Lord's money to buy a gold-plated dog kennel.

Nevertheless, televangelizing was a phenomenal success with an estimated 47 percent of Americans watching at least one religious program a week. Later televangelists incorporated podcasting, Internet streaming, mass mailing, and database organization into their repertoire. The strategy availed itself of the vast fundraising resources that existed in audiences who were happy to give a hundred dollars to the Lord. By the end of the twentieth century there were an estimated seventy million evangelicals in America—most registered as Republicans—who were opposed to homosexuality, Darwinism, and abortion.

However, in the 1970s, they still had not wrestled back the kind of political control they had before the Scopes Trial. They needed a leader to guide religion beyond television and into the White House. Their call summoned up one of the most influential but controversial figures produced by American society in decades.

The Birth of the New Christian Right

Born to a long line of respectable bootleggers and atheists in 1933 in Lynchburg, Virginia (the town named after the brother of Irishman Colonel Charles Lynch, who ran an irregular court to try British Loyalists during the Revolutionary War), Jerry Lamon Falwell accepted Jesus Christ as his savior in 1952. He went on to become a Baptist pastor, televangelist, and leader of the fundamentalist charge into political activism.

His evangelizing prowess was evidenced from an early age. At twenty-three he founded the Thomas Road Baptist Church in Lynchburg with a membership of thirty-five. That same year he began airing his sermons on radio's "Old-Time Gospel Hour" and moved into TV six months later. Over the course of his career, his Lynchburg church grew from thirty-five to twenty thousand members. He founded Liberty University, a liberal arts college with over sixty thousand registered students, and became a leading spokesman for the fundamentalist Baptist Bible Fellowship.

His political activism began in 1976 when he embarked on a series of "I Love America" rallies across the country to raise awareness of the social issues he believed were hurtling America into disarray, namely abortion, feminism, and gay rights. Then in 1979, despite the Baptist principal of separating religion from politics, he founded an organization called the "Moral Majority" that would grow up to be the largest political lobbying group for evangelical Christians in the United States. It waged political warfare to lead a new generation of fundamentalists beyond simply denouncing cultural trends and back into an engagement with contemporary life.

He got off to a fast start. Within two years the Moral Majority had persuaded legislators in fourteen states to introduce laws requiring the creationist views be taught in science class. Falwell's message that that Church was the cornerstone of a successful family, the center for spiritual guidance, and the gathering place for socializing with like-minded individuals resonated throughout the nation. Americans continued to respond to his message of personal morality, free enterprise, capitalism, and the maintenance of military superiority.

As an advocate for conservative family values, he famously criticized Tinky-Winky the Teletubby for being a gay role model and a moral menace to America's youth.

"He is purple—the gay-pride color," he wrote in his magazine the *National Liberty Journal*, "And his antenna is shaped like a triangle—the gay-pride symbol."

He also noted that Tinky-Winky carries a purse. The Teletubby production company, Itsy Bitsy Entertainment, denied that Tinky-Winky was a gay role model and said the purse was a "magic bag."

Larry Flynt, pornography publisher of *Hustler Magazine*, couldn't resist. In 1983 Flynt ran a parody of a Campari ad featuring a photo and a fake interview with Falwell during which "the preacher" described his first sexual experience "with Mom" in an outhouse while both were "drunk off our God-fearing asses on Campari," and that "Mom looked better than a Baptist whore with a $100 donation." Asked if he still drinks Campari, he answered, "I always get sloshed before I go out to the pulpit. You don't think I could lay down all that bullshit sober, do you?"

Falwell sued Flynt for libel, invasion of privacy, and emotional distress. He lost.

Shaking himself free of the Flynt controversy, the preacher wielded his real power in the realm of domestic politics. He noticed a wing of the Republican Party shared his Christian conservative values: support for prayer in school, the teaching of creationism, and opposition to abortion, pornography, homosexuality, and sex education. With these issues, Falwell mobilized the Christian soldier to do battle in defense of their values. In 1980, those values were embodied in presidential candidate Ronald Reagan.

Other Christian leaders like Billy Graham criticized Falwell's political involvement, but he was undeterred; he was successfully turning conservatives into activists. Four million strong, the legions of the Moral Majority knocked on doors, distributed literature, organized rallies, and did whatever the cause demanded. On presidential Election Day in 1980, they delivered two-thirds of the white, evangelical Christian vote to Ronald Reagan.

After Reagan's victory, the Moral Majority wound down, but its banner was picked up by other Christian right, evangelical, parachurch organizations that worked across denominations to engage in social welfare and proselytizing.

An up-and-coming campaign manager closely studied Falwell's lessons on the politics of religion. Karl Rove, George W. Bush's political adviser, knew his candidate was going to have to appeal to the conservatives on their terms to get elected. While Bush talked about scripture and faith, Rove was making sure millions of evangelicals got out to the polls to vote. In May 2004, gay and lesbian couples won the right to marry in Massachusetts. In November 2004, just in time for presidential elections, constitutional amendments codifying marriage as an exclusively heterosexual institution appeared on the ballots in eleven states. Conservatives galvanized to vote in the amendments were predisposed to vote for Bush while they were in the booth. The Republicans garnered an estimated four million votes from conservatives who seemed more concerned with the sanctity of heterosexual-only marriage than with Washington politics.

Falwell succumbed to sudden cardiac death in 2007. The following year the Republicans lost the White House despite having the devoutly conservative Republican vice presidential contender, Sarah Palin on the ticket. Conservate activism was on the wane.

"They're probably coming back," predicted one psychology professor looking ahead to 2012. "You can never count them out."[30]

Jimmy Morrow

Pastor Morrow closed the church doors and took his box of serpents back home. He was happy; it had been a good sermon. His eyes lit up and his mood elevated when he was given the opportunity to preach the word of God; he seemed just like the high-spirited "Little Rowdy" again. The joy he found in delivering the Lord's word compelled him to welcome all of Jesus' believers to his church. Last year a group of Japanese and Australian students had come to hear him speak, and a group of American students were expected any day. The BBC taped a show about his church, and the Animal Planet channel was coming soon to make a documentary. Morrow said millions would watch those programs and hear him preach—just as the Lord promised when he was only six.

Morrow drove twenty miles home along the dirt roads to his simple cabin where he fed the snakes before tending to his garden. It was all the land he had left since the big corporations drove out the small farmer in the 1950s. That night, like every night, he and Pam made dinner and then listened to a religious program on the radio. Afterward he would paint or do some more research about the history of the area and his ancestors.

Out there in the remote Appalachian Mountains of Tennessee, where a hog trail of flattened grass constituted a road, he was as removed from Washington politics as his ancestors had been from the colonial government and ecclesiastical authority of the East. He had little interest in denominations or politics. They could squabble about candidates or values or scriptural differences; Morrow knew he had a blessed life ever since God spoke to him fifty years earlier. Nothing took precedence over the direct word of God.

"I just believe what the Bible says, and they can do what they want to,"[31] he smiled.

CHAPTER 4

AMERICAN SOLDIER

"We'd been told it was bad before, but this was for real."[1] With bullets whizzing past his head, Lieutenant Colin Layne was calling in radio positions for artillery support. Then he saw red tracer dots on his legs—someone was about to open fire with a machine gun. Layne grabbed his radio operator and made a run for cover in a hail of automatic gunfire with only one thought in his head, "Shit, shit, shit, this is gonna hurt real bad."

Layne was part of the 3-2 Stryker Brigade tasked to take back the city of Baqubah, the headquarters of Al Qaeda in Iraq (AQI), the place General David Petraeus called "the heart of darkness."[2] Three of the brigade's companies under the command of LTC Bruce Antonio had been sent north to hold Baqubah in early 2007 but they were taking heavy fire. After four relentless months it was clear they needed to call in the cavalry.

Colonel Fred W. Johnson, a smart, dogged, tough-as-nails Scots-Irishman with a drawerful of war medals, strapped on Antonio's request and set out from the brigade's tactical operating center in Baghdad. He took two Strykers—the army's new all-terrain armored vehicles loaded with machine guns, grenade launchers, surveillance and communications equipment—and headed for Baqubah. The plan was to liaise with Antonio, assess the terrain, find the city's former leaders, and determine what assets were needed to rout the enemy.

"We were shot at the whole way up," Johnson said. "Bullets were pinging off the Strykers, but we couldn't ID anyone to shoot. Bruce's guys were ducking; they said it was a light day, but it was wide open like cowboys and Indians."[3]

The next morning his detachment left Forward Operating Base (FOB) Warhorse with two Strykers and a Fox armored vehicle. They

Colonel Fred Johnson with the 3-2 Stryker Brigade, Baqubah, Iraq, 2007. Courtesy of Michael Yon www.michaelyon-online.com.

weren't a hundred feet outside the FOB when the Fox was blown up by a roadside bomb.

Life outside was a disaster. Baqubah's local government had collapsed, basic services were nonexistent, half the population was starving, and corruption was rife. The Sunnis in Baqubah wanted their city back; a small group of citizens had armed themselves to fight but couldn't outman or outgun the Al Qaeda foreign fighters. The Americans needed to go in and find the resistance fighters, but AQI was dug in—they needed to go in hard.

On March 14, 2007, seventy-seven Strykers, six tanks with a platoon of Bradley mounted infantry, and almost a thousand men rolled out of

Baghdad, men who were hardened from the intensity of house-to-house combat in places like Haifa Street and Mosul. They also knew the dreaded silence of asymmetrical warfare that preyed on jittery nerves as they peered into the darkness waiting for the next ambush. The 3-2 Stryker Brigade only had thirty days left of their deployment when word came that not only was their time being extended, they were being thrown back into hell. Driving up from Baghdad that night, they had an uneasy feeling that they were on borrowed time.

"Tired and smoked," is how one commander described them, "and wondering when is it going to end."[4]

Al Qaeda had been warned that the U.S. Army and its technical might were about to descend on the city. This would usually make them scatter, but not this time. These were hard-core foreign fighters, prepared for a long siege.

Day one beyond the wire was filled with deafening explosions and thick smoke. The entire battalion engaged in heavy firefights across the city. For the next three days everything seemed to be exploding. Mines were planted every fifty yards. A seventeen-ton Stryker drove over a deeply buried IED and was blown upside down. Remote controlled IEDs detonated with deadly precision. F-16s screeched overhead, dropping five hundred pounds of explosives on booby-trapped houses. Contact explosions wore on the soldier's nerves; no one on the ground could tell what was happening. Only one fact was certain—AQI had reached a new level of sophistication.

Fighting raged for ten days and nights: relentless small-arms fire, constant ambushes. AQI used citizens for cover, which increased the risk of collateral damage and made artillery support impossible. Except for calling in phosphorous clouds for cover, the soldiers had only instinct and raw nerves to counter the onslaught. Rarely sleeping and dragging seventy pounds of body armor, weapons, and ammunition in 120-degree heat, they became exhausted, edgier, and more aggressive. They kept pushing westward to the end of the city, battling, securing, and holding territory as they advanced. Winning "hearts and minds" wasn't part of this plan. This was all-out kinetic combat.

"Enemy contact," someone yelled.

Suddenly out of nowhere thirty fighters opened fire on them from every direction. It was a close ambush—no one survived a close ambush. With all the smoke and yelling and small-arms fire, no one could ID the targets.

Layne ran to the roof of the nearest building for a visual—there were too many citizens in the surrounding houses to call in artillery from Warhorse. "Retaliation—think quickly—what was the plan for retaliation?" His men on the ground let rip a bone-chilling yell, threw grenades, and ran headlong into the machine-gun fire, picking off fighters as they went. Two squads took position on the rooftop and shot down the rest.

It was over. Everyone was alive. They did it. They survived a close ambush. Hooah! It would take days to come down off that high. This was life in wartime, volume turned way up.

"Higher than any high, lower than any low," said Layne. "Going from crying to elation within ten minutes."[5]

Suddenly a massive explosion rocked the city. A few blocks away Lieutenant David Stroud ran in the direction of the black smoke plumes. A squad had kicked in the door of a booby-trapped house, and the whole thing detonated and collapsed on them. Stroud's men went digging through the rubble to pull out survivors so the squad's own platoon wouldn't have to see their men cut and bleeding. That was part of the soldier's ethos: there was nothing worse than watching your own men injured. They called for a medevac and kept digging for the other five men but it was too late.

Standing there helplessly in the rubble, Stroud's heart sank. It was a long way to El Paso, Texas, where he got the idea that the army would be a life of adventure. This wasn't adventure—this was just the day from hell that wouldn't end.

Layne's platoon found a local police station. Military strategy in Iraq included incorporating Iraqi army and police elements into the war effort, so they went to investigate. As they left they were blasted by small-arms fire, mortars exploded around them, then four men careened towards them in a suicide car bomb. The squad ran to the Stryker for cover. Two of Layne's soldiers were hit and lay bleeding outside the station. Suddenly, an Irish kid, Sergeant Matt Andrews, jumped out of the Stryker into the hail of bullets, ran to the injured soldiers, opened fire on the car that was barreling down on them, and killed all but the driver, who screeched off leaving the fallen fighters behind. Andrews gave first aid to the fallen soldiers. He was awarded a bronze star for valor.

Layne inherited some of the hardy Scots-Irish bloodline from his tough old grandmother who hid Billy the Kid in open defiance of the law, but this relentless, screaming barrage of booby traps and surprise attacks in endless days of kinetic combat was brutal. Someone had informed AQI they were at the station, and AQI were able to respond with a complex attack. Layne's men had taken all the fighting they could; they were killing fighters left and right but they just kept coming back.

Johnson had seen too much warfare in Bosnia, the Gulf, and Iraq to believe that battling and beating the enemy were enough to extract the brigade. If he didn't identify the root of the problem, they'd get caught in months of kinetic fighting. They'd rout AQI, but they'd just come back when the army left. Baqubah had all the makings of a quagmire or the first round in a long game of Whac-A-Mole™.

Johnson was chewing over the quandary in the blistering hot desert summer: what does a warrior do when battlefield victory isn't enough?

Revolution

"Those pestiferous Presbyterians," snapped King George III of England about the Scots-Irish in America. "They are always in unrest and will be until they are wiped out."[6]

Unfortunately for the English monarchy, the Other Irish never did take to the yoke of oppression. Their hard-won economic success in northern Ireland had been undermined by British rules and taxation, their religious freedoms had been quashed, and their land rights impinged. When they sailed away from those northern Irish harbors in the early 1700s, they brought their burning hatred of the traitorous English and a warrior ethic forged by centuries of warfare, during which loyalty was to the laird and even that honor had to be earned. In the New World, loyalty was to kin, and any army that tried to subjugate them or any government that betrayed them would meet the time-honored maxim of the defenders of Derry: "No Surrender."

This didn't deter the British from making the same mistakes in America that they'd made in Ireland. Tired of the strain America was putting on the British Royal treasury, the British reasoned that colonists should pay for the honor of colonial rule in the form of new taxes. This turned out, unsurprisingly, to be so unpopular that one collector killed his horse under him galloping to escape an angry mob. The British deployed six thousand soldiers to Boston to keep the mobs in check, thus adding rancorous occupation to increased taxation. It was downhill from there.

In 1775 after five years of inflicting massacres, injustices, and coercive legislation, the British marched on Lexington and Concord in Massachusetts to destroy a store of military supplies. At Lexington they were met by seventy local militiamen. A shot rang out, and in the ensuing skirmish eight patriots died. It was the beginning of the American Revolution.

Word of the attack spread rapidly from settlement to settlement, and incensed colonists rallied to the cause. One man loaded up his rifle and ammunition, told his young son to stay behind and take care of his mother, and galloped off to the fight. As soon as the father was out of sight, the boy borrowed a rifle and set out for the skirmish.

By the time the British soldiers arrived in Concord, they faced a motley bunch of stout and hardy patriots dressed in white frocks and round hats, with remarkable musketry talents honed from life on the frontier. On the soldiers' march back to Boston, the patriots sniped them from behind stone walls and trees. The British called "their twisted guns the worst widow and orphan–makers in the world." An eighty-year-old Samuel Whittermore "opened fire, killing the soldier he aimed at . . . With one pistol he killed the second Briton, and with his other fatally wounded a third one," reported a British soldier. "They rushed to the spot, clubbed him with their muskets and pierced him with their bayonets until they felt sure he was dead." Whittermore lived eighteen more years, dying in 1793 at the age of ninety-eight.[7]

In May 1775 a newly formed Continental Congress convened in Philadelphia and created a Continental Army under the supreme command of war hero and respected Virginian, George Washington. The new army was tested a month later at Bunker Hill near Boston when they faced off with the British who were trying to capture the surrounding countryside. After a bitter fight, the patriots lost the battle when they ran out of ammunition, but while they had it, they inflicted heavy casualties on the enemy.

In the north of Ireland women supported the cause by making clothing for those who were fighting for the cause of liberty in the New World. One schoolteacher gave his pupils a half-day off whenever there was news of a patriot victory. Unfortunately those days came less and less. Over the next two years, after major defeats at the hands of the British, the patriots lost New York and the nation's fledgling power base in Philadelphia. The British incited the Cherokee to attack the entire southern frontier, unleashing months of bloody attacks on the Scots-Irish pioneers.

A lightning war ensued, where skirmishes erupted rapidly with devastating carnage inflicted on both sides. Rarely having time to bury their dead, patriots put them in piles and covered them with old logs to spare them from preying animals. After one battle in New Jersey, some soldiers found time to dig two graves, but when they returned with the bodies, they found some Pennsylvanians had put corpses in the holes. After a long argument, the Jersey men prevailed; the Pennsylvanians removed their bodies, put them under a shallow heap of brush and stones, and rushed back to the front.

Washington soon realized he couldn't beat the British, and then began a war of attrition in the hope of wearing them down to the point of collapse. Months and years dragged on with the positions of both armies changing little. The militias found themselves fighting battles hundreds of miles from home for extended periods of time while their settlements lay vulnerable to Indian attacks. Their families depended on the harvest to survive—these men couldn't afford the luxury of playing soldier. As one Southerner said, "go fight the battle at once, and not be Shilly Shally in this way, until the Poor people are ruined."[8]

The Scots-Irish remained by Washington's side, doggedly determined through the cold and hungry winters. Their patriotism and zeal to beat the British coupled with their Calvinist work ethic that equated failure with unworthiness. Remaining as ardent as ever, they filled the ranks of the militia and the regular army, along with twenty-five leaders.

"Half the rebel Continental Army were from Ireland," one British officer testified before an exasperated parliament.[9]

The Scots-Irish militia brought their unique warrior ethic to the front lines. Their brand of soldiering came with a strong sense of individuality that chaffed at rules that weren't of their own making. They insisted on thinking for themselves. They showed up for a battle and pitched their tents where they wanted. They insisted on electing leaders based on valor and cunning, as was their tradition; they caused all sorts of disruptions to the ranks when untried men from higher social classes claimed to be their superiors. A North Carolina man said he "would shoot the first officer that would offer to Command him," and a South Carolina man said he wouldn't serve under a man he could "lick."

In the fall of 1777, thousands of militia swelled the ranks in the north, overwhelming British soldiers and Hessian mercenaries at the Battle of Saratoga, where they exacted the surrender of nine thousand British soldiers. It was a critical victory that secured America from further attacks from Canada and convinced the French to enter the war on the side of the Americans.

"Call this war by whatever name you may," declared a beleaguered Hessian captain. "Only call it not an American rebellion, it is nothing more or less than a Scottish Irish Presbyterian rebellion."[10]

In the South, the Scots-Irish were fighting an asymmetrical war. They were so numerous that once the British left a location, the militia streamed in and took back control. They intimidated local Loyalists with vigilante courts, the most famous belonging to Virginia planter and son of Irish Quaker immigrants, Charles Lynch. Lynch ran an irregular court on his lawn that gave summary trial to Loyalist suspects and handed down sentences like whipping and property seizure. The tar and feathering of collaborators happened on an impromptu basis throughout the colonies without the need for a trial. Detailed instructions were printed and issued throughout the settlements, and defendants often had to pluck their own ducks before being drummed out of town.

Meanwhile the British, reeling from defeat at Saratoga, devised a "southern strategy." At the end of 1778, they took the rebel port of Savannah, Georgia. They massacred unprepared settlers at Waxhaw Creek, South Carolina, with such ferocity that they radicalized a twelve-year-old boy named Andrew Jackson. They pulverized Charleston with a force of ten thousand men and fourteen war ships.

"Every man that I saw was endeavoring by all sober means to escape from death or captivity," a soldier said. "Which at that period of the war was almost certain death."[11]

Meanwhile Indian allies of the British were plundering settlements left unprotected by men who had gone off to war. Soldiers' wives were forced to beg from door to door. Southern treasuries were empty and unable finance an army. American currency was worthless. Washington, whose soldiers were weak and starving, could provide no help.

"Except for occasional small guerilla parties," President Theodore Roosevelt wrote later. "There was not a single organized body of American troops left south of [its] broken and dispirited army. All the southern lands lay at the feet of the conquerors."[12]

Despair settled over the South, till out of nowhere came a Scots-Irish skirmish in the backwoods that changed the entire direction of the Revolution.

British officer Major Ferguson—tasked with protecting the left flank of the British main advance on Charlotte, North Carolina, under Lord Cornwallis—issued a directive to the frontier rebels in September 1780 to lay down their arms or he would "Lay waste to their country with fire and sword." Patriot leader Isaac Shelby jumped on his horse and galloped forty miles through the Tennessee wilderness to the Holston Valley home of John Sevier. They agreed to muster as many frontiersmen as possible. On September 25, the day of the muster, the whole countryside seemed to gather at Elizabethton, Tennessee: 1,100 hardy Scots-Irish called "Overmountain Men" came from across the Appalachians, 200 came from Virginia, and 160 from North Carolina.

Old men and young boys showed up to defend the settlements from Indian attack while the men were away. Women turned out to mend and sew clothes, the mills ground corn to make bread for the army, men mined lead for bullets. When they were ready, a high-spirited Presbyterian circuit rider, Reverend Samuel Doak, galloped into Elizabethton to deliver a blessing.

"Brave men, you are not unacquainted with battle," he thundered. "Your hands have already been taught to war and your fingers to fight. . . . Go forth then in the strength of your manhood to the aid of your brethren, the defense of your liberty and the protection of your homes." He then called down God's blessing, "Oh God of Battle, arise in Thy might . . . smite those who exalt themselves against liberty and justice and truth."[13]

The men with horses saddled up, others followed on foot across the harsh mountain terrain. Word of their march spread through the settlements. Four nights later, three hundred and fifty more men from North Carolina and fifty Georgian artisans emerged from the woodland hills to join their ranks. In the usual Scots-Irish fashion, they elected their overall commander, Colonel William Campbell, known as "bloody tyrant of Washington County" for his harsh treatment of Loyalists. The next night they met a British force twice their size at Kings Mountain.

"The sky was overcast with clouds, and at times a light mist of rain falling, our provision were scanty," wrote one militiaman. "Each [man] felt his situation; the last stake was up and the severity of the game must be played; everything was at stake—life liberty property . . . seemed to depend on this issue."[14]

The Overmountain Men came within a quarter mile of the enemy before being discovered, but once the alarm was sounded, the British drums began to beat. Redcoats jumped to their positions firing musket balls that rained over the rebels' heads.

"Shout like hell and fight like devils," yelled Colonel Campbell as he charged at the head of his men, and they let loose their infamous bloodcurdling "Rebel Yell."

At once one of Ferguson's officers, horrified to hear that all-too-familiar sound, tried to warn his superior of the danger they faced. "Those yelling boys are here again," he stressed, but Ferguson was unfazed.

The rebels divided into six columns. As one charge was beaten back by British bayonets, they reloaded at the base of the mountain and regrouped while another column rushed from behind. The rebel units inched their way toward the British through the thick smoke. Loyalist bodies were strewn all over the mountain. In a desperate effort to break through their lines, Ferguson wielded his sword in one hand and charged at the patriots. A marksman cut him down. The British surrendered an hour later, and after nine executions, the Scots-Irish, true to their warrior ethos, disbanded and went home.

News of the victory rallied Americans across the land.

"This brilliant victory marked the turning point of the American Revolution,"[15] President Theodore Roosevelt later wrote.

On hearing of Ferguson's defeat, the main British forces retreated from Charlotte back to Yorktown, Virginia. The French transported Washington's army by sea and blockaded British reinforcements along the coastline. Cornwallis was outgunned, outnumbered, and unable to resupply. On October 19, 1781, he capitulated.

"There is no use crying about it," British Prime Minister Horace Walpole told his parliament, laying the blame at the feet of the Scots-Irish. "Cousin America has run off with a Presbyterian parson, and that's the end of it."[16]

After the Revolutionary War, Congress saw no further need for a large national army, and the people who had an inherent distrust of armies—even their own—agreed. The veterans mustered out, leaving a two-tier structure consisting of a minuscule standing army and a militia that would be called on only in the cause of national defense. It suited the Scots-Irish ethos. Their natural rebelliousness didn't respond well to coercive military duty, particularly at the hands of unproven officers. They did, however, undertake their militia duty reliably and patriotically as long as it was on a volunteer basis. For the next two hundred years, the army underwent multiple changes, but the warrior ethic at the heart of these soldiers of the South stayed the same.

Shoot Low, Boys! Shoot Low!

The British Empire was about to be humiliated by the orphan child the redcoats beat. Not that he went spoiling for a fight—although that was typical of his nature—but thirty-four years after the young Andrew Jackson's face was sliced up by a British officer during the Revolutionary War and his older brothers and mother were killed in the line of duty, he had his chance to wreak revenge.

When yet another war broke out between Britain and France in 1793, America claimed neutrality but continued trading with France. The British responded by making a menace of themselves on the high seas. They seized neutral vessels and made them pay duties; they impressed thousands of American men into their Royal Navy. On land they kept up their usual frontier mischief of inciting the Indians to attack settlements and continued to amass a presence on the Canadian side of the Northwest Territories, lest the Americans forget their old foe was close at hand.

In response to their misconduct on the seas, President James Madison accused them of flagrantly disrespecting America's hard-won sovereignty. He was ignored. On June 18, 1812, Congress was left with no options but to declare war on Britain.

"Here's the Stuff! Wake up! War! War with England!!"[17] the president's express-rider, Bill Phillips, yelled as he tore through the countryside, his long hair streaming in the wind before he disappeared in a cloud of dust. The country rallied to the call.

The main theater of battle was focused in the North and at sea. Northern generals stressed the necessity of retaining control of Lake Erie to prevent Detroit and Chicago from being lost to British armies in Canada. A small American force advanced northward but were beaten back and lost the city of Detroit and the Michigan territory in the process. They launched a second invasion a few months later through the Niagara Peninsula, but were again defeated. The only victories won by the Americans were Jackson's defeat of the British allies—the Creek Nation—at Horseshoe

Bend, and by the tiny U.S. Navy that captured and destroyed three heavy British frigates at sea.

In 1814, Napoleon, emperor of France, surrendered to the British. Divested of their war with the French, the English now turned their entire armed forces loose on their former colony. They landed in Virginia with five thousand battle-hardened troops. Not knowing what to do, President Madison, his generals, the navy secretary, and the attorney general fled to a camp outside the city in a "scene of disorder and confusion which beggars description."[18] The British strutted into an undefended capital and spent the next five weeks humiliating the city. They set fire to the Capitol building, piled all the White House furniture into the parlor and set it alight. Fire at the treasury building and navy yards burned until it was put out by a thunderstorm.

"I know not where we are in the first instance to hide our heads," said Madison.[19]

America was humiliated and in desperate need of a savior. He emerged from the frontier wilderness in the shape of Andrew Jackson and his diehard Tennessee militia.

As commander of the U.S. Army in the southwest, Jackson was responsible for the city on which the full force of the British army was about to descend. Eight thousand disciplined regulars, many of them veterans of the Napoleonic wars, expected to punch their way through New Orleans, sail up the Mississippi, and meet their troops coming south from Canada. The plan, according to the British foreign secretary, was to capture "all the rivers of the Mississippi valley and the [Great] Lakes [, making] the Americans little better than prisoners in their own country."[20]

Jackson arrived in New Orleans on December 1, 1814. Three weeks later, ten thousand British troops landed under the command of General Edward Pakenham to fight Jackson's motley army of four thousand militiamen, regulars, Indians, and pirates.

At daybreak on January 8, two Congreve rockets exploded overhead signaling the order to attack. The entire British army seemed to be moving toward the Americans in the early morning fog. They charged two Tennessean batteries, thinking them a weak spot in the line, but the Kentuckians rallied behind their kinsmen and readied three cannons to fire.

The British responded with heavy artillery fire, and then under the cloud of gun smoke, ran a bayonet charge with ladders and ditches to scale the parapet.

"An Irishman born, came running along," one soldier reported. "He jumped upon the brestwork and stooping a moment to look through the darkness as well as he could, he shouted with a broad North of Ireland brogue, 'Shoot low, boys! Shoot low! Rake them—rake them! They're comin' on their all fours!'"[21]

The American batteries opened fire, cutting the redcoats to pieces, and sent them running for cover in the ditches. Another company of redcoats ran into the woods to attack the Americans from the swamps but was driven back by the Louisiana militia. To the right, twenty-five hundred British marched on a small American artillery force that managed to keep firing just long enough for a retired French officer who had volunteered his services to fortify them with four hundred of his men.

The constant rolling of cannons and muskets was said to sound like claps of thunder followed by the lightning flashes of a furious electric storm as the noise and carnage raged on. The Americans kept loading and firing as fast as they could, hardly able to see their targets through the smoke. One soldier, who had no gun, picked up a barrel and flung it at the British, then found an iron bar and started beating them.

Pakenham rode out to try to rally his broken ranks and was shot dead.

Then in the afternoon, the disgraced British ceased firing and raised a white flag. The smoke cleared, and for the first time, the battlefield carnage was revealed.

It looked to the Americans like a sea of blood before they realized it was covered in the prostrate bodies of redcoats. Some crawled out from under bodies where they'd taken shelter and ran off. One squat soldier ran about two hundred feet, then thinking himself out of range, turned and made obscene gestures. A Tennessean fired, and the squat redcoat fell over dead. The squat soldier didn't know that the frontier, a man who couldn't hit the head of a squirrel from two hundred yards was considered a bad shot.

The battle was over. Surviving British officers testified they had never witnessed anything like the stubborn fierceness of the American force, or the carnage that befell the British army. There were seventy-one American casualties compared with over two thousand British. One of the mightiest armies of Europe had been humiliated by a small force of rag-tag frontiersmen under the leadership of a rough-hewn Scots-Irishman.

Later they heard that a peace agreement had been reached in Ghent two weeks before the battle, but it didn't matter that the war was over before the battle began. Victory at New Orleans infused the nation with a sense of pride witnessed not even after the Revolutionary War. Years of humiliations perpetrated by the British were thoroughly reversed.

The Scots-Irish general and his band of rugged patriots came to represent the true warrior spirit of America. Thus the nation's love affair with its solders had begun.

The War of Northern Aggression

Events might have unfolded differently had it not been for a 1749 case of grand larceny in London. The unfortunate John Jackson, of Country Derry in northern Ireland, was convicted of the capital crime of stealing 170 pounds while living in London and sentenced to a seven-year indenture in America. Meanwhile, Elizabeth Cummins, a six-foot-tall, blonde Londoner had been convicted of stealing nineteen pieces of silver, jewelry, and fine lace. The two were transported on the prison ship *Litchfield* that departed London in May 1749 with 150 convicts. John and Elizabeth met on board, and by the time they docked in Maryland, they were madly in love. They served their sentences in different places, but six years later they found each other and married. Twenty years later John Jackson and their two teenage sons fought at the Battle of Kings Mountain. Three generations later, Thomas J. Jackson was born the son of a poor farmer. Seven years later, he was orphaned and sent to live with an uncle for the rest of his unhappy childhood. He was withdrawn, uneducated, and didn't make friends easily. He was one of few farm boys who had no instinct for farming.

His personal mantra "You may be whatever you resolve to be," coupled with his absolute faith in God, somehow led the poor orphan to struggle his way into the U.S. Military Academy at West Point. After graduation, he deployed to the Mexican-American War, where he won three awards for gallantry and became known for his honesty and dedication. It seemed his ancestors' warrior ethic was coursing through his veins. He also inherited his ancestors' rebelliousness—manifested in the civil disobedience caused by running a Sunday school to teach black children to read and write. Virginia's law prohibited the education of slaves. For the most part Jackson's actions were overlooked. In fact, there was little about him that ever drew attention. He cut a shabby figure in plain uniform but was a devoted husband, loyal servant of God, and lived a quiet unassuming life.

"There was not a particle of gold lace about him," one soldier said. "He rode a horse as quiet as himself. His seat in the saddle was ungraceful. His well-worn cadet cap was always tilted over his eyes."[22]

However, Major Jackson's days of simple life were numbered.

By the mid-1800s the population of the industrial North exploded with the arrival of millions of poor immigrants. This elevated the established Americans into the middle class. More interested in industrial productivity than military duty, they shunned the compulsory annual militia training and paid a fine instead. Those who couldn't afford the fine were ridiculed as "rabble" and "scarecrow militia" playing at military drills without any real weapons or uniforms.

The South was different. The Scots-Irish had settled the frontier and imbued it with their strong warrior ethic that valued qualities like skill and valor. They believed the North had become soft and only they embodied the rugged individualism and principles on which the nation was founded. The mountains in particular made fighting men. Religion and war were pillars of Scots-Irish culture. With their staunch faith in their Lord and Savior, death meant everlasting life and so they feared no enemy. Mountain men were tougher than most men—they could do without, they weren't accustomed to luxuries, they lived tough every day.

Military preparedness took on greater significance in the South as the 1800s progressed. The North was imposing protective import tariffs that benefited their manufacturing interests but hurt the agrarian South. The congressional balance of power was also shifting. The population of the North was rising much faster than the South's. Once the North had larger voter rolls, they would have political control of the country. The rural Southerner was fearful of becoming a minority at the mercy of Northern whims; such fears were exploited by the "slavocracy" that wanted to create a "Solid South" to stand defiantly against Northern political and economic oppression. Ninety-five percent of rural Southerners didn't own slaves and had no interest in helping the planters keep theirs, but they did respond to outside threats to their hard-earned right to liberty and self-determination.

By 1861 the already charged political environment became untenable with the election of abolition sympathizer Abraham Lincoln. Eleven of the fifteen slave states seceded. They set up their own Confederate government and demanded that all federal property in the South be turned over to their authority. When President Lincoln refused, the Confederates signaled the start of the war with a forty-three-gun bombardment on Fort Sumter in South Carolina. The American Civil War had begun.

Southerners enlisted in droves, driven by their commitment to independence and liberty and a passionate hatred for the tyrannical "Northern Invaders."

"Everyone seems to know that his life liberty and property are at stake," said one Tennessee man. "Hence we never can be whipped."[23]

Northern forces mobilized to fight for the high and noble concept of the Union. They had little interest in slaves or racial equality. One commander with a black unit admitted he assigned them to "do every particle of the dirty work." A New York major resolved that if this was "an ablation war . . . I for one shall be sorry that I ever lent a hand to it. This war [must be] for the preservation of the union [and] the putting down of armed rebellion, and for that purpose only."[24]

Jackson hoped his home state wouldn't secede but when it did, he decided his loyalty to Virginia was greater than his loyalty to the United States. He packed up and rode out to take over as brigadier general in the army of General Joseph E. Johnston, a fellow veteran of the Mexican-American War.

In eastern Virginia another Southerner faced a dilemma. Born in 1807 into a wealthy Virginian family that fell on hard times through poor business acumen on the part of his father, Robert E. Lee was a proud Southerner, unwilling to ever accept defeat. At eighteen he entered West Point determined to restore his family's reputation. Having built an illustrious military record with some key victories during the Mexican-American War in 1846, Lee restored his family's pride and standing.

At the outbreak of the Civil War he was offered the job of supreme commander of all Union forces. Where did his loyalty lie—Virginia or the Union? Eventually, he came to the same conclusion as Jackson and penned the letter he never wanted to write.

General:

Since my interview with you on the 18th instant I have felt that I ought not longer to retain my commission in the Army. I therefore tender my resignation, which I request you will recommend for acceptance. It would have been presented at once, but for the struggle it has cost me to separate myself from a service to which I have devoted all the best years of my life & all the ability I possessed. . . . Save in the defense of my native State, I never desire again to draw my sword.

Be pleased to accept my most earnest wishes for the continuance of your happiness & prosperity & believe me most truly yours.

R. E. Lee[25]

For Lee as a soldier of the South, self-determination and loyalty to kin were of utmost importance. With equal doggedness, his men supplied their own horses and often their own weapons. They left their homes not because they were looking for a fight but because a fight was put upon them, but once attacked they refused to be bested.

On July 21, 1861, the Union army of 33,000 men amassed around Washington to march a hundred miles on the Confederate capital of Richmond; they believed its capture would bring a short, sharp victory to end the Southern rebellion.

Confederate forces under the command of Louisiana-born General Beauregard intercepted the Union army north of Richmond at Manassas, Virginia, near the Bull Run tributary. Beauregard telegrammed Johnston in the western theater for reinforcements. Johnston telegrammed Jackson in the Shenandoah Valley to the west of Richmond.

Jackson had been keeping the Union army busy chasing him around the valley. His little Confederate army consistently won victories over much larger Union forces—attacking and then melting into the forest. They disrupted transportation and supply routes and delivered a series of blows that confounded the enemy.

"Always mystify, mislead, and surprise the enemy," he said with all the cunning of the Scots-Irish warrior. "And when you strike and overcome him, never let up in the pursuit so long as your men have strength to follow; for an army routed, if hotly pursued, becomes panic-stricken, and can then be destroyed by half their number. The other rule is, never fight against heavy odds . . . a small army may thus destroy a large one in detail, and repeated victory will make it invincible."[26]

Lincoln eventually grew tired of Jackson and ordered additional troops into the Shenandoah Valley to neutralize him, but they also failed. Eventually, even the Union troops admired him.

"[Jackson's] chief characteristics as a military leader were his quick perceptions of the weak points of the enemy, his ever readiness, the astounding rapidity of his movements, his sudden and unexpected onslaughts, and the persistency with which he followed them up," said a Union officer. "His ruling maxim was that war meant fighting, and fighting meant killing, and right loyally did he live up to it."[27]

On July 18, fifty miles from Bull Run, Jackson received Johnston's telegram.

"Our gallant army under General Beauregard is now attacked by overwhelming numbers," he told his brigade. "The commanding general hopes that his troops will step out like men, and make a forced march to save the country."

The soldiers shouted with joy, packed up, and marched for two days across hostile terrain, wading rivers and resting little. If they did stop for a few hours, Jackson himself kept watch so they could rest. Meanwhile the battle at Bull Run was raging and the Union was gaining the upper hand.

The Confederates were forced to retreat. The bodies of the dead and dying were strewn across the ground, three and four deep. The trees were splattered with their blood. A New York regiment charged on the Confederates, shattering their line and sending the troops fleeing toward a plateau. Alarmed by the unanticipated strength of the Union, Johnston looked anxiously toward the mountain gap, hoping for more reinforcements. Then he saw Jackson standing on the ridge with six thousand men pulling up the rear.

"They are beating us back!" General Barnard E. Bee cried out.

"Then, we will give them the bayonet!" Jackson replied.

"Look at Jackson!" Bee yelled riding back to his South Carolina soldiers. "There he stands like a stone wall! Rally behind the Virginians!"

With renewed courage the Confederates reformed their broken ranks, let loose their infamous rebel yell, and charged at the Union relentlessly all afternoon. The Union eventually exhausted their artillery shells, and their line quickly melted away.

"They started like a flock of sheep every man for himself and the devil take the hindermost," said a Union soldier who watched his comrades rush back to Washington leaving much of their equipment in the field. "While the rebels' shot and shell fell like rain among our exhausted troops."[28]

The Confederates were elated. It was clear evidence that their skill, courage, cunning, loyalty, and refusal to be bested won the day. The Union was humiliated. Lincoln called up half a million more men and prepared for a long war.

In battle after battle "Stonewall" Jackson and Lee delivered devastating blows to their Union enemies, but Lee's first invasion of the North ended disastrously at Antietam Creek in September 1862. The defeat not only discouraged European powers from coming to the aid of the South, it prompted Lincoln to capitalize on the victory by issuing an Emancipation Proclamation that freed slaves in all rebel states. Slavery remained legal in only the four slave states that had stayed with the Union: Maryland, Delaware, Kentucky, and Missouri. For the Southern soldier, the legislation proved what they believed all along—the North was willing to impose rules on the South to which they themselves didn't subscribe. They felt vindicated in fighting against tyrannical oppressors.

In 1863, almost two years after their victory at Bull Run, Lee and Jackson beat an army twice their size at Chancellorsville, Virginia. It was called Lee's "perfect battle" when his risky decision to split his army paid off. Jackson's brigade crushed the Union flanks to deliver the final battle blow. When Jackson and his army returned to the Confederate camp after completing their mission, darkness had already fallen.

"Halt! Who goes there?" shouted a guard to the approaching soldiers.

Jackson's men tried to identify themselves.

"It's a damned Yankee trick! Fire!" shouted an officer.

Jackson was hit three times. When he finally got medical attention, the doctor had to amputate his arm but remained optimistic that the general would survive.

"Give General Jackson my affectionate regards," Lee wrote. "And say to him: he has lost his left arm but I my right."[29]

Jackson developed pneumonia, which at the time couldn't be cured.

"Presently a smile of ineffable sweetness spread itself over his pale face," the doctor remembered. "And he said quietly, and with an expression, as if of relief, 'Let us cross over the river, and rest under the shade of the trees.'"[30]

He died on May 10, 1861, brought down by friendly fire.

After Jackson's death, Lee's attempt to get the fight out of war-torn Virginia resulted in the bloodiest battle of the entire war. At Gettysburg, twenty-eight thousand confederate casualties were suffered, and the backbone of Lee's army was broken. To finish him off, Lincoln unleashed Ulysses S. Grant on the South.

Grant's family left County Tyrone in northern Ireland about the same time as Stonewall Jackson's great-grandfather was being dispatched on a prison ship. Like his kinfolk, he shared the same grim determination, courage, and genius for warfare. He served alongside Lee in Mexico, but as an Ohioan, he had a genuine desire to crush the traitorous rebels and restore the Union for the patriots. He pulverized his enemies without mercy. "The only terms I can offer are immediate and unconditional surrender," was his modified Scots-Irish motto.

Grant left General William T. Sherman—America's incarnation of Oliver Cromwell—in the western theater to lay waste to the entire infrastructure of the South. He went east to destroy Lee's army and march triumphantly into Richmond. Lee successfully fended off every attack. For six weeks the two armies struggled in combat throughout the state. Grant was losing two thousand men a day, and despite accusations from the North that he had no respect for life, Grant could replenish his ranks. Lee could not. Finally they ended up in a ten-month-long siege around Richmond, with Lee powerless to stop the devastation being wreaked by Sherman on his March to the Sea.

Finally Lee was forced to flee south to resupply the hungry and battered remnants of his army. Grant gave chase for a week. Lee knew he couldn't win. Finally on April 9, 1865, at the Appomattox courthouse, they met to discuss the terms of surrender. Lee, the proud Southern cavalier, appeared dressed in full uniform with ceremonial sword and spurs. Grant, the down-to-earth Scots-Irish warrior, came in muddy boots.

Grant committed their terms to paper and then, of his own volition, included a clause that allowed Confederate officers to keep their personal side arms. Lee added that his cavalry supplied their own horses and asked that they be allowed keep them. The Southern soldier without might or money had brought his sense of moral obligation and most valued possessions to the defense of the South. Grant agreed and Lee signed. They shook hands. Lee bowed to the other officers present and took his leave. Outside, Union general Horace Porter watched him as he waited for his horse.

> While the animal was being bridled the general stood on the lowest step and gazed sadly in the direction of the valley beyond where his army lay—now an army of prisoners. He smote his hands together a number of times in an absent sort of way; seemed not to see the group of Union officers in the yard who rose respectfully at his approach, and appeared unconscious of everything about him. All appreciated the sadness that overwhelmed him, and he had the personal sympathy of every one who beheld him at this supreme moment of trial. The approach of his horse seemed to recall him from his reverie, and he at once mounted. General Grant now stepped down from the porch, and, moving toward him, saluted him by raising his hat. He was followed in this act of courtesy by all our officers present; Lee raised his hat respectfully, and rode off to break the sad news to the brave fellows whom he had so long commanded.[31]

And so with that time-honored respect for valor, nobility, and the incorruptible qualities that define the warrior, the war ended. An estimated 620,000 Americans had died. The South had been laid to waste, its land torched, its infrastructure demolished, yet the Southern spirit never died. Lee became one of the most revered generals in American history, and his soldiers were forever remembered for their fine, true qualities of courage, patriotism, and the spirit of independence that were at the heart of America.

Lead Me, Follow Me, or Get Out of My Way

A massive dust cloud erupted in the distance as three armored vehicles blasted through the vast desert wasteland with the bodies of two dead

Mexicans lashed to the hoods like hunting trophies. The ten men inside the blistering hot vehicles had just engaged in wild firefight with officers subordinate to Mexican revolutionary Pancho Villa near the rugged Sierra Madre Mountains. Villa had torched towns and killed American citizens in surprise attacks on U.S. soil. Now payback was skidding to a stop outside mission headquarters in Dublan, Mexico.

"We have a bandit in our ranks," declared the commander Brigadier General John J. Pershing when he saw them arrive. "This Patton boy. He's a real fighter!"

Journalists were standing by to immortalize the young mission leader into a national hero. George S. Patton, otherwise known as Pershing's legendary "bandito," certainly knew how to make an entrance.

The Patton family legend had been going strong for seven generations in America. The patriarch was shrouded in mystery (no one knew exactly from whence he came), but the family mythology held that—much like Stonewall Jackson's patriarch who was chased out of London—he was a wanted criminal who fled Scotland in the early 1700s and assumed the name of fellow passenger Robert Patton, who died on the journey. Robert Patton settled into the redoubtable Scots-Irish settlements of Virginia, where his offspring made themselves champions of the culture's noble, warrior ethic. They fought in the Revolutionary War and the Mexican-American War. Uncle John served under Stonewall Jackson, and grandfather George was a renowned Confederate colonel. It seemed like every member of the Patton family made their way into the Confederate ranks, in fact, every generation of Pattons seemed to show up in one war or another.

When George S. Patton was born in 1885, he was weaned on his ancestors' stories of battlefield glory. He decided that he too would be a war hero. After graduating from West Point, he showed his fierce Scots-Irish competitive streak during the first ever modern pentathlon at the 1912 Stockholm Olympics. He not only proved his mettle as an athlete, he excelled at the skills every soldier should possess: shooting, fencing, swimming, horse-riding, and running.

The days of the motley militia were long gone; the determination exhibited during the Civil War brought respectability to the ranks, and the army became a means of social and political advancement. Even the militia evolved into a voluntary and more cohesive National Guard force that became the formal reserve component of the U.S. Army. The ranks were filled with professional soldiers. A disproportionate number came from the South, where the military tradition was strong. As far as they were concerned, the frontier tradition made them superior soldiers; they were proud that they could ride better and shoot straighter than any Yankee. In the twentieth century their ethos evolved as a world force.

It started in 1914 when the Germans invaded Belgium, Luxembourg, and France but were brought to a halt in Paris by the combined French and British armies that had scrambled to launch a counteroffensive. Meanwhile on the eastern front, the Russians were fighting Germany's ally, the Austro-Hungarian Empire. In the western theater both sides were dug into a bloodbath of trench warfare. The Battle of Verdun in 1916 almost brought France to the brink of collapse. Later that year the Battle of the Somme inflicted over 600,000 casualties on the Allies and almost half a million on the Germans. Still, no major advances were made on either side.

Everything changed in 1917. Russia withdrew from the war after a communist revolution overthrew the czar. German U-boats sank seven U.S. merchant ships, and America obtained intelligence that the Germans were wooing the Mexicans into an alliance against them. Congress declared war on Germany on April 6.

The British and French were delighted to witness American soldiers arriving in France at the rate of a quarter of a million a month. They joy was diminished when they learned that Pershing, the supreme U.S. commander planned to train his draftees with the goal of forming an American army fighting under American command. His soldiers would not to be used as replacements in the decimated French and British ranks.

Major Patton landed in France in 1917 with the newly established United States Tank Corps. He received ten tanks in March 1918—and being the only member of the corps with tank-driving experience—backed seven of them off the train himself. Patton had a lot to teach his men, including his mantra, "You're never beaten until you admit it," and his strategy for discovering enemy positions, "Just drive down that road, until you get blown up . . . then report back."[32] He was a warrior's warrior—a tough, outspoken, fearless, straight-shooting, all-American winner, and his men revered him.

By August 1918, Pershing had created the U.S. First Army, trained and ready for an independent offensive to break the German lines and capture the railroads at a fortified town near St. Mihiel in northern France. The Allies had a different idea.

"[Their] plan . . . would require the immediate separation of the recently formed First American Army into several groups, mainly to assist French armies," Pershing wrote in his final report to Washington. "This was directly contrary to the principle of forming a distinct American Army . . . the strategical employment of the First Army as a unit would be undertaken where desired, but its disruption to carry out these proposals would not be entertained."[33]

The supreme Allied commander had to do it Pershing's way.

On September 12, 1918, five days of heavy wind and rain had turned the roads of northern France into marshlands. Over half a million soldiers were knee-deep in mud as they advanced behind engineers who tried to clear dense nests of barbed wire with Bangalore torpedoes. Patton's tanks got stuck in the mud or developed engine trouble from the pouring rain, making them an easy target for German artillery.

As a brigade commander, he had been given orders to watch his reserve and to direct operations from his post, not from a tank on the front lines. But his Scots-Irish warrior ethic and competitive spirit couldn't abide watching the "most irritating sight" on the battlefield—his tanks stalling in the trenches. Before long he left his adjutant in charge of the command post telephone and, calmly smoking his pipe, walked onto the battlefield where he directed operations from on top of a tank—technically not disobeying his orders that stipulated he was not to be *in* a tank.

He was later reprimanded for "swanning" around the front area. Nevertheless, the battle was a success—the Germans retreated and the Allies carried the day.

An American army was an accomplished fact, and the enemy had felt its power," Pershing's report continued. "It gave our troops implicit confidence in their superiority and raised their morale to the highest pitch."[34]

On September 26, after a three-hour barrage from French artillery, Patton's tanks went grinding forward, leading the army's 1st Division through the dense cloud of thick fog and shell smoke on the Allied mission to route the Germans from the Meuse-Argonne region in northern France. The battle was hell; the shelling and German machine-gun fire were deafening. Some soldiers got lost in the fog and were wandering around looking for their units; others panicked and were retreating when they bumped into Patton, who ordered the men to stay with him, and five tanks to attack the machine gunners.

"Let's go get them! Who's with me?" he yelled as they advanced.

That ancient Scots-Irish battle cry inspired a hundred or so infantrymen to fall behind him. At the top of the hill, they encountered fierce fire that cut down men on every side. Patton and a handful of soldiers pushed forward. One by one they were shot down, leaving only Patton and Private First Class Joe Angelo to advance. In the cloud of gun smoke over the German lines, Patton thought he saw his warrior ancestors and said calmly, "it is time for another Patton to die." Suddenly a bullet struck him in the left upper thigh, leaving an exit wound the size of a dollar bill. He was carted off by cattle car to a hospital near Dijon. Six weeks later an armistice was announced. The Great War was over. It was Patton's thirty-third birthday, and he'd been promoted to full colonel.

"Peace was signed and Langres was very excited. Many flags," he wrote in his diary. "Got rid of my bandage. Wrote a poem on peace."[35]

Old Blood and Guts

"We'll win this war," General Patton told the Third Army in England on the eve of battle in 1944. "But we'll win it only by fighting and by showing the Germans that we've got more guts than they have; or ever will have . . . . We're not going to just shoot the sons-of-bitches, we're going to rip out their living Goddamned guts and use them to grease the treads of our tanks."[36]

In two decades since the Meuse-Argonne offensive, everything but Patton's attitude had changed. He cultivated a flamboyant image complete with polished helmet, riding pants, high cavalry boots, and flashy ivory-handled revolvers. His vehicles had large insignias and loud sirens that suited his profanity-ridden but much-quoted vernacular. His philosophy was as simple as ever: "All real Americans love the sting and clash of battle. . . . Americans love a winner. Americans will not tolerate a loser. . . Americans play to win all of the time."[37]

He was the quintessential Scots-Irish warrior: an all-American hard-ass, defiant, competitive, and self-reliant fighter poured white-hot out of Scots-Irish culture. His confidence was legendary—while Stonewall Jackson inspired his troops with his unwavering faith in God, Patton inspired them with his unwavering faith in himself.

Lieutenant Colonel Lyle Bernard, Colorado, 30th Infantry Regiment and a prominent figure in the second daring amphibious landing behind enemy lines on Sicily's north coast, discusses military strategy with Lieutenant General George S. Patton. Near Brolo, Italy, 1943.
Courtesy of National Archives Local Identifier 111-SC-246532.

On September 1, 1939, Nazi Germany invaded Poland. Britain and France declared war on Germany. In 1941 Germany invaded the Soviet Union; the Japanese bombed America's naval base at Pearl Harbor; Germany declared war on America. Before the year was up, the whole world was at war.

The sneaky nature of the Japanese attack united America more than it had ever been. The entire country mobilized in the war effort. The defense of the nation became a shared burden. The standby army of fewer than 150,000 troops shot up to 18 million. There was no question in people's eyes that they were on the side of good and that their soldiers were virile, brave heroes fighting to liberate the world from Nazism. Patriotic sensibility soared, and the American soldier was its symbol.

"I have nothing but the best in my Army. I don't care what color you are as long as you go up there and kill those Kraut sons of bitches," Patton told the elements of his army. "Everyone has their eyes on you and is expecting great things from you. . . . Don't let them down and, damn you, don't let me down!"[38]

With that, Patton went back to war. Three years later, on June 6, 1944, the Allies launched the largest amphibious assault in the history of warfare. After storming the beaches of Normandy, they secured the beachhead and consolidated the initial landings. A month later, Patton was where he wanted to be: leading the Third Army through France in a ferocious dash toward the German lines.

The Soviet army was closing in on the eastern front, while strategic Allied bombing was wreaking havoc on German cities. The Nazis needed to regain some battlefield initiative and made a strategic decision to launch a major offensive through the Ardennes forest in Belgium, a weak point in the Allied lines. Some lightly armed members of the 101st Airborne at a little known town called Bastogne stopped them in their tracks. The town was critical to the Nazis because it was a hub where seven main roads intersected; if their Panzers were to make the rapid progress necessary for a victory, the Germans had to control those roads.

The 101st Airborne and the 10th Armored Division—two severely battered units—were rushed into the small town with orders to hold it at any cost. There, they were trapped in an arctic landscape; snowstorms froze their weapons; the men had to urinate on them to thaw them; trucks had to be kept running to prevent the engines from freezing; the ground was so hard they could barely dig foxholes. They had no cold-weather gear, ammunition, food, or medical supplies, and the weather made tactical air support and resupply lines impossible.

By December 21 the German forces had them surrounded. Their superior firepower pulverized the Americans, who found themselves in a reversal of normal battlefield conditions—they were a small lightly armed force facing off against a well-supplied, heavy-armored enemy. What they lacked in brute force they made up for in endurance, skill, and ingenuity. They commandeered three artillery battalions that could unleash the firepower of twelve howitzers. They rounded up forty light tanks to create a mobile "fire brigade" that scampered around the battle zone repulsing German armor, like a mechanized version of the old frontier musket snipers.

As the 101st strained to hold the perimeter, a note arrived from the German commander requesting the surrender of Bastogne. Acting commander Brigadier General Anthony C. McAuliffe turned the paper over, wrote the word "NUTS!" and sent it back. For the "battered bastards of Bastogne" as they were later dubbed, there couldn't have been a greater morale booster, even though they knew their chances of holding out for much longer weren't looking good.

All around the countryside, scattered American units were engaging the enemy, repelling furious attacks, blocking the enemy's northern advance. To the south Patton was involved in heavy fighting along the Franco-German border. General Eisenhower ordered Patton's Third Army to stop its offensive to the south and relieve Bastogne. He was told of McAuliffe's dire position and given three days to arrive with reinforcements.

"Any man who is that eloquent deserves to be relieved," Patton said when he heard McAuliffe's response. "We shall go right away."[39]

Patton already had three plans worked out in anticipation of Eisenhower's order. With a tactical maneuver that seemed to defy logistical ability, Patton disengaged the forward elements of the Third Army and swiftly faced his men north.

"Drive like Hell!" he ordered, and they drove like fiends for six hundred miles. At Bastogne his 4th Armored Division attacked the German Panzers from the rear, broke through the surrounding enemy lines, opened a corridor to the town, facilitated the resupplying of the 101st, and paved the way for an Allied counterattack in January 1945. It was a fatal blow to the Germans.

"This is undoubtedly the greatest American battle of the war," British Prime Minister Winston Churchill told his parliament. "And will, I believe, be regarded as an ever-famous American victory."[40]

But the Scots-Irish warrior wasn't interested in waiting around for accolades; he resumed his mechanized race, chasing Germans across France, Belgium, Luxembourg, Germany, and Austria. By the time the Nazis surrendered, Patton's advance units had punched into Czechoslovakia where they met the Red Army.

The war in the European theater was over, but in the Pacific the Japanese were still grinding on. Soldiers were jumping from island to island as the enemy dug in even deeper. Fighting was getting harder; casualties were escalating. President Harry S. Truman was handed the plan for an invasion of Japan that projected a quarter of a million American casualties. The alternative was to drop the atomic bomb. If it worked, it would demonstrate to the Japanese that America would use any means necessary to defeat them. It would also show the Russians that the United States had the military power to prevent the spread of communism. The bomb was dropped. Five days later Japan surrendered.

The war was over, but Patton—now considered one of the greatest military figures in history—predicted that without a common enemy, the Soviets would cease to be a U.S. ally.

"Let's keep our boots polished, bayonets sharpened, and present a picture of force and strength to these people, the Soviets. This is the only language they understand," he advised. "Tell the Red Army where their border is, and give them a limited time to get back across. Warn them that if they fail to do so, we will push them back across it."[41]

They were portentous last words. On December 9, 1945, his car was involved in a low-speed collision with an army truck. Patton was paralyzed after hitting his head in the impact. Like Stonewall Jackson, the predecessor with whom he shared the warrior bloodline, his own men inadvertently cut down the indefatigable fighter. He died twelve days later and was buried, as he requested, "with my men" at the Luxembourg American Cemetery.

The New World Order

The Soviet alliance splintered just as Patton predicted, and the atomic bomb signaled the start of the nuclear race. Americans recognized they were involved in an ideological and political struggle with the Soviet Union and reconciled themselves—for the first time in history—to the idea of a large peacetime standing army. But it was a new army and military tradition, transformed by the new world order. The Soviet Union started to flex its muscles, first by trying to drive the British and French out of West Berlin and later by detonating an atomic bomb. The Communist Party took control in China.

The "red" menace continued to spread. World War II ended thirty-five years of Japanese colonial rule of Korea. The peninsula was divided along the 38th parallel, with the Americans occupying the south and the Soviets the North until free elections could be held. Instead of elections, the North Korean Communist army, in Soviet tanks, ran roughshod across the 38th parallel and all over the South Koreans. The United States, supported by the United Nations, came to South Korea's aid.

This was a new kind of war. There was no mass mobilization, no declaration of war; the American soldier went to fight in a distant land for reasons he vaguely understood while the nation went on about its business. No one knew that President Truman had signed a document in September 1950 that established American strategic goals. For the next four decades, classified report NSC-68 identified ultimate victory in this new ideological Cold War—the collapse of Soviet power and the emergence of a new world order based on American capitalist values. The United States as "the center of power in the free world" had an obligation to contain the Soviet hegemony.

As Truman wrestled with the nature of the new enemy from the ruins of the old world order, a select group in Washington may have understood the emerging political objectives. But on the battlefield they were murky, confusing, and subject to a bewildering number of changes—as World War II hero and strategic genius, General Douglas MacArthur discovered when he was ordered to the peninsula to eject the communists from South Korea.

MacArthur accomplished his military objectives by driving the communists back into the North. Then Truman, with the United Nation's endorsement, changed the objective to unifying the peninsula. MacArthur invaded the North, but China came to its defense and drove the Americans back into South Korea. Then MacArthur was told to hold a line until the United States could bring about a negotiated settlement. The general was furious that he was ordered into a strategic defensive position and openly criticized Truman's policy. In one of the most unpopular decisions in presidential history, Truman relieved him of duty. The ensuing public outrage accentuated how cherished the American soldier had become in American society. Despite public allegiance, the warrior ethic continued to be defeated by an ill-defined enemy and vacillating political objectives that would become the hallmark of the era. For the American soldier— symbol of the nation's finest, truest qualities—the question became: Are we in this to win?

American Tragedy

"Now this is the way it's going to be," Lieutenant James Webb told his new platoon on the ground in Danang. "Anything you say to me I will believe. If you tell me the sky is brown, I will believe it. If I ever find out you lied to me, you're dead meat."[42]

Jim Webb was a twenty-two-year-old rookie with an attitude. Fresh out of the Marine Corps base at Quantico, he was thrown into the dense Vietnamese jungle to lead a platoon of soldiers on search-and-destroy missions. All over the countryside soldiers were marching for weeks at a time, weighed down with heavy packs full of food, water, weapons, and ammunition. They were eaten by mosquitoes, covered in blood-sucking leeches from wading waist-deep through rice paddies, and exhausted from hacking their way through dense vegetation. It was hot, humid, and miserable.

Worst of all, as they scoured for an enemy that knew the land intimately, they were on a tense hair-trigger alert for sudden ambushes and mines that riddled the jungle.

"You go out on patrol maybe 20 times or more and nothin', just nothin'," one soldier explained. "Then, the 21st time, zap, zap, zap, you

Soldiers carry a wounded comrade through a swampy area. Vietnam, 1969. Courtesy of National Archives Local Identifier 111-SC-651408.

get hit . . . then [the enemy] fades into the jungle before you can close with him."[43]

On Webb's first night on patrol, they walked into a vicious firefight at a heavily fortified North Vietnamese stronghold. He called in air strikes and directed the counterattack. Brigade command had just about given them up for dead, when the whole platoon returned to base without casualties. When the same thing happened the following night, it became clear that Webb was a warrior's warrior—a twenty-two-year-old who could lead men into battle and get them out alive.

Fighting, courage, and self-reliance coursed through Webb's Scots-Irish veins. His family were frontier fighters long before the Revolutionary War. His father was a World War II air force officer, and Webb grew up trailing him from one dusty base to another. Webb Sr. was the epitome of the Scots-Irish ethos—loud, demanding, sharp, and his son's greatest hero.

When he was four, his father, a veteran of World War II and the Berlin Airlift, would clench his fist and hold it out:

Are you tough?

Yes, I'm tough.

Then hit my fist.

Jimmy swung, crushing the knuckles of his tiny hand.

Is that as hard as you can hit? Hit it again.[44]

The exchange echoed of Elizabeth Jackson scolding her son two hundred years earlier.

"Stop that Andrew, do not let me see you cry again, girls were made to cry not boys," she admonished. "What were boys made to do?"[45]

"To fight," little Andrew Jackson replied.

Webb shared a lot of traits with Jackson: both were warriors, born leaders, determined, persistent, independent thinkers, and both would always prevail. Now young Webb, the latest generation to embody his culture's warrior ethic, was in the jungle trying to learn how to lead troops. He studied warfare, strategy, tactics, and leadership, trying to learn why generals made the decisions they did. He had no political views about the war; he trusted the country's leadership.

Those were the early days in Vietnam.

For more than a millennium, the Vietnamese had been ruled by imperial China yet never lost their cultural distinctiveness and never wavered in their relentless, violent resistance. In the 1600s, it was an independent country, albeit divided in half by two powerful Vietnamese families who engaged in civil war for the next four decades. In the 1800s, the French colonized the country, but after World War II, a communist revolutionary, Ho Chi Minh, declared Vietnamese independence. The French responded militarily, but after eleven years of fighting, they negotiated a ceasefire at the 1954 Geneva Conference. Vietnam split officially at the 17th parallel into a communist-controlled North Vietnam and democratic South Vietnam. France withdrew.

In its zeal to contain communism, the United States propped up a corrupt, dictatorial South Vietnamese government, while the Soviets backed a fiercely proud and independent North Vietnamese regime. China quietly observed events in its former colony, while the political subterfuge spawned military ambiguity replete with poorly defined objectives.

President Lyndon B. Johnson promised he had every intention of keeping "American boys" out of Vietnam. However, when U.S. Navy destroyers in the Gulf of Tonkin reportedly came under attack by the North Vietnamese, and when the Viet Cong—communist guerrillas from South Vietnam—stepped up their attacks on U.S. forces, Johnson authorized massive air strikes called Operation Rolling Thunder and a troop buildup half a million strong.

Initially the troops went to Vietnam filled with a sense of patriotism. Morale was high; they still believed containing communism was necessary for the defense of the nation. Most of them were sons of World War II veterans and felt a strong sense of duty, especially in the American South where the Scots-Irish ethos still honored the image of the noble Civil War soldier, the true American patriot and defender of liberty.

At the outset, fully two-thirds of those who served were volunteers; the other third were drafted. Draft exemptions were made for medical reasons and for those in college, meaning the middle-classes were granted immunity. The poor rural and inner city kids were caught up in the machine. There were other draft-dodgers fleeing to Canada, but as a Tennessee infantryman said, "If [a Southerner] ran they knew they'd never be welcome back in society in the South . . . it's always been this way."[46]

Troops landed in Danang expecting to be greeted by the South Vietnamese as liberating heroes—they were greeted with distrust and suspicion instead. The Viet Cong (VC) was virtually unidentifiable; they could blend into villages as easily as they could melt into the jungle. The troops never knew whom to trust, but they knew they were being watched. They learned to sense if the enemy had been in a village before them, partly because the villagers never tripped the land mines. It was as though they were told where not to step.

"Here's a woman of twenty-two or twenty-three . . ." one soldier said. "She [says] her husband works in Danang and isn't a Viet Cong. But she watches your men walk down a trail and get killed or wounded by a booby trap. She knows the booby trap is there, but she doesn't warn them. Maybe she planted it herself."[47]

Over time, as mines and booby traps killed and injured more American soldiers, they became increasingly frustrated with trying to fight an enemy they could not see. It could take an entire day to hack their way through two miles of jungle. They'd secure a village, search it, leave, but the Viet Cong returned when they were gone. Some began to take their frustrations out on officers who seemed more interested in their own glory than the welfare of their men, particularly those who directed combat missions from the safety of command posts, or from helicopters overhead.

It wasn't Webb's way—he was the incorruptible warrior, forged from the values of the frontier and devotedly loyal to kin. He wasn't interested in currying favor with commanders, and neither would the ethos coded in his bloodline permit him to take half-baked orders from superior officers who hadn't earned his respect.

When his platoon was sent in to support an infantry company that was taking heavy casualties, a captain ordered Lieutenant Webb to provide cover for an advancing unit by taking up position in an open rice paddy about two hundred meters away. Webb questioned the decision; his men would be sitting ducks out there, he explained.

"I'm giving you a direct order," said the commander.

"You're not my company commander, sir," Webb said. "I'm not going to do it."[48]

Webb took his platoon to a position that made sense. He was going to make sure people were thinking before sending them off on a knucklehead maneuver. When the assault started, his machine gunners killed eight

Viet Cong. That was the last time someone questioned his judgment. As General George S. Patton had always said, "It takes brains and guts to win wars. A man with guts but no brains is only half a soldier."[49]

That first summer in Vietnam, medals started piling up. He earned the Navy Cross when they came under grenade attack from three bunkers. Webb fought back, disabled the enemy, and found intelligence data. When a grenade was thrown at one of his men from the third bunker, he simultaneously fired his weapon, jumped at his soldier shielding him from the blast, and then threw a grenade into the bunker to destroy the last elements of the VC ambush. It became routine for one of his troops to wander up to the company commander and say, "Skipper, lieutenant earned another medal last night."[50]

By the end of 1967, the U.S. soldier had reportedly killed 90,000 Viet Cong. At Christmas, the American public were thrilled to hear the enemy were close to defeat. A month later, 70,000 Viet Cong launched a well-planned surprise attack on more than a hundred Vietnamese towns called the Tet Offensive. Fighting was intense, but U.S. soldiers managed to kill or capture almost 40,000 VC within several weeks and inflict a devastating blow to Minh's army. It was a tactical triumph for the American warrior.

Unfortunately it was a public relations disaster. That the VC could muster so many men after losing so many during the previous years suggested they had an inexhaustible supply of fighters. Victory was nowhere in sight. American journalist Walter Cronkite had already announced after the Tet Offensive that the country was mired in a stalemate and that the war probably could not be won. The anti-war movement at home exploded.

Few knew that the Department of Defense had issued highly restrictive Rules of Engagement: a village couldn't be bombed without warning even if the soldiers had been fired upon first; a communist village could only be attacked once civilians had been removed. Surface-to-air missile sites couldn't be bombed while under construction, only after they were operational. MiGs couldn't be bombed while sitting on a runway, only when airborne and showing hostile intentions. Bases couldn't be bombed.

Commanders were issued wallet-size cards warning them to "use your firepower with care and discrimination, particularly in populated areas." The DOD didn't want edgy U.S. soldiers mistakenly destroying non-combatant villages. In reality, the soldiers rarely knew which villages were friendly. Some were forcibly occupied by guerrillas who used villagers for cover; most villagers just stood by, not warning them that they were about to walk into a minefield or ambush. They neither cared nor believed that the American soldiers were in Vietnam dying for the cause of their liberty.

After the Tet Offensive the morale of the U.S. soldier was in rapid decline, as he grew frustrated with the strategy of endless search and destroy missions that seemed to risk lives without any clear purpose.

"The military mission became to inflict casualties and the primary reason for existence became to minimize your own casualties," said Webb. "And you were sort of walking that tightrope the whole time. Ethical confusion is the only word that I can use. It just sort of mounts."[51]

Troops kept hoping that they would be given permission to really fight: to get in, get the job done, and get out. But they were so hindered by the Rules of Engagement they began to believe that the government wasn't in to win, at least not militarily, probably for fear that if they were unleashed, it would provoke China into World War III. Instead, they fought a war hampered by a host of political objectives against an enemy whose objectives were simple—destroy the American invaders.

Some soldiers started taking their anger out on the villagers. Some beat up women, children, or elderly men who refused to give them information. Others burned down huts and destroyed food supplies. As bombing missions and combat patrols destroyed thousands of villages, the Vietnamese were forced to live as refugees, which only hardened their support of the VC cause. In 1968, frustrated troops exploded in the tiny South Vietnamese village of My Lai. They raped, beat, tortured, mutilated, and killed almost five hundred unarmed Vietnamese civilians, including women and children. Three servicemen tried in vain to stop them.

The media reported the war crimes with horrific photos that caused domestic and international outrage. Anti-war sentiment exploded with an intensity virtually unprecedented in U.S. history. Americans believed their own government had betrayed them, but their anger was not only unleashed on the politicians who began the war, for the first time it was directed at the troops in the field. Ninety-seven percent of those who served were honorably discharged, yet this undeclared, unpopular war destroyed the hard-won mythology of the warrior as the liberating hero.

In 1971 President Richard Nixon started a two-year phased withdrawal. As the veterans trickled home, they found that no one distinguished between the war and the warrior. The public blamed the troops for the debacle. They also blamed them for not winning, even though the soldiers never actually lost a battle. As the war progressed, the military had adapted to prevailing battlefield conditions. If the war was lost, they believed it was by a lack of political will in Washington.

"There's not a comprehension of the level of performance of people who were in Vietnam," said Webb. "If you look at the actual battlefield results, there's no comprehension of how competent our military really was."[52]

Eventually the nation settled into a distrustful and indifferent mood. Unlike the World War II veterans, no one cared to hear their war stories. Even the Veterans Administration, the government agency charged with their care, was wholly inadequate.

"Ignoring the Vietnam vet was just one part of the more general phenomenon of ignoring the nation's entire, shattering, unhappy Vietnam experience in all of its aspects,"[53] lamented one historian.

The draft was abolished in the 1970s, which helped to remove America's resentment toward its own military. When the Rules of Engagement were declassified in 1985, the public finally grasped the impossible situation in which the soldiers had been placed. They began to see them as ordinary men doing their job in an unpopular war. The nation resolved that if it fought another war, popular or not, they would never again crucify the soldier who went out to fight. After all, the American warrior came from the American people; he was the heart and soul of the nation.

The Screaming Eagles

Fred W. Johnson grew up in a small town in southern Illinois about sixty miles from the Missouri border in a family built on the two pillars of Scots-Irish culture: fighting and religion. His mother was a devout Pentecostal and took her young son to the church where the seven gifts of the Spirit were regularly manifested. It was there the young boy saw people speaking in tongues, curing the sick, and being slain and saved by the spirit. At seven years old he felt himself become filled with the Holy Spirit and got such a fright that he ran out of the church and never went back.

His father had served a couple of years in the army, and as a boy, Johnson was happiest running around in his Dad's old army fatigues and listening to him sing "jodies," the old songs soldiers sing as they march double-time in formation. He also had that fierce Scots-Irish competitive streak that manifested in college basketball and running marathons. Then in 1982, his college basketball scholarship was cut and Johnson found himself joining the Army's Reserve Officer Training Corps program as a way to make it to graduation. Once in, however, he was immersed in the Southern military tradition that had endured since the first hard-living, hard-drinking frontiersmen ran the British off Kings Mountain in 1780. He was surrounded by like-minded guys who liked to fight, compete, and drink beer and be inspired by the ethos of warrior leaders.

"I'm talking Vietnam vets, guys who were shot up—incredible," he said. "In fact my battalion commander, Zannie Smith, I think the story was that he went up Hamburger Hill a sergeant and came down a lieutenant."

Smith never did get a battlefield commission but the legend spread all the same.

After Drum he was promoted to captain and assigned to the 101st at Fort Campbell. He was going to be a company commander with the legendary division that told the Germans where to stick their surrender during World War II. Unfortunately his superior officer, the lieutenant colonel (LTC), was a huge disappointment. True to Scots-Irish form, Johnson couldn't serve under a weak character and weak leader. Only five years in the army, at the age of twenty-nine, he wrote a letter he never thought he'd write—his resignation. Then Operation Desert Storm was announced and he tore it up.

"There was no way in hell I was going to miss the war."[54]

One of the most versatile divisions in the army, the 101st Screaming Eagles fired the first shots in the offensive by taking out Iraqi radar sites on January 17, 1991. They were tasked with making the longest and largest air assault in history, airlifting two thousand men, fifty transport vehicles, artillery, and tons of fuel and ammunition deep into Iraqi territory. They had a field full of aircraft including two hundred Black Hawk, Apache, Chinook, and Kiowa helicopters. The Screaming Eagles were ready.

The LTC gathered the men together on the eve of war.

"We were all assembled in this mess tent and this guy was gonna come up and give us our, what we hoped would be our Patton speech . . ." Johnson recalled. "And he gets up and he starts babbling and crying, 'I don't want to come back here and fight,' you know it was very uninspiring. So we all filtered out."

Outside the demoralized division got ready to fly. The LTC had a death premonition and decided to drive, taking the 101st anti-tank assets on the road with him. When the troops landed, the LTC was hours behind—they were on the front with no commander and no technology. Their orders were to seize Highway 8, which was used to resupply the Iraqi army from Baghdad. There they were, standing in the middle of the desert, without their anti-tank missiles. Forced to improvise like the "battered bastards of Bastogne," they rounded up what they had, which was a platoon of old TOW anti-tank missiles that they could launch off their Hummers.

"All we did was fire, beginning with a vehicle that came through and did not stop," Johnson said. "We just shot at whatever came at us."[55]

Hours later the enemy stopped advancing, and the shooting stopped. After a few minutes of silence, they were amazed to see their little low-tech assault had stopped the enemy and disrupted their ability to resupply.

By the time the LTC arrived, the four-day ground offensive was over. Johnson was awarded his first bronze star. The battle and the kinship among warriors were a defining point in his life. He kept photos of that day to remind himself of his greatest fear—cowardice.

New Kind of War, New Kind of Win

Sixteen years later, Captain Johnson was the much more seasoned Lieutenant Colonel Johnson, but this time in the desert nothing seemed as straightforward as that impossible task of using TOWs to stop Saddam Hussein's army during Desert Storm.

After the World Trade Center attack, patriotic duty swelled in the hearts of men and women nationwide, especially in the South where new enlistments were almost double those of the North. The military's new motto became "There's nothing on this green earth that is stronger than the US Army because there's nothing on this green earth that is stronger than a US Army soldier."[56] But soldiering had suddenly become a complex and multitasked job, not just about the dramatic explosions that brought media glory. The new war in the post–September 11 world required that warriors possess both an instinct for killing and the smarts to be peacekeepers. However, the kind of men who were attracted to the military sought hardship, challenge, and adventure; they wanted to blow things up. How would the warrior fare being told to stand things up?

Johnson was chewing over this quandary in the blistering heat of an Iraqi summer. Battling and beating AQI out of Baqubah had already proved to be a temporary solution. The only way to defeat them was to stand up its police force and army, restore its power center and basic services, and get food to the people. They needed to make the city so secure that it could protect itself so AQI couldn't fight its way back in. Colonel Antonio suggested they start by liberating the food rations that were locked up under the Shia-controlled government in Sadr City, Baghdad.

At first light, Johnson headed to the provincial center and sat in the suffocating heat of a small cramped room with the shy, chubby mayor and deputy governors to find solutions to the city's predicament. The Sunni city of Baqubah was starving; the Shia government had kept their food rations locked up in Baghdad for over a year. If they could get the food distribution system running, that might help to get city services running. With flour, the mills could open, and people could get back to work. That would be the first step toward reconstructing the city. Johnson decided that since the warehouses weren't going to provide assistance, they would just do it themselves.

The mayor found ten "ratty, old, civilian trucks" and rounded up ten men who could drive them. The trucks had no gas. Johnson had them fueled up by a tanker from the base. Eventually the rag-tag convoy of ten trucks was assembled, interspersed with six Strykers, an anti-tank platoon, a Fox armored vehicle, and four Iraqi army Hummers. They were about to set off when a strange man started walking toward them; something bounced under his shirt. In Iraq this usually meant one thing—suicide bomber.

Johnson drew his pistol, aimed, and shouted a warning for the man to stop. The Iraqi stopped. He waved his arms and shouted back. The soldiers finally realized he was speaking English. "I know all these people," he said. "I'm a part-time police officer." Osama, as the Sunni driver was called, heard about the convoy and came to offer the services of five trucks and drivers.

The Sunni convoy finally took off for the food warehouse in Shia-controlled Sadr City, the heartland of the Madhi army in Baghdad. The anti-tank platoons led from the front; the Strykers were intermixed through the fifteen trucks, with one at the back for rear protection and to make sure no one scampered off.

"It's right over here, it's over here," Osama yelled out of his truck window in the busy northeastern quarter of Baghdad. The trucks pulled into and parked in the warehouse lot. Johnson anticipated that they would just drive up, take Baqubah's food allocation and go, but nothing was ever that simple in Iraq. The warehouse was closed for the evening, and the manager told them they'd have to come back tomorrow. Ructions erupted; everyone was yelling and arguing. They objected to staying in Sadr City overnight. The drivers, the Iraqi army soldiers, and the mayor tried to take off, but Johnson refused to let anyone leave. Finally the drivers agreed to stay on the condition that both armies leave; military presence made them a target for Shia insurgents watching nearby. They'd take their chances alone.

The Iraqi army left and promised to return at six a.m. The American soldiers went to the nearest base. Chances were good that the Strykers would arrive the next morning and find the truck drivers had cleared out from the parking lot and gone home, but Johnson had little choice. At six a.m. the next morning, the American detachment returned to Sadr City, and to the colonel's surprise, everyone had assembled.

"Follow me," said Osama, and all the trucks roared out of the parking lot and lined up at the warehouse loading docks.

With the mayor in tow, Johnson went in to negotiate with the warehouse manager. Minutes later a grenade exploded outside. The warehouse manager scuttled behind the door and told them to come back another time. Johnson blocked the door, told him General Petraeus was talking to Prime Minister Nouri Al-Maliki. Everyone knew that Al Qaeda had been routed and it was safe to start sending the humanitarian assistance to Baqubah again. Johnson pointed out a reporter with him. The manager's actions that day would become a matter for world news, he warned—he could be a hero or not.

The situation grew more tense. The warehouse workers weren't afraid of the American army because the Madhi army was right across the street. They were more afraid of being in trouble with their superiors for causing political embarrassment. Finally, the perplexed warehouse manager filled out the paperwork and released the food. Johnson ushered the mayor to the front so it would appear to the people that Baqubah's own leadership had restored the public distribution system. The colonel slipped into the background.

Out of nowhere, fifty-five more trucks arrived from Baqubah with a platoon of Iraqi police. They were sent by an Iraqi army general who had been monitoring the situation from behind the scenes. The most enormous convoy that probably ever left Baghdad headed back to Baqubah with so much food, flour, tea, and sugar that every warehouse shed in the starving city had to be used for storage. The mayor was a hero, his credibility forged in the Sunni-Shia standoff in Sadr City.

For the next forty-nine days, the Iraqis stood up other essential services like water and electricity. The Iraqi army and police took over security. The flour mills reopened. On September 22, 2007, after a fifteen-month-long deployment and the loss of twenty-seven American lives, Baqubah was strong enough to keep Al Qaeda out by itself. The four thousand warriors that had adapted to the complex, asymmetrical warfare that simultaneously demanded killer instinct, guts, cool heads, and brains—came home.

Johnson was awarded another Bronze Star for valor.

"It was really earned by everyone that was there doing the missions—I'm just the 'keeper' of the medal," he said. "I'm not being modest or anything. That's how I feel."[57]

It was a medal that honored the continued sense of brotherhood that permeated the Scots-Irish warrior ethic. It honored the same resourcefulness that existed since the militia pitched their tents and collectively worked out their battlefield strategy in 1775. It was recognition of the warrior ethic that still informed what was good in the armed services—patriotism, honor, and a dogged determination to be victorious.

As General Patton said, Americans always play to win.

CHAPTER 5

GOVERNMENT OF, BY, AND
FOR THE LITTLE GUY

"That sorry, good for nothing son-of-a-bitch Herbert Hoover never would admit there was a depression," railed Otto Harlow to his long-suffering wife and seven hungry children in their run-down shack in the inaccessible mountains of southwest Virginia.

Years after the Great Depression, he still told tales of how little children were starving and folks were living in fields and sleeping in haystacks. Every story ended with him cursing Hoover for the mess. In the 1940s, it seemed to the seven Harlow children that they never did get out of the Depression. Up there in Slaughter Hollow, they squatted in one leaky shack after another until someone eventually found them and ran them out. There were no roads, electricity, running water, or plumbing, and it was a good half-mile hike to the creek for seven hungry children to fetch water in their little buckets.

Every day Marvin and Ed Harlow, the eldest and youngest boys, climbed up into the cherry tree beside the house and sat there for hours eating cherries like a pair of possums. They had a staple diet of berries three times a day. Still, Otto insisted, it was worse during the Depression.

"I don't really see how it could have been worse," mused Ed Harlow. "But he said that it was." [1]

For most of Ed's childhood, Otto worked in a woodworking factory. He left each morning at six a.m. and hiked two miles down the mountain to catch a bus to work. His job was part of President Roosevelt's Works Progress Administration that put millions of people to work during the Depression. Otto loved Roosevelt. With typical Scots-Irish pride, he'd never take a handout, but he'd grab any opportunity for an honest day's work and a fair wage. That's what Roosevelt gave him.

Marvin Harlow (back right) and Ed Harlow (front center), ca. 1950, in front of their shack with cherry tree in the background. Reprinted with permission.

The Harlows would have lived fairly well except for one problem—Otto loved freedom and whiskey. On Friday nights he'd bring some groceries as far as the bus stop. The boys would take their mule along the two-mile trek to get them before Otto went off drinking. When he sold their mule for whiskey, their mother made the four-hour round trip to Bristol every Friday to collect half of Otto's paycheck before he disappeared into some honky-tonk for the weekend.

During the Republican administration of Herbert Hoover, Otto hoboed trains looking for work, like a drifter straight out of a Hank Williams song. There was no way to survive in the mountains; the land was too scrappy to farm, and the Depression had closed down all the mines. Otto was a handsome, likeable man who was wild, restless, and adventurous. Being a hobo suited him well until 1938 when he met Cleo Fleenor at a corn husking. They got hitched, and he traded his restless life for a WPA job in a Virginian factory. He was twenty-two; she was fifteen. The following year Marvin was born, and as more and more children were added to the fold, Otto spent evenings regaling them with stories of romance and adventure about how he used to find empty houses and barns to sleep in and how to get on and off boxcars without getting hurt or caught. Stationmasters watch for hobos, he warned his avid audience of children; he had to wait till the train pulled out and reached a certain speed before he could chase it and jump on.

Otto never did get those wayward days out of his blood. Cleo was left alone to fend for herself and her children. She knew everything that could be picked and eaten from the land. The boys went out fishing and hunting for squirrels, rabbits, and possums. It didn't take much to thin out the wildlife, but as Ed said in his idiomatic southwest Virginian drawl, "If they were caught they were eat." Cleo was a strong-willed woman; she made sure if there was any food, the children got it; she did without or she ate what was left. After a breakfast of berries, the children walked miles to school and stayed hungry most of the day. There were no school lunches in those days, not that they would have taken them anyway—pride wouldn't let mountain folk take anything for nothing.

From time to time, they'd go to fetch water and find Otto passed out in the creek after some failed attempt to get home.

"Serves you right," Ed always would say and leave him lying there.

"If it hadn't been for our mother we wouldn't have had a prayer," Marvin explained.

Marvin grew up to be handsome and fun loving, smart but largely uneducated, musical but self-taught. His easy manner and southwest Virginian drawl helped him be the peacemaker of the household, especially between their parents, who argued continuously. Once when they were trapped after the creek flooded, Marvin scaled the mountain and brought back some groceries. He hunted for game and gathered and chopped wood so Cleo could feed the children. At fifteen, he got a job in a grocery store making $18 for a seventy-hour week. He walked two miles each way from the mountain shack in the dark, the rain, and the snow. The company he worked for was started by a Confederate captain who won $800 playing poker with the guards while in prison and used the money to start a business when the Civil War ended. That's how Marvin learned how to get ahead—by grabbing opportunities.

"I knew there had to be something somewhere better than we had," Marvin said. "I worked my way out of it. I had nobody handing me nothing. Thing is, you'll make a way if you have to."

After Marvin left in 1955, little Ed wanted to grow up and get a job too. He was a smart, hyperactive boy who was often in trouble at school and hated being stuck in the mountains. When he was twelve, they moved to their uncle's farm where he got a job clearing land for fifty cents an hour. He saved it to put himself through school.

Meanwhile Marvin was making good money as a sales rep. He had a good work ethic and always seemed to make the right decisions. Ed idolized him.

"He taught me how to play music and made sure that I did it right. He was a demanding older brother in his own way," said Ed. "I always admired him."

That was until 1964 when Marvin voted for a Republican. From that day on, the two brothers who grew up hunting squirrels and sitting in a cherry tree could no longer be in the same room when it came to politics.

"Marvin's thinking is: I made it on my own, you make it on your own, it's up to you," Ed said in total dismay at his brother's new Republican ideas.

That year the Democratic nominee, Lyndon Johnson, won the White House. Marvin supported Johnson's Civil Rights Act because he believed it was wrong to keep anyone down, but other than that, he couldn't find another redeeming feature in the president's policies.

"We started going wrong when Johnson started getting socially and fiscally liberal . . . making us a socialist country," [2] Marvin declared confidently.

"Many of Johnson's programs brought the mountain people out of poverty," Ed retorted. "There's always going to be someone that needs help. It's the responsibility of government to provide for its people. It's not a handout—it's an opportunity."

"We just don't need all that government," Marvin insisted. "We started this country because we wanted to get away from people ruling us and telling us every move to make and what we could and we couldn't do."

The two brothers are freedom-loving, self-reliant, and independent. They share that deep-seated Southern distaste for having issues forced on them; what they don't share is how that translates into the government's role in people's lives.

"What we accomplished in two hundred years was great," Marvin said proudly. "If you turn the people loose and let them go they'll take care of themselves."

He's a disciple of small government because he's convinced a big one will just meddle in his life and hurt him in the end. He's adamant—there's only one way out of poverty and that's to work your way out. Ed agreed. As a Bristol City Democratic councilman, he worked hard to bring decent jobs into the city. He's the first to say, there's no such thing as something for nothing, but you'll always be poor if the government doesn't stimulate the economy and provide opportunities to do better.

"Only people who can bring jobs is the businesses, not the government," Marvin balked. "Liberals hold people down, they make people feel like they can't do nothing. If these people could get some pride in them . . ."

"Republicans [say] programs to help people are nothing more than a give-away for lazy, good for nothing people who won't work and don't deserve it," Ed interrupted. "It plays into government mistrust . . . since Reagan anyway."

"Ronald Reagan was the best president we ever had," declares Marvin, coming to the defense of this idol. "Reagan put a lot of pride back in people, got things going."

"Bullcrap," snaps Ed. "The wealthy people only care about their wealth, they don't care about the working man, they're not gonna give you anything to get you wealthy. They need your services to work; they'll keep you as poor as they can."

The argument has been raging for fifty years, and each time it ends with each brother more deeply entrenched in his own viewpoint than ever. Ed voted on economic issues because it was his way out of poverty. Marvin voted for his values because he believes the best thing the government can do is leave people alone. Each is convinced the other has become deluded by media bias and needs to be deprogrammed.

They return to their corners with the question unresolved: was it big government or big business that got these half-starved little guys out of the cherry tree?

"Mac-ocracy" of the Backwoods

Rebellion was brewing in the backcountry.

Since they arrived on the frontier, tax hikes and colonial government interference had been a thorny issue for the Scots-Irish settlers especially in North Carolina, where they were subjected to corrupt officials, dishonest sheriffs, and excessive taxes. If the sheriff came unexpectedly to collect taxes, the farmer would have to try to borrow money from neighbors. Many times the sheriff would sell the property—often to his friends for a sum well below its value—before the farmer had time to find the cash.

These immigrants arrived from Ireland with little or no political experience or education. They had no lawyers, judges, or politicians. The Great Awakening, however, imbued them with a sense of confidence that came from knowing they had a role in their own salvation, so they asked why not their own governance. A "Mac-ocracy" began to emerge in the backwoods, marked by a deep and abiding distrust of government. It would become the bane of the ruling class on the eastern shore as it spread through the South.

By 1764 the backwoodsmen were threatening sheriffs, tax collectors, registrars, court clerks, and judges. Four years later they banded together to form the Regulators in an effort to eliminate the corruption and regulate their own affairs.

When the sheriff took a farmer's horse and saddle for nonpayment of taxes that April, more than sixty Regulators rode into the county seat in Hillsborough, seized the horse, broke up the court, and dragged corrupt officials through the streets. On the way out of town, they fired on the house of Colonel Edmund Fanning—the most corrupt of all colonial administrators. The colonial governor, William Tryon, denounced them as "riotous and disorderly persons" and ordered the militia of adjoining counties to be "held in readiness."

A month later Fanning ordered a raid to capture some of the organization's dominant figures. That summer, Tryon arrived in Hillsborough to try them on charges of "inciting the populace to rebellion."

Four thousand Regulators arrived in town to face off against Tryon's militia of fourteen hundred. Three Regulators were convicted but pardoned by the governor in the hope that leniency would settle the matter. Once Tryon left, the corruption resumed.

In 1770 the settlers finally exploded in anger at the tax bill they were expected to foot for the building of "Tryon's Palace," the governor's home.

"We are determined not to pay the Tax for the next three years, for the Edifice or Governor's House, nor will we pay for it," declared one member.

Regulators were hauled up for trial again. In response, hundreds of men armed with sticks and switches descended on Hillsborough, dragged the chief justice from the bench, and put the attorney general on mock trial. Others found Fanning, beating him so severely that "one of his eyes was almost beaten out." They destroyed his house, drank his liquor, and terrorized the rest of the town.

The colonial General Assembly passed a Riot Act replete with harsh punitive measures for protesters and ordered Tryon to march the militia against the main Regulators encampment at Alamance Creek. Two thousand men gathered in what would be the culmination of years of backwoods skirmishing. Regulators' Captain Benjamin Merrill started out on a daylong march with his men to join them; without him the backwoodsmen had no leadership or battlefield strategy.

Their superior numbers did not intimidate the governor. He refused to negotiate but gave them an hour to return peacefully to their homes or to be fired upon.

An hour later he sent an officer out to receive their reply.

"Fire and be damned!" was their answer.

The governor gave the order to fire, but the militia hesitated.

"Fire! Fire on them or on me!" he yelled standing up in his stirrups.[3]

A cannonade was unleashed. The Battle of the Alamance began. Some Regulators managed to drive off the gunners and captured one of the cannons. Unfortunately they were no match for Tryon's well-trained and well-equipped troops. Two hours later the battle was over, and they were defeated.

Tryon left the battlefield with thirty men in chains. He issued a proclamation offering a pardon to those who took an oath of allegiance to the colonial government. He disarmed the locals, burned their houses, destroyed their crops, and took their beef and flour for his army. He held courts-martial, where he prosecuted civil and military offenses, "extending their jurisdiction even to ill-breeding and want of good manners."

The battle was over before Merrill arrived, so he disbanded his men and went home. Fanning came knocking, put Merrill in chains, and dragged him off to Hillsborough. He was tried and given a death sentence despite not having been in the fight. He went to the gallows professing his faith in God and his hope of heaven. One of Tryon's soldiers reportedly declared that if all men went to the gallows with a character such as Captain Merrill's, "hanging would be an honorable death."

Tryon moved to New York, where he was notified by the king's officials that the Battle of Alamance "fully answered" the need for crushing "the Dangerous & desperate Designs of those lawless disturbers of the public Peace."[4]

The Scots-Irish backwoodsmen who refused to take the oath of allegiance were forced to move farther into the wilderness of Tennessee and Kentucky. Theirs had been a protest of the "illiterate, injured multitude" against the wealthy ruling class who comprised five percent of the population yet had total control of the government. They lost at Alamance, but they set the stage for the emergence of a distinctly American style of democracy, one built from the bottom up, with a government of, by, and for the little guy.

The People's President

"There is nothing certain but that the will of Andrew Jackson is to govern," said a rival during the president's first term in office.[5]

When the strong, shrewd, patriotic, military genius who restored the nation's pride after the Battle of New Orleans came to power, he discarded the wigs, buckles, and stagecoaches of the old guard for the leather bodkins and horseback riders of the new—he became the symbol of a democratic uprising, an assertion of the people's right to govern themselves. His popularity with the common man allowed him to amass so much power some believed the Constitution was in jeopardy; certainly no politician who valued his career could challenge his authority and survive.

Yet the political career of the man who created the distinctly populist style of American democracy got off to an inauspicious start in 1796 when Tennessee was admitted to the Union and voted in Jackson as its elected representative. He rode eight hundred miles on horseback, with his long hair tied in an eel-skin, to join the Washington elite for a brief and uneventful career in Congress, where he spoke only twice, and followed this up with an even less distinguished career in the Senate, where he didn't speak at all.

"His passions are terrible . . . he could never speak on account of the rashness of his feelings," said one senator. "I have seen him attempt it repeatedly, and as often choke with rage."[6]

Two years Jackson withdrew from the political fray and returned to the frontier as a circuit-riding judge meting out justice to scoundrels. He eventually bought a small ramshackle plantation outside of Nashville called "The Hermitage" and began planting cotton. He itched to return to politics, but even the governorship of New Orleans was denied him because of his reputation as "a man of violent passions, arbitrary in his disposition, and frequently engaged in broils and disputes."[7]

As major general of U.S. forces he was responsible for preventing slaves from escaping into the Spanish colony of Florida a territory filled with remnants of the Creek Nation, adventurers, Spanish freebooters, Irish roustabouts, and other sundries that were ready for any foray across the border that promised booty. Jackson saw Florida as a territorial threat and wrote to President Monroe requesting authority to invade. Without waiting for an answer, he took three thousand men into the peninsula, blew up a few forts, and forced a surrender. President Monroe found himself in the embarrassing position of having to smooth ruffled Spanish feathers to the tune of five million dollars. Calls for censure echoed in the Senate chamber, but fearing a backlash from the people, the president put Jackson in the unenviable position of Florida's military governor. He was back in politics but not quite the way he had hoped.

"I am sure our stay here will not be long," his wife wrote to her brother. "This office does not suit my husband."[8]

Nine months later, Don Andrew Jackson was bored with administrative duty. He retired from public life and was back at the Hermitage entertaining political leaders and men of distinction. Then in 1821, his friends suggested he run for the White House.

"'No sir; I know what I am fit for," he wrote to a friend. "I can command a body of men in a rough way; but I am not fit to be President."[9]

Nevertheless in 1822, at the behest of a clamoring public, he threw his hat in the ring. He had two chief competitors: one was a prominent New Englander and secretary of state, John Quincy Adams, a frigid man considered out of touch with the people; the other was Henry Clay from Kentucky, an "impetuous, willful, high-spirited, daring, jealous, but, withal, a lovable man."[10] Clay was more of a Virginian than a frontiersman and appealed to the educated, businessmen, and property owners. Jackson was the rough-hewn "tough as old hickory" Scots-Irish brawler of Tennessee who personified the self-confident nationalism of the interior.

Jackson won the popular vote but not more than half the electoral votes needed for a clear victory. The decision fell to the House of Representatives. Clay assigned his votes to Adams in exchange for the job of secretary of state. None of Kentucky's electors wanted Adams, so Clay was accused of circumventing the will of the people to curry political favors. There was a public outcry: the "man of the people" had been robbed by the "corrupt aristocrats of the East."

Adams—a representative of old-school politics—introduced a monstrous government that undertook all sorts of federally funded programs. They were to be financed by selling public lands at the highest prices and imposing a tariff on imports. His plan was universally unpopular, particularly in the South where farmers found themselves buying manufactured goods at artificially high prices in a closed, protected market but selling their tobacco and cotton in an open, competitive market.

Within six months the country split into Jackson men and anti-Jackson or administration men. A new two-party system arose: the Democratic-Republican Party, or Democrats, and the National Republicans, or Whigs. The backbone of Jackson's support came from voters mainly in the South and West who favored minimal government interference and free-market opportunities for individual enterprise.

In 1828 Jackson ran again. The campaign was brutal—Adams was denounced as a corrupt aristocrat. Jackson was painted as "a usurper, an adulterer, a gambler, a cock-fighter, a brawler, a drunkard, and withal a murderer of the most cruel and blood-thirsty description." His mother was called a prostitute and his wife a bigamist. Still, he won by a landslide, carrying every Southern and Western state, leaving only New England to Adams. Unfortunately his wife Rachel died from ill health suffered by the stress of the Adams' campaign allegations.

Almost fifteen thousand people thronged to Washington on Inauguration Day to usher out the old regime of the northeast and usher in the new regime of the people.

"A monstrous crowd of people," wrote one senator, "is in the city. I never saw anything like it before. Persons have come five hundred miles to see General Jackson, and they really seem to think that the country is rescued from some dreadful danger."[11]

Others described it as an inundation of northern barbarians into Rome. For the first time Pennsylvania Avenue was crammed with everything from splendid carriages all the way down to ragged wagons. When Jackson rode to the White House on horseback, it seemed as if the entire crowd had followed—clothes were torn, ladies fainted, and china was smashed. Servants eventually got the mob out of the house by bringing liquor out onto the lawn. Meanwhile, because Jackson harbored a hatred of Adams whom he blamed for Rachel's death, he refused to make the usual call of the incoming on the outgoing executive.

Once the celebrations were over, Jackson settled into tirelessly long workdays. He replaced over two thousand administrative officials with his own supporters in what he called the "Spoils System." It was really a display of inefficient partisanship, justified by claiming the "rotation in office to be the cardinal principle of democracy."

"Were it not for the outdoor popularity of General Jackson," wrote a senator, "the Senate would have negatived more than half his nominations."[12]

Jackson—or "King Andrew the First" as Davy Crockett facetiously called their new omnipotent executive—believed the United States was destined, perhaps even divinely ordained, to expand from the Atlantic seaboard to the Pacific Ocean. Later this philosophy would be honed into the Manifest Destiny, but in the early 1800s, it led Jackson to open territories in the West for settlement and claim all lands held by the Indians east of the Mississippi. Having expanded the nation Jackson looked around for the next cause on which he could sharpen his "scalping-knives."

The president was convinced that if left unchecked, the elite would serve their own interests at the expense of the many. In his time, those interests were being met by the Second Bank of the United States, which was chartered in 1816 for twenty years with a capital of thirty-five million dollars. Before 1816, money was printed by private commercial banks in various states. The national bank's goal was to control the notes issued and rein in over-speculative private banks. By 1823 it had become a financial behemoth led by an autocrat, a Philadelphia lawyer called Nicholas Biddle who led a monopolistic charge across the nation. He restricted loans and caused fluctuations in the economy that were regulating both small farmers and enterprising little guys out of existence. When Jackson's advisers told him Biddle and his bank had worked against him during his campaign, the "People's President" decided the institution was a menace to democracy by virtue of the financial power it wielded over politicians. He decided to wage a prototypical anti-lobbyist, anti-trust war.

"This worthy president thinks that because he scalped Indians . . . he is to have his way with the Bank. He is mistaken,"[13] said Biddle, who tried to weaken Jackson's popularity by curbing loans and calling in debts and political favors.

This was Biddle's blunder. When the bank's charter was up, it had to come before Congress for renewal. The ensuing face-off between Biddle and Jackson was perceived as a power struggle between the common man and the financial control vested in the conniving elite. Congress voted to reissue the charter, but Jackson crushed it with a presidential veto on the grounds that it was only making rich men richer. Government funds were withdrawn and deposited in twenty of Jackson's loyal "pet banks" nationwide. The national bank lost its special status as keeper of the nation's treasure, as well as all of its power, and within a few years it was bankrupt.

"I have . . . put to death that mammoth of corruption and power, the Bank of the United States," he declared triumphantly. "Biddle shan't have the public money to break down the public administration with. It's settled."[14]

Under Jackson the economy burgeoned during his first term, as revenue from indirect taxation and land shot up. He reduced the size of government and eliminated the national debt. He expanded suffrage beyond the landowning class to all white male adults, thus extending the populist vigor at the heart of the American democracy. The voters liked this frugal, minimalist, popular style of government without pomp and pretension. Under Jackson's guidance, American-style democracy, driven by the power of the common man, became enshrined in the heart of the U.S. political system.

American Idealism and a New World Order

"The state exists for the sake of society, not society for the sake of the state,"[15] wrote Thomas Woodrow Wilson in an early twentieth century moment of Jacksonian sentimentalism.

Times had changed since Andrew Jackson went out to bludgeon the conniving elite of the Northeast on behalf of the proud, self-determined pioneers of the Southern frontier. The Civil War industrialization had the power to demolish the South. By the dawn of the twentieth century, the industrialists had grown to such titanic proportions, they threatened to trample little guys everywhere. The engine of honest, hard-working, enterprising self-reliance that drove American democracy was being threatened by the financial behemoths Jackson fought to kill.

Then along came Wilson.

Wilson was a Virginian of devout Scots-Irish Presbyterian stock whose grandfather came to America from a little farm in County Tyrone in northern Ireland in 1807. He was born in 1856 and grew up in the scarred Civil War–era South. One of his first memories was of Jefferson Davis being hauled to prison in chains through the streets of Augusta, Georgia. His father was a Presbyterian minister, staunch Calvinist, and part-time teacher who had great influence over his son. Wilson himself experienced an "awakening" in his youth and believed himself, by the grace of God, to be one of the Elect. He strove for the rest of his life to prove his worthiness through good works, inspiriting leadership, and education.

"My life would not be worth living," he told a friend in 1915, "if it was not for the driving power of religion."[16]

Yet the future world leader was physically weak, suffering from headaches, gastric problems, colds, and depression. He was all but illiterate till he was twelve years old, when he discovered his passion for government. This presented his first opportunity to prove himself worthy of God's good grace. With his newfound zeal for politics and education, he graduated first from Princeton University, received a PhD from

Johns Hopkins University in political science and in 1902 was appointed president of Princeton University.

Always a man of the people, he saw abuse of money and power at Princeton that set him at odds with the establishment. He believed the college's "restless, rich, empty-headed people" were defending the class privileges of the wealthy. If the United States wanted to avoid another revolution, its institutions "must become saturated in the same sympathies as the common people. [The] country must be reconstructed from top to bottom."[17]

In a major departure from Jacksonian democracy, Wilson convinced America that in the industrial age, a big benevolent government with wide powers of intervention was the best way to protect the common man from corporate power. He launched a revolutionary program that called for economic fairness and equal opportunity—New Freedom.

"No one but the President seems to be expected . . . to look out for the general interests of the country," he said, and "We must abolish everything that bears even the semblance of privilege or any kind of artificial advantage."[18]

Wilson launched a war to overhaul the banking sector and the tariff system that had run amok since Jackson's day. The tariff was a relic from the days when the nation's fledgling economy needed protection from European powers. A century later, it had become an unwieldy system of intricate shelters that protected industry and created exploitative monopolies that diminished any sort of enterprising worker, preventing him from effectively competing in the marketplace. In effect, taxes benefited the large trusts and kept the little guys down.

In April 1913, Wilson went to war to battle the privileged on behalf of the poor. The public galleries in the House of Representatives were crammed with commoners eager to see their president face down the establishment.

"We have seen tariff legislation wander very far afield in our day—very far indeed," Wilson said. "We long ago . . . sought in our tariff schedules to give each group of manufacturers or producers what they themselves thought that they needed in order to maintain a practically exclusive market as against the rest of the world. Consciously or unconsciously, we have built up a set of privileges and exemptions from competition."[19]

He also proposed that control of the banking system must be "vested in Government itself, so that the banks must be the instruments, not the masters, of business."[20]

The Senate debated the issues all summer, and then in the fall, the commoners once again crowded into the galleries to hear whether fair taxation and credit reform would go into effect and give them a fighting chance to get ahead. The outcome was announced—the bills passed. The galleries erupted in cheers and applause; the common man faced down the behemoths and won.

"I feel tonight," Wilson said, "like a man who is lodging happily in an inn which is half way along the journey."[21]

Wilson was only getting started. Loans were issued to give farmers the chance to finally buy their own land. He promoted labor union growth, supervised agriculture and food production, granted women's suffrage, put restrictions on child labor, and established the eight-hour day for railroad workers.

"Wilson is making friends because he fights," said William Jennings Bryan, who was leader of the liberal wing of the Democratic Party at the time. "The people like a fighter."[22]

Unfortunately, Wilson's trailblazing reform campaign was abruptly halted by what he called the criminal stupidity of European governments. War had come to Europe. Wilson had no interest in embroiling the country by "going abroad in search of monsters to destroy." But his plans to keep American out of the war were undermined when Germany started sinking American ships and courting Mexico into an alliance against the United States. In 1917, Congress declared war on Germany.

The American war effort tipped the balance; bringing victory to the Allies. Wilson seized the opportunity to promote his idealistic notion to unite world leaders in "a general association of nations . . . affording mutual guarantees of political independence and territorial integrity to great and small states alike."[23] Wilson's version of the Manifest Destiny rejected territorial expansion in favor of the exportation of American democratic principles—he wanted to extend the benefits afforded the little guys in America to the world at large.

In December 1918, he set out for Paris on an epic quest to establish a League of Nations. The Paris Peace Conference of 1919 was grueling. The European allies wanted to impose a brutal "Carthaginian peace" on Germany, but Wilson, who had witnessed the backlash from the punitive Reconstruction efforts in the post–Civil War South, pleaded with them to treat Germany with leniency. The French prime minister Georges Clemenceau called Wilson pro-German and stalked out of the room.

Wilson was in bad health. Racked by "asthmatic coughing" and fevers, he pressed on, but his health caused him to swing between rage and depression and was openly hostile to any proposed Allied alterations to the terms. The burden of responsibility was "enough to crush the vitality of a giant," Wilson's wife said. "There would come days when he was incapacitated by blinding headaches that no medicine could relieve."[24] Wilson, however, wouldn't let any other American politicians attend the conference. Power and glory were to be his alone.

The conference culminated in the summer of 1919 with the signing of the Treaty of Versailles that ended the state of war between Germany and the Allied countries, with terms that humiliated Germany. It included a covenant to form the League of Nations.

Wilson returned to Washington to request Senate ratification of American membership in the league. The Republicans would accept it only with modifications proposed by their Senate majority leader, Henry Cabot Lodge. Wilson refused. Cabot was resolute; he wouldn't agree to any covenant that required America to deploy its troops in a conflict that didn't threaten its own national security. He would allow no American to serve under "a mongrel banner invented for a league."

"Mr. President, you are licked," a Republican senator advised. "There is only one way you can take the United States into the League of Nations."

"Which way is that?"

"Accept it with the Lodge reservations."

"Lodge reservations? Never!" Wilson answered in a rage. "I'll never consent to any policy with which that impossible name is so prominently identified."[25]

Stymied in Congress, Wilson decided to take his appeal to ordinary Americans, hoping he could rally the people against the evil Republicans. By now his headaches had become unbearable, his moods were erratic, and his heart unsound. His doctor advised against a month-long trip across the country but Wilson was resolute.

He made one speech daily to clamoring crowds, but four days after his return to Washington he had a stroke and was paralyzed on the left side. Meanwhile the Senate did not ratify the covenant. As the president lay incapacitated, Lodge gloated that the league was "as dead as Marley's ghost."

On Armistice Day, 1923, Wilson despite having won the Nobel Peace Prize was a failed and broken man. His dream of a new world order was dead. While he was trying to export American democracy he neglected to extend its principles to black American citizens, 300,000 of whom had fought for its defense in the trenches of Europe. Riots, lynching, and disenfranchisement continued to shame the nation.

On that cold November day in 1923, three months before his death, he appeared in the doorway of his Washington house to address the hundreds of people for whom he had fought so hard and for so long. They came to pay him tribute. His voice was weak and barely audible; at times he wept. He turned to go inside, then turned back to the people with an afterthought.

"I cannot refrain from saying it," the Scots-Irishman offered as his final and most prophetic words. "I have seen fools resist Providence before, and I have seen their destruction, as will come upon them again, utter destruction and contempt. That we shall prevail is as sure as that God reigns."[26]

A Fair Deal

That "Roosevelt nonsense" was over at last. In the spring of 1945, during his twelfth year in office, President Franklin D. Roosevelt, whose Scots-Irish ancestors sailed from Larne in 1729, passed away. Republicans and conservative Democrats paid tribute to the man, but breathed a sigh of relief that they'd seen the last of his big-spending, liberal, Depression-era government.

The seemingly unremarkable vice president, Harry S. Truman, a Missourian of Scots-Irish and English extraction, stepped into the job and into a world rent by the war of Wilson's prophecy—the Third Reich had risen out of the humiliations inflicted on Germany at the Treaty of Versailles. Truman never wanted the top job, but eighty-two days after being inaugurated as vice president he became the thirty-third president of the United States. It was now up to a failed haberdasher and son of a Missouri mule-trader to end the second world war and create a new world order.

No one was exactly sure how Truman ended up in the Oval Office—no one but his closest friends knew he was "one tough son-of-a-bitch of a man." His resolute hardiness was encoded into his thick Scots-Irish blood. His grandparents arrived in Missouri in the mid-1800s having left their Kentucky farm with a wave of Scots-Irish kinsfolk in search of a better future on the harsh frontier. They were uneducated, plain, hardworking people who idolized Andrew Jackson as one of their own.

Like all stalwart Scots-Irishmen, Trumans served in the Revolutionary War, fought with Jackson in 1812, and were Confederates in the Civil War. After the Civil War, Grandfather Truman, who had been driving cattle and wagon trains across Western plains, settled down into a life of farming on the line between a free and a former slave state. They suffered from roaming bandits and Union "occupation." His mother, a strong, resolute woman never shed her fierce animosity toward the North; she claimed till her dying day "If there are any good Yankees, I haven't seen one yet."

Harry Truman's humble life began in 1884 in a tiny house in rural Missouri amidst this culture of racial acrimony and segregation. Two decades after the Civil War, schools and neighborhoods were segregated; lynchings of blacks and whites were never reported, but everyone knew they happened.

Young Harry Truman had little schooling but was a regular at the town library, where he read voraciously. He was small and studious, with little glasses that earned him no end of teasing. He always remained cheerful, active, and amiable but gave no hint of his potential to be a giant world leader.

At fifteen he got a full-time job as a railroad timekeeper where he said he learned "all the cuss words in the English language—not by ear but by note."[27] At twenty-one he joined the Missouri National Guard and was called to active duty by President Wilson in 1917. By the time they reached France he was a captain, dragging horse-drawn gun carriages with the hundred men in his command up steep, muddy roads in northeastern France. They fired off five hundred rounds but when they started taking heavy enemy fire, horses bolted and broke away from gun carriages; the company dissolved into chaos.

"Run, boys! They've got a bracket on us!" yelled the first sergeant.[28]

The once small, bespectacled, unassuming Truman roared a string of those old railroad profanities and got the "no-good Irish sons-of-bitches" back in line. By the time he came home from the trenches, he was battle-hardened and quietly confident in his ability to lead.

In 1945, ninety days after assuming the presidency, the humble boy from small-town Missouri was getting war reports from the front in World War II, making decisions about atomic bombs, dealing with leaders like Josef Stalin and Winston Churchill, helping to rebuild Europe, devising doctrines to make the world safe for democracy, and working to establish international organizations like NATO, the IMF, and the United Nations.

Meanwhile the American forces were demobilizing, and twelve million men and women were flooding back home to compete for jobs while billions of dollars in defense contracts were canceled. The country was facing the biggest housing shortage in history. Five million Americans were living in firetraps and slums, often two families to a house. Fears of another Depression loomed. It was coming, they said "as sure as God made little green apples" and would be bad enough; fathers told their children to "curl your hair."

Truman responded with a massive twenty-one-point plan called the Fair Deal, in which he went all out for the little guy. He proposed tax, health care, housing reform, and farm bills. He vetoed legislation that tried to limit the power of labor unions. They said not even Roosevelt asked for so much "at one sitting." But the American polity, having already had enough of the little guy reforms of his predecessors, began to tire of the Democratic behemoth.

On the international front, America stood militarily triumphant, economically prosperous, and carried real international weight. The new United Nations, with its headquarters in New York, issued a landmark Declaration of Human Rights in 1948. Fully supported by Truman, it included provisions that closely echoed the American Constitution: the rights to life, liberty, security, property ownership, to think freely in conscience and religious beliefs, to express opinions freely and assemble peacefully.

But America had a credibility problem: publicly it advocated human rights for people worldwide, but at home it denied those rights to its own black citizens. The problem was exacerbated by the nation's attempt to absorb its enormous wartime army back into society. Racial violence flared.

"My very stomach turned over when I learned that Negro soldiers, just back from overseas, were being dumped out of army trucks in Mississippi and beaten," he wrote back. "Whatever my inclinations as a native of Missouri might have been, as President I know this is bad. I shall fight to the end evils like this."[29]

If America was to hold itself up as the beacon and protector of democracy in the new world by exporting its principles and its populist heritage, it needed to mandate federally protected civil rights for little guys of all races. To that end, Truman went further than any president since Lincoln in the cause of equality for all Americans. In the election year of 1948, he submitted a Civil Rights agenda to the Hill, calling for a federal law against lynching, statutory protection of the right to vote, and fair employment practices. That summer he issued executive orders to integrate the armed forces and federal government. The right to police its own citizens was taken away from the states. Their historical anathema to government interference was kindled.

"We have a higher duty and a greater responsibility than the attainment of our own national security,"[30] Truman insisted in his 1947 State of the Union address. "Our goal is collective security for all mankind. If we can . . . fulfill this solemn obligation which rests upon us . . . the spirit of the American people can set the course of world history."

Most Americans, however, were unconcerned with issues facing blacks in the United States, and there was little support for federal civil rights reform. While the Republicans contrived to use their power to stop the domestic agenda of Truman's monstrous government, the Southern Democrats readied for the opening salvo in their own battle against their fellow son of the South.

At the head of the Southern revolt was Strom Thurmond, descendent of Palatine Germans, who grew up in the wild west of South Carolina where men still gathered in the town square for target practice. He fathered a black daughter before absconding to Florida to seek his fortune in real estate. He launched a political career as superintendent of schools, responsible for white and black students alike, and worked to eradicate black illiteracy. He became state senator as a "progressive Democrat," a circuit-riding judge, and governor of South Carolina. He called for the largest lynching trial in the nation's history after thirty-one men were accused of taking a black man from jail and hanging him. He believed the South's problems rose from economic disparity between the industrial giants of the North and the colonial status of the South and warned people "not to trust their economic future to the tender mercies of the Republican Party." He fought for better pay and working conditions to bring economic and racial stability to the region. He championed the underdog of both races and was highly regarded by black leaders.

By 1948, it was apparent that South Carolina's progressive governor's fight for the little guy of both races existed within the confines of segregation. Once Truman threatened the social order, Thurmond became a champion of states' rights and a symbol of the Southerner as the oppressor of the black man.

The Rupture of 1948

"I was reasonably sure, far in advance of the convention, that there would be a splintering off of the South or at least a portion of it," Truman rued.[31]

The Democratic Convention in Philadelphia in the summer of 1948 was nothing if not memorable. The party made a valiant attempt to deflect attention from the racial controversy by attacking the opposition on the grounds of a populist platform.

"Ours is the party which was entrusted with responsibility when . . . twelve years of Republican neglect . . . had blighted the hopes of mankind, . . . had squandered the fruits of prosperity and had plunged us into the depths of depression and despair," read the Democratic manifesto for its convention in 1948. "Ours is the party which rebuilt . . . a shattered economy. Ours is the party which introduced the spirit of humanity into our law."[32]

They could denounce the Republicans all they wanted, but everyone knew they needed the South to win. Truman supporters, desperate to hold on to some Southern voters, proposed a plan by which each state would have the exclusive right to police itself. When Truman rejected it, they came back with various "softened" versions of the civil rights manifesto. Truman responded with the same stubbornness of his Scots-Irish presidential predecessors. Like Wilson he believed citizens' basic dignity was the responsibility of the government; unlike Wilson he believed this extended to all Americans regardless of race.

Abhorred by "Ideas flagrantly repugnant to the South," the Alabama and Mississippi delegations grew increasingly furious at their own party's interference in their states' rights. Even the band was dragged into the political fracas. The conductor was approached by "two dignified men" who offered him $500 to play "Dixie" at certain strategic times that night, hoping somehow it would bring patriotic unity to the party and prevent the Alabama delegation from walking out. Later a man from Mississippi made him an offer to play "Dixie" so the Alabama delegates would follow the Mississippi delegation that was preparing to walk out. An hour later both delegations walked out in a dramatic flourish, but no one was whistling "Dixie."

Two days later the disaffected Democrats met in Alabama to create a new party called the States' Rights Democrats, or "Dixiecrats" as the press called them. They nominated Thurmond for president. The Republicans nominated the popular New York governor Thomas E. Dewey. Many Democrats feared the split would deliver the South to the Dixiecrats, thus destroying the Democratic Party by eroding the support from its traditional Southern stronghold.

When asked why he was breaking with the Democratic Party when Roosevelt had made similar promises on civil rights, Thurmond responded, "Truman really means it." Truman never deigned to mention his nemesis, except to tell the director of the Democratic National Committee, when she asked what name to use for the Dixiecrats, "I don't care what you call them—you can make it as unprintable as you choose."

In Thurmond's mind it wasn't a racist fight, "it was a battle of federal power versus state power," with the "racial integrity of each race" hanging in the balance. He never lost an opportunity to fuel the Southerners' fear that their social order was crumbling and another Northern "occupation" of the South was looming.

"To bring all this about, the federal government would set up a super–police force with power to rove throughout the states and keep people in constant fear of being sent to a federal jail unless we accepted the decrees turned out by a bunch of anti-Southern bureaucrats in Washington."[33]

As the campaign wore on, he called the big government programs that were established to help the little guy as "communistic," said the forced integration of the armed forces was "un-American," and stressed "no decent and self-respecting Negro would ask for a law to force people to accept him where he is not wanted."

No one believed Truman could win—not the party, not his staff, not even his wife. The only person who had faith in Truman was Truman. He launched his famous integrated Whistle Stop Tour of rural America in the brutally hot summer of 1948, during which he covered almost twenty-two thousand miles and delivered three hundred speeches. He was showing his true colors—he was a man of the people, engaging, empathetic, honest, and most importantly, a dogged, committed fighter. The people responded. Huge crowds started showing up at his Whistle Stops. Half a million people turned out in Michigan; a full million came to a ticker-tape parade in New York.

"Give 'em hell, Harry!" someone famously shouted at a rally in Missouri.

The night of the election, the *Chicago Tribune* set the next day's headline "DEWEY DEFEATS TRUMAN." Truman went to bed while the ballots were counted. At four a.m. he got up, turned on the radio, and heard he was ahead by two million votes.

The South had not rallied en masse behind the Dixiecrats. In fact Thurmond only won the four states where he was listed on the ballot as a Democrat—Alabama, Mississippi, Louisiana, and South Carolina. Truman held seven of the eleven former Confederate states, along with the rural vote in the West. It was the most stunning comeback in American political history.

The attempt to drive a racial wedge into the South had failed—at least in 1948. Thurmond only got 2.4 percent of the ballots cast. Those votes, however, were the first chink in the armor of the Democratic Party's Southern base. It wouldn't take the Republicans long to find a way to turn it into a fissure.

During the inauguration parade in 1948, Thurmond took off his hat and waved in a sign of respect to President Truman. The vice president went to wave back; Truman grabbed his arm and was overheard to say "Don't you wave to the S.O.B."[34]

Thurmond went on to be classified as the longest-serving—and least effective senator.

Four years later Truman left the White House at the end of his second term. His Fair Deal had met with mixed success, he banned racial discrimination in federal government but failed to secure passage of a federal anti-lynching law; he increased the minimum wage but left office in the midst of a faltering economy. The Korean War ended in a return to the status quo.

"I have tried to give it everything that was in me," he said leaving office.

By Christmas in 1972, at the age of eighty-eight, he was admitted to a Kansas hospital with lung congestion. Over the next three weeks his vital organs failed one by one. His nurse said he was "warm, sweet and most appreciative of anything I did for him." By Christmas day he was in a coma. The next day he passed away.

Almost seventy-five thousand people lined up for half a mile to file past his flag-draped, light-mahogany casket in the Truman library. Outside, 250 howitzers roared a twenty-one-gun salute. The *New York Times* obituary reminded the American people that Truman made "decisions many of us would pale before." As social upheaval and political scandals rocked the country in the ensuing years, Truman became a political folk hero who exemplified old-fashioned integrity and accountability.

How the South Was Lost

In the 1930s the low-spending, small-government, laissez-faire, Jacksonian-style democracy took a radical left turn largely due to the Great Depression. The Democrats had been introducing plans to protect the little guy since President Wilson's New Freedom programs. Successive Democrat governments believed it was their moral responsibility to protect and provide opportunities for Americans to help themselves.

In the 1940s, the South was America's poorest region mainly because of lack of infrastructure and over-reliance on farming. The Southerner— descendents of the rugged Scots-Irishmen who vanquished the hostile frontier—was a hardworking Calvinist who lived by the credo "no man suffers from poverty unless it is more than his fault, unless it is his sin."[35] He was born of a culture that believed power rests with the individual, not with the state. He emerged from a landscape where there was a lot of land that afforded less need to compromise, but it required a greater need for self-sufficiency, self-reliance, and self-defense. He was the symbol of true American grit and patriotism. He didn't want a welfare state that rewarded people for laziness; he just wanted a fair shake.

In the 1960s, President Lyndon B. Johnson continued the party's social conscience by unleashing a war on poverty. He passed over a hundred initiatives that extended the federal government's role in education, housing, culture, health care, and environmental issues. In 1964 he successfully passed the landmark Civil Rights Act that outlawed segregation and enfranchised all African-Americans. The courts banned prayer from public schools, introduced new gun controls, and suspended the death penalty. Prisoners and even pornographers were given new rights. The crowning glory of what was widely considered the drift of abominations was the 1973 legalization of abortion.

As the entrenched social order of the South unraveled, the nation was beginning to look like Europe, complete with assaults on religion and an ever-burgeoning government. It was becoming everything their ancestors sailed across the ocean to escape.

Under a relentless liberal assault, the South's discontented rumblings were being heard on the other side of the aisle. In the 1970s, the country not only continued its spiral into leftist politics and moral depredation, it was humiliated when Iranian militant students stormed the U.S. Embassy and held sixty-six hostages for 444 days. The Democratic leadership was not just an affront to their self-reliant, religious, and conservative traditions; it was an outrage to their patriotic sensibilities. They needed a new leader.

"Get the government off our backs," was the popular message California governor Ronald Reagan delivered to cheering opponents of the dreaded welfare state.

Although Irish-Catholic in ancestry, his campaign did a spectacular job of attracting the Scots-Irish by appealing to their cultural conservatism, individualism, patriotism, and disdain for government interference. But Reagan was also playing on a Southern strategy that had been devised in the early 1960s to rally Dixie against Johnson's Civil Rights Act. By 1980, race issues had become far less divisive, but his team managed to exploit lingering racial tensions by wrapping them up in renewed talk about states' rights and the need to curb the power of the federal government.

He opposed affirmative action, which provided advantages to minorities under the genial guise of promoting self-sufficiency for all Americans and reducing their dependence on government programs. The Southern strategy expanded from its initial racial premise to include a range of social and tax issues that would attract lower- and working-class Southern whites without direct references to race. It was a populist message tailor-made for the South and delivered to perfection. No one could pitch the right-wing reactionary script better.

"Reagan gives this really heartfelt, sincere pitch that only he can do. He's a master at it," said one of Thurmond's staffers. "He comes through with his philosophical pitch. Real simple, direct answers . . . . they're the same ones every time—pop-pop-pop . . . They're worked out where they sound really off the cuff, but they aren't."[36]

He had a jingle for every occasion that convinced the Southerner that he understood their culture. "Government's first duty is to protect the people, not run their lives," he said to the proponents of small government.[37] "The problem isn't people are taxed too little, the problem is Government spends too much," he said to those who favored low taxes over services. For the pro-lifers he said, "I've noticed that everybody that is for abortion has already been born."[38] To the Second Amendment devotees whose hunting and defensive impulses had been genetically encoded since the time their ancestors tamed the frontier he said, "As long as there are guns, the individual that wants a gun for a crime is going to have one and going to get it. The only person who's going to be penalized and have difficulty is the law-abiding citizen."[39]

He never made a speech that didn't invoke America's greatness; he roused national pride with statements like "Let's Make America Great Again." He insisted the American spirit was still there and ready to blaze back into life by exercising some good old-fashioned common sense. He listened, he understood, and it was music to their ears.

On religion he agreed with the Christian Right and Jerry Falwell's Moral Majority that the country was in the midst of a moral crisis. He spoke of God and democracy as indivisible, and he promoted a vision of America grounded in faith and morality.

"I'll confess that," he said, momentarily faltering during his closing speech at the 1980 Republican National Convention, "I've been a little afraid to suggest what I'm going to suggest."

He paused.

"I'm more afraid not to. Can we begin our crusade joined together in a moment of silent prayer?"

Everyone in the auditorium bowed their heads, until he concluded:

"God bless America."[40]

Hundreds of red, white, and blue balloons dropped from the rafters as the band played on. Across America the Christian Right mobilized to register voters and get them to the polls.

Reagan had promised to restore the nation's morality, its military strength and pride, and its economic health with a balanced budget and tax cuts for the wealthy that promised to increase national output so much that the benefits enjoyed by the rich would trickle down to the poor. On Election Day he won by a landslide. The Scots-Irish no longer saw the Democrats as champions of the working class and their values. They were offered a choice between morality, dignity, and patriotism on one hand and moral obscenities, dependency, and weakness on the other. There was no contest—Reagan had made conservatism respectable again.

As promised, he brought "Seven Fat Years" of economic prosperity. He ended the Cold War with America triumphant. Huge corporations that had been muzzled under every Scots-Irish president since Jackson flourished. The country became committed to small government again. It was accomplished by cutting health care, education, firing striking workers, and declaring government programs inefficient. Federal government spending on projects for rural America fell from $10 billion to $1 billion. The federal debt somehow soared, and the trickle-down effect trickled out to cheaper labor in India and China.

When there was a hue and cry, the Republicans reminded citizens that the tax-and-spend liberal Democrats who rewarded the lazy and inept would let issues like abortion and homosexuality run amok and eradicate creationism, religion, and gun rights. The three-G's of "God, Gays, and Guns" replaced economic fairness in a country whose historical distrust of government was intensified by the Calvinist belief that success is the responsibility of the individual and a mark of his divinely ordained salvation.

It was easy pickings. Besides, the Democrats gave them nothing to vote for—if they voted on economic issues, they had to accept moral repugnance. The Republicans at least understood their culture. The Democrats retreated without a fight, abandoning 35 percent of the electorate, and for the first time in forty years declared the South "not their demographic." The little guys—bastions of the party since their idol Andrew Jackson rode in to revolutionize the White House—were lost to the New Right.

"You haven't left the Democratic Party," Reagan said. "The Democratic Party left you." He got that one right.

The New Jacksonian

"Fear not," Andrew Jackson once said. "The people may be deluded for a moment, but cannot be corrupted."[41]

Forty years after Reaganomics promised prosperity across the land, not only had jobs trickled out to Asia instead of down to the workers, 25 percent of existing manufacturing jobs in the South were shipped overseas. Once upon a time, a CEO made twenty times what a worker earned, but starting with the Reagan years it grew to four hundred times.

Some said it was the natural result of a competitive society; a sort of Calvinism turned social Darwinism. Regardless of the name, it amounted to America's top tier growing disproportionately richer.

The days of proud self-reliance were fading. These descendents of the independent Scots-Irish, who always wanted fairness and never wanted a handout, began to feel the effects of the same government betrayal that had rallied their ancestors to rebellion on two occasions. Basic services were disappearing, pipes were rusting, and children were getting sick from dirty water; more miners were dying of black lung, sons were being sent to Iraq, and their jobs were being outsourced. Meanwhile, corporations were banking billions. Finally, one man had had enough. Out of the mountains of southwest Virginia, a defiant Scots-Irishman and Vietnam War hero charged toward Washington on a new populist crusade.

"In the early days of our republic," Jim Webb warned in his January 2006 response to President Bush's State of the Union address. "President Andrew Jackson established an important principle of American-style democracy—that we should measure the health of our society not at its apex, but at its base. Not with the numbers that come out of Wall Street, but with the living conditions that exist on Main Street. We must recapture that spirit today."

In the mountainous corner of Virginia where the hardy Scots-Irish culture imprinted itself on the American frontier, a group of virtually destitute workers gathered to hear the Beltway outsider make his case for a seat as their state's senator in Congress. Blending in with the crowd in his jeans and sense of indignation, the workers knew he understood them. They had been disregarded by political powers; they were living below the poverty line with few opportunities to get back to work. They were suffering from poor health and education, family breakdown, crime, and drug abuse.

When Warren Buffet, America's second wealthiest man, who benefited from the $50 billion in corporate tax breaks in 2003, admitted, "if class warfare is being waged in America my class is clearly winning," mountain folk were hitting bottom. But history had shown, in times of oppression, the Scots-Irish were liable to develop revolutionary tendencies.[42]

For two hundred years the Webb's lived in Big Moccasin Gap, which cut through Virginia's Clinch Mountains to the Wilderness Road out to the West. They pushed through those mountains to create some of the first frontier settlements in Tennessee and Kentucky. From there they traveled by covered wagons into Arkansas, crossing the Mississippi River on a flatboat, where they built their own wooden roads through the swamps by cutting down saplings. They grew up chopping cotton and picking strawberries, finding some schooling where they could, slept on corn-shuck mattresses, and brushed their teeth with twigs.

Webb came from the blue blood of the warrior aristocracy in which a fighting spirit ran deep. His father was an Air Force officer, and by growing up on military bases all over the country, Webb learned to fight hard and fight young.

Having become a decorated war hero, he was secretary of the navy under Reagan and stayed in the Republican stable until Operation Iraqi Freedom. As he watched his son ship out to Iraq with the Marine Corps, Webb's vehement opposition to the war drove him back into the Democratic Party fold and into the senatorial race.

As one of the most highly decorated veterans of the Vietnam War and member of a proud Southern military family, Webb could never be called unpatriotic. He was almost a lone voice of opposition when the country was clamoring to invade Iraq. He warned it would be the "strategic blunder" of a confused, misdirected, vulnerable foreign policy, when the real threat was China, Iran, and North Korea. He said a Middle East strategy required diplomacy, a walk-softly-and-carry-a-big-stick approach, as well as the involvement of regional leaders including Syria and Iran. Speaking to one's enemies was as important as speaking to one's friends.

Everyone said he was crazy thinking he could run for senate in Virginia as a Democrat. He was up against the well-financed Republican machine with a candidate endorsed by the "Who's Who" of Washington. Even the Democratic Party was supporting someone else. But along came Webb with a collection of war medals, no money, and no congressional record, campaigning in a suit and tie and a pair of his son's combat boots. His only credentials were a sense of outrage, a fighting spirit, and an old 1998 Jeep Cherokee in which he traversed thousands of miles to three or four meetings a night.

When Ed Harlow got a call to say a new guy in the Democratic Party was coming to Bristol campaigning for the senate seat, he was hopeful. The Republicans were running Virginia's former governor, a snuff-chewing Californian in a cowboy hat who was passing himself off as a little guy. As far as Ed was concerned, George Allen was a complete phony. Marvin Harlow, on the other hand, thought Allen was the best governor the state ever had. He was a man of integrity, "when he said something you could believe it."

Webb was trailing in the polls; word was he hadn't a hope of winning, but when Ed met Jim Webb at the Bristol train station in the middle of a freezing winter workday, he knew they were wrong. This man had something. He had a proud military bearing, and he was amiable. Having given a thirty-minute speech to a crowd of fifty or so people, he took a stroll down State Street, shaking hands and chatting with locals. People were smitten; "regal" some people called him.

"His independence impressed me," Ed remembered. "He reminded me of an Irish guy, who, if you say something he doesn't like, he'll put you out."

A populist candidate meeting the populace face to face was an age-old strategy, but it was working. A populist message par excellence was being received loud and clear.

"Webb is not afraid to take a stand," said a Bristol voter. "His ideals are strong. He truly cares about the common man, and he's not in this just for himself."[43]

Ed watched Republicans try to demonize him on moral issues and fail. He wasn't too far right or left, Ed decided, just the kind of man the South needed. Ed Harlow went all out to help get Webb elected.

"I don't trust him," mumbled Marvin. "He's a Democrat. If Webb brings in a job, he'll get me somewhere else."

Someone needed to bring in jobs—big businesses hadn't come of their own volition. It was said the American dream was dead out there in the mountains. After years of political manipulation and neglect, the region had become one of the most depressed places, spiritually and economically, in the country. Webb was tired of corporate exploitation of poor Southern whites and blacks. He was tired of the Southern white man being blamed for keeping the black men down, and tired of the political manipulations that drove a wedge between the blacks and whites in the South. In 1982 he fought to have a black soldier added to the statue at the Vietnam Memorial in Washington, saying those who fawned over the abstract wall of architect Maya Lin could "kiss my ass."[44]

Webb was convinced that the greatest realignment in U.S. political history would happen if the Southern whites and the African-Americans were allied. It would be a unified stand by all the little guys. Meanwhile he careened across the Southern wasteland, veering left on economic fairness and right on moral issues, while the Republicans predicted a moral apocalypse if the Democrats were allowed into power. They would permit more gay marriages, more murdered babies, the demonizing of religion, the confiscation of their guns, and the transformation of the entire nation into a welfare state.

The Democratic Party played into their propaganda by focusing on appeasing their own liberal, anti-gun, pro–gay marriage, pro-choice secular base. Unfortunately, the Democratic base wasn't large enough to win the White House without winning at least part of the South. Webb was a Second Amendment devotee and advocate of American military power. He was religious but left God out of political controversy, a decorated veteran who left his medals at home, and a proponent of economic fairness. He was living proof that the Democratic Party needed only to understand the Scots-Irish inspired Southern culture: its patriotism, religion, independent spirit, right to bear arms, and social and moral conservatism. They didn't have to agree with them; they just needed to care about his convictions and leave him alone.

"If Jesus Christ went down through the Appalachians and he didn't embrace the culture," explained one of Webb's political advisers. "He wouldn't get any votes."[45]

Coming round on the outside track without campaign funding or political support, Webb became America's most unlikely senator, winning 46 percent of the vote in a region where 80 percent of the population were registered Republican. It was a watershed moment that exposed cracks in the Republican armor just like the one they exploited in the Democrats' armor back in 1948.

At the subsequent White House reception for new members of Congress, Webb declined to stand in the presidential receiving line to have his picture taken. President Bush found him just as he and his heavily pregnant Vietnamese wife were about to leave.

"How's your boy?" Bush asked without acknowledging Mrs. Webb.

"I'd like to get them out of Iraq, Mr. President," Webb answered.

"That's not what I asked you," Bush said. "How's your boy?"

"That's between me and my boy, Mr. President," Webb replied.[46]

It could have been President Andrew Jackson refusing to pay the traditional call on the outgoing executive more than two hundred years earlier; certainly Webb was subjected to media comments about his manners. But Webb didn't want a photo with President Bush, and it was just that simple. To the blogosphere he was a folk hero. He was the new Jackson, a Scots-Irish warrior with the same brash, unpolished style and faith in the inherent goodness of the little guy. Both demanded strong leaders and wouldn't tolerate anyone who thought himself above his fellows. The only obvious difference was that Webb wore a suit with his boots instead of leather and eel-skin. Besides, many Virginians believed Webb should be living in the White House, not visiting it. Many considered him to be the new Jacksonian, that man who comes along once in a generation that could change world history.

"Have you ever read the *Leadership Principles of Attila the Hun*?" asked a political adviser. "When times are rough, the toughest and the darkest, the tribe always leans to the meanest, baddest, son-of-a-bitch in the tribe."[48]

Ask any Virginian—except Marvin Harlow—and they'll say that man is the all-American patriot, James Webb.

CHAPTER 6

THE ABOLITIONIST AND THE ARISTOCRAT

Willy Haslerig's palms were sweating. There he was in the blistering heat of an Indian summer, driving a rickety old milk truck full of clattering bottles to the one place on earth he should not be.

"Don't let the dark catch you up there," Grandpa George warned him when he was a child.

Beads of sweat rolled down his forehead and stung his eyes as the fifty-three-year-old spit-cleaned the dusty windscreen and saw the mountain looming in the distance. Grandpa George was born in the foothills of Sand Mountain, Tennessee, in what he liked to call the third year of freedom. He grew up hearing how Sundown towns popped up after the "Freedom War." They were places where blacks weren't allowed after dark.

Sand Mountain was different. The large plateau in north Georgia that stretches westward into northeastern Alabama wasn't a no-blacks-after-dark place, it was a no-blacks-anytime place. They said it was full of inbred hillbillies and snake-handlers that hung the sign of a black man running on the dirt road at the bottom of the hill. Willy, always a curious kid, wanted to know what would happen if he went up, but Grandpa would just answer with something like "don't mark me or I'll light that butt up."

If George Haslerig knew what happened on the mountain to scare blacks away, he took the story with him to the grave. There were no official reports of violence at that time, but it didn't stop the mystery of the mountain from becoming entrenched in local lore. Some people said it was the isolation that fueled the mystery, since no one really came out of that community and no one had any reason to go in. Others said something happened during the Reconstruction Era after the war. Whatever it was,

Haslerig Milk Delivery Truck. East 8th Street, Chattanooga, Tennessee, ca. 1950. Courtesy of the Haslerig Family.

subsequent generations accepted—without quite knowing why—that going up there meant you weren't coming back down alive. Yet here was Willy Haslerig driving out of Chattanooga up the forbidden mountaintop. And it was all because of Ernest Collins.

Collins delivered milk for Happy Valley Farms where Willy worked as a supervisor. One day Collins's driver up and quit, leaving him with a truckload of milk that was about to curdle. He needed help and there was only one person available that day.

"Go with me, Willy, up to Sand Mountain and deliver milk to a school up there," Collins pleaded.

"That place has been blocked off to me my whole life," Willy replied shaking his head.

Collins enlisted the help of their manager, and both men tried to convince him to take the ride.

"We'll look after you," the manager promised.

"What that meant exactly was hard to determine since the plant was more than fifty miles from the mountaintop. Collins had been up there many times and swore there wouldn't be any trouble. Finally they wore Willy down and he consented to ride up.

The men set out on a hot Tennessee afternoon, driving fifty miles in complete silence along the dusty country roads, broken only by the clinking bottles in the back of the old truck and the steady hum of the hot engine.

Willy's early life was spent in the shadow of that great ridge. His father Charles, a proud, handsome, black man with a great head for business, scraped enough money together to buy his own tract of farmland, where he grew fruit and vegetables. He eventually bought a few dairy cows and started a little milk run. As his business prospered, he built a nice home with four or five rooms for his family of ten. It was the cream of the neighborhood where most other families were sleeping four or five to a bed.

Then came that night in 1924. The house was already filled with smoke when Willy's mother ran into his room, woke all her children, and rushed them outside. Standing there in pajamas in the middle of the night, the Haslerig children clutched their parents while they watched their lovely house and everything they owned burn to the ground. Mrs. Haslerig looked behind her into the darkness and saw someone had broken the necks of all their chickens.

Somebody was unhappy that a black family was doing well. They were lucky, the neighbors said. A man in Alabama was lynched when his farm started doing well; his body was left hanging from a tree for three days before the sheriff cut him down.

There was nothing Charles could do except take a job mining ore alongside poor whites and other blacks, while his sons helped rebuild the business.

"Poor white people—they suffered a lot," Willy remembered with surprising compassion. "They were trying to organize a union to protect themselves, and the owners put them out of their jobs and their homes."

The responsibility of rebuilding the farm fostered Willy's entrepreneurial skills. A few years later he took over the family business, built a little plant to pasteurize milk, and expanded their milk round into Chattanooga. Within a few years he had a fleet of nine trucks and a little army of employees.

"It was a big business at one time," he said proudly.

But as the sixties drew to a close, big business started eating up the little guy. Willy was forced to sell out to Happy Valley Farms in Chattanooga and take a supervisor position with them. He did pretty well for himself, until today.

As they approached the mountain, Collins's big talk left him, and he began to feel stress. The infamous sign of the black man running wasn't there when Willy began to climb the dirt road uphill to the mountaintop. It didn't matter. All he could think was that this day in 1972, at the age of fifty-three, he, Willy Haslerig, was about to die.[1]

The Abolitionist and the Aristocrat

Within a two-hundred-mile radius of where Willy's ancestors were slaving on the plantation of a Mr. Westfield, two Scots-Irish children were growing up in abject poverty on the wild frontier, but they were destined to take radically different paths in life. John Rankin would become one of the most ardent and effective abolitionists in American history; John Caldwell Calhoun would become a brilliant politician, pro-slavery advocate, and champion of the South. Both men were quintessential Scots-Irishmen: independent, rousing leaders with an indomitable fighting spirit and a passionate dedication to their cause. It seemed inevitable that they would end up as archenemies in the life-and-death struggle that tore the Union apart.

John Rankin's great-grandfather was born the year the defenders of Derry were still celebrating their great victory in Ireland. He was thirty-six when James Logan—his kinsman from the north of Ireland and manager of the great pacifist colony of William Penn—extended an invitation to his countrymen to settle in Pennsylvania. The Rankin patriarch took his wife and three-year-old son Thomas and joined the second wave of hardy emigrants who set sail in 1724 for the New World.

Pennsylvania was a haven for the abstemious, hardworking Rankin family and for fifty years their small independent farm prospered—until the Revolutionary War scorched their land. Starving soldiers on both sides stole whatever grain and livestock they could find to survive. Thomas made the unfortunate mistake of selling his farm for Continental money, which was worthless by the end of the war. Reduced to abject poverty, he was forced down the Great Wagon Road into the wilds of Tennessee to forge a life on the pitiless frontier like thousands of his kinsmen before him.

Thomas was a resilient man who garnered considerable respect in a frontier Presbyterian settlement. He believed wholeheartedly that occupation was a religious duty in life, and success the only way a person could demonstrate he was among God's chosen people. Recognized in the community as one graced by God, Thomas Rankin was elected an elder in the Presbyterian church.

"He had no wealth to bestow on his numerous offspring," John Rankin said of his grandfather. "But by pious example, and truthful teaching, he opened to them a fountain of spiritual life that widens as it flows and will descend to the remotest generation."[2]

When John Rankin's father moved further into Tennessee to raise his own family, they were among the first settlers in Jefferson County—a land that was still in "its wild and natural state." He bought a thousand acres of scrappy land for almost nothing, and it yielded almost nothing. They were frequently attacked by Indians, and many times John Rankin's father and the other men of the settlement had to ride out after them.

Unlike the pious community of his grandparents, the settlement in which John Rankin was reared was populated by a "low, ignorant, and immoral class of people" who believed education only produced rogues. Preachers recited passages from memory because they couldn't read their Bibles—not that it troubled them, since they professed they needed a calling, but no "larnin'."

From the moment Rankin was old enough to hold a hoe, he was put to farming, and the rest of his childhood was spent in all work and no play. For the three months between harvest and planting, his mother sent him to school where they sat on logs and learned from Dilworth's Spelling Book and the Bible. The teacher sat in the corner with a switch, was usually drunk, and if he knew any arithmetic, he didn't pass it along to his students. Rankin, however, was ravenous for knowledge. He listened avidly when his father read the Bible and history books aloud. Whenever he could, he snuck into the woods and wrote articles on any subject that came to mind, then pretended he was delivering speeches by reading them aloud where no one could hear him.

At the time eastern Tennessee was typical of mountain communities: most of the settlers were independent small farmers who couldn't afford a slave. Most of the farmers had no clear position on slavery, but Rankin's parents were fervent anti-slavery advocates who passed on this conviction to their children.

When his father finally managed to scrape enough money together to get him away from his drunken teacher and to a real school, Rankin was packed off to Washington County to be taught by the Reverend Samuel

Doak, who delivered the rousing speech and fiery blessing before the Battle of Kings Mountain.

Doak was descended from Presbyterian immigrants from the north of Ireland and shared their characteristic mettle. After he graduated from Princeton, Doak leapt onto his horse and became a circuit rider in Virginia, logging thousands of miles each year preaching to the most dangerous, outer reaches of the Scots-Irish settlements. After the Revolution, he channeled his energy into the abolition of slavery and ran one of a network of anti-slavery Log Colleges next to the church.

Without fail, Rankin traveled fourteen miles each day to Doak's school. He was the poorest student there, the only boy in homespun clothes and moccasins that he'd made himself. During these years he grew into a man who stood erect, a little shorter than most, clean-shaven, with a broad forehead, keen eyes, and a kindly expression. He became an outspoken youth with an unparalleled intellect who was passionately opposed to the institution of slavery.

In 1814, a tragic event galvanized his position.

Rankin's older brother David—a fervent patriot—volunteered to fight with General Andrew Jackson at Horseshoe Bend. When the call to storm the Cherokee fortress was sounded, David charged in advance of his company through a hail of arrows. He was driven back with the rest of the Tennessee militia, but when he saw Sam Houston reach the top of the barricade, David Rankin resumed his assault, only to be shot in the chest. He died within minutes.

"He was two years older than myself, and was my companion from childhood to manhood," mourned Rankin. "He was a kind-hearted brother. The news of his death caused me inexpressible sorrow."[3]

After the war, the government sent an allowance to the Rankins to compensate for their son's death. The money was used to pay for John Rankin's education.

"All events are part of one great plan by which the greatest good will ultimately be accomplished,"[4] he wrote after David's death. From that day on Rankin devoted himself, and the education David's life had bought him, to something far larger than himself and to a cause worthy of his brother's sacrifice. He would fight to the bitter end against any foe, no matter how powerful, or wealthy, or formidable, for the liberty of all men. That resolve set him on a collision course with the vice president of the United States and the champion of the South.

Like Rankin, John Caldwell Calhoun was descended from the same plain stock of Presbyterian immigrants from the north of Ireland. He had a brilliant mind and a fervid nature, but lacked Rankin's humility. He was a Yale-educated, South Carolina farmer determined to rise above his class. He was ambitious, aristocratic, and consumed by burning desire to be the country's most powerful politician.

Nine years after the Rankins set sail out of Belfast Harbor, Patrick Calhoun Sr. and his wife Catherine followed suit, all the way across the ocean and down the beaten path from Pennsylvania into a Virginia farming community. When Grandpa Patrick died eight years later, his wife Catherine and her children undertook a fateful move to a Scots-Irish settlement in Long Cane, South Carolina—the heart of Cherokee country.

For a decade the Calhouns worked hard in the Carolina backcountry, but by the 1750s tensions between the colonists and the Cherokee were mounting. By 1759 the Cherokee declared war. In 1760 word reached Long Cane that the Cherokee were attacking isolated farms in the area, stealing, and slaying any settlers they found.

Two–hundred fifty Scots-Irishmen packed their wagons and left for the nearby Fort Tobus in Augusta, Georgia. They hadn't gone far when they were surrounded by the terrifying sound of Indian war whoops. Seventy-six-year-old Catherine Calhoun, her son, and granddaughter were scalped. Two other granddaughters aged five and three were captured and raised as Indians. Calhoun's Uncle William cut a horse loose from a wagon and sent his pregnant wife and five-year-old son to Fort Tobus, Augusta. It was the last time she saw her husband alive. Calhoun's father Patrick Jr. was left alone to watch the Cherokee burn and massacre the settlement. The horror of seeing his mother, brother, and niece scalped and discarded in the dirt only made him tougher and more combative—it was a trait his children would inherit.

When John C. Calhoun was born in 1782, his father had become a respected landowner, member of the legislature, and anti-government activist. He was also an Indian fighter of some renown. His hat, which became a family treasure, had four bullet holes in it from riding out after war parties. In the South Carolina legislature he fought for settlers' right to vote. He was among those who organized the church and school and tried to civilize the place at a time when the Regulators were rampantly meting out their own kind of justice. Patrick Calhoun was a giant of a man in his son's eyes.

One evening the young John Calhoun watched his father ride home from a legislative session in Charleston much like he always did, but this night Patrick Jr. was leading a slave straddled on a horse behind him. It was unusual to find slaves among humble log cabins of backcountry farmers. With Adam's arrival, John Calhoun's whole life changed; his future was woven into the system of slavery that became a normal part of life

The Calhouns weren't idle or wealthy. The sons all worked long, hard days, plowing fields in the "brilin' sun" like every other poor Scots-Irish farmer in the backcountry. There was only one difference—they worked alongside their slave. As Patrick Jr. prospered, the Calhouns acquired almost a hundred slaves.

Whether the young Calhoun ever smelled the stench of a slave ship, or witnessed the crushed lifeless bodies chained to the lower decks, fighting and rabid for a drop of water, or people chained together on an auction block, the women with their heads and breasts bare, is not known. Real as the horrors of slavery were, the Calhouns like other slave owners insisted that cruelty was an abuse of the system.

Like Rankin, Calhoun was a voracious reader and showed early signs of being a great orator. At eighteen, his father sent him off to study with his brother-in-law Moses Waddell, a Presbyterian preacher who ran a Log College in Georgia. Unlike Rankin he was not humbled by homespun clothes and self-made moccasins. Calhoun was a confident, well-dressed youth, with courteous manners and a strong sense of honor.

At Waddell's Academy he grew up to be a tall, handsome man with thick, dark hair that fell down over his temples and deep-set eyes that people said were either blue or gray depending on his mood. He was an original thinker with a commanding intellect and a strong grasp of philosophy, history, and economics.

When Patrick Jr. died in 1796, Calhoun left Waddell's Academy and returned home to take on the responsibility of managing what had now become a family plantation. He took responsibility for its slaves with good conscience and with high ideals. He was reputed to be a kind master and very attached to his slaves, although he was known for whipping them for misconduct. Slave children, however, were delighted when they saw a man riding home "just 'kase he were Marse John C."

"Give the Planters Free Trade, and let every Planter be the parent as well as the master of his Slaves," he wrote. "Let the Slaves be made to do their duty as well as to eat, drink, and sleep; let morality and industry be taught them, and the Planter will have reason to be satisfied."[5]

He often cited a story of a slave he once freed who came back cold and starving from the North begging to be taken back into bondage. This was an indictment of Northern callousness that it would allow a man and his family to starve in the streets and be driven back into bondage to survive.

"When I told him that I would do all I could for him, he seized both my hands in his, and expressed his fervent gratitude," Calhoun said. [6]

This event bolstered Calhoun's argument that blacks in America would share the fate of the Jamaicans who squatted and starved after the Britain abolished slavery. As far as this planter was concerned—the slave needed the master, and the master needed the slave, and the South thrived on the efforts of both.

The National Stage

In 1811, Calhoun successfully courted and married his cousin Floride Bonnie Calhoun—an heiress from an aristocratic Charleston family. Her small fortune transformed him from a South Carolina backwoodsman into a person of stature in Charleston society. The abstemious and unromantic Calhoun was able to pass for a Southern gentleman and a member of the planter class. The next step was politics.

After a six-year stint in the House of Representatives, where he developed a reputation as an ardent nationalist and war hawk, he was made secretary of war in the Monroe administration. He was only thirty-five. At forty-one he won the vice presidential race—which at that time, was run separately from the presidential race—to join the administration of John Quincy Adams. The two thrashed around the question of slavery.

"What of liberty, justice, the rights of man?" Adams asked.

"The principles you avow are just," Calhoun replied. "But in the South, they are always understood as applying only to the white race."[7]

"If the Union must be dissolved," Adams said prophetically. "Slavery is the question upon which it ought to break."[8]

But these were early days, and the issue of slavery was not forefront in the minds of the majority. There was more immediate business like taxes, war, and industrialization.

While Calhoun was solidifying his reputation as a wealthy, brilliant, and formidable politician, Rankin was becoming a passionate orator with clear, honest convictions and an anti-slavery doctrine. In 1816 the shy young man who never associated with ladies proposed to a local woman, Jean Lowry, "who had a high reputation for industry and good nature." In a ceremony diametrically opposite to the Calhouns' union, Jean spun his wedding coat, and he made his own shoes, and after the pious, simple ceremony, the twenty-four-year-old John Rankin was married.

As soon as he was licensed to preach, he took to the pulpit to deliver such fervent anti-slavery sermons that the congregation feared he'd incite a rebellion among the slaves. He was told to consider leaving Tennessee if he planned to speak against slavery again, but he refused to compromise his beliefs or his debt to David. He finally announced they were moving to the free state of Ohio, which at that time was still wild and unsettled land. His father-in-law gave him a horse, a two-wheeled carriage, and seventy dollars in silver; the young couple with their newborn son packed their meager possessions and prepared for an arduous trip to free soil.

Rankin and the Underground Railroad

In the early 1800s, the land occupied by hostile Indians above the Ohio River was simply called "Red Country." There was one little town that overlooked the twisting river and the forests of the slave state of Kentucky beyond. Ripley was a bustling dockland town overrun by itinerant rabble in search of labor and replete with shootouts, fistfights, saloons, and muddy wagon wheels that splashed through puddles in the dirt roads. In this town there was one constant, "drinking, frolicking, and dancing."

By the time Rankin arrived in Ripley, fugitive slaves were attempting to reach Canada by crossing the Ohio River, and mercenaries were showing up to hunt them down and collect rewards. Even free slaves were captured and sold downriver into the plantations of the Deep South from where there was no escape.

In 1822, John Rankin took the position of pastor of the First Presbyterian Church and its total congregation of thirty-two where he used the pulpit to expound the evils of slavery. No one else was interested in giving up drinking, gambling, or womanizing to come to church, and no one cared about the plight of the slaves.

Rankin took a house on the riverfront, and word spread that it was a safe house for any runaway slave who managed to find a skiff and traverse the icy Ohio River. Gradually more anti-slavery crusaders gravitated to Ripley to help the fugitives they found climbing the riverbanks or creeping down alleys in the dead of night. A network of escape routes and safe houses evolved, as the town became a busy depot on the Underground Railroad that conducted slaves safely to Canada. This "hellhole of abolitionists" began depriving the state of Kentucky of hundreds of thousands of dollars' worth of their property.

Rankin's house became the first stop for slave hunters when they came to town, so he moved his family to a modest but more secure house high on a bluff that had a clear view of the entire town, the river, and the woodlands of Kentucky on the other side. Every night he placed a lantern in the front window that could be seen for miles. Word slowly spread that it meant freedom if a slave could get to this light.

As Rankin's sons grew, conducting slaves to freedom became a family business. Fugitives who managed to cross the Ohio River and make their way up the steep hill to the Rankin house would be escorted by one of his sons or a neighbor for miles under the cover of darkness to the next safe house on the Underground Railroad.

They wrote cryptic notes to be passed along the line: "Dear Sir, by tomorrow's mail you will receive two volumes of the 'Irrepressible Conflict' bound in black. After perusal, please forward and oblige."

They varied routes and depots. Each homesteader would then decide what the next stop would be, and so on until the slave reached freedom. If a slave arrived in daylight, Rankin dressed them in his children's clothes and marched them out of town as if they were his own. He hid as many as twelve fugitives at a time on some nights, hiding a few in the barn and a few others in the basement and tiny attic in the house.

One night a man climbed to the hilltop with twenty men on his tail. He told Rankin that planters were trying to scare slaves by telling them the abolitionists were really conspiring to capture them and sell them downriver.

"I was sold anyhow," the man told Rankin. "And I thought I would try it."

Rankin took him to another depot and bade him farewell.

"How good to find friends," the man said. "Can't I come back from Canada and see you all?"

"No," Rankin replied. "The laws are against you. You cannot come back."[9]

Rankin House on the hill overlooking Ripley, Ohio, 2010. Photo by Karen McCarthy.

One winter morning when the Ohio River was almost frozen over, a young woman overheard her master planning to sell her two-year-old child downriver. She grabbed her baby and ran through the woods toward the riverbank where she'd heard a story about a light on the hill that led to freedom. With dogs barking behind her she plunged down the bank and stepped onto a pack of ice but fell into the freezing water. She somehow managed to throw her child onto the ice and pull herself out. She didn't know a slave-catcher was watching her from the opposite bank as she navigated her way across the treacherous ice, clutching her cold, drenched child. She fell two more times and almost drowned before she dragged herself and her child onto the free land on the Ohio side. She was lying half-dead from hypothermia when the slave-catcher seized her arm and dragged her up. She had barely the energy to whimper.

"No [slave] was ever caught that got to his house," he said pointing to the light.[10]

He dragged her through the alleyways to the foot of Rankin's hill and let her go. Maybe he admired her courage, or was moved by a moment of compassion, but she never knew why he let her go. When she climbed up to the house, Jean Rankin gave her dry clothes. Two of Rankin's sons were woken and took the woman to the next stop. Later Rankin told his friend Professor Stowe, and his daughter Harriet Beecher Stowe, of the flight of the slave mother across the Ohio River that night. "Terrible, how terrible" was all Harriet could say. She later wrote the young woman into her novel *Uncle Tom's Cabin* as the character Eliza.

Rankin's work as an abolitionist continued in this way, until he got a letter from his brother Thomas, a prosperous Virginia merchant who mentioned he had "recently purchased a negro slave." Rankin was horrified that his own brother, reared by the same moral, abolitionist parents could disgrace their virtue. He wrote a series of thirteen letters, had them printed in a local paper called the *Castigator,* and mailed Thomas the newspapers.

"I consider involuntary slavery a never failing fountain of the grossest immorality and one of the deepest sources of human misery," he wrote. "It hangs like the mantle of night over our republic and shrouds its rising glories."[11]

This was the beginning of a huge body of writings that became known as *Letters on Slavery.* They were published eighteen times in America and Britain by different papers, before being bound in book form. The Anti-American Slavery Society published a few editions for which he took no money but garnered a national reputation. Many anti-slavery societies were formed using his books as a guide.

In the preface he stated that the safety of the people and the nation depended upon the extermination of slavery, but its abolition must come by fair discussion and other lawful means. There were many ideas within the anti-slavery societies on how to abolish slavery—some advocated immediate emancipation, others gradual emancipation. Many said blacks could not coexist with whites and had to be repatriated to Africa. Rankin was one of the few that recognized the abolition of the institution could destroy the Southern economy and that the Southern response would likely be so rabid it could destroy the Union. He advocated that the government buy all the slaves and set them free, but his proposal was ignored.

Planters and even abolitionists believed in the inherent inferiority of the black race. Rankin believed if the slaves were educated they could be viewed as equals and become industrious members of society. In this way prejudice against them could be eliminated and the paternalist argument for continued bondage dropped. To prove his point, he set up a little school in an empty house for free blacks in Ripley. A mob broke through the door and forced them out with clubs. Rankin moved his school into a friend's kitchen but the mob came back. After weeks of being chased around with the threat of violence, his students were afraid to return and he had to close his school.

He knew he needed to rally, not just Northerners, but his fellow backcountry Scots-Irishmen. Ninety-five percent of them didn't own slaves and had no vested interest in slavery. He needed to appeal to their moral barometer, to convince them that slavery was a vile institution and stain on the nation's character. Meanwhile his nemesis was appealing to the same farmers that slavery was their "highest and most solemn obligation" and fundamental to their best interests.

Calhoun's Compromises

The truth was, the South was in trouble. Calhoun recognized this as early as 1820 when Missouri petitioned to join the Union. It was imperative to the balance of power between the free states of the industrial North and the slave states of the agrarian South that each be entitled to an equal number of seats in the Senate to eliminate any danger of one encroaching on the other's interests. The South could count three-fifths of its disenfranchised slaves as part of its electorate to qualify for more electoral votes and allocation of tax revenues. However, the population of the North was rising faster than the South, and more non-slave states were being added to the Union. Once the northern states had larger voter rolls and more electoral votes, they would have political control of the country.

"The day that the balance between two sections of the country—the slaveholding states and the non-slaveholding states—is destroyed," Calhoun, now vice president under Andrew Jackson, warned, "is a day that will not be far removed from political revolution, anarchy, civil war, and widespread disaster."[12]

After a long bitter debate, Missouri joined the Union as a slave state with Maine joining simultaneously as a free state to maintain the balance of power. Slavery would also be prohibited in any future states formed north of the 36°30' parallel. Not that the North was any bastion of equality—Illinois, Ohio, and Pennsylvania, believing blacks had a greater propensity to commit crimes, required them to post a five-hundred-dollar bond when entering the state as a guarantee of good behavior. Enterprising free blacks were caught in the injustice that drove whites into the Revolutionary War fifty years earlier—taxation without representation. Most northern states didn't admit blacks to their schools.

As a shift in power toward the North became only a matter of time, Calhoun canonized himself as a rabid advocate of states' rights on a crusade to wrestle more control away from the federal government. He had drafted a proposal for nullification in 1828, contending that the Constitution was a compact among the sovereign states; therefore, any one state could declare an act of Congress unconstitutional and refuse to enforce it within its borders. Jackson fumed that picking and choosing laws would reduce the fledgling nation to a loose coalition of states that would undermine American democracy.

"Our union, it must be preserved," Jackson toasted at a dinner to commemorate Thomas Jefferson's birthday.

"The Union, next to our liberty, the most dear," added Calhoun.[13]

Calhoun's first order of business was to fight a protective tariff that had been introduced in 1828 to protect American manufacturers from European competition. The duties on foreign imports were increased so that American manufactured goods could be made more competitive. Unfortunately the South consumed, but didn't produce, manufactured goods, so they ended up buying manufactured products on a protected market and selling their agricultural goods on an open market. The North also benefited from the revenue the tariff generated that was used to build roads, railroads, and canals for which the South had little purpose. South Carolina decided that imposing this tax was an act of usurpation on the part of the federal government. It announced it would cease collection of this "Tariff of Abominations."

In 1832 Calhoun resigned as Jackson's vice president and reentered the Senate to fully engage in South Carolina's cause for nullification.

"Tell [the nullifiers] from me that they can talk and write resolutions and print threats to their hearts' content," Jackson told a South Carolina Congressman. "But if one drop of blood be shed there in defiance of the laws of the United States, I will hang the first man of them I can get my hands on to the first tree I can find."[14]

They said when Jackson talked about hanging it was time to look around for the ropes. Jackson put the navy on alert and threatened to collect the revenue by cannonade if necessary. Calhoun responded on the Senate floor with a speech delivered with "satanic Majesty . . . clenched fists . . . and his great white eyes."[15]

"Death is not the greatest calamity," he thundered. "There are others still more terrible to the free and brave, and among them may be placed the loss of liberty and honor . . . her gallant sons will stand prepared to perform the last duty—to die nobly."[16]

Neither of the stubborn Scots-Irish leaders would yield. Finally an eleventh-hour compromise was reached to reduce the tax to a level that appeased both North and South. The crisis was averted, but the nullification cause was lost. However, Calhoun became more resolute in his determination to protect the South from what he perceived as the encroaching threat of servitude to the industrial North.

"Let it never be forgotten that where the majority rules, the minority is the subject," he warned.[17]

Calhoun urged Southerners to "look to her defenses" and unite within a single party and on a single issue. Only through its autonomy could the South be preserved—if one of its institutions could be subverted by the federal government so could they all. The institution of slavery, he decided, was the issue around which the South could unite.

"I hold concession or compromise to be fatal," he urged. "If we concede an inch, concession would follow concession—compromise would follow compromise, until our ranks would be so broken that effectual resistance would be impossible."[18]

Calhoun had told John Quincy Adams years before that slavery was an economic necessity for the South, the only means by which they could produce the tobacco, sugarcane, and cotton on which their economy survived. Moreover, it was a matter of self-determination—the states should be able to decide whether to be free or slave.

"I anticipated that he would prove an ornament and a blessing to his country," President Adams wrote in his diary about his vice president. "I have been deeply disappointed in him, and now expect nothing from him but evil."[19]

Calhoun was determined to convince poor whites and backcountry farmers—almost 95 percent of whom owned no slaves and had no particular interest in helping the slave owners keep theirs—that slavery was fundamental to their survival. Furthermore, he warned the South that abolitionists like Rankin were "deluded madmen" who were "stirring heaven and earth" to destroy the Southern economy.

The Truth, the Whole Truth, and Anything but the Truth

"Slavery is a great cuss . . . the greatest there is in these United States," one North Carolinian told a journalist in 1822.[20]

The reporter, Frederick Law Olmsted from Connecticut, had grown frustrated by the pious posturing of abolitionists, as well as the "moonlight and magnolias" picture painted by planters. He convinced two newspapers to send him, as a roving correspondent, into the American South to discover the real truth. He found what Calhoun feared, that mountain folk generally seemed to have had equal contempt for slaves, their masters, and the system of slavery itself.

"[It] would be a great deal . . . better for the country . . . if there was not a slave in it," a Tennessean told him.[21] Another wished there had never been any blacks in the country, but didn't think there could be "any better way of getting along with them than they had."[22]

The majority of small independent farmers who dominated Southern agrarian life worked where slavery didn't exist at all. However, where slavery did exist, white laborers hated the competition and the opportunities owning slaves afforded the planters. During the antebellum period, the South prospered well enough that competition wasn't an issue and racial tensions were minimized. In fact, there was more prejudice against the planters than the blacks. The slave owners controlled local politics, regulated wage rates, prevented public schooling that would require they pay more taxes, and, since they owned all the land, could prevent landless whites from becoming landowners. They kept the poor white man down, then demeaned him for laboring on another man's farm.

"Poor white folks would never had a chance," said a northern Alabama slave. "The slave holders had most of the money and the land and they wouldn't let the poor white folks have a chance to own any land or anything else to speak of. These white folks weren't much better off than we was."[23]

Despite all the negative stereotypes, plain folks, whether they were landless or small farmers, began to take pride in their culture. They valued virtues like independence, courage, love of freedom, and a sense of adventure. From this evolved a distinct folk culture that grew from gathering on each other's porches to tell stories or play music. Aristocrats called them idle, but they continued to hunt, fight, drink, and compete as they had always done on the frontier.

"To stand on his head in a bar, to toss down a pint of raw whiskey at a gulp," recorded one writer. "To fiddle and dance all night, to bite off the nose or gorge the eye of a favorite enemy, to fight harder and love harder than the next man, to be known eventually far and wide as a hell of a fellow—such would be his focus."[24]

As Olmsted moved through the mountains, he found fewer slaves and began to see how slavery created cultural and social stagnation. It robbed farmers of their Calvinist work ethic or any incentive for self-improvement. As a labor force, slaves proved inefficient. The lack of incentive made them work slowly and poorly. It was in their interest "to work as little as they can" since the drudgery was never going to end. He watched an entire field of women stop work after their overseer passed, then start again when he came back. This work ethic in turn affected whites, who developed "unfaithful, meritorious, inexact and non-persistent habits of working."[25]

Olmsted's findings bolstered Rankin's argument that slavery induced immorality and idleness in the slaveholding class, cultivated a spirit of cruelty and tyranny, and increased the gap between rich and poor.

"There was . . . many a man who had gone to the bad world, who wouldn't have gone there if . . . he hadn't had any slaves," one farmer said. "It made the rich . . . people, who owned the [slaves], passionate, and proud and ugly, and it made . . . the poor people mean."[26]

"People that own [slaves] are always mad at them about something," another farmer added. "Half their time is spent swearing and yelling at them."

Calhoun meanwhile argued that slaves reflected the character of their owner: ignorant, degraded slaves were usually owned by a master of the same qualities, but Olmsted insisted that the most pleasant house he visited in his mountain travels was in an area where there were no slaves.

"Compared with the slaveholders," Olmsted wrote, concluding that slavery had an adverse affect on whites, "these people are more cheerful, more amiable, more sociable, and more liberal. Compared with the non-slaveholders of the slaveholding districts, they are also more hopeful, more ambitious, more intelligent, more provident, and more comfortable."[27]

Slavery in the Southern Mountains

In many Appalachian communities, if a free black was found spending time "in idleness and dissipation, or having no regular or honest employment," he was arrested and bound out for three to ten years. The poorhouses also bound out free children of single black women. One woman in North Carolina indentured her five young children because she was too poor to take care of them.

The binding out of slaves to work alongside free blacks and whites made interaction between the races in the Scots-Irish dominated Appalachians different from the rest of the South. Integrated workforces were particularly common in mines and mills. A British traveler noticed over two hundred whites and blacks working together weaving and spinning in a mill.

"There is no difficulty among them on account of color, [they are] working together without apparent repugnance or objection. . . . I have witnessed . . . that the prejudice of color is not nearly so strong in the South as the North."[28]

When gold was discovered in Georgia in 1828, men rushed in from everywhere. Every summer Calhoun reassigned twenty of his slaves to work his Dahlonega mine until cotton harvests. Some slaves hid gold dust and small nuggets in their hair. One evening one overseer made them shake their hair out and several ounces of pure gold were recovered. They still managed to bury little treasure troves in the hills, which would later buy a ticket to freedom.

Towns exploded into existence across the mountains to cater to the influx of miners, speculators, and general degenerates. One visitor wrote, "I can hardly conceive of a more unmoral community than exists . . . around these mines; drunkenness, gambling, fighting, lewdness, and every other . . . vice exist here to an awful extent."[29]

Many blacks, free and slave, capitalized on the new market by convincing their master to allow them to open shops and tanneries and share their profits. Some opened saloons if they had a guardian to get a liquor license.

"Slaves are trained to every kind of manual labor," one visitor wrote. "The blacksmith, cabinet-maker, carpenter, builder, and wheelwright . . . The Negro is a third arm to every workingman who can possibly save money to purchase one."[30]

Skilled boatmen were in huge demand on Southern waterways. The Tennessee River hired five hundred slaves annually from Appalachian counties in northern Alabama. Many of these slaves transported goods without supervision and developed the skills to traverse rivers that were believed to be impassable.

"Sometimes that river take your boat round and round like a merry-go-round" explained a black steersman. "Then it swing from that whirl into a swift stream that take you a mile a minute. . . . Then you see a tree a-coming right straight at you."[31]

Unfortunately for slave owners, the more ingenious the slaves became, the more likely they were to escape. Many just walked off the boats when they reached a free state or dug up their gold nuggets and paid their way to Canada. Newspapers were covered in advertisements that offered high rewards for the capture of skilled slaves. One offered a hundred-dollar reward for the return of Anthony Page, who was "a slave of great capacity and considerable ingenuity."

Others protested their bondage by refusing to work. At one Alabama coal mine a slave refused to pump water from the pits. His manager complained that he "lay there on a plank and went to sleep insisting that it was not necessary to haul any more, and in fact did not haul any more."[32] In other workplaces, fights started to erupt. One slave threatened to burn down the factory if his master didn't dismiss his overseer. Another burned down his master's gin.

"I expect to kill someone about it yet,"[33] the master said.

Southerners started to blame slave uprisings on these industrial slaves, since artisans led almost all the black insurrections. A free black carpenter called Denmark Vassy led a small army in a general revolt to win their freedom in Charleston. It was brutally suppressed, and thirty-five slaves were hanged. Ten years later, another carpenter, Nat Turner, led a rebellion that raged for weeks and resulted in the deaths of fifty-eight white people. It amplified Southerners' terror at the prospect of slave revolt.

Free blacks were increasingly perceived as a menace. Whites feared being killed or absorbed by the black race. In 1793 thousands of white refugees from the slave revolt in Haiti fled to the South and told the story of how black freedom was unfolding on their island: the mass meetings in forests, the walls of fire and smoke as plantations burned, the human carnage, and the subjugation of the white population to barbarian control.

As rebellions swept across the South, fear and paranoia grew. Gradually people with no vested interest in slavery began to view Rankin as part of a lunatic fringe that would "Africanize" the South and have them all murdered in their beds. This fear played into Calhoun's plans to create a solid South united in its defense of its institutions.

The Information War

In the summer of 1835, the American Anti-Slavery Society declared an information war on the South by sending more than one million copies of anti-slavery publications, including Rankin's letters, from New York into five Southern states to "overthrow slavery by revolutionizing the public sentiment of the country."[34]

Calhoun took to the Senate floor railing against the abolitionist's effort to incite slaves to insurrection with incendiary publications. They were "dividing the country with hatred more deadly than one hostile nation ever entertained toward another," he warned. Since the nullification crisis, Calhoun believed the industrializing North would take advantage of, and eventually oppress, the South. Now citizens of one state were meddling with the legal domestic institutions of another, thus violating their sovereignty. If the Union were to be saved, the agitation must be stopped, but if they had to rely on the power of the federal government to protect the South, that implied the federal government also had the power not to protect them. The South, he decided, would stand united in its own defense.

Calhoun's "peculiar institution" was now a question of liberty and self-determination, two incendiary and fundamental issues for the Scots-Irish. Southern leaders rallied behind Calhoun, warning farmers and laborers that the day would come when the free blacks would take their jobs. It was in the interests of the small farmers to cooperate with the planter by keeping the blacks out of economic competition. It was also imperative that they prevent industrialism from crushing their agriculture. The North had already tried to tax them into subservience, and its outraged, hypocritical morality should not be allowed to prostitute the agrarian South industrial power.

Gradually, Southern whites began to equate slavery with independence and economic necessity. Rankin continued to travel around giving speeches and sermons and writing letters trying to convince them otherwise while his sons conducted slaves to freedom. Finally the state of Kentucky offered a reward of three thousand dollars for the abduction or assassination of Rankin and his cohorts.

Cincinnati was overwhelmed by the deluge of slaves escaping on the Underground Railroad through Ohio. Several hundred white men stormed its free black community, burned buildings, dragged women from their beds, and beat them with sticks and clubs. Cincinnati was forced to enact "black laws" for the first time. The city required each free black to post a five-hundred-dollar bond as a guarantee of good behavior. Riots erupted again when a white mob destroyed a black confectionary store. Violent clashes lasted for six hours, by which time part of the city was under martial law.

Fear took root in the backcountry in places where there were only one or two slaves working fields alongside their masters, and even in places where there were no slaves.

"I reckon the majority would be right glad if we could get rid of the Negroes," one farmer said. "But it wouldn't never do to free them and leave them here."[35]

In 1837 Calhoun began to rally the South in a passionate defense of slavery. He genuinely believed the slave system was a benign institution. He stopped calling it a "necessary evil," as it had been called since Jefferson's time, and began to call it a "positive good."

"Look at the sick, and the old and infirm slave, on one hand, in the midst of his family and friends, under the kind superintending care of his master and mistress," he argued, with a barb at the North, "and compare it with the forlorn and wretched condition of the pauper in the poorhouse."[36]

In Charleston, a mob of citizens raided the post office and stole and burned a sack of abolitionist pamphlets. Across the South, slave hunters grew more violent, killing whites helping runaway slaves and sending the blacks downriver. Conductors and slaves were lynched, murdered, and their houses burned. In a Mississippi river town in Illinois, a mob struck at a printing press of Presbyterian minister and abolitionist Elijah P. Lovejoy. Called the "minister of mischief," he edited a St. Louis newspaper until his anti-slavery editorials provoked mobs to ruin his press. In July 1836, he bought a new printing press that was left on the dock overnight till he could move it the next morning. He came back to find it shattered into little pieces, floating down the river. When he got a third press, a mob began throwing bricks at his building and setting it alight. He ran outside to stop them and was shot to death. It was two days before his thirty-fifth birthday.

"Lovejoy . . . died a Martyr to liberty and righteousness and deserves a place on the brightest page of history," Rankin said from the pulpit that Sunday. "Slavery has abolished both the liberty of speech and of the press in the slave states and is attempting to do the same in the free states."[37]

Rankin had been spared this kind of violence largely because he had twelve children, five of whom were grown men and were heavily armed. This provided the family with effective security for many years—until 1841 when everything changed. One night when he was away on a speaking tour, and two of his older sons, David and Calvin, hadn't returned from conducting a slave the night before, seventeen-year-old Samuel heard a commotion and came outside to see men with a pistols and dogs approach the house.

"Halt! If you come one step farther I will kill you," he shouted brandishing a shotgun, despite being outnumbered six to one.[38]

A few minutes later, horses thundered through the thicket. Word had spread that mercenaries were climbing the hill just as Calvin and David returned from their midnight ride. They rounded up eight or nine men from the town and drove the intruders off. But the attacks got worse. Another night a noise abruptly woke Calvin, who instinctively grabbed a shotgun, ran out outside, and opened fire on the intruders. His cousin and two older brothers scrambled to join him. Flames blazed from the barn. The brothers rushed to put out the fire while Calvin held the intruders at

Rankin Family Portrait, ca. 1861–1865. Courtesy Ohio Historical Society.

gunpoint. After a frenzied effort, the fire was extinguished; three minutes later and the whole place would have gone up.

Rankin responded to the attack by taking the light out of his window, erecting a thirty-foot pole outside, and hanging the beacon to freedom even higher. The Underground Railroad had already conducted between fifty thousand and a hundred thousand slaves to freedom, and Rankin was more determined than ever to do his part in relieving slave owners of thousands of dollars in "property" by aiding fugitives and writing letters.

In 1837 Calhoun was on the Senate floor like "a man racked with furious passions" delivering his speech on the "Reception of Abolition Petition." Abolitionists had sent more than a hundred and thirty thousand petitions to Congress asking for the abolition of slavery. He fumed that they were plotting a civil war and proposed action that would prohibit the circulation of "incendiary publications intended to instigate the slaves to insurrection." The South, he said, had the right to hold slaves without interference from the "frivolous, absurd, unconstitutional, immoral, and impious" activities of the American Anti-Slavery Society.

The House passed a gag rule that automatically "tabled," or postponed action on, all petitions relating to slavery without hearing them. Free speech was being subverted; but the greater fear came from the abolitionists' activities. Rankin was pummeled with eggs. During a sermon to a black congregation, people hurled stones through the church window. With typical Scots-Irish stubbornness and resolve, he responded with more articles, commentaries, and pamphlets against slavery.

Presbyterians and Quakers who had fostered the anti-slavery movement realized they were terrifying the nation with their fervor and could bring down the Union. It didn't help that Calhoun was thundering on the Senate floor that "Abolition and the Union cannot coexist" and that slavery cannot be abolished without "drenching the country in blood." The churches were getting jittery, but Rankin wanted them to make a public stand against slavery. He raised the question, "Ought not all anti-slavery Presbyterians withdraw from the present branches of the Presbyterian church in the United States?"[39] He called for the expulsion of all slaveholders, and by doing so precipitated a conspiracy that engineered his downfall.

Throughout his life, Rankin had poured his own money into founding schools and churches. A few years earlier, he was trying to survive financially and care for thirteen children and seven other dependents. He issued bonds on parcels of his land to two of his sons who paid him monthly until the bond was paid off. They were legitimate deals, but whispers started that he was trying to hide assets. Perhaps, they said, he wasn't the paragon of virtue he professed to be. When the whispers grew loud enough, his faceless enemies had him dismissed from the church.

In the autumn of 1846, after twenty-four years of serving the Ripley Presbyterian Church, Rankin locked the heavy oak door behind him for the last time. Its majestic steeple shaded under a canopy of breezy trees still towered over the town. Behind it, far up on the bluff, his tiny house was visible with its long wooden staircase that had carried thousands of slaves to freedom over the years—all of those steps honored his dead brother, Thomas. Rankin started this church in the midst of a lawless, debauched town with a meager thirty-two members. Over the years, his hard work, perseverance, and pious example had coaxed another two hundred feckless drunks and gamblers inside its walls.

"This was one of the greatest afflictions of my life," he wrote. "I never endured at any other time such agony of spirit. To see a church that . . . had always been harmonious, and for which I had labored twenty-four years and made for it every sacrifice in my power, now violently torn asunder was heart rendering."[40]

A Conspiracy of Slave Power

As the 1840s closed, the crutch of compromises that supported the Union for twenty-eight years was visibly buckling. At the end of the Mexican-American War, new states were being added to the Union, and the compromises that had maintained a delicate balance of power for three decades were threatened. California, a territory "full of black abolitionists" joined the Union as a free state. The South's fear of becoming a political minority at the mercy of Northern vagary was being realized.

Calhoun, more than ever, needed to rally the South into a single political vision. In 1848 he held a caucus of Southern senators and representatives in the Senate chamber and gave his "Address of the Southern Delegates in Congress to their Constituents," determined to rouse the independent nature and fighting spirit of the South.

"Slavery is a domestic institution. It belongs to the States, each for itself, to decide whether it shall be established or not," he demanded. "And, if it be established, whether it should be abolished or not. Such being the clear and unquestionable rights of the States, it follows necessarily that it would be a flagrant act of aggression on a State, destructive of its rights, and subversive of its independence, for the federal government, or one or more States, or their people, to undertake to force on it the emancipation of its slaves."[41]

He was hitting all the right cultural chords. Forty Southern senators rallied behind him, bolstering the power of the "slavocracy." The abolitionists called it the "Address of John C. Calhoun and Forty Other Thieves," but the senator had successfully sounded the alarm of inevitable Northern aggression. To appease the South, the Fugitive Slave Act of 1793 was revamped with the stipulation that anyone helping a slave escape, in any state in the Union, could be fined up to a thousand dollars and incarcerated for six months. The North was forced to collaborate with slave power and slaves were safe nowhere.

"The Fugitive Slave law is a standing monument of the most highhanded wickedness ever a nation did," Rankin proclaimed.[42]

The constitutional duty of the non–slave-owning states to hand over escaped slaves intensified Northern hatred, anger, and fear of a "slave power conspiracy." The escalation of tensions continued when Kansas became eligible for admittance to the Union. Pro- and anti-slavery residents of surrounding states poured in to influence the legislature in its decision to join as a free or slave state. In May 1856 a mob of pro-slavery advocates attacked the anti-slavery headquarters. They set fire to a hotel and people's homes and destroyed a printing press, killing several townspeople in the process.

Three days later John Brown, a radical abolitionist and advocate of armed insurrection, hacked five pro-slavery settlers to death. In 1859 he led another raid on the federal armory at Harpers Ferry, Virginia. Seven people were killed. Local farmers and militia rose up against him, and with the aid of U.S. Marines, Brown and his conspirators were captured and hanged.

Rankin and many other anti-slavery advocates were horrified by the extreme acts of these abolitionists, but Southerners believed it was just the beginning of the onslaught.

Rich and poor, they found renewed solidarity in their passion for independence and distrust of government. Just as planters respected the small farmer's independence, farmers began to support the right of planters to keep what they owned. When the institution of slavery was threatened, so too was the very principle of ownership in the South.

"If they can take . . . our [blacks] away from us they can take our cows or hosses, and everything else . . . we've got!" said one defiant Southerner.[43]

Whatever distaste these non–slave-owning small farmers felt for slaveholders and the entire institution, it was less offensive than outside interference in their way of life. "Racial solidarity" came to mean "self-preservation." Rankin lost the battle to win the South over to the abolition of its "organic sin."

Calhoun didn't live to see the implementation of the new Fugitive Slave Act. Tuberculosis was racking his body. He continued his crusade to the painful end, knowing without a doubt that the South would not permit itself to be destroyed by Northern aggression, or be degraded by subjugation. She would protect herself just as he predicted "should it cost every drop of blood and every cent of property."

On March 31, 1850, he died, crying the final words: "The South! The South! God knows what will become of her!"[44]

A Fire Bell in the Night

Ten years later the son of a poor Kentucky frontiersman, Abraham Lincoln, campaigned for the White House against the expansion of slavery.

"A house divided against itself cannot stand," he said in 1858. "I believe this government cannot endure permanently half slave and half free.... It will become all one thing, or all the other."[45]

And so the battle lines were drawn. As Lincoln's victory looked more certain, the South looked to her defenses.

Fearing their enemies in the North were about to take control of the government, seven Southern states declared their secession from the Union before Lincoln took office on March 4, 1861. The Confederate States of America led by Jefferson Davis authorized an army to take control of military installations in the South, namely Fort Sumter that guarded Charleston Harbor in South Carolina. When Lincoln refused to give up the fort, Provisional Forces of the Confederate States opened their batteries on April 12, 1861, and fired a shot that burst a hundred feet over the harbor. Every man, woman, and child in Charleston jumped from their bed to watch the onslaught of war explode in horror.

An estimated three quarters of a million Confederate soldiers were about to go to war against an estimated two million Union troops. Among them were five of Rankin's sons and one grandson. The enthusiasm of young Southerners was almost unequaled in history. Less than 5 percent of them had slaves, yet they enlisted in droves, not to protect the rights of the elite to keep their slaves or because they burned with a hatred of blacks. They were driven by their commitment to independence, self-determination, and survival, or as Davis wrote, to protect their rights against "unlimited, despotic power."

They fought the "War for Southern Independence" with the indomitable spirit of the frontier: optimistic, confident, and chaffing at the idea of enslavement to the North, willing to die driving "the evading host of tyrants form our soil." Defense of the homeland is one of the most powerful combat motivations, and it manifested in the doggedness of the Confederate soldiers so markedly that it startled Union officers.

"We are fighting for the Union ... a high and noble sentiment, but after all a sentiment," wrote an Illinois sergeant in 1862. "They are fighting for independence and are animated by passion and hatred against invaders."[46]

The fatalities were enormous. Two hundred and fifty-eight thousand Confederate soldiers and three hundred and sixty thousand Union soldiers went to their death. The Confederate states suffered an estimated $7.4 billion worth of property damage. At the start of the war the slave states held 30 percent of the country's wealth; ten years later this had collapsed to 12 percent. It would take almost a hundred years for Southern agricultural output to return to 1860 levels, and a hundred and fifty years before the freed blacks would gain their civil liberties.

Rankin's heart was broken.

"I lived to see four million slaves liberated, but not in the way I had long labored to have it done," he lamented. "More than fifty years ago I published an article in a religious paper . . . urging the setting of the slaves free by purchase. A thousand million would purchase all the slaves in the Union . . . a million lives would have been saved from a bloody death. The prime men of the nation were slaughtered and sorrow and weeping pervaded the entire country."[47]

On March 18, 1886, at the age of ninety-three, Rankin's own life was lost in a battle with cancer. That night was desperately cold with gale force winds blustering around his house on the hill. Six free black men stood on the icy wharf of the Ohio River on a nightlong death vigil. The next day, along with four of Rankin's sons and two sons-in-law, they served as pallbearers to carry the unconquerable spirit of this resolute Scots-Irishman to the tiny cemetery in his adopted home of Ripley.

"Who abolished slavery?" Harriet Beecher Stowe's brother Henry was asked.

"Reverend John Rankin and his sons did it," he responded.[48]

The Beginning of Race Hate

When Willy Haslerig's grandfather, George, was born in 1866, the hope for a new era of black liberation was turning into one of the most corrupt and oppressive periods in American history. Three years earlier Lincoln had issued a Proclamation of Amnesty and Reconstruction to restore the Union based on forgiveness, not punishment. Southern states were to be readmitted once 10 percent of their registered voters swore an oath of allegiance to the Union. They could then draft revised state constitutions and establish new state governments. A full pardon would be granted to everyone except high-ranking Confederate army officers; all private property except for slaves was guaranteed. Lincoln hoped for a swift return to normalcy.

Like many freedmen, the Haslerig men wandered the countryside, flexing their newfound liberty and looking for new opportunities. It seemed to them that many Republicans in Congress wanted to transform Southern society for their benefit. What they didn't realize was that the Radicals in government wanted to punish the South. They wanted to disband the planter aristocracy, redistribute land, develop industry, and guarantee civil liberties for former slaves. Confiscated land was to be leased in forty-acre tracts to former slaves and poor whites with an option to purchase later. But before George Haslerig had time to catch a glimpse of forty acres, everything changed. President Lincoln was assassinated. Hopes for a peaceful restoration of the Union died with him and the "Tragic Era" was about to begin.

Lincoln's successor tried to continue Lincoln's plan of leniency. The states were required to ratify the Thirteenth Amendment. This prohibited slavery but didn't mandate suffrage. The Southern states agreed, believing compliance was the only way to get rid of federal soldiers and take back control of their own affairs. They assumed that the management of their free-black population would be left to them, and they intended to introduce a caste system that would keep freedmen segregated, restricted, and subordinate to the whites.

The Radicals were horrified; they overruled the Southern states, took charge of Reconstruction, passed the Reconstruction Act of 1867, and dramatically changed Southern politics. Radical whites and newly enfranchised blacks went to the polls and voted Republican governments into power in every state.

Many blacks were voted into office; unfortunately most were illiterate. The real power was in the hands of carpetbaggers who had come from the North to exploit the prostrate South, and scalawag Southerners who colluded with the Radicals. In the hands of these scoundrels, inefficiency and corruption in the new Southern state governments were endemic. Bonds were issued for railroads that were never built, pay increases were awarded at will, and bribes were needed to get any legislation passed.

The outraged planters screamed that the North had imposed "black dominion" on them. It was a rallying cry across the South that united whites in a hatred of the "reconstructed" governments. It galvanized them in the cause of ridding the South of legions of villains, plundering carpetbaggers, disloyal scalawags, and black politicians. Before the war most whites condescended to blacks, many feared them, but now they were learning to despise them, as the Haslerigs soon discovered. A new South was being formed based on racial hatred.

In 1865 a secret society of vigilantes, the Ku Klux Klan, was formed to intimidate supporters of the Radical Republicans and their state-imposed governments. They murdered carpetbaggers, organized race riots, and terrified the black and white Radical voters away from the polls. Before 1900, mobs lynched as many whites as blacks. Two-thirds of those lynched in Kentucky were white, but with each passing decade, as bitterness deepened, the number of black victims increased.

Planters were unable to hire workers to do the work of former slaves so a system of sharecropping evolved whereby blacks and poor whites worked sections of a planter's land and paid him a share of the crop at the end of the year. George Haslerig was trapped in this system of subsistence living for sixty-five years. Like all blacks he had to borrow seeds from the landowner at the beginning of planting season, so when they returned the crop quota after the harvest, he still needed to borrow seed for the next season. After years of hard work, he finally managed to deliver the crop quota and pay the landowner for the seeds he bartered. He should have escaped from the yoke of debt, but the landowner denied the debt repayment. Papers disappeared; it was a black man's word against a white. He ended up like all the other blacks—tied in a backbreaking existence to a tract of land, not much better off than his father had been in the years of bondage.

With few options available in the devastated South, landless whites also found themselves living the sharecropper's life. They were incensed to find themselves oppressed by a political system and caught in an economic system that equated them with blacks. They never owned slaves, but while there was a man in bondage, the poor whites were never on society's bottom rung. Now they were. Their rage surfaced sporadically in racial violence and attempts to drive blacks from the land. Between 1890 and 1930, blacks were expelled from three thousand communities across the South, including Sand Mountain.

"You tell us what to do and we'll say no thank you," explained one angry local, reflecting the general attitude toward the imposition of Reconstruction governments. "The Klan was always around somewhere but we don't need them either."[49]

Gradually, through a combination of terror and politicking, the white majority took back power. Federal troops were withdrawn, the abhorred state governments collapsed, and Reconstruction crumbled. The South drafted new constitutions and settled into a system where the landowners had political control and the blacks remained landless peasants without equal civil rights. Despite ratifying the Fourteenth and Fifteenth Amendments that guaranteed citizenship and suffrage, blacks were subjected to strict voter eligibility laws, literacy tests, and poll taxes that prevented them from voting.

George Haslerig's travels through the land as a free man were over, and his fleeting suffrage was gone. The Jim Crow laws were enacted in 1876, mandating segregation in all public facilities. They were supposed to guarantee a "separate but equal" status for black Americans, but in reality they were anything but equal.

The restoration of white supremacy ignited one of the greatest internal migrations in American history. Thousands of blacks started moving north and west in 1877, causing huge social, housing, and cultural problems. The result was race riots on a scale never before seen in America. The black issue was now a Northern problem and Northerners quickly had enough; they reasoned that only Southern conservatives knew how to restore economic and political stability. They grew bored hearing the Radicals cry about "Southern outrages." Many felt that the nation had done enough for blacks, and now they should be able to fend for themselves.

"We've tried this long enough," was the new attitude. "Now let the South alone."

The next three generations of Haslerigs lived a separate but not-equal existence, segregated from whites, aware of the many places they weren't welcome. In 1948 they watched President Truman try to push through Civil Rights legislation. In 1955 they heard Rosa Parks refused to give up her seat to a white man on a bus and sparked a boycott of the buses in Montgomery, Alabama. They watched federal troops oversee the forced desegregation of Little Rock High School in 1957 and the rise and assassination of Reverend Martin Luther King Jr. in 1968.

Then one day in 1964 long after Grandpa George had passed on, Willy Haslerig witnessed the passing of the Civil Rights Act. Finally, one hundred years and three generations later, blacks had equal rights under the law.

Sand Mountain

Of course, equal rights didn't change the fact that Willy Haslerig knew better than to park his milk truck in front of a school on Sand Mountain in 1972. He shaded his eyes from the glaring sun and saw a group of locals approaching. This wasn't good. He'd heard what happens next—at best he'd get a beating, at worst they'd be cutting him down from a tree in a few days. His heart was pounding as the locals rounded the truck, peered in at the white bottles, and walked right up to him. An eternity passed in silence. When someone finally spoke, it was to thank him for driving the milk all the way up the mountain. They were a group of isolated, working-class rural folks, most of whom had never seen a black man, all of whom were happy their children's milk had arrived.

Willy's heart stopped racing.

"I found human beings on that mountain," he said in astonishment. "The nicest people that I ever worked with up there." [50]

After three generations of instilled terror based on a story his grandfather took to the grave years before, this fifty-three-year-old man finally discovered the myth had outlived its relevance. People learn to fear and don't know why, he mused later; others are reared with hatred in their hearts, and they don't know why.

"After they outgrow that, they turn out to be some of the nicest people you'd want to meet," he said. "That's the reason why I learned, 'don't go by what they say.'" [51]

A little time later, he applied for that milk delivery round and for the next fifteen years, until the day he retired, Willy Haslerig and his milk truck were regular fixtures on the Mountain.

CHAPTER 7

MAYBELLE AND THE MOUNTAIN

odney Crowell blew it. If the singer, poet, and quintessential Scots-Irishman was going to dig himself out of his sinkhole he needed someone to throw him a line and quickly. A woman with a mane of auburn hair and enigmatic smile, sidled up to him.

"I think the first thing I'm going to have to do to get you properly seasoned is sit you down at the blackjack table with Mother Maybelle," June Carter told him, referring to her mother.[1]

To the poor kid from Houston who grew up listening to the Carter Family on the radio, Maybelle was a goddess, and the idea of sitting with her at a blackjack table in Lake Tahoe, hoping to be forgiven and admitted to the fold of the First Family of Country, had him nervous as hell and praying for a miracle.

June was married to Johnny Cash and Crowell was dating his daughter Rosanne. Two tickets arrived in the mail inviting the couple to visit Johnny and June at their home in Jamaica. Crowell feared he was about to be clobbered for living in sin with his daughter and started drinking on the plane. By the time they got to the house, he was well oiled, irascible, and like any lifelong Johnny Cash fan, dead set on proving he was his own man.

"Son," Crowell remembered his future father-in-law saying. "I don't know you well enough to miss you if you were to leave."

The only way out of the mess was to impresse Maybelle.

The good news was that the Carters and the Crowells shared a sensibility that evolved from a unique frontier experience where rural isolation and the lack of religious guidance created a fissure between a desire for salvation and unregulated heathenism. Out of this deep chasm in the mountains came authentic songs about absolute human experiences. The anguish of loss, starvation, and death crept in like ghosts from the Civil War, along with the themes of patriotism, independence, and a fighting spirit.

"Somewhere at three a.m. the devil and God exist side by side," said Crowell.

"That moment [is] where the myth exists . . . mystery, human debauchery, redemption, and death."[2]

It's the moment in which generations of Scots-Irish dangled between good and evil, sin and redemption, the devil and Jesus. For these Presbyterians you're either good or bad; you're either saved or damned. Jesus died on the cross for your sins, so to be saved you only have to ask—but you have to mean it, you have to commit to the right side of the fissure for all time. The entire culture wrestled under this burden. The Book of Romans explained that salvation is a once-and-for-all spiritual event after which you "consider yourselves dead to sin and alive to God in Christ Jesus." So the Scots-Irish lived by either ignoring the enormous story of ultimate sacrifice or making that vast, life-changing commitment.

"Saturday night sinning and Sunday morning going to church," is how Crowell described it. "You're going to get drunk as shit on Saturday night, and then you're going to go and see what kind of deal you can cut on Sunday."[3]

The bad news was Maybelle had come down from the mountain with hymns and songs of innocence that somehow transformed the misery, debauchery, and death into a rural mystical Eden. She chose God in the moment when Crowell all too often found himself on the side of the devil.

Crowell saw it firsthand growing up in a family of poor and uneducated sharecroppers. From the age of eleven—the year he was baptized in the putrid waters of the Emmanuel Temple Pentecostal Church's glass-enclosed baptismal—he was playing drums while his father sang in infamous Texas honky-tonks. He grew up around reprobates, drunks, and bar brawls. His grandfather who led the line singing at their Pentecostal church on Sundays was a "drop dead drunk." His uncle Porter was the archetypal Scots-Irish tragic-comedian. Crowell watched him get drunk, wrap his car around a tree, and walk away, then borrow another and run it up a telephone pole. He was whistling when they hauled him off to jail.

"Ha ha, got away with it," Uncle Porter laughed, and for some reason that his nephew couldn't yet understand, out there in the mountains that somehow made perfect sense.

Crowell lived a typical life of the rural poor; Saturday nights they pushed the furniture aside in his aunt's farmhouse, and those that could, played music, while those that couldn't danced. Music was their only solace out there in the hills. One of Crowell's earliest memories was hearing Johnny Cash and Carl Perkins on the radio for the first time. He was a six-year-old, dirt-poor, free-spirited child in Houston, "When those rockabilly rebels / Sent the Devil running right through me."[4]

Crowell became obsessed with the visceral tones that told stories of sin, torment, and redemption and led many men down dark alleyways to their own destruction. In there, he found his own raw feelings bleeding through the words of heart-wrenching ballads, sometimes tragic, often comedic, always autobiographical and authentic.

"It'll spot a fake a mile away," he said of the Scots-Irish culture. "Anything manufactured, that's not conjured from the ghost stories' that's not from the culture, that true, native, authentic sensibility."[5]

When he sat down at the blackjack table in Tahoe that night, Crowell wasn't the Grammy and Lifetime Achievement Award–winning inductee into the Songwriters Hall of Fame he later became. He certainly wasn't walking on the same side of the fissure between midnight and morning as Mother Maybelle. He was just a barefoot heathen, forged by poetry, tragicomedy, honky-tonk reprobates and rockabilly rebels, facing the most revered woman in country music who sang of God, love, and salvation.

He was mesmerized watching Maybelle. He loved the sound of her voice, her sensual eyes, the fact that she was Maybelle Carter, the Queen of Country Music. It was rumored she put men in their place without ever uttering a word. She'd just fix her pale blue eyes on them, "Mama just whips us to death with those eyes," one singer said. Crowell's chances weren't looking good.

Maybelle turned to him.

"Are you country or are you rock and roll?" she asked.

"I'm, uh, country," he answered.

"Good you can stay here and gamble with me," she replied.

Instant relief. Regardless of whether he was sinning or saved, he shared the primitive, honest, rooted sensibility that tied the people of the mountains to their history and folklore. That's what mattered to Maybelle.

Crowell was lucky. He had done his Saturday night sinning and managed to cut a Sunday morning deal.

The First Family of Country

The Carters were the earliest and most fiercely independent settlers in Poor Valley, Virginia, a little community at the foot of Clinch Mountain. In the aftermath of the Civil War, Robert Carter, a typical free-spirited wanderer, and his tough mountain wife Mollie, were left with Confederate currency that they said was worth about as much as a two-legged mule. They had a one-room cabin that housed a family of eight. They lived off the land, growing vegetables, rearing hogs for meat, and raising corn and tobacco for bartering.

When Mollie was pregnant with her eldest son, Alvin Pleasant or A.P., a bolt of lightning struck a tree and then shot a streak of fire across the ground close to where she was gathering apples. When A.P. was born his hands trembled; Mollie believed he was marked. Her fear was validated the day he went off with his savings and came home with a fiddle—the devil's instrument as far as she was concerned.

A.P. loved three things: wandering the mountains, selling fruit trees, and music. In 1926 all three collided when he heard a sensual female voice singing a lonesome somber song about the death of a railroad engineer. It took a few visits, but he persuaded Sara Dougherty to marry him and move to his side of the mountain. When her cousin, Maybelle, a beautiful sixteen-year-old came to visit, A.P.'s younger brother Eck—a rascally wanderer with a fondness for moonshine—was smitten. Maybelle was well able to deal with the devil. She came from a long line of intrepid mountain folk; her father was a farmer, mill operator, storekeeper, and moonshine maker.

A.P., Sara, and Maybelle shared a deep love of music. Sara had a sultry, earnest voice, A.P. a baritone, and Maybelle could play the guitar, harp, and banjo like no other.

Music was deeply rooted in the hills. When the immigrants from northern Ireland tumbled down into the Appalachians, they brought their passion for singing ballads and playing the fiddle. Many sang old traditional songs about King William and their great victory in Derry in 1689. But these "Billy Boys" weren't fussy—they'd make music out of

A.P. Carter's birthplace. Poor Valley, Macon Springs, Virginia. Photo by Karen McCarthy.

anything that made a noise: comb and paper, harmonicas, whatever they could get their hands on.

When Mollie grew up in Poor Valley, the South had retreated inward to soothe itself from the devastation of the Civil War. The hill people were cocooned in their own culture and worship. The church was the moral censor and cornerstone of the community. Singing gospel hymns brought back the fire of evangelical revivalism and its message of salvation that brought rapturous relief from a life of misery. Like everyone else out there, the Carters learned to sing in church, and because there were no songbooks available, someone would line the hymn, singing two lines at a time, waiting for the congregation to repeat them.

"I am bound for the Promised Land / I am bound for the Promised Land / O who will come and go with me / I am bound for the Promised Land."

From this necessity came the invention of simple melodies and refrains that gradually seeped into hill country music whether they were songs about God or heathens. Later the African banjo infused their traditional music with new rhythms. The hill country sound became distinct from the balladry of the old world and reflected the unique culture of the new.

For the most part, entertainment consisted of going to someone's house on a Saturday night, taking all the furniture out of the room, and having an old-fashioned square dance. Songs reflected issues close to the heart of the rural Southerner like death, love, family, God, but given their natural tendency toward mischief, the night would inevitably end with drinking and fighting. Occasionally a medicine show would find its way into these towns, luring in the crowds for hours of music, magic, comedy acts, clog dances, and minstrel routines before a snake-oil merchant pitched his cure-all remedy.

It was also inevitable that their competitive nature would turn music into a contest. Fiddle conventions popped up with barefoot crowds arriving with their Sunday shoes hung over their shoulders. The fiddler became the knight-errant of the mountains, traveling around to tournaments, playing those old Irish tunes that had been handed down from their ancestors. He regaled audiences with tales about making moonshine, hardscrabble farming, and jail-time. The Carters, however, sang about feelings somebody had, about death, love, loss, and hope for the afterlife. They stirred something powerful in people, something haunting and authentic: ghost stories and dreams that everyone understood.

In 1927 when A.P. saw an advert in a Bristol, Tennessee, newspaper announcing that the RCA Victor Company was coming to town with a recording machine and would be paying a whopping fifty dollars for every song good enough to record.

"Ain't nobody going to pay that much money to hear us sing," Sara said.[6]

A.P. prevailed and the trio piled into Eck's old Ford and bounced twenty-five miles along the uneven, curving mountain roads to Bristol. It was a sweltering summer day. A tire burst. A.P. put a patch on the inner tube, but the heat kept melting it away. It was almost dark when they arrived, but the thriving railroad town was bustling with people arriving for the audition by bus, buggy, in trains, or on foot. One of those people was a free-spirited rambler who'd been traveling with a medicine show since the age of eleven. He lived lavishly, drank heavily, and fraternized with reprobates. He was the antithesis of the Carters' wholesome simplicity, but together they sparked the "big bang" of country.

Sarah (left), Maybelle, and A.P. Carter, ca. 1930. Courtesy of Carter Family Memorial Music Center.

The Father of Country Music

Jimmie Rodgers lived a life that burned twice as bright and half as long. In 1897 Meridian, Mississippi, he was molded from the same clay as the Carters but grew up to be a streetwise kid and unrepentant drifter with an affinity for the company of vagrants. He was cheerful, rowdy, and loved music. He trolled every Meridian barbershop, opera house, theater, and hotel lobby, wherever he could find music.

Rodgers's father was a railroad foreman who reared him alone after his mother died. Following his father from place to place, the boy developed a love of unfettered freedom and had zero education. He loved the railroad tracks and spent hours around working gangs. He hung out in black neighborhoods where he listened to men talk about women and work. He absorbed the rhythms of black popular music that earned him the title of "a white man gone black." At thirteen he launched a stage career treading the boards of a medicine show. His father found him and brought him home. Later he ran off with his sister-in-law's bedsheets, turned them into a tent, and started his own show. His father caught him again, brought him home, and made him reimburse his sister-in-law.

When Rodgers sang, he strummed simple cords on his own guitar. He rarely sang a traditional ballad and only ever sang one gospel song, and even that was accidental. He sang about life on the other side of that fissure between midnight and morning, about hardworking, hard-loving men, hobos traveling in boxcars, small towns, and lost loves. He was funny, sentimental, wild, and evocative. He could yodel like no one else.

"Jimmie's yodeling songs sounded as if they might have been composed by a lonesome Texas cowboy or a hobo kicked off a freight in Tucson or Albuquerque," said a folklorist.[7]

Sadly, in 1924, at the age of twenty-seven, he contracted tuberculosis and spent the next few years drifting between railroad work and entertainment. Between shows he wandered to the rail yards of New Orleans, Texas, Florida, and Arizona. It was a hardscrabble life, but it radiated with adventure, freedom, and poetry. He was happy to exploit the hillbilly image of a hard-drinking, gun-loving rascal. Rodgers would use any story for the sake of a good song.

At the beginning of August 1927, when the Carters were getting into their Sunday best to go to Victor Records' audition and sing about family traditions, religion, morals, and rural simplicity, Rodgers strode in like an outlaw with the wandering, drinking, fighting spirit of the Scots-Irish.

The Hillbillies

Ralph Peer was a fast-talking man who had helped American record companies discover the blues. In 1925, four musicians from Virginia showed up at his studio in New York. When Peer asked them their name, one responded, "We're nothing but a bunch of hillbillies from North Carolina and Virginia. Call us anything."[8] Peer loved the name and appropriated the term as a general moniker for hill country music. The fact that Southerners considered it a fighting word since it was always used disparagingly—usually by Yankees—didn't bother him. He went the whole hog, putting hillbillies in publicity shots standing in cornfields dressed in overalls; and for reasons he couldn't understand, their haphazardly recorded phonograph records were selling.

In 1927 Peer decided it was time to head South. He put an ad in the Bristol paper, set up a makeshift studio in an empty furniture store on State Street, and hoped to attract some new hillbilly talent. On August 1, the Carters sang some soulful ballads that had drifted through the hills for generations: "Broken Down Tramp," a tale that warned young men about drifting into a life of drunken dissolution, and "Old Ladies' Home," which painted a picture of the lonely lives of abandoned old women. Immediately Peer knew he'd struck gold. Sara's voice resonated with those who lived the same joy, or disappointment or tragedy, in her songs and Maybelle could make her guitar talk.

"They were good," Peer told his son. "But they didn't seem to know how good they were."[9]

The eighteen-year-old Maybelle was more interested in the recording system and the microphone that ran off electricity. She couldn't wait to get home and tell Eck all about it.

The Carter Family cut six songs in all and were paid three hundred dollars. Then they bumped twenty-five miles back to Poor Valley and went on with life as usual.

Two days later, Rodgers wandered into the studio. He recorded a tragedy and a lullaby. A few months later the brash singer persuaded Peer to record another session that included characteristic Rodgers sentiments like "Blue Yodel," about a man who plans to buy a shotgun after his girl has run off with another man to "Shoot That Rounder / that Stole My Gal."

It was a catchy song about cheating and revenge, full of yodels, refrains, and bluesy tones, with Rodgers strumming simply on his guitar and his voice doing all the work. It was a smash.

Two months later Maybelle and Eck were in town when Maybelle heard their recording of "The Wandering Boy" being played over the loudspeaker in the store and drifting outside into the streets where a big crowd had gathered to listen. They bought a copy and rushed home. Their uncle had already arrived back in Poor Valley with a copy, and he didn't even own a phonograph. He brought it to his neighbors, and everyone came around. They cranked it up, and out came the old songs of the valley. There was great excitement buzzing through their little community.

After that, A.P. started traveling the mountains visiting trappers, miners, and farmers, anybody who could share interesting music with him. He brought a black blues guitarist named Lesley Riddle, who would memorize the music while A.P. wrote down the words to all the forgotten pieces of music that were being lost in the mountains. He came back and "worked them up" with Sara and Maybelle. The Carter Family recorded almost three hundred songs that became staples for generations of folk singers.

They toured around small mountain towns, setting up plank stages and hanging kerosene lamps. A.P. nailed his own homemade posters to trees, assuring people "The Program is morally good." Meanwhile "Blue Yodel" had propelled Rodgers to stardom. With his wild cowboy image and irrepressible personality, he was filling huge venues. He epitomized the spirit inside every Southerner who wanted to escape the drudgery of post-Depression existence for the wild life and adventures about which he sang. He cultivated his hard-living, hard-drinking lifestyle as part of his image. He identified strongly with the Texan spirit of self-reliance and individualism, and he was only too willing to travel down the wrong side of the fissure and sing about it when he came back.

It seemed so unlikely that Rodgers and the Carters could appeal to the same audience. But together they embodied the conflict at the heart of the Scots-Irish culture, and its eternal rupture between godliness and depravity. The conflict was clear in the four-hour recording session they did together in the summer of 1931 in Louisville. Rodgers did two vocal duets with Sara, including "The Wonderful City," which was the only gospel song he ever recorded. All four joined in on the particularly amoral, and un-Carterlike 1896 ragtime song "Hot Time in the Old Town Tonight," even though none of them apparently knew the words.

"[It was] the wildest, most audacious thing on the record—a scant twenty seconds of country scat," wrote Rodgers' biographer. "Sara in the lead, Maybelle solidly behind her, A.P boldly bursting in, Rodgers filling in the gaps with the shimmering little yodels."[10]

During the session, he asked A.P. to "go get the ole boy (Rodgers) a little squirt," playing to his consummate roguish image, despite the fact that he was rapidly deteriorating after seven years of suffering from tuberculosis. He was so weak, Maybelle had to play his guitar during parts of the session. Still, he managed to find the energy in his dilapidated state to make certain advances on the young girl, or so the story goes. It was the furthest thing from appropriate for a married woman at the time. Maybelle, who would never speak ill of anyone, endured his wild behavior and volcanic temper and never mentioned his iniquity.

It was the first, but wouldn't be the last time Maybelle forgave a scoundrel who medicated his physical pain or tormented soul with alcohol and drugs.

Two years later Rodgers went on a sightseeing tour of Coney Island in New York with his nurse. That night, he died when his lung hemorrhaged. He was only thirty-five.

His body was taken by train back to Meridian, Mississippi. As it pulled into the station, with Rodgers's coffin in the baggage car, the engineer blew the whistle long and hard, a sorrowful tribute to their beloved son who had sparked their imaginations and regaled them with adventures.

"His was an America of glistening rails, thundering boxcars, and rain-swept night, of lonesome prairies, great mountains and a high blue sky," read his memorial. "He sang of the bayous and the cornfields, the wheated plains, of the little towns, the cities, and of the winding rivers of America." [11]

Sunshine Station between Nations

Texas became the epicenter of country music owing to Doctor John R. Brinkley's particular talent for circumventing regulations. He was a self-made millionaire, surgeon, and snake-oil merchant who fled to Mexico with a number of malpractice lawsuits hot on his tail. He built a lavish studio in Texas, planted a monster transmitter in Mexico where there was no federal limit on wattage output, and blasted radio signals that had ten times the amount of power the United States would allow from domestic stations. For the next two years XERA blanketed America, reaching remote regions that had no electricity, where battery operated radios were the only contact with the outside world.

In 1938 Brinkley offered the Carters a job, and they found themselves once again bumping across gravel and dirt highways in blistering heat for ten hours, this time in A.P.'s dust-covered Chevrolet. The same night they were rushed into the studio where began a schedule of broadcasting two shows a day, six days a week.

Maybelle missed her three daughters and brought them all down out of the mountain into the desert. Her middle child, June, couldn't stay on key.

"If you're gonna be on the world's largest radio station with us," Maybelle said. "We'll need some kind of miracle."[12]

By the end of Brinkley's reign, A.P. and Sara had divorced. A.P. quietly went back to the Virginia hills and opened a country store. He never performed and never spoke about his heartache. Eck however wasn't prepared to let Maybelle and his daughters retire. They were now a household name, so they went back out as Mother Maybelle and the Carter Sisters. By 1950 an offer came from the "mother church of country music," the Ryman Auditorium in Nashville, home of the Grand Ole Opry where the best in country music had been broadcast since 1925.

"It was where everyone wanted to be," said June, "and we were like everyone."[13]

The Ryman was an uncomfortable place; lack of ventilation and bright lights had performers in their spangled costumes sweltering. Audiences sat on hard oak pews, but people drove for hundreds of miles to get tickets; some nights five thousand would line up outside. Those who couldn't get to Nashville tuned in their radios every Saturday night to hear the country stars perform. Ever since they appeared on Brinkley's border radio station, kids all across the South tuned in to hear the Carters sing. The Stanley brothers from the same Clinch Mountains imagined what it would be like to be famous like them. Earl Scruggs, a kid in Shelby, North Carolina, was learning to play guitar by listening to Maybelle's picking style. From their farmhouse in Dyess, Arkansas, Jack and Johnny Cash were intrigued by Maybelle's voice and June's ability to make everyone laugh. In Texas, Rodney Crowell, the poor kid from Texas, would listen to the Opry over the coming years as he hauled his drumset through honky-tonks following after his father.

They were a whole new generation of devotees ready to launch and make their own mark on country.

Folk Music in Overdrive

In Kentucky, a young boy was listening to the ghost in the mountains, to the whispered stories of men and women long dead about their loves, losses, and hopes for reunion in heaven. He could crawl through the fissure between midnight and morning without careening into depravity as Rodgers had done. But unlike A.P., who played folk music simply, Bill Monroe played "with an overdrive."

Monroe was a reclusive, cross-eyed kid who was relentlessly bullied by his older siblings. He was born in 1911 in Rosine, Kentucky, a town where they said "they'd just as soon fight you as look at you." Like most other rural kids, he worked the farm from the moment he could wield a hoe. His mother who imbued him with a love of music died when he was only ten. He belted out songs like "Old Joe Clarke" when he was working the fields alone and nobody was around to make fun of him.

When he was old enough, he hopped on a horse behind his eccentric Uncle Pen, and the two would set off to play fiddle and guitar at a square dance in somebody's home. From Uncle Pen, he developed a deep love of folk music. In Rosine he developed a love of the blues from an old black man who hauled freight from the train to six or seven stores in town.

"He would be riding on a mule on those muddy roads just whistling the blues, and you could tell by the way he whistled he was the bluest man in the world," Monroe said.[14]

Being the youngest, Monroe's brothers took all the best instruments in the house, and he was left with the one no one else wanted—the mandolin. For a while he traveled around with two older brothers, playing house parties and appearing on some radio shows. They were even signed by RCA Victor, where they had a hit with a song about the ever-popular theme of sin and redemption, "What Would You Give in Exchange for Your Soul?" Unfortunately, their fame was short lived. The brothers never got along and had to go separate ways. Monroe decided he was going to be the best mandolin player in the business.

Off in Shelby, North Carolina, a kid called Earl Scruggs was trying to figure out how to play the guitar. He lived in an isolated, rural enclave that, left to their own devices, had developed their own cultural nuances, including picking to their own beat on a five-string banjo that they played in the three-finger banjo-picking style.

The area was devastated by the Depression and tuning into XERA radio to hear the Carters sing "There's No Depression in Heaven" was a tonic for this hardworking farming community that was struggling to survive.

"I grew up in Depression days with nothing much for enjoyment, and that helped me enjoy music more," Scruggs recalled during an interview later. "Playing was something that made me feel good. Like my daddy. He had an old banjo probably wasn't worth three dollars. It made him feel better."[15]

Unfortunately his father died when he was four, so for Scruggs there was only one way left to learn.

"My idol at the time . . . was Momma Maybelle Carter, so that's who I copied," he said. "She played the fire out of the guitar."

One day he got into a fight with his brother, and his mother sent them to opposite ends of the house. Scruggs picked up a banjo that was lying around and started playing one song over and over till he discovered he could pick the syllables of the words. By the time he was ten, he was clipping the rhythm, adding licks, and playing so rapidly he brought a whole new dynamic element to old-time music.

Back in Virginia, a haunting voice was emerging from a shy, small child running around the woods in the Clinch Mountains, a few miles from the Carters' homestead. Ralph Stanley and his older, more gregarious brother Carter loved the mountains where they could run around like rabbits, get lost, and imagine great adventures. They didn't have much music around; his father sang snatches of old ballads that caught his fancy. His mother had played the banjo at square dances, and people would dance till dawn.

In 1936 when Stanley was nine, the family finally got a radio and heard music shows for the first time. Every morning before dawn, he took a little kerosene lantern and his radio out to the barn and listened to Maybelle Carter's five a.m. sunrise show while he milked the cows and slopped the hogs. When he heard "My Clinch Mountain Home" he started realizing that there might be a whole other life out there.

His first step was to sing at the local church. It was a Primitive Baptist church that had plank benches and a woodstove for heat. It allowed no instruments, so the leader's voice echoed through the room. One morning his father asked him to lead the hymn. It would have been easier for his affable older brother, but for this backward little boy who never mixed well with people it was terrifying. He took a deep breath and sang.

"Salvation O! The name I love, which came by Christ the Lord above."

The words seemed to hang in the air and fade away. He thought he'd made a mistake but after a brutally long silence the congregation sang the verse back exactly as he had sung it. It was like one big voice that made his "heart swell up like to bust." He continued to the next verse and so it went till the hymn was done. That's how he learned "fear ain't anything to be afraid of."

Later his mother brought him to see his aunt who had a litter of hogs. The aunt was charging five dollars for a piglet, or five dollars for an old banjo she had.

"Which one do you want?" his mother asked. "I'll buy you one of them but I can only afford one."[16]

He'd no idea how to play the banjo, but in the choice between a pig and a banjo, he chose the banjo.

When Stanley was twelve, he tuned in to the Opry one Saturday night and heard Monroe with a new band he put together called the "Blue Grass Boys," named after the bluegrass of his home state of Kentucky. They sang a speeded up version of Jimmie Rodgers' "Mule Skinner Blues" and got a standing ovation, the first encore call ever at the Opry.

A few years later, Monroe was looking for a new banjo player when he happened upon Scruggs and his revamped style. Banjo players had been the hillbilly comedians in minstrel shows since the early 1800s and usually provided the drumroll for punch lines in stand-up comedy, but in Scruggs's hands it was serious business.

"I had never heard anybody pick a banjo the way he did," said Monroe's guitar player, Lester Flatt. "He'd go all over the neck and do things you couldn't hardly believe."[17]

Together Monroe and Scruggs reinvigorated the old homespun songs the hillbillies abandoned. They increased speed, added African rhythms, blues, gospel, and Irish balladry. Most venues they played had only one microphone, so they'd move in and out of center stage to sing their parts, which gave them a dynamic stage presence. One of their tour dates was with a hillbilly package show that came to the remote Clinch Mountains. Stanley had never seen anyone play live, but there was no way he was missing an opportunity to see Monroe. He saved up his money and climbed miles down the mountain to the venue. Monroe and Scruggs were like him—simple, authentic men with those mountain ghost stories running through their bloodline.

The Blue Grass Boys inspired the Stanley brothers to take their music out to the neighborhood. Encouraged by the response, they went with couple of friends to audition for a spot on a local radio station. It was 1946, and these rural boys were so nervous, even the ever-confident Carter couldn't calm them down, but when their turn came Stanley said, "We gave 'em everything we had." They got the spot—it didn't pay, but it was free advertising to make money on the road.

They started living life just like Monroe and the Blue Grass Boys, driving around in a '37 Chevrolet sedan, a bass fiddle strapped to the top and a few instruments in the trunk. Three of them squashed into the backseat, chattering and laughing. They traveled up to a hundred miles a night, seven days a week, barely making enough money for gas, but people kept showing up at their venues, hungry for their blend of old-time music and all the old themes.

"If you feel a song and sing it like you really feel it," Carter used to say, "They'll recognize that feeling, and they'll respond to it. Then you've done your job as a singer."[18] It was similar to Monroe's sentiment—he never sang the same song the same way twice because he would never feel it exactly the same way twice.

Initially Stanley covered a lot of Monroe's songs but sang them in his distinctive high, lonesome voice. People called it weathered, "something you'd hear moaning in the woods late of a night and not from the mouth of a young'un."[19] It was like a lament for the remote green hills of Virginia, an evocative sound that had been drifting over the mountains since the first Scots-Irish settled there, so when A.P. started a little festival on Clinch Mountain it was inevitable that he'd invite the Stanleys to play.

"He had . . . no seats, just a little stage that he built himself in the middle of the mountains," said Stanley. "He didn't want a fence because he didn't want to spoil the view. It was supposed to be $1 admission, but he never turned nobody away."[20]

When it came their turn to play that Sunday afternoon, A.P. took to the stage.

Ralph (left) and Carter Stanley Cincinnati, Ohio, ca. 1963. From the personal photo files of Ralph Stanley.

"Friends, we've got the Stanley Boys here this afternoon," he said. "They sing good old-time songs. As far as I know, they're good boys. I'd never heard nothing bad on them."[21]

It was a typical A.P. introduction, simple and genuine, without any showmanship or pizzazz. This was his way of blessing the boys. Stanley sang "Man of Constant Sorrow," a song older than the hills that his father used to sing on the front porch.

"You can bury me in some deep valley / For many years where I may lay / Then you may learn to love another / While I am sleeping in my grave . . . / Maybe your friends think I'm a stranger / My face you'll never see no more / But there is one promise that is given / I'll meet you on God's golden shore."

Meanwhile, the Blue Grass Boys were becoming a musical sensation. Fame, however, had its downside; Monroe toured like a maniac and Flatt and Scruggs couldn't take the pace.

"The road seemed endless," said Scruggs. "We would travel sometimes for days without pulling our shoes off in that old stretch limousine."[22]

They quit and formed the Foggy Mountain Boys in honor of the Carter Family song "Foggy Mountain Top." Monroe was so furious that he had them barred from the Opry.

"I don't want you talking to any of them Foggies," he told the rest of the band.[23]

Monroe collected feuds, they said, like other men collected coins.

The following year the Stanleys got a contract with Columbia. It had been a long-time dream to be at that label, because that's where his hero Monroe was signed. Instead of being happy to have another band singing what had now become known as "bluegrass" music—Monroe was furious. He wanted to be the only bluegrass musician there. He left for Decca Records and regrouped with a new "high lonesome" version of the Blue Grass Boys.

One day his new fiddler found him staring off into space.

"Listen, can you hear that?" Monroe asked.

"No," answered "Tater" Tate.

"It's the ancient tones and don't you ever forget it boy."[24]

Monroe loved those authentic tones, so it seemed peculiar to snub shy young Ralph Stanley who not only could hear them, but could channel them in his wistful voice.

"I was born and raised in the mountains," said Stanley. "That's all I ever knew, all up through my childhood and through high school and everything. I'm just a mountain man."[25]

Eventually Monroe relented and invited the Stanleys to play with his band, but Ralph couldn't handle the grueling schedule any more than Flatt and Scruggs. He had to stop, but they remained friends. Monroe was like "a great big oak tree on a hill," Stanley said, "where you went for shade and to get some strength to get you through the storms."[26]

Perhaps it was A.P.'s blessing that day on the mountain or maybe it was something more ethereal, but as the people Stanley loved passed on, he found himself compelled to sing more gospel songs. He wasn't a preacher, but he was heavily influenced by the Baptist hymns of his childhood. People often told him they got more out of his singing than any preaching they'd heard. Then he began to notice that everyone seemed to be getting something from his hymns except him. He had never even been baptized; he sang about salvation but he had never actually chosen God. He'd never asked Jesus to save him—salvation meant reformation.

"I ain't ashamed to tell you," he admitted. "I was too afraid to go through with it."

There were so many temptations on the road, so many wrong turns and distractions from the right way. He knew he was rambling down some alleyways that should be avoided. For decades he had dodged God and the devil. One night in that moment between midnight and morning when he was tossing and turning, God made the choice for him.

"I tell you God gets hold of you," he said. "I woke up at about four o'clock in the morning and I couldn't lay still, I couldn't do nothing. I was just torn to pieces, I just . . ." [27]

His voice trailed off.

"You know what I had to do?" he finally added. "I had to call the preacher at about four o'clock in the morning and tell him I wanted to be baptized that day. The preacher said it was the best news he ever heard in his life."

With that, Stanley hung up the phone and fell straight to sleep.

The next morning he waded out into the river with the preacher and was put under. When he was raised up, he felt different, like that intangible burden had been lifted.

Down in Texas, the young Crowell saw the same behavior Stanley had witnessed in Virginia—people drinking, dancing, and fighting in the honky-tonk as they teetered under that burden of choice between sin and salvation. That's where he learned that Saturday nights were for sinning and Sunday morning was for going to church. But even at eleven years old he knew Sunday morning piety wasn't the same as being saved.

"A long time ago Jesus died on the cross for your sins and all you have to do is admit that you sinned and you're saved," Crowell mused. "How do you reconcile yourself to the quiet life of books, poetry and a garden, when . . . Jesus died on the cross and this is the giant ghost story that you live beneath?" [28]

It was the conflict buried at the heart of mountain music, the reason why people vacillated between hard drinking and church going. It was even more apparent for Stanley. When he sang gospel songs in honky-tonks, people jumped up half drunk and shouted like they were lining it out on a Sunday morning at church.

"There used to be a saying that when you heard a Stanley Brothers record," he smiled. "You'd either want to get drunk or go to church and get saved."[29]

Blood Buckets and Honky-tonk

One man was destined never to make it to church. When Maybelle and her daughters arrived at the Opry in 1950, he was a young, pale, handsome, liquored-up skeleton of a man, with a disarming smile and a small, light voice with a range that could sing gospel, blues, melodic, and sorrowful songs with simple but believable sincerity. Even his guitar style was a simple, pared-down chord and rhythm that kept the focus on his painful lyrics. His style made him Nashville's brightest star, yet he was its most tortured soul.

One night Maybelle's youngest daughter Anita stood in the wings at the Opry listening to the young man sing about his wife's "Cold, Cold Heart" with an ache that bled through every line and seeped into the hearts of the audience. He sang about how he was growing to care for her more and more yet helplessly watched them drifting apart, unable to "free your doubtful mind / And melt your cold, cold heart."

Anita started crying—it was the saddest and most beautiful song she ever heard.

King Hiram "Hank" Williams was the embodiment of the mountain culture contradiction—a poet that could move people to tears with his sincerity, yet terrify them with his violent self-destructive streak. He was a poor Alabama kid born in 1923 with a spinal defect that caused him great pain all his life. His father was a part-time farmer and log train engineer until illness forced him into retirement at a VA hospital where he was apparently diagnosed with dementia. His mother Lilly was a church organist who imbued her son with a love of music, especially the hymns and gospel tunes from their fundamentalist Baptist church.

"My earliest memory is sittin' on that organ stool by her and hollerin'," he said. "I must have been five, six years old and louder'n anybody."[30]

Wednesday nights he'd sit on the fence with his childhood friend and listen to the prayer meeting at the local black church.

"The most beautiful music in the world," said the friend. "The breeze came from the south and it would undulate the sound. One minute soft, next minute loud, like it was orchestrated. One night, Hiram looked up at me and said, 'One day, I'm gonna write songs like that.'"[31]

From the age of eight, he was singing on the streets while he shined shoes and hawked peanuts to support the family. One day he spotted a black street band playing played guitar, fiddle, and a base made out of a tub and broomstick. Williams started following the bandleader Tee-Tot around, begging him to teach him how to play.

"I'd give him fifteen cents or whatever I could get hold of for a lesson," Williams remembered. "When I was about eight years old, I got my first guitar. A second-hand $3.50 guitar my mother bought me."[32]

Before he knew it, he'd learned to play "My Bucket's Got a Hole in It."

"One time I was playing at the entrance of a penny arcade on a Sunday afternoon," he said. "I was sitting on a shoeshine stand playing my guitar just to entertain my own self. Pretty soon there was eight or ten or maybe a dozen people stopped to listen. Afterward they threw nickels, quarters and dollar bills at me. I added it all up. It was $24. I never saw that much money in my life."[33]

The young singer was smart enough to pack up his shoe-shining business and relocate to the entrance of the local radio station, where, just as he hoped, he was called into the studio to perform for people who wanted to hear the "Singing Kid." At thirteen he showed up at an amateur night contest dressed as a cowboy to regale people with his song "The WPA Blues," about President Franklin D. Roosevelt's Depression Era Works Progress Administration. Since most of the audience worked for the WPA at the time, they cheered, and Hank got the $15 prize.

With that he formed his own band, the Drifting Cowboys, and set off on the road to play in schoolhouses, medicine shows, barn dances, and honky-tonks. Unfortunately, sitting in the car exacerbated his back pain, and he started medicating his agony with alcohol. The life of the happy, precocious little kid who sang as he polished shoes was about to become one of harrowing self-destruction.

Honky-tonk bars were like a homing beacon for working-class folks and habitual drunkards. After the Texas oil boom, dingy bars with little dance floors popped up and spread through the South. They became the Saturday night watering holes for rural workers who had been driven by poverty into urban factories but retained their affinity for hill country songs of broken hearts and "Heading Down the Wrong Highway." The notoriety of the honky-tonk peaked in the 1940s when drunken servicemen and defense workers flooded in and started brawling. In Williams' home state of Alabama, they were called "blood buckets," with the musicians often getting into as many fights as the customers.

Simple, homespun songs were discarded to reflect the new rowdy circumstances of the displaced country boys. Musicians pumped out raucous songs that roused people into dancing and hard drinking, but they also sang of broken hearts, despair, and the Sunday morning guilt of going to church with a hangover. The fundamental Protestant culture was only ever a scratch below the surface.

Williams stripped country and western music down to its roots, doing away with conventional instruments and slowing down the beat. He focused on the lyrics, emphasizing themes of working-class life, the tragedy of lost love, cheating, drinking, loneliness, and self-pity. He blended gospel and honky-tonk into a unique style with his versatile voice and simple strumming. He could sing sorrowful songs with a broken heart in "Why Don't You Love Me?" followed by soul-stirring songs such as "Are You Walkin' and A-Talkin' for the Lord?" He was a master at conjuring the feelings of guilt and despondency associated with waking up drunk—because he knew them intimately.

In 1943 Hank joined a medicine show touring south Alabama and met his first wife, Audrey Sheppard. Their relationship became a torturous, mutually destructive tragedy that gushed into Williams's lyrics. The pair got caught in a vicious cycle where alcoholism caused marital problems and marital problems fed his alcoholism.

His reputation for drunken unreliability prohibited him from getting a spot on the Opry. Instead he found fame in Shreveport, Louisiana, a busy steamboat port of muddy roads, taverns, and gambling houses where men were shot dead over card games. The town was part agricultural, part frontier, all sin, and some salvation—perfect fit for a kid driven by his own demons.

"My ears have been almost continually ringing with vile blasphemy . . . against God," wrote one horrified traveling preacher. "Oh, the fuel that Satan will get in Eternity from Shreveport alone . . . the majority of citizens are: stealing, . . . gambling, swearing, lying, drinking."[34]

Every Saturday night at the *Louisiana Hayride*, Williams's voice was pumped into millions of homes. He got sober, hoping his career would take off if he could prove his reliability. In 1948 he had a smash hit with an old Tin Pan Alley song, "Lovesick Blues." The Grand Ole Opry couldn't snub him any longer. He left the *Hayride* in the summer of 1949 with the audience calling for seven encores of the last verse of "Lovesick Blues." When he arrived at the Opry, they called him back for five. It was the most remarkable performance in the show's history. The host pleaded with the crowd to stop howling and let the program continue, such was the mesmerizing power he held over his audience.

"He had a voice that went through you like electricity, sent shivers up your spine, made the hair raise on the back of your neck with the thrill," read one account. "With a voice like that he could make you laugh or cry."[35]

In Nashville he stayed sober for months. Songs came "busting out," inspired by his tormenting marriage, but by the end of 1949 marital stress and increasingly severe back pain led him back to binge drinking, which further alienated his wife. A year later Audrey had an illegal abortion and ended up in the hospital with an infection. When he went to see her, he bent down to kiss her but she pulled away.

"You sorry son of a bitch," she spat. "It was you caused me to suffer this."[36]

He went home and wrote "Cold, Cold Heart."

Williams had come to define a new style of music called honky-tonk—the most enduring and influential style of country music ever created—and he set the tone for the honky-tonk singer: raw, emotional, and out of control.

"When a hillbilly sings a crazy song, he feels crazy," he said. "When he sings 'I laid my mother away' he sees her a-laying right there in the coffin ... He sings more sincere than most entertainers because the hillbilly was raised rougher than most entertainers."[37]

The night Williams saw Anita Carter cry in the wings listening to him sing, he asked her on a date. It was entirely inappropriate considering they were both married, but she agreed and showed up for dinner with the whole Carter family. Williams immediately adopted them as his surrogate family. He adored Maybelle and called her "Mama." Many nights he sat at her kitchen table, eating homemade biscuits and gravy or corn bread crumbled in milk, crying over Audrey or flying into a rage. If he was with Audrey, he was despondent; if they were apart, he was jealous. Maybelle's quiet, non judgmental ways that had helped the troubled Jimmie Rodgers now soothed Williams. She listened, she counseled, and no matter how bad he acted, she was never scandalized and always forgave. She and June tried to convince him to stop drinking, and sometimes he'd really give it a try.

"I'd see him down at the newsstand, buying a whole bunch of comic books: *Captain Marvel, Superman*, and all that stuff," a record producer recalled. "This was his reading material when he was trying to go straight. Be he would call his wife at two o'clock in the morning and she would be out cutting around. And that drove him to drink."[38]

Williams would never find God in the moment between midnight and morning.

By the end of 1949, he'd become addicted to the morphine prescribed for his back pain. He flew into violent jealous rages over Audrey that even Maybelle couldn't ease. He started showing up at the Opry so drunk that the Carter women had to drop what they were doing to try to sober him up enough to go on. Maybelle watched him standing out there under the stage lights, thin, pallid, trying to endure the pain, a lonely, unhappy twenty-four-year-old who poured out his feelings in a steady stream of melancholy songs. There was nothing she or anyone could do.

In 1952 he deteriorated rapidly. One day he almost ran June off the road thinking Audrey was in the car. Maybelle confronted him. With her jaw clenched and her pointed finger trembling, she told him he would regret it if he ever hurt one of her girls.

"But Mama . . ." he tried to explain.

"Don't you call me Mama?" Maybelle snapped.

"That was the harshest thing I ever heard Mama say," her daughter Helen recalled. Williams shuddered as if he had been whipped.[39]

Maybelle cooled toward him after that but never banned him from the house. She knew he didn't have long; his habitual drunkenness had sent him into a tailspin, and all she could do was stuff food into him and let him cry.

In 1952 the Opry fired him, and Audrey filed for divorce. He went home and recorded his final and most prophetic song, "The Angel of Death," wondering if he was ready to meet death as its dark shadow crept over him.

On New Year's Eve, 1952, he hired a college boy to drive him from Knoxville, Tennessee, to a concert in Canton, Ohio. He had morphine shots just before he left to alleviate his back pain and spent most of the trip sprawled in the backseat with chloral hydrate tablets, vodka, and whiskey. When the student pulled over in Oak Hill, West Virginia, he found Williams' blue and lifeless body lying in the backseat.

The twenty-nine-year-old was pronounced dead on New Year's Day 1953.

His funeral in Montgomery, Alabama, was one of the most spectacular the South had ever seen. The air was filled with the harmony of gospel songs. Twenty-five thousand people gathered in front of the Montgomery municipal auditorium; several thousand filed by the casket. The Carter women along with many other stars of country listened to the mournful eulogy delivered from the pulpit.

"Years ago, one of America's greatest doctors said, 'If you have something that represents the genuine need of humanity, though you live in a cottage deep in the forest, mankind will beat a trail to your door.' Hank Williams had something humanity universally needs: a song with a human heartfelt message."[40]

The Man in Black

Two years had passed since the industry lost its greatest legend. It was still searching for his successor when a juggernaut passed through Nashville, crushed everything on his way from Memphis, and left country music reeling for decades. Only Bill Monroe saw it coming. Others thought it was funny watching the self-titled "Hillbilly Cat" jerking around the stage singing a high intensity version of Monroe's "Blue Moon of Kentucky." Monroe knew this kid would push them all off the radio.

Elvis Presley, known in school as the trashy kid who played hillbilly music, was a hybrid: part Scots-Irish, part Cherokee, with a little dash of French. His music was a similar fusion. He integrated black and white cultures, hillbilly, gospel, and blues, with an attitude and sexuality that burst out of the confines of conservative Southern culture and captivated the emerging youth culture nationwide.

"If I could find a white man who had the Negro sound and the Negro feel," said Sam Phillips, owner of Sun Records in 1953, "I could make a billion dollars."[41]

Once Presley showed up "hillbilly" was out and "rockabilly" was in.

"Elvis just about starved us out," admitted Ralph Stanley, who had to go back to farming part-time. One winter he had to sell thirteen cows to pay the band's wages. Even Monroe, a mainstay of the Opry, began to falter in the avalanche of rock and roll.

Nashville responded by fusing pop elements with country to create the Nashville Sound. It replaced the fiddles and steel guitar with pop elements like string sections and background vocals. The iconic image of the old Caddy rattling along dirt roads, five people piled in and a bass fiddle strapped to the top, disappeared. It was the end of an era.

The industry really needed a new Hank Williams, a superstar with crossover potential who could survive in Presley's slipstream, and they found it in the self-proclaimed "biggest sinner of them all."

As a kid Johnny Cash picked cotton on the family's small tract of land, singing as he went. He was the epitome of the cultural contradiction that was wracked between sin and redemption. His father was a Baptist preacher who was fond of a drop of whiskey, and his mother baked "scripture cakes," which used only ingredients found in her Bible. His internal conflict was intensified by feelings of guilt over the accidental death of his brother in a sawmill when Cash was off fishing. For the rest of his life, he lived in the shadows like an outcast hell-bent on self-destruction.

"There is that beast there in me," he told the *New York Times*. "And I got to keep him caged, or he'll eat me alive."[42]

Cash was a smash from the moment he took the stage at the Opry in 1956 singing "Cry, Cry, Cry"—a song he wrote after Sun Records allegedly told him to go off and sin and come back with something they could sell. People were suspicious that he was playing an inauthentic form of music with his backup band playing a "boom-chicka-boom" or "freight-train" rhythm that became known as the Johnny Cash sound. But Earl Scruggs saw something primitive in him and made him feel welcome.

Maybelle Carter, "Mama" to many lost souls that trod the boards at the Opry, watched Cash closely. She may have had a premonition that this star would give her a cross much heavier than either Rodgers or Williams had.

Cash became a crossover sensation. He fused singing, storytelling, and grueling life experience into captivating, hard-hitting ballads like a mother pleading with her son in "Don't Take Your Guns to Town" or "The Ballad of Ira Hayes," the true story about a patriotic Indian who raised the flag over Iwo Jima but came home to find "No water, no crops, no chance / At home nobody cared what Ira'd done."

He sang stripped-down songs about everyday people, coal miners and sharecroppers, convicts and cowboys, railroad workers and laborers. Most of his heroes were usually plagued by guilt and seeking God's forgiveness.

Even his love songs, "I Walk the Line" and "Ring of Fire," are about a man fighting temptation.

In Cash's world, love and depravity lived side by side, and America loved it.

In the 1960s Maybelle and her daughters started touring with the Cash show.

"Having her in my show was a powerful confirmation and continuation of the music I loved best," he wrote in his autobiography. "It kept me carrying on the traditions I come from."[43]

Even though he was married at the time, Cash had been in love with Maybelle's daughter June from the moment he saw her. June was his antithesis: light, funny, giving, and a devout Christian who was terrified he was going down the same road as Williams. She was right—in 1962 they saw him popping pills and feared they were about to repeat the years they spent trying to force food into Williams's emaciated body, pleading with him to sober up, and eventually having to watch him die. Still, Maybelle wouldn't turn Cash away. She invited him to stay over when he was in a terrible state, but even Maybelle and June's positive, simple, homespun, Christian influence wasn't enough to stop him from drinking heavily, getting high, and leaving wreckage in his wake. By the mid-1960s he'd accidentally set fire to hundreds of acres of California's National Forest; he was arrested by a narcotics squad in El Paso, Texas, for carrying prescription drugs across the border. He wrapped June's car around a utility pole, totaling the car and smashing his face. Finally, just like Williams, the Opry fired him.

The whole time she'd known him, June had been hiding pills and trying to sober him up; by 1968 she told him she'd had enough. He responded by getting high and crawling into the Nickajack Cave with his guitar to die. Exhausted and lost in the darkness of that cavern, he had an experience like Ralph Stanley—God got hold of him. He felt the presence of God in his heart, and in that moment he made the vast confession and chose God and sobriety. In 1968, after Cash and June were married, he joined a small church in Nashville.

"God never let him go," said June. "And neither did I."[44]

Cash returned to the industry in 1969—everything had changed. He got his own TV show where he tried to present real country and gospel music, but the flavor of the show was overwhelmed by the demand for pop. Not only was country contending with Presley, it was being devoured by the British invasion, the punk era, and rock giants like the Rolling Stones. A folk revival in the 1970s helped rejuvenate country somewhat, but its liberalism and identification with sexual and racial equality weren't suited to a Southern culture steeped in conservative values.

Cash—the titan of country—learned his TV show and recording contract were dropped.

Good Night. I Love You

Through the 1970s, groups of folk musicians from California were fighting to bring traditional American music back to popular attention. For John and Bill McEuen, Maybelle Carter and Earl Scruggs were their guitar and banjo picking idols. They traveled to Nashville in their twenties to catch a glimpse of the country legends but couldn't get in. They stood on their tiptoes straining to hear Lester Flatt announcing "we're going to bring Mama Maybelle Carter out here to do the 'Wildwood Flower.'"

"Seeing Maybelle walk out on that stage to do that song was one of the most powerful moments of my life," said John.[45]

They formed The Nitty Gritty Dirt Band and tracked Scruggs down to a hotel in Colorado where they persuaded him to record with them. To the Dirt Band's delight, Scruggs called Maybelle.

"I may do 'Wildwood Flower' on the audio harp, if you all don't mind," she said at their recording session. McEuen was astonished.

"To me it was exactly like Jimmy Hendrix saying 'I'd like to play "Foxy Lady" in E with a flattened thirteenth, if you all don't mind.' I was thinking, 'just line us up and tell us how to do it.'"[46]

They recorded a triple album that day called *Will the Circle Be Unbroken* in honor of the song adapted by A.P. Carter. It was chosen to reflect the album's effort to bind together two generations of musicians. They included songs from the Carter Family, Hank Williams, Scruggs, and the Foggy Mountain Boys. The album went platinum. Newspapers called Maybelle a legend; *Rolling Stone* magazine called the album "one of the most important recordings ever to come out of Nashville."

Before Maybelle had a chance to enjoy any kind of popular resurgence, a stroke left Eck mute and his heart weakened. He was wasting away, with Maybelle never leaving his side. She watched Williams and Rodgers die, she prayed while Cash almost destroyed himself, but sitting with Eck after forty-eight years of marriage diminished her. By the time his coffin went into the ground in 1974, she was drawn and skeletal.

Despite her family's entreaties and Cash's pleas, she never sang again. She spent her final years indulging her only vice—a visit to the dog track or a few hours playing slot machines or bingo. Then on an unusually hot October day, she invited everyone around for a cookout. She put steaks on the grill and went picking berries with her friend Peggy. That evening she went to bingo, won fifty dollars, and she carried it home crumpled up in her hand. She watched a little TV then turned to Peggy and said, "Good night. I love you."

She passed over quietly sometime between midnight and morning; with her went the idealization of a simple, old-timey mountain life.

The Devil Must Have Made You Do It

"Country singers now are so commercial you can't really tell that they're country singers," lamented Ralph Stanley.[47]

In its attempt to compete with new musical styles, the nostalgia and romance of the mountains, the treacherous walk of a tortured poet along that fine line between God and the devil, and the ancient tones that had drifted across the mountains and into the rural simplicity of people's lives were crushed under the engine of bottom lines.

A whole new type of pioneer was about to launch herself onto the scene: a brash, self-assertive woman who came from the culture of the Great Smoky Mountain and used "good old horse sense" to become a generous, genuine, high-spirited, and immensely popular multi-millionaire in less than two decades.

Dolly Parton was born the fourth of twelve children into a dirt poor family in a one-room, dilapidated cabin, delivered by a doctor who was paid with a sack of cornmeal. They had no electricity, running water, or plumbing. They grew their own vegetables since their independent, self-reliant nature made them determined to stay off the welfare rolls. Her father was a sharecropper and a moonshine maker; her mother sang those "crying, hurting songs." Music and religion were everywhere in their home. Her grandmother was a gospel songwriter, her uncle a local entertainer who gave her her first guitar. Parton was composing songs before she could even read or write.

"I was singing to my brothers and sisters and the chickens and the dogs with a tin can as a make-believe microphone," she laughed.[48]

When she was twelve, Ralph Stanley came to play at her school. She sat in the front row, mesmerized by his haunting voice. The day after her high-school graduation, she packed her cardboard suitcase and headed for Nashville, where she started writing songs and eventually landed a recording contract with Monument Records. She broke into the Billboard charts with "Dumb Blonde," letting people know she might be blonde but she's nobody's fool, and "Something Fishy," with the traditional theme of cheating men.

Parton could sing both ends of the scale and write about any experience that faced the contemporary woman, and she did it all with a thick country accent. She was a true blue-collar heroine who was proud of her origins and breathed working-class dignity into her songs. She wrote of her humble beginnings in "My Tennessee Mountain Home."

Perhaps it was because she had to vie for attention among twelve siblings that Parton became a consummate exhibitionist, with a great sense of humor, who sparkled in the limelight. Perhaps she simply had the horse sense to know how to market herself. She exploited her diminutive frame and country glamour for all it was worth.

"The first time my Mama saw me all done up with blonde bleached hair all piled up, and my lips, cheeks, and nails red as I could get them, she screamed to the Lord, 'Why are thou testing me this way?' and she told me the Devil must have made me do it. 'Heck no.' I told Mama. 'Let's give credit where it's due. I did this all myself.'" [49]

When she landed a job on the popular Porter Wagoner syndicated TV show, she was propelled into the perfect forum for the racy, effervescent personality of the poor kid from the sticks.

After a couple of years with the TV show, she left in search of a solo career. She wrote "I Will Always Love You" about her professional split with Wagoner. By 1976 her country-pop sound earned her a number of top ten hits, and she became the first female country singer to get her own syndicated TV show. Then she launched into movies, making saucy choices like *The Best Little Whorehouse in Texas*. She showed up in magazines that ran the gamut from *Good Housekeeping* to *Playboy*. However, the more she became an icon of popular culture, the more she moved away from her roots. Instead of country having elements of pop, it became pop with a residue of country. But Parton was making money—lots of it. She had huge hits with her duet "Islands in the Stream" and with the royalties from Whitney Houston's cover of her song "I Will Always Love You." Within a couple of decades, she went from living on a sharecropper farm in a patched-up coat, to being a multi-millionaire, seven-time Grammy winner, Oscar nominee, and winner of five Country Music Association Awards. She had a string of movie hits, twenty-five hit songs, became a member of the Country Music Hall of Fame, landed on the *New York Times* bestseller list, opened a theme park, received the United States Library of Congress Living Legend Award, and became a respected philanthropist. It was genius. It was all-American. But it wasn't country.

The man who financially eclipsed Dolly moved country even further from the visceral fissure in the mountains. He merged her country-pop sound with rock and roll. He didn't come from mountain culture and didn't grow up listening to the tones seeping through the valleys. His childhood wasn't full of the Pentecostal or Evangelical fire from an isolated community church or makeshift barn dances on a Saturday night.

Country's new superstar was a college-educated, marketing whiz from Tulsa, Oklahoma, who loved rock, pop, and country. When Garth Brooks graduated college in 1984 with an advertising degree, he was equipped with the tools to independently market himself to superstardom. He developed a huge repertoire of favorite themes about men gone wrong and put them into modern songs that imitated that old idea of Saturday night sinning and Sunday morning redemption.

Brooks's genius was in integrating spectacular stage shows of the rock genre with simple country songs. The formula earned him twenty number one hits and six Diamond-certified albums. He even outsold Elvis in domestic record sales.

Brooks spoke to a new generation of people who projected their finances and made decisions not for art but for profit. As radio stations were bought out by corporations, they begin micro-managing their quarterly earnings—the days when shows like the *Louisiana Hayride* could take chances to find new talent disappeared.

"The ghost-stories went out the window and music slowly became a corporate business," said Crowell. "It was a cottage industry . . . it became something different."

For the poet steeped in the ancient culture of the hills, country is only country if it is true and primitive and if the songwriter had lived or died in the fissure between hard times and heaven. It took a dark side to really sing to people's dreams and pain. But now that Brooks made country a billion-dollar industry, more and more people were singing the old themes without the spiritual conflict or authenticity of the mountains.

"As rootless as country music is right now," country legend Marty Stuart lamented in an interview. "It sure needs Johnny Cash."[50]

American Recordings

Cash had spent years trudging around the country fair circuit in the 1980s and early 1990s when rap producer Rick Rubin approached him with the idea to do a series of cover albums called *American Recordings*. Rubin revived Cash's bad boy image and his torturous yearning for both self-destruction and redemption, recognizing it had a soulfulness for which America yearned.

Cash recorded in his living room in the Virginia hills—just him and his guitar. He often got up in the middle of a session and walked out into the mountains with a pair of headphones. Out there is where he heard the primitive tones. His son John Carter Cash, associate producer on the album, set up a makeshift studio outside and spent days with his father recording in the remote hills behind the cabin. John Carter—third generation of the revered First Family of Country—had long since learned to just go with his parents' creative impulses. He recorded the album "Wildwood Flower" with his mother June on the front porch with crickets chirping in the background.

"The spirit is in the simple houses not studios," John Carter said in the shadow of the Clinch Mountains of Virginia. "It's more important to have the right environment. Here it's more authentic."[51]

A few years earlier, Cash's lungs were damaged by pneumonia, so *American Recordings IV* was a bare bones country-folk album sung in sparse, somber tones. The video released for his cover of the track "Hurt" was filled with images from his life and feelings of loss and regret. It had a sincerity as though he was recording his own eulogy.

American Recordings IV was released in 2002 and became Cash's most acclaimed album in decades. It went platinum, won him eight Grammy Awards, and exposed him to a new young alternative music audience. It was also his last album. He died on September 12, 2003, less than four months after June passed away after heart surgery.

With his final albums, Cash stirred the old sensibilities just as Williams had done.

Dolly sensed it too. Frustrated by her failure to secure a solo hit for almost ten years, she went back to her roots and released a critically acclaimed traditional folk album *The Grass Is Blue*. She included two original songs—one a heart-wrenching rendition of a woman with a broken heart not wanting to live—and bluegrass versions of two previously released songs. She won a Grammy Award, the International Bluegrass Music Association's Album of the Year, and was credited with bringing a fresh interpretation to bluegrass.

The old tones were quietly lingering, waiting for a spark to reawaken the authentic sensibility of the American consciousness.

It's a Wild, Whacked-Out Wonder

The spark came in the unlikely form of an adventure movie set in Depression-era Mississippi, full of criminals, politicians, comedy, authenticity, and restlessness. All the old themes were there: failed marriages, superstition, rascals, and redemption. There couldn't have been a better medium for reawakening the old ghost stories. The collection of primitive mountain songs that made up the soundtrack of *O Brother, Where Art Thou?* became a multi-platinum, five-time, Grammy Award–winning album.

The adventure centered on a fictitious jail-breaking trio—Everett, Pete, and Delmar O'Donnell—who escape from a chain gang and set out to find the $1.2 million that Everett supposedly stole from an armored car. The treasure is buried behind his old shack in a valley that is about to be flooded as part of a new hydroelectric project.

On their odyssey, they meet up with a young guitarist Tommy Johnson—whose character was based on the real-life alcoholic, itinerant musician who claimed to have sold his soul to the devil to be able to play the guitar. Hoping for some quick cash to finance their adventure, the four drop into a radio station and record the hundred-year-old song Stanley learned from his father in Clinch Mountains—"Man of Constant Sorrow."

Calling themselves the "Soggy Bottom Boys"—a tribute both to Flatt and Scruggs' Foggy Mountain Boys and Maybelle Carter's song "Foggy Mountain Top"—the three criminals make their way through Mississippi singing old-timey music filled with old macabre themes of God and death, sin and redemption. After two hours of what *Rolling Stone* magazine called "wild, whacked-out wonder," the film finally ended with justice and redemption, and the reconciliation of lost loves.

The soundtrack's producer, T Bone Burnett, recorded the music before the film was shot with the idea that the musical tones would lend authenticity to the movie. The voices behind the Soggy Bottom Boys were well-known bluegrass musicians like Ralph Stanley and Dan Tyminski who sang all the old classics. There were upbeat songs like the Carter Family's "Keep on the Sunny Side," haunting songs like Stanley's "O Death," in which he begged the grim reaper for more time, and the dark humor of Jimmie Rodgers's "In the Jailhouse Now," in which his gambling, thieving friend Ramblin' Bob refuses to listen to advice and ends up in jail, with Rodgers following hot on his heels.

The soundtrack was a smash, and traditional American folk music was propelled back into the mainstream complete with sinning, drinking, rascals, and repentance.

"Kids with nails driven through their noses come up to me and say, 'Man, that record rocks!'" said Burnett.[52]

The old-timey musicians who had stuck to their roots through the decades suddenly found themselves with an audience that spanned three generations of Americans. Roots music—as old-timey and bluegrass music was now called—became the latest thing.

Ralph Stanley, who had been awarded an honorary doctorate of music from Lincoln Memorial University in Tennessee and had been named a Library of Congress Living Legend—to which he joked "I'd rather be a living legend than a dead one"—took his seat at the Grammy Awards ceremony in 2002. He was seventy-five years old and nominated for a Grammy for Best Male Country Vocal Performance for "O Death." He was running against Johnny Cash, Willie Nelson, and Tim McGraw. He didn't believe for one moment he had a chance; no old-time country singers had ever won, so when they opened the envelope and called Dr. Ralph Stanley's name, he didn't hear a word until his wife prodded him to get out of his seat.

He sang for thousands in the audience and millions who watched from home.

"[They were] probably wondering who was this little white-haired man and how in the world did he wander out on this stage without security getting properly notified," Stanley smiled. "There I was, Lucy Smith

Stanley's backwards little boy, standing in the spotlight all by myself, no musicians or nothing to back me up."[53]

He was a long way from being a scared kid in the Primitive Baptist Church of southwest Virginia. He just sang the only way he knew how—raw, haunting, and weathered—the way an old man would beg Death for more time.

"O, Death / Won't you spare me over til another year . . . / My head is warm my feet are cold / Death is a-movin upon my soul / Oh, death how you're treatin' me / You've close my eyes so I can't see . . . / You run my life right outta my soul / Oh death please consider my age / Please don't take me at this stage."

Death cruelly replied, "Well I am death, none can excel / I'll open the door to heaven or hell . . . / No wealth, no ruin, no silver no gold / Nothing satisfies me but your soul."

Dr. Stanley's song had special meaning for one man who hailed from the same Clinch Mountains with whose family Stanley had had an enduring friendship for generations.

"[It's] all from the heart with a constancy in character and strength in spirit," John Carter Cash mused. "Listening to Ralph Stanley brings me back full circle to my roots."[54]

After the film's release, the fictitious band became so popular that T Bone Burnet decided the real musicians needed to come down from the mountain for an old–fashioned, barnstorming tour. In a reversal of normal rock tour conventions, Crowell watched twenty buses and one equipment truck drive down the road.

"More humanity than technology," he mused.

The roots music convoy traveled from city to city playing classics of folk, bluegrass, and old-time country in the "Down from the Mountain Tour." For three hours before the show every day, Dr. Stanley sat at a table signing autographs for crowds of fans. Crowell, who had been weaned on these legends, emceed the show. After he introduced them at the Starlight Theatre in Kansas, he sat in a big comfortable chair in the wings and listened to them sing. Out in the audience, he watched hip-hop fans hang their head in sorrow when Patty Loveless sang "You'll Never Leave Harlan Alive" and listened mesmerized to Stanley lining "Amazing Grace."

"It feels great to know this authentic music is still alive and well," Crowell said. "Now I find myself trusting my instinct to go back and express that rural ghost story . . . to the moment between midnight and six a.m. where the myth exists. It's where 'Man of Constant Sorrow' slipped through and reawakened . . . our genetic memory."[55]

After the tour, Crowell's former brother-in-law, John Carter Cash, went back to Maybelle's simple home in Poor Valley and set up a temporary recording studio to record some tracks with Dr. Stanley. While he waited for the living legend to make his way through the snowy mountaintops that winter morning, he baked some corn bread and reflected on their culture. He was convinced *O Brother, Where Art Thou?* reminded Americans of how great it was to connect to its roots. The album had brought people back to the idea of that wholesome idyll even if they had never lived in a cabin or walked through the farm-dotted backcountry valleys. It was the authentic voice passed down from the first Americans who braved the frontier to give birth to the nation.

"There's something about these Clinch Mountains," Dr. Stanley said. "They've been around a hundred million years and they'll be around for a good while more, I reckon. They keep you humble. They put you in your place. I'm going to see if I can maybe make one hundred years myself. I figure that's what I'll do and then I'll go right back into the ground that raised me."[56]

CHAPTER 8

RACING MOONSHINE

It was the wildest race in Daytona history.

While a massive snowstorm buried the Northeast, CBS readied itself for the first ever, live broadcast of a stock car race to a captive audience. Southern superstars prowled the starting line of the 1979 Daytona 500 in two tons of steel packed with enough ambition, ego, and vengeance to mangle anyone hunting for first position. After four of the most wreck-racked hours in Daytona history, a spectacular crash in the final lap caused a fistfight in the infield that captivated the nation, took racing beyond its Southern roots, and throttled it across the country.

It was Scots-Irish fury at its best.

The all-star lineup included Cale Yarborough, a young daredevil forged from a hardscrabble existence in South Carolina. When he was a child, he wrestled with an alligator after falling into a river. He was once bitten by a rattlesnake, but it was the snake that died. He leapt out of an airplane with a bad parachute and walked away unscathed. He said there were only two places in racing, winning and losing, and he was going to run flat out to win.

Pulling up beside him were the Allison brothers, who were ready to run over everyone. Bobby and Donnie Allison had been racing since their high-school days in Florida when they took their school cars to an abandoned track and banged and crashed their way around. A few years later, Bobby hitched his jalopy to his pickup truck, Donnie jumped into the passenger seat, and the pair rolled into Montgomery, Alabama, looking for the nearest racetrack. By 1979 Bobby had become a sly, cagey driver who would stalk and hunt down the competition.

Bobby Allison had a beef with Yarborough and his team owner: one of NASCAR's all-time best racers and its most notorious renegade Junior Johnson. A few years earlier, Junior unceremoniously dumped Allison off his team in favor of the driver Junior considered the best on the track at the time. That driver was Yarborough. Bobby would make them both pay for having suffered the insult.

Lined up alongside the two rivals was Richard "The King" Petty. Petty was stock car royalty and hugely popular. His father Lee had been a NASCAR pioneer and one of its first superstars. It might have been sour grapes, but Allison considered Petty an overindulged son of a well-financed family team, who drove expensive racecars when Allison could barely afford a new set of tires. Not that The King had it easy. When he pulled up that day, he was recovering from a surgery that had removed 40 percent of his ulcerated stomach and had been given strict orders not to race. He had once been NASCAR's top dog, but in 1979 Petty was running a forty-five-race losing streak and desperately needed a win.

Heavy rain the night before the twenty-first Daytona 500 set the event up to be the most disastrous in history. At the starting line, the track was still soaking and hazardous to the drivers who were about to pound it at 190 miles per hour. The stands were packed with a hundred thousand fans. They said their traditional prayer, sang the national anthem, and watched F16s screech overhead before the adrenaline pumping words: "GENTLEMEN, START-YOUR-ENGINES."

Racecars howled across the starting line. Donnie Allison quickly took first position with Yarborough coming up third and Bobby Allison fourth. Seventy miles later the brothers were side by side, generating a wind tunnel draft that dragged Yarborough along behind them. At the second turn, Bobby tagged Donnie's left fender and almost flipped him upside down. Donnie spun out of control, taking all three cars spinning with him into the swampy infield and placing them laps behind.

Yarborough sputtered to the pits for repairs that put him three laps down, an almost impossible gap to close.

"It'll be some story if Cale Yarborough can come back and make up those laps," the commentator said. "But if anyone can do it he's the one."

By lap 55 four cars ran out of control and piled up against the track wall. It looked more like a demolition derby, but the carnage allowed Yarborough to make up time. Sand was scratching and pitting his windshield, making it almost impossible to see, but he made it back into the leading lap. The crowd jumped to its feet, cheering him on as he pulled into the second spot behind Donnie Allison.

"Cale will probably stay in the draft," Junior told the commentator.

Junior Johnson with his Holly Farms racecar, ca. 1963. Courtesy Junior Johnson Collection.

"He'll sling shot past him on the last lap."[1]

With one lap to go, Bobby Allison was still three laps down with no hope to make it back to the front. Petty had his foot to the floor, giving it all he had to break his losing streak but was half a lap back with the pack, too far behind to be a contender. No one took much notice of The King's struggle; all eyes were fixed on the battle raging at the front.

Yarborough came down on the inside to pass, but Donnie swerved to block him. The two drivers smashed into each other, crashed into the wall, then skidded into the infield where their spinning, mangled cars came to a stop.

The cameras swung to the backstretch to find the new leader. Cheers erupted from the crowd when they saw the famous blue and red car number 43 break from the pack and take the lead. Petty was back in the race, blocking everyone who tried to swerve and dodge past him. He screeched by the smoking wrecks of the former leaders and roared across the finish line first. The crowd went wild. CBS camera crews scrambled into the Petty pit to capture the triumphant return of The King.

Unfortunately the celebration was cut short by a clash in the infield. Cale Yarborough and Donnie Allison had clambered over their wrecked cars, punches and helmets flying, while pit crews rushed into the fray. Yarborough thought the Allisons had set him up. When Bobby Allison pulled over to help his brother, Yarborough smashed him in the face with his helmet. Bobby Allison's account of the Southern-style brawl was simply, Yarborough "went to beating on my fist with his nose."[2]

Junior was mad as hell about losing his car and the race. He knew the fastest car out there was his Chevrolet. Yarborough had passed the younger Allison four times in it that day, but that didn't matter. Junior was well aware that Allison would rather wreck Yarborough than be beaten by him. "Stupid," he called it. "Absolutely stupid."

As a result, Yarborough did the only thing he could and abided by the unwritten rule—if you don't win the race, you've got to win the fight.

"It ended with really what it was all about," Junior admitted. "You mess with me and I'll beat you to a pulp."[3]

The fight landed stock cars on the front page of the *New York Times* sports section the next day, and snowbound Northerners everywhere were talking about the crazy redneck race they'd watched on TV and the mayhem that followed it. They'd never seen anything like the danger, fearlessness, and passion that fueled the speed demons' commitment to win at any cost. As Yankees caught Southern racing fever, NASCAR hit the jackpot. Subsequent races were media frenzies. Races would soon rake in billions of dollars in TV revenue, with over two hundred thousand people attending races, and tens of millions more tuning in each week. Stock car racing went national, garnering respectability, sprouting beyond its redneck roots, and shedding its dirty secret—the sport was not invented by NASCAR founder and president Bill France, but began with dirt-poor Scots-Irish braggarts and rascals running moonshine in jacked-up Fords through the rural South. Of all these scoundrels, it was Junior Johnson who reigned supreme.

King Moonshine

The Johnson clan tumbled off the boat from Belfast and down into the Blue Ridge Mountains in the 1700s, with nothing but the recipe for *uisge beatha*, or "whiskey" as the British called it. In the Appalachians, they made it from corn by the light of the moon and were about as interested in paying taxes on it to the British government in America as they had been in paying them in Ireland. Whiskey was the lifeblood of the South, in spirit and economics, and as far as they were concerned, it was their God-given right to make it and haul it without government interference.

Robert Johnson Sr. was no exception. When the Johnsons settled in Wilkes Country, North Carolina, Robert Sr. quickly recognized no matter how hard he worked the land or ran his sawmill, there wasn't much of a living to be made in farming, and even less so in the winter. By the time Robert Glen Johnson Jr. was born in 1931, the family was on the verge of starvation.

Junior grew up to be a lot like his father; both were well-built and determined men, but the younger Johnson is much quicker to laugh. He almost always wears a bright cheeky grin that lights up his round face and makes his mischievous nature even more alluring.

Junior spent most of his youth working the family farm. In worn-out overalls and bare feet, the teenager plowed big Southern fields with his favorite old mule, giving commands to the animal in his soft Southern drawl. The neighbors knew his easy manner belied his wild nature, but they wouldn't have expected that thirty years later this rural teenager would be donned the "Last American Hero" by *Esquire* magazine and have a stretch of North Carolina's highway named after him.

His path to becoming an American icon started with an unlikely family venture that allowed him to stop plowing and start tearing up Wilkes County's dirt roads. Robert Sr. had a particular skill—making good moonshine. When his fearless son turned fourteen and started hauling, it meant fast money for the whole family.

"He was a great father and a great provider and he'd make whiskey, didn't make any difference what they did to him," Junior recalled. "He was not going to let his family starve."[4]

At the time, Wilkes County was soaked in moonshine, but no one had as big an operation as Robert Sr. Junior estimated his father ran about a thousand stills at one time, most buried deep in the woods. Even after Prohibition ended in 1933, the market for tax-free, cheap moonshine was still greater than for the legal, more expensive taxed whiskey. The Bureau of Alcohol, Tobacco, and Firearms (ATF) would come to shut them down, but there would always be a still someplace else to fire up.

"He had so much whiskey that it was stored throughout the house,"

Junior said. "It was stacked up in cases so high we had to climb over them to get to the bed."[5]

ATF agents, or "revenooers" as the locals called them, were regulars at the Johnson home. Mrs. Johnson, never short of Southern hospitality, would always have coffee and pie ready when they came to confiscate the stock and take away her husband. The revenuers set up long planks on the stairs, slid the cases down, and carried them off. As a little kid Junior and his friends, barefoot and in overalls, would hop on a case and ride it down the planks like a sled.

"We thought it was funny," Junior said. "The lawmen didn't, they'd say 'You damn kids get off them cases,' and we'd say, 'You get outta here—this is our house.'"[6]

In 1935 federal agents raided the Johnson house and discovered over 7,100 cases of moonshine, the largest single haul of illegal whiskey ever made in America. When the ATF released its reports of whiskey busts in the moonshine belt that year, that one haul made Wilkes County the moonshine capital of the South and knocked its rival Dawsonville, Georgia, right off the top. Robert Johnson Sr. had unintentionally snagged precious bragging rights for the county. Bragging right were golden. Back then there wasn't much else to do except to try to outdo your neighbor.

"They'd brag about anything down here," Junior laughed. "They'll brag about I can grow a better tomato than you."[7]

When the ATF took Robert Sr. off to jail, the family kept his business ticking over until his return. When he came home, he went right back to making moonshine.

"Pride," Junior calls it. "I never seen a man with so much pride in my life."

Junior started working around the house and the farm before he was ten. His father taught him to do things right. Robert Sr. only had a third-grade education, but he was innovative; if he needed a piece of equipment he made it. "Crafty," Junior called him.

Junior didn't have an auspicious start in the craftiness department. At eight years old he had his "hind end wore out" for dismantling a mower engine that he couldn't put back together. It was, however, the start of a love affair with machinery. By nine he was driving his father's pickup truck, and at fourteen he'd retired from high school and started hauling liquor. He was too young to have a driver's license but as he explained, "I wasn't going to stop so I didn't need no driver's license."

If there was one thing Junior was determined to do, it was to find some sort of advantage with which to beat his adversaries. NASCAR would later call his tactics cheating, but in the 1940s world of bootlegging it was called good business. In order to get ahead, cars were modified to be lighter and faster.

Junior saved up for a 1936 Ford and figured out how to overhaul the engine and the suspension. He sat on a stump in North Carolina and built an engine that mechanical engineers up North wouldn't invent for years. He took the rear seat out and perfected the art of stacking jars like a pack rat so when he made hard turns they acted like a brace for his body. He could pack 120 gallons of moonshine into one run at a profit of about $450 a night—as long as he didn't get caught.

"You got to understand it takes so much to get the car to turn and you got to learn that," he said. "You just practice and practice and practice and some things you'd miss. I ended up in ditches while I was practicing, and bent the car. I'd have to keep fixing it till I learned how to do it."

Junior eventually perfected the "bootlegger turn," an ability to turn 180 degrees without stopping and head back in the same direction. The

Policeman standing alongside wrecked car and cases of moonshine, November 16, 1922.
National Photo Company Collection. Courtesy of the Library of Congress.

cops chasing him had to struggle with a three-point turn, giving Junior ample time to escape. It wasn't long before Junior was a legend, tripping whiskey down Route 421, and the bane of every highway patrolman assigned to the night shift.

Jim Rhyne was a green patrolman when he first came across Junior. He was a tall, handsome twenty-two-year-old, who beat out four hundred applicants for the coveted job on North Carolina's state highways. His salary was a meager $100 a month, a fraction of what a tripper would make on one whiskey run. They gave him a sleek new Ford Coupe, known as the "silver bullet" that had no heater or air conditioner and got better radio reception from South America than North Carolina. His first assignment was to patrol Yadkin County, and it wasn't long before the "bullet" burnt rubber on every dirt road and paved highway chasing liquor cars.

He clocked many hours waiting off dark, crooked roads in Wilkes County. Rhyne was on the lookout for speeding Fords jacked up at an angle because of the white lightning weighing it down in the rear. He caught most of them, but one always got away.

"I chased Junior Johnson so many times. I got after him one night and after about a mile or two he went around a sharp turn and came back to meet me," Rhyne remembered of Junior's bootlegger turn.[8]

Junior sped by so fast Rhyne didn't even have time to shift into gear, and the few times he did try to get after him, he sped straight into a ditch.

"He was too good a driver for me," he said. "I plowed out more ditches than the highway department did."[9]

The bootlegger got a kick out of tormenting law enforcement. Instead of avoiding blockades, he got a siren for his car and raced down 421 with the "sir-een" screeching. Officers would pull the blockade, thinking it was one of their own, then watch Junior race by. When they got after him, he'd turn the valve and let oil run into the hot exhaust pipe.

"It'd fill the road with smoke and they couldn't go no further because they couldn't see," Junior chuckled. "I'd do it for fun."[10]

When they got a radio, he got a radio. He'd hear the cops discussing where they were putting up roadblocks, and if he was heading toward one, he would suddenly turn the other way, laughing as the officers muttered "that lucky dog" over the airwaves.

Hauling a lot of whiskey means having enough gas to get to where you're going and finding gas someplace to get back, if the law is on your tail that gets a little tricky.

"One time I was out of gas and I'd just got away from the law and pulled into a farm and they didn't know where I went. I went to the door— there weren't nobody home. They had a big tractor out there and it was full of gas. I backed my car up . . . took a hose out, put it in the gas tank and topped my gas up. It was only twenty-five cents for a gallon of gas or something. I put a ten dollar bill on the seat with a note on it, "I got twelve gallons of gas here's ten dollars for it."

About six months later Junior was coming back up the same road when he saw the farmer again and decided to stop and tell him he was the one who took his gas.

"Sir you don't know me and I don't know you but, I'm here to thank you. I was in an awkward position and I got twelve gallons of gas out of your tractor and I put the money on the seat. Did you get the money?" asked Junior.

"You gave me a lot more money than you got gas," the old man said reaching for his wallet and handing Junior his change.

He wouldn't take it and that made the farmer mad.

"I don't want to make you mad because you saved me . . . I'm a bootlegger and they was going to catch me because I was out of gas," he explained.

"I don't care what you do," the farmer insisted. "I'm gonna give you your change."

Junior took it and was grateful. The farmer thanked him for being honest.[11]

Wilkes County was devoutly religious. They held weeklong revivals where the community would camp out and hear different preachers speak, and socialize with friends and neighbors. But there wasn't a whole lot of excitement for a teenager hopped up on outrunning the law.

"Most of the time, I was either working the saw mill or I was working the still at night or I was hauling whiskey," he said. "Bill and Charlie Monroe would come from Nashville and you'd pay a quarter to listen to them. Saturday you'd go to the movies, or play ball, that's the kind of life people lived."[12]

They invented a new kind of entertainment. Every night on 421, he'd come across other whiskey-trippers in their jacked-up cars. In the moonshine business, everybody wanted to have the fastest car, and before long they were racing each other along the highways.

"It got to be a big thing to where you'd meet and race till somebody won," he said. "It was bragging. They wanted bragging rights."[13]

There was nothing Junior loved more than a bit of competition, and nothing he hated more than losing. But he quickly outgrew the rough-and-tumble racing on Route 421 and began to yearn for recognition in a legitimate racing sport. Unfortunately, the only official racing at the time were the World Speed Trials of Daytona Beach. These were exclusive races for rich men who could afford to build sophisticated, expensive, experimental automobiles. Not even whiskey money could put a Southern farm boy in a league with the likes of Sir Malcolm Campbell or Henry Ford whose specially engineered cars smashed world speed records. Even the popular Indianapolis 500, which was attracting over eighty thousand spectators since its inception in 1909 was dominated by the deep pockets and specialty cars of the international racing elite. By comparison Southern racing was a poor man's oddity, an ad hoc sport of jerry-rigged cars driven by outlaws and rascals on dusty highways.

A Gentleman of Inestimable Character

Across the state line, a wild bunch of bootleggers in Georgia had faced the same dilemma a decade earlier. Even if they could afford it, they would never be welcome in those Northern races. They needed their own Southern sport and were now primed to do something about it. Dawsonville had already declared itself the moonshine capital of the world and was about to crown itself the birthplace of stock car racing.

The roads of Dawson County were lined with chest-thumping, bragging, law-ignoring, self-reliant Scots-Irish the whole way to the federal penitentiary. A mark of pride in a county that never could quite figure out what side of the law the law was on.

The man who put Dawsonville on the map was a peculiar kind of Scots-Irishman, a tall, quiet, competitive, moonshiner, racketeer, ex-con with an eighth-grade education called Raymond Parks. Born in 1914, he dragged himself out of the Great Depression and Southern despair to become what the Atlanta papers called a "gentleman of inestimable character." He became known as the "moonshine baron" and later, the "Godfather of NASCAR," both before he reached the ripe old age of thirty.

The Parks patriarch had tripped off a northern Irish boat and into Philadelphia a couple of hundred years before. Great-great-grand-uncle Benny trekked down the mountains and entrenched the family at the edge of the world, living alongside hostile Indians and other fierce, ungovernable immigrants from northern Ireland, who were happiest lost in the wilderness: hunting, fishing, and distilling their own liquor from corn.

One day Benny tripped while out hunting and discovered gold, but unfortunately he sold his lease to future Vice President Calhoun for what he thought was a good price, leaving an untapped fortune hiding in the dirt. Luck and lousy instincts were common traits in the Parks's genome.

"All of the family are pretty smart," said Violet, Raymond Parks's fourth wife. "But you can be pretty smart and pretty dumb in the same sentence."[14]

The Parks clan included every variety of outlaw, fornicator, and criminal that could fill the pages of the Dawson County Superior Court records. Raymond's father was a drunken sot who fathered sixteen children in a tiny house without water or electricity. As the eldest, Parks took care of his siblings, worked his grandparents' farm, grew corn, and raised sheep on the rocky land that wasn't good for anything else after Sherman's March and the Great Depression.

In the wintertime there was no way to survive except by making moonshine. The ATF estimated ten thousand gallons a week poured from the Georgia mountains along Route 9, which was the moonshine artery from Dawsonville into Atlanta. Everyone was in on the action; even a local deacon stashed liquor and sugar in his church and moved it out of the way on Sundays. The pastors who weren't making moonshine were quite happy to see their Sunday service plate full of cash even if it came from nefarious activities.

Although Parks's father didn't make moonshine, he drank his fair share of it. One night, while running a regular errand to get a bottle of whiskey for his father in the family's rag-tag 1926 Model T Ford, the fourteen-year-old Parks was stopped. Prohibition wouldn't be repealed for another five years, and the local sheriff wanted to make an example of someone, even if that meant incarcerating a minor.

"Everyone knew he wasn't eighteen and they put him in jail anyway,"[15] Violet said.

Jail turned out to be his ticket to fortune. Inside he met a bootlegger who promised him a bright future as a backwoods moonshine maker. When he was released four months later, Parks tossed his farm tools and headed off to the whiskey still.

Parks was quiet, studious, and a shrewd six-foot-tall willowy boy. Unlike his ancestors, he planned on making and keeping his fortune. He invested his moonshine earnings in a 1925 Model T Ford and got into the whiskey-tripping business in Dawson County. A couple of years later, he went to Atlanta to work in his uncle's service station and ran liquor after dark. Atlanta was Parks' ticket out of the overalls and the hills and into the bright lights of the big city. From then on he only ever wore a suit. Perhaps it was insecurity about his uneducated, country roots that fueled his desire for recognition and respect.

While running liquor, Parks was careful not to attract attention. He ran his Ford up and down "Old Number Nine" in a suit and tie. If there was too much police activity, he'd call it a night and let them chase someone else. He kept a bucket by a river on the outskirts of Atlanta where he'd stop and wash the red clay from his tires after a night's hauling, then just blend in with the morning commuters. Over the next few years he made a fortune in legal and not so legal ventures. He bought up half the neighborhood, ran a numbers game, and put cigarette and game machines all over the city. In his early twenties, he owned six liquor stores when it was legal to own only two. He believed the best way to beat the law was to employ them, so he kept a roster of cops on his payroll.

"He likes to be in control," said Violet. "He'll connive to figure out a way to beat you at something."[16]

In 1935 at the age of twenty-one, the law finally caught up with him. They couldn't nail him for racketeering or moonshining, but after arresting many of his drivers, they amassed enough evidence to charge him with conspiracy. He was sent to the federal reformatory in Chillicothe, Ohio, for nine months, the same place Junior would later wind up. In prison the semi-illiterate jailbird took a few classes; he said his sentence was like going to college. When he got out he was a changed man. Bootleggers were God-fearing people, but they were still delinquents. He wanted to wash the red clay off his soul and be known for something more. His first order of business was to hand the driving over to his younger cousins Lloyd Seay and Roy Hall.

"Lightning" Lloyd Seay was a handsome, wild but gentle boy, born into a dirt-poor, illiterate, drunken house of thieves, felons, and fornicators, most of whom died violent deaths. He was raised by moonshine-swilling uncles who taught him three things: how to sign his name with an X, drive fast, and make moonshine. Seay was on the fast track to the family plot.

(Left to right) Andrew Bearden, Roy Hall, and Raymond Parks, ca. 1950. Courtesy of Gordon Pickle.

His cousin "Reckless" Roy Hall was undisciplined and angry. He was orphaned at the age of ten and brought to Atlanta by an uncle where he grew up on the streets. He was running numbers for cousin Parks by the age of twelve and hauling moonshine by fourteen.

The cousins joined a pack of thirty or more Georgia speed demons that shared the philosophy that the best way to escape revenuers was not to outsmart them as Parks had done, but to outrun them. Two of the wildest whiskey trippers in that pack were Bob and Fonty Flock who hailed from a family of daredevils in Alabama. Newspapermen called Bob Flock the "wild-eyed Atlantan," who "had no respect for life or limb." His nutty brother Fonty was reputedly handsome, smart, and mischievous. Fonty started hauling whiskey on a bicycle as a kid, and when he finally got a car in his mid-teens, it was just for fun.

Only these four daredevils with a death wish would have fun running on Old Number Nine from Dawsonville to Atlanta. It was a twisted, perilous road lined by deep ditches and towering trees. The cargo of many a moonshiner's car crashed in those ditches over the years, and the rusting carcasses of a few Ford V-8s sank into their muddy depths. It was crawling with the law. The four Georgia trippers learned to go eighty miles an hour forward and sideways simultaneously, skidding along the narrow, winding roads, handling one hundred gallons of shifting liquor and three thousand pounds of machinery and still stay out of ditches. They had to drive fast enough so that if they passed an agent sitting on the side of the road waiting, they'd be long gone before the law could even get a start. The revenuers couldn't keep up.

One afternoon in 1941, the police chief got after a '39 Ford Coupe speeding by on its way back to Dawsonville after dropping its cargo in Atlanta. The driver pulled over and held two five-dollar bills out the window.

"Dammit Lloyd, you know the fine for speeding ain't but five dollars," said the chief.

"Yeah," replied Seay, "but I'm gon' be in a hurry coming back, so I'm paying an advance."[17]

Seay, Hall, and the Flocks became folk heroes: masters of machinery who wore fancy clothes and went to glitzy nightclubs in Atlanta. Everyone wanted to be like them.

Farm kids who had little chance of escaping a subsistence-level existence aspired to the exciting, daredevil life of speed and defiance and riches. Instead of playing cowboys and Indians, children played bootleggers and revenuers, flipping coins to see who would play Seay, Hall, or the Flocks and who'd get stuck playing the law. As Parks found out, bootlegging could make you somebody, and that was worth risking prison or death.

It wasn't always so easy for the law and the bootleggers to stay on opposite sides of the same business. On one occasion the sheriff of Dawsonville—who made whiskey stills on the side—saw "federal revenuers" chasing a liquor car and shot at the agents' tires to flip their car over. When they yelled at him for shooting at the wrong car, the sheriff reprimanded them for chasing trippers in the town and endangering its citizens. In reality they were endangering the moonshine-making livelihood of Georgia voters, and that just wasn't good politics for an ambitious lawman.

Of all the moonshine-hauling voters who were running two or three loads of liquor a day down Old Number Nine, Seay, Hall, and the Flocks emerged as the craftiest and fastest. This inevitably led to disputes over who was the top dog.

Tim Flock, the youngest of the Flock clan remembered the day they all started arguing about who had the faster car. "Finally they found a place right outside Atlanta, down on Highway 54, a great big field. They started racing these bootleg cars on Sunday and betting against each other, and then people started coming. The bootleggers would pass old helmets around the fence, and the spectators would put quarters in them, half dollars, and the drivers would collect quite a bit of money on Sunday afternoons. That was the very start of stock car racing."[18]

The Unruly Birth of Stock Car Racing

In 1935, the elite World Speed Trials on drivers who had been racing at Daytona for over twenty years took their sophisticated, specialty cars and left the beach for the more stable surfaces of the Bonneville Salt Flats in Utah. The city of Daytona was hurting for tourism when they heard about the strange new phenomenon on the Southern whiskey trails. Word was spreading that bootleggers were racing each other on the highways in jacked-up Fords and Chryslers, and that hundreds of people were coming out to watch and lay bets. Seeing dollar signs, Daytona city officials decided to capitalize on this new popular pastime and organize a race of Fords and Chryslers themselves. Their race was on a track, not Southern highways, and the participating cars weren't modified to outrun the law, they were the same factory-built or stock cars that average people drove. Daytona believed fans would be interested in seeing a competition between cars that looked just like theirs and so promoted their race with the gimmick, "Will the car like you drive win over the kind driven by your friend?"

The event was sanctioned and certified by AAA, making it the first official stock car race to take place in America. Unfortunately, at that time there weren't any official stock car racers. There were only bootleggers driving "creative" stock cars and even they were way off on remote Appalachian whiskey trails running moonshine and trying to beat each other for bragging rights.

An assortment of Indy racers and regular people showed up to compete on Daytona Beach, but the whole event was a mess. Thousands of fans got in without paying. When the race started, cars got stuck in the sand and had to be towed. Some mangled hulks of crushed metal were left behind obstructing the course. One racer was flung out of a tumbling convertible and other cars rolled into the surf. The race was cut short, and even then only ten of the twenty-seven starters finished. No one could agree on how many laps anyone ran, or who won the race. The city of Daytona and AAA lost a lot of money and swore no profit could ever be made from this ridiculous sport.

The fans loved it. They were hooked on the chaos, the wrecks, and the danger. While officials licked their wounds and went home, one driver stayed. He was a twenty-nine-year-old mechanic who crossed the finish line fifth. Bill France recognized the potential in the fan frenzy.

Born in Washington, D.C., France descended from immigrants out of northern Ireland on his mother's side. His only discernible Scots-Irish qualities were his leadership skills and a competitive nature. He wasn't in the liquor business, but he did share his Southern cousins' passion for cars. As a teenager he worked as a mechanic during the week and traveled around on weekends in search of races in Maryland, Pennsylvania, and Atlantic City. He secretly raced the family Ford until his father began wondering why the tires were wearing out so fast.

France became a six-and-a-half-foot-tall intense, ambitious, ruthless man with a silver tongue that could talk anyone into anything. Over the next few decades, the Scots-Irish would find out just how calculating, persuasive, and treacherous he could be.

In the early 1930s, France packed up his wife and children and headed south in search of sunnier pastures and less Depression. He stopped at Daytona Beach where he happened upon the city's ill-conceived stock car race. He was sure the mishap could become a giant sport.

France had a vision of an "everyman" race with great possibilities for Sunday afternoon shows that would attract the whole family. Unlike the elitism of the drivers up north who had the money to build exceptional cars, Southern racing would allow people to race in their own factory-made "stock" cars. They didn't need to be rich, they just needed skill. To make sure the emphasis in Southern driving stayed on the driver and not wily mechanics, when France promoted a race he included inspections to stop the whiskey boys from making bootlegger modifications to the cars. He knew if he didn't harness Billy Boys' craftiness, they'd end up filling their engines with rocket fuel and blasting off the starting line.

France obsessively launched himself and his family into the business of racing. His wife managed the books and tacked the publicity posters to poles. His kids worked the concessions stands and collected tickets. France even directed fans in the parking lot and cleaned up the trash after everyone left. Whether he did it for money, passion, or power, no one knew, or at least no one dared to speculate. Whether it was his booming voice, towering presence, or ruthless intensity, everyone knew it was dangerous to cross Big Bill France.

The first race France organized made a modest $100 profit, but in 1948 he organized his second race, which drew a respectable five thousand spectators. France made sure everyone paid through the turnstiles this time by posting "Careful Rattlesnakes" signs all around the fences. Up north, Indianapolis was dishing out prize money of $32,000; at Daytona the prize included $240, a bottle of rum, and a case of cigars, and it was won by a gun-toting gambler and bootlegger called Smokey Purser.

Purser was as tough as they came. Since his teenage years, he'd been running moonshine out of Florida and up the Mississippi in a boat, around the county in a van marked "Florida Fresh Fish," or dressed up as a Roman Catholic priest. When Smokey crossed the finish line, he shot through the pits, took off from the track, and headed down the beach. France was convinced Smokey had made illegal modifications to the car and had sped away to retro-engineer them so he wouldn't fail the post-race inspection. When Smokey returned a few hours later, a furious France stripped him of first place and awarded the prize to the second-place driver—himself.

This was the beginning of France's compulsion to write rules to suit the way he believed the race should be run. It also marked the birth of the love-hate relationship he would have with whiskey haulers for the rest of his life. He resented the outlaws who spoiled the squeaky-clean family entertainment image he was desperate to present. France was convinced that if it remained in their renegade hands, the sport would never grow beyond its Southern bootlegging roots.

In November 1938, two months after seeing potential in France's Daytona effort, Atlanta decided to promote a stock car race at a former horseracing track in Lakewood. Seay and Hall convinced Parks to build a couple of sterling racecars. It cost Parks thousands. He said later the best way to make a small fortune was to "take a huge fortune and then go racing." It was, however, the opportunity he'd been looking for since his release from prison. While the Northern racers were old-money gentlemen, Parks was a shady-money Southern gentleman with something to prove.

"He enjoyed that persona, the gangster type-person," said Violet. "He also was trying to legitimize racing at the time, he was giving it respectability by going there with nice cars and his men always dressed nice too."[19]

Parks showed up with the best cars and the best drivers. He had machine shops build parts that no one else could get. The rest of the liquor boys put their cars together from junkyard parts. They'd put the hydraulic brakes from a '39 Ford on the lighter body of a '37 so they could get around the track better, but they just couldn't beat Parks.

The ramshackle, jerry-rigged getups that passed for stock cars at the Lakewood starting line weren't the sport to which France aspired, but he still came up from Florida. It was here he met Parks. The men were radically different in disposition and had little in common beyond racing. Respectability was the one, perhaps the only, point on which Parks and France agreed; although their uneasy, lifelong friendship eventually forged the biggest spectator sport in America.

"The reason he came," Junior said of France's appearance in Georgia, "was because the bootleggers had money and he didn't and nobody would listen to him because they thought he was crazy, wanting to start organizing and racing competitively."[20]

The hype in Atlanta was unprecedented. It was promoted as the biggest racing event in two decades. Newsmen promised "speed and maybe some gore." Since the track ran around a lake and had no banks, carnage was possible at every turn. Racers could speed off the track, crash into the lake and drown still strapped into their cars. Others could crash and burn. Kids turned out to see their outlaw heroes, women to see the dashing, untamable men, and gents to see the danger. The city added special buses, streetcars, and taxi services. Twenty thousand spectators showed up. Lakewood dwarfed France's effort in Daytona.

The day started off with inevitable squabbles as the disreputable bootleggers showed up in whiskey cars packed with mechanical magic under the hoods. Parks's mechanic had craftily assembled more than one car from the superior parts of others, patching them all together to be better, faster, and tougher than anything that was rolling off the showroom floor.

When thirty cars started up their engines, it exploded into an ear-piercing roar that Atlanta hadn't heard since the Civil War. Dirt and red clay were whisked up into a savage tornado drowning the spectators in a sandstorm and blinding the racers on the track.

Hall and France and Seay—who drove with a broken arm propped out of the window—navigated through the wreckage piled up around the track. After two and a half hours of carnage, Seay crossed the finish line first to win $100, a fraction of his earnings from a night tripping whiskey but well worth the priceless bragging rights that came with winning Atlanta's first official race.

The whole day was a smashing success. It was everything the Southern spectators expected of their heroes—careening along the razor's edge, on the brink between life and death, wild, fierce, competitive, lawless, and working-class, just like them. Seay and Hall's legendary status exploded. More than ever, the handsome twenty-one-year-olds symbolized everything the poor hopeless farm boy aspired to be. Not only did they have fancy clothes, money, and nerve—they were champions.

That day in 1938 was everything France loathed. Despite Parks's efforts, it lacked respectability, rules, and regulations—all words the whiskey boys didn't understand. None of them really knew how many races they'd won or how much money they'd earned; nobody kept records because nobody wanted to pay taxes. France was determined to get racing out of their felonious hands and into his own backyard at Daytona, but he needed these moonshine stars to draw the ticket-paying crowd.

By 1945, thirty thousand people were showing up regularly at Lakewood to watch the stock cars racing. Atlanta was dwarfing Daytona as the cradle of racing and France was fighting a losing battle until the city of Atlanta came to his aid. City ministers decided to denounce a sport that put criminals in the role of heroes, and they pressured municipal officials to ban felons from racing. That put Seay, Hall, the Flocks, and practically every other moonshine-hauling stock car driver in Georgia out of racing.

At the next Lakewood race, spectators saw a mysterious driver with a handkerchief over his face circling the track. A police car cruised through the gates, then another. A buzz erupted among the crowd.

"They got down to the lower end, and had him hemmed up. He ran through the fence, and broke some boards," said one fan. "He took off through the field, and went up on the highway, with these police cars chasing him. We found out later that it was Bob Flock, trying to slip in there to race."[21]

After Flock was run off the track, there was no one left at the starting line. The Atlanta-Daytona rivalry came to an end, and Daytona won by default. France was finally in a position to take matters into his own hands.

The Organization of **NASCAR**

Despite their rather disastrous experience on Daytona Beach in 1935, AAA had continued to endorse some stock car races, but by the mid-1940s they'd had enough of the mayhem and decided to get out of the sport altogether. Independent stock car associations started to spring up to fill the vacuum, but each had its own rules and scoring system, and the result was a sport run by squabbling, splintered governing bodies.

Racing had been structured so that a driver didn't just win a cash prize from individual races but gathered points. These points were accumulated over the course of the season, and at the end of the year the driver with the most points was declared champion. Unfortunately all the new associations calculated their points differently. Points from one didn't count in the other, so an ultimate champion couldn't be determined. Drivers ended up traveling around like mercenaries, running in whichever race offered the most prize money. They would often go to collect their winnings to find the purse had disappeared along with the promoter.

France was convinced more than ever that, no matter how lawless the Scots-Irish were, the sport needed some consistency and regulation to drag it out of chaos.

In the late 1940s he founded his own sanctioning authority, the National Championship Stock Car Circuit (NCSCC), and set rules that appealed to the unruly top drivers who only cared about winning and prize money. Like the other associations, he offered a purse to the winner of each individual race along with points that could be accumulated over the course of the season; he also sweetened the pot. In his races, the driver with the most points at the end of the season won a $1,000 bonus and the NCSCC championship title. His association offered money on top of race prizes and the ultimate bragging rights.

In a plan to quash all other governing bodies, he declared that any driver who raced for another promoter would be stripped of his points and banned from NCSCC races for a year. In 1947 he devised a scheme to bring the sport under one official organization. He invited racers, drivers, promoters, and mechanics to meet at the Streamline Hotel in Daytona Beach on December 14—ironically the date Alexander Hamilton first proposed taxing whiskey to create the Bank of the United States in 1790.

France's proposal was ambitious. It wouldn't be easy to govern law-breaking, whiskey-tripping Scots-Irishmen, who were impossible to control and hostile to authority. France made the conference more palatable by inviting a number of girls from the local charm school and supplied free booze. After three days, France had inspired the attendees with his grandiose visions of the future. They agreed to form a committee and voted him president of the new association. Parks's mechanic came up with the name, the National Association for Stock Car Auto Racing, or NASCAR. No one would realize for many more years that something was not right about that meeting. A savvy businessman like Parks, who might have sensed something was wrong, was more interested in the female guest in his hotel room that day than he was in the meeting downstairs.

The drivers who did attend were happy to have an organization that brought a consistent paycheck, but most of them were uneducated, and no one wanted to handle the actual business, so they left it all to France. No one realized until too late that by not putting the stockholders and committee members' names down on paper, they had inadvertently given France complete control over the sport. Despite France's seeming support for a democratically elected committee, he knew there would be too much infighting and dissidence for stock car racing to survive as a democracy. It needed the iron fist of a dictator, so he quietly set up the corporation without them.

"He used his lawyers to draw up legal papers giving him all rights to our organization," Parks said later. "That's how Bill France stole NASCAR."[22]

Parks was loyal to a fault. He didn't expect to be hoodwinked by the man who was supposed to be his friend, but whatever Parks's personal feelings were about France's betrayal, he kept them to himself. When France couldn't pay the purse in NASCAR's early races, Parks privately kept the sport going by sending carloads of cash to his aid. He said France paid him back, but it would be fifty years before anyone learned that the Scots-Irishman and his whisky money had saved NASCAR in its infancy.

As the decade closed, Parks decided he'd had enough and retired. It was hard to believe he'd been involved in the sport for less than twelve years. He pumped money into the racing when it was a money-sucking hobby. He delivered the original champions, the fastest cars, and the only respectability the sport had ever known. France would never admit it, but without Parks he could never have turned the unruly hobby into a lucrative sport. It was impossible to imagine racing without him, but one day, as quietly as he came, the godfather of NASCAR was gone.

The Bootleggers' Last Stand

By the early 1950s the whiskey-tripping legends of early days were dead, retired, or in prison. "Lightning" Lloyd Seay was shot to death by his cousin over a misunderstanding on a moonshine deal. He was only twenty-one. "Reckless" Roy Hall, who was a wanted criminal most of his life, was caught and sentenced to six years. In the mid-1950s, Bob Flock retired after breaking his back in a track accident, and after a close call at Darlington, Fonty Flock decided to walk away while he still could.

With the passing of the old guard, France began to fixate on ways to make NASCAR bigger, faster, better, and richer. He continued to consolidate his authority, chipping away here and there, slipping in an innocent rule or two. He quickly banned moonshine from the pits, which severed an artery to the sport's origins.

He also wanted to get rid of the rabid red dust of the dirt tracks that sent everyone home with red clothes and raccoon eyes. He wanted families to show up after services in their Sunday best and spend a lazy afternoon picnicking and socializing. When an opportunity to collude with a South Carolina peanut farmer on the construction of a massive paved track at Darlington appeared, France jumped at the chance. This was going be a huge leap forward for his dreams of a dust-free, respectable, family-oriented, law-abiding Southern stock sport.

Yet, much to France's annoyance, the bootleggers didn't fade away. Instead they passed their torch to a new generation of whiskey trippers who became NASCAR superstars. The new drivers drew huge crowds who loved their hard-charging, reckless ways. One was the indomitable Junior Johnson who, at twenty-two hit the big racetracks like a tornado, crushing NASCAR's superstars like he outsmarted every highway patrol officer in Wilkes County. In his first year, he won five races and finished sixth in the Grand National points standings. His success and aggressive driving style earned him the name "The Wilkes County Wild Man."

"I was a very rough driver; it was a style of driving. If I hit anybody or anything it was not intentional," he said. "They didn't race me as hard as somebody else because they knew I was determined to go to the front and I'd do it regardless."[23]

Junior raced to win because he just couldn't stand to lose. Even in his early twenties he was a savvy businessman, but he wasn't in it for the money; he made more hauling liquor. He ran for the satisfaction of outwitting his competition, and for the bragging rights. Those days were about to change. The ATF were going after tax-evading bootleggers more aggressively than ever. Unfortunately for Junior, just as his illustrious racing career was taking off, he was busted while firing up his father's whiskey still and carted off to the same Ohio reformatory where Parks had resided years before. He served eleven months of a two-year sentence.

After his release, Junior went back to racing and to bootlegging, but in 1960 his moonshine-running exploits earned him a bounty on his head. Junior knew it was only a matter of time before someone ratted him out. It was time to retire; he stopped breaking the law and took up breaking France's rules instead.

The only thing Junior liked better than winning was finding an advantage over his adversaries, and his proudest moment came during the 1960 Daytona 500. His car was running twenty miles an hour slower than the top cars in the race. During a practice run, a Pontiac sped past and he noticed that when he got in behind it there was a slipstream, a current of air that dragged Junior along at higher speeds than his Chevrolet was capable of. On race day, he sat rear bumper of the leader Bobby Johns and got sucked along in the draft. When Johns pitted so did Junior. Then luck gave him an added bonus. Johns' rear window popped out and flew into the air, creating a suction that spun him into the grass. By the time Johns got back on the track Junior was too far ahead to be caught.

The slipstream he discovered that day became a staple of every NASCAR driver.

After his victory Junior went back to plain old cheating. People started noticing that he was always in the lead because he was somehow able to keep driving when everyone else had to pit to refuel. While bewildered drivers watched from the pit, Junior just kept on circling the track. NASCAR took his car apart. It turned out his roll bar was full of gas and connected to his gas tank, which was giving him extra mileage.

Junior wasn't discouraged. With his newfound fondness for physics, he arrived with cars subtly adjusted for better aerodynamics. France thought he put an end to bootleggers' modifications way back in the days of Smokey Purser, but Junior kept showing up with something that almost—but didn't quite—break the rules.

When the bootlegger built a car for another driver, France decided, rule or no rule, he'd gone too far. The front of the car sloped downward, the roof was low, the rear end was raised, and it was painted yellow. It was known as the "Banana." It eventually passed inspection but it was the first and last time the Banana was allowed to race. NASCAR told him not to bring it back.

Eventually France had templates made to put over the body to make sure he'd never lay eyes on a Banana again. From then on all cars had to meet exact design specifications dictated in the rulebook. They said that rulebook was written by Bill France to stop Junior Johnson from doing what he was doing.

That put an end to the era of bootlegger craftiness. It took him twenty years, but France finally won the "strictly stock" fight he started back on Daytona Beach. NASCAR was to be an "everyman" sport that kept the skill firmly in the hands of the driver and out of the hands of engineers and mechanics. Of course in the old days, it cost $500 for the junkyard parts to build a whole car; but the sport had grown, and it now cost $500 per tire. The "everyman" sport was no longer so everyman, but that seemed to be a minor point. France had quashed the last mutinous straggler and solidified his autocracy—until the Blonde Blizzard of Virginia blazed onto the track.

Curtis Turner hailed from Floyd, Virginia. He'd been running moonshine in his father's convoy of Oldsmobiles from the age of ten. By eighteen, the blue-eyed, blond-haired Tuner was tall, slender, popular, and successful. In his lifetime he made a fortune, lost it, and remade it. He owned three sawmills, a fleet of heavy machinery, and a private plane. He held court everywhere he went and threw the biggest wildest parties anyone ever saw. He loved soaring in the air and speeding around the track. As his friend, actor James Garner said, "he knew he was a legend and therefore he lived it."[24]

Turner raced even harder than Junior, and the two beat and bashed each other around the track during many races. Losers left the speedway in cars that were still pretty and shiny. The winners' cars bore the scars from "mixing it up" to get across the finish line first. Everyone knew Turner's car; it was the one locals said was "beat up all to pieces."

Turner became a NASCAR superstar when he threw his car sideways and slid it the length of two football fields past all the other cars on the track. The crowd immediately loved him. Unlike most drivers who ran fifty miles, slowed down for fifty, and ran for fifty more, Turner ran hard for the whole five hundred. His competitors never really knew what to expect. Some days he'd show up ready to bang them up and run them over, but other days he'd show up so drunk he didn't know his own name.

"I don't really think I'd be happy if I wasn't in some sort of trouble," he said.[25]

Turner was always in trouble. In the late 1950s he decided to get in on the super speedway trend and build a huge paved track in Charlotte just like those at Daytona and Darlington. Despite his millions, the project was underfinanced and besieged with so many problems that he had to carry a gun to protect himself from hostile workmen. Finally, his shareholders forced him out.

When the track opened, Turner was bitter and almost broke. He desperately needed a $750,000 loan, so he turned to the one place he knew had deep pockets. The Teamsters Union wanted to branch into pro sports, and just as Turner expected, they were happy to oblige him if he organized the NASCAR drivers. Turner knew this would be a direct challenge to the dictatorship France finagled in 1948. If the drivers got union representation, it would diminish his power and give the Teamsters more say in the sport. Challenging France was risky, but impending poverty left Turner no option. Besides, almost all the drivers agreed that it would be good to have a union to represent their interests and provide them with benefits and a pension plan that NASCAR didn't provide.

France was furious. He called a meeting of all the drivers and mechanics before a race at Winston-Salem and announced that no union member would be allowed to compete in NASCAR races. France banned Turner both from the meeting and from racing for life. Turner expected the boss to relent as he had always done, but this time was different. It didn't matter that Turner was the star attraction; Turner directly challenged France's authority. This was France's operation; it didn't answer to some hedonistic whiskey-tripper.

While Turner was in exile, NASCAR's other famous bootlegger decided to retire from driving. In the mid-1960s, after fifty victories and a ranking in the top fifty racers ever, Junior decided to get out of his car and into the pit. At thirty-five-years of age, he decided to build the cars and contract other people to drive them.

"I'd accomplished practically everything I'd set out to accomplish," he said. "The thrill was gone, even the excitement of the speed had gradually worn off. I'd run faster in a liquor car than I ever did on racetracks."[26]

The year before, as stock car racing was ignored by the rest of America who thought it was some sort of redneck demolition derby, author and journalist Tom Wolfe heard about the renegade origins of the sport. On assignment from *Esquire* magazine, Wolfe trekked to North Carolina in a Yankee suit and a pair of spats to talk to the locals.

"I wasn't in the South five minutes before people started making oaths, having visions, telling these hulking great stories, and so forth, all on the subject of Junior Johnson," wrote Wolfe.[27] He finally understood the mythology when he met the man himself and was impressed by the "old boy culture" and "pocket of courage" that Junior possessed, although the bootlegger didn't know what all the fuss was about.

"I didn't figure he'd get much of a story," he said modestly. "But somehow he got the local people to talk to him and his story turned out to be pretty doggone good and accurate."[28]

The story *The Last American Hero Is Junior Johnson. Yes!* ran in *Esquire* in 1965 and was considered one of the six greatest stories the magazine ever published. Twentieth Century Fox later adapted the story into a movie starring Jeff Bridges that took Junior's name beyond the Wilkes County line and made him a national icon. In 2004 the state of North Carolina renamed his old whiskey-hauling Route 421—Junior Johnson Highway. There was a strange irony in Junior's sudden thrust into the national spotlight. While the Northern racing elites looked down on his kind and his sport, this Scots-Irish outlaw and braggart became the "Last American Hero" right under their noses.

Meanwhile, back in Columbia, South Carolina, France finally relented and allowed Turner back into the fold. Four years in exile was punishment enough; besides, when Junior retired into the pit, there was no one left on the track that could draw the ticket-paying crowds.

One of the prodigal son's first races was for Junior Johnson's team. NASCAR heavily promoted the event that involved two racing legends running on the same side. The officials warned Turner not to cause any trouble and instructed him to wear a suit if he wanted to compete. Instead of a racing suit, Turner showed up in a spiffy business suit.

"You didn't specify what kind of suit," he told officials.[29]

With thousands of fans hyped up for the big event, NASCAR had no choice but to let him run.

"He was still wearing a tie when he put his helmet on," Junior said.

It was Turner's last act of defiance. A few years later, his plane crashed into the side of a mountain in Pennsylvania. Some believed he put it on autopilot to take a nap in the back as he liked to do and was unaware of a problem with the navigational system; other reports said he was fighting to regain control until his very last breath. It was inconceivable that a giant like Turner was suddenly gone. He was the last big liquor hauler on the track, the last man running at full throttle on and off the speedway. When Turner died the party ended.

The Modern Era of Southern Stock

As the 1970s dawned, a new era in NASCAR began to unfold. Monstrous speedways began to crush the little tracks. Local venues that proudly opened their gates in the 1950s perished beneath the escalating sanction and insurance costs. The giant paved super-speedways snatched racing from the hands of the working-class folks who once put cars together with spit and glue. Dirt-track drivers didn't understand the cost of hosting a race; they thought the track owners were making thousands at the gate but were refusing to pay out their winnings. All across the South the small track owners just quit, turned out the lights, and went home. Their tracks fell victim to rust, overgrowth, and the passage of time. There was no more call for the guy with the fiddle to show up, or for the ordinary folks to race their ordinary cars, drink moonshine, and party all night.

As super-speedways were dominating the circuit, big car manufacturers in Detroit were pouring research and development money into constructing better engines and faster body styles. Aside from garnering prestige by beating other carmakers on the racetrack, they realized that if their racecar won, it increased their consumer car sales dramatically. Detroit technically became NASCAR's first advertiser.

The proud old V-8 Fords that once showed up at the dirt tracks on a Sunday with their fenders missing, roofs sawn off, hydraulics from one welded onto another, headlights taped up or missing altogether, and some white shoe polish number on the door had returned to the junkyards from which they came. In their place were high-tech, newly designed, specially constructed machines. Stock car racing began to look more like the World Speed Trials that had once belittled the Southern racing oddity. Prohibitive costs pushed out the old motley pack of drivers. Those who survived didn't care about bragging rights or theatrics or banging around the track. They recognized this was now a high-stakes game, and they needed to operate it like a business. This ushered in an era of highly specialized, money-driven teams.

The man who emerged as the most influential in this new big-finance, team-driven age was Richard Petty. He was a second-generation racer in a NASCAR dynasty. The racing bug bit him at the age of eleven when he watched his father Lee compete in one of NASCAR's earliest races. Lee Petty was a religious, sober family man who worked hard as a bakery truck driver to provide for his family. France's prize money would go a long way toward that end.

Lee borrowed a neighbor's Buick and showed up at the starting line for the fledgling race in Charlotte in 1949. Richard, his mother, and his brother Maurice watched with pride as their father roared through the red dust clouds holding his own with the rest of North Carolina's speed demons. Then they gasped in horror as he lost control and rolled four times with pieces of the neighbor's Buick flying into the air. Lee wasn't seriously injured but the family had to hitchhike home. Richard didn't care, he was smitten. It didn't matter that his father's car ended up as a mangled wreck; he'd never seen anything like the fury and power.

The Pettys didn't live too far from the Johnsons and other moonshiners in rural North Carolina but they steered clear of that lifestyle. In Lee's time, bootleggers made most of their money from whiskey and raced for the challenge, but once he began competing, his income and his family's livelihood relied solely on winning. He ran his racing career like a business. His wife kept the books, Maurice built the cars, and Richard worked with the pit crew. His motto was simple, "stay out of trouble, make money." He formed Petty Enterprises with the goal to provide a better life for his family. He let nothing get in his way even if that meant being a dirty driver when it came down to the money lap.

"God help you if you got in between Petty and a paycheck," they said in the pits.[30]

Once Turner spun him into the wall. Afterward, Lee smacked him unconscious with a tire iron wrapped up in a newspaper.

Richard Petty grew up to be a handsome man, always smiling, and devoutly loyal to his clan, his sponsors, and his fans. He shared his father's fierce competitiveness, but he dwarfed his achievements. He won both the Winston Cup and the Daytona 500 a record seven times and acheived an astounding two hundred victories throughout his career.

Richard was a religious man and a teetotaler who never had alcohol in the house. He grew up around moonshine but, like his father, wanted no part of that trouble. Building the family business was his priority but not at the expense of his integrity. When Busch beer offered him some financial support, he turned them down because he didn't want a beer decal on a Petty car door.

"Richard is a special type person," said a friend. "He is very intelligent and he's a giving person. What other person would sit and sign autographs like he does? At his picnics I've watched him sign from sunup to sundown, two lines going down the highway as far as you could see."[31]

Richard became the champion of champions—The King, the greatest NASCAR driver of all time, and one of the most accessible. He never begrudged the fans, and they loved him for it. He was one of them, working hard in a family enterprise, with Southern values they could relate to and a mythology they could aspire to.

Everyone wanted to see The King cross that finish line first, and he rarely let them down. He was never a daredevil whiskey-tripper outrunning the law, but he was a tenacious opponent. During one race he almost broke his neck but kept his injury hidden from NASCAR officials knowing they'd stop him racing for fear another wreck would kill him. One thing fans could count on was that as long as The King could drive, nobody was getting him off the track.

His popularity helped NASCAR fill the hundreds of thousands of seats at the super-speedways. While he didn't always like the way France did business, he agreed with him on one thing—the growth of the sport depended on it becoming clean family entertainment, and that meant saying goodbye to the wild, whiskey-tripping, rough-and-tumble attitude that still prevailed.

"As it cleaned itself up from inside, then it got a better class of fans," he said. "The newspapers got interested in it 'cause it was a family sport. The more press you get the more people you get to come so it helps everybody."[32]

Ticket sales were critical, but they didn't bring in nearly enough revenue. As the 1970s progressed, the energy crisis was crippling the car manufacturers who had largely supported the sport. Finally, after numerous disputes with NASCAR over engine schematics, they decided to pack up their toys and go back to Detroit.

The teams needed a cash infusion to keep them afloat, and they needed it quick. It was then that Richard Petty's popularity really paid off. He quickly attracted the attention of sponsors eager to capitalize on the advertising potential of his superstar status. They were willing to pay large sums of money to see their decal on the hood of his blue number 43 car as it invariably crossed the finish line first. In 1972 he signed with STP motor oil and became the first NASCAR driver to secure a major sponsorship deal. This ushered in a new era of big finance that changed the rules for everyone. No one would be able to compete again without serious corporate backing. The little teams were forced out and off the tracks.

The sport may have gotten away from the rest of the bootleggers and into the hands of teetotalers and big corporations, but there was one Scots-Irishman from whom it wasn't getting away. Junior was busy building a formidable team of his own and was already working to get his own sponsorship deal. He had survived starvation, the law, and prison; he was going to survive the onslaught of big business.

When a federal ban prohibited tobacco companies from advertising on television, Junior decided to pay a visit to RJ Reynolds—the second biggest tobacco manufacturer in America. He planned on talking them into sponsoring his team in exchange for advertising their tobacco products on his cars. What he found waiting was a suitcase of money much larger than he'd imagined and much more than he needed.

He called in Bill France.

"I realized with the way the sport of racing was itching to take off and with the money Reynolds could put behind it, it would turn out to be something good," he said.[33]

It was one of the biggest turning points in NASCAR history. Reynolds came in with $100,000 for the Grand National Championship—a fortune at the time. It was a far cry not only from the $100 Lloyd Seay triumphantly won thirty years earlier, but also far from the millions that the cup would be worth thirty years later. The Grand National Championship was renamed the Winston Cup, and the top tobacco brand overcame the TV advertising ban by landing on the tongue of every racing commentator and radio sports show host. From that point on all races less than one hundred miles were cut from the circuit, making stock car racing bigger and richer than ever. The modern era of NASCAR had officially begun.

Junior brought in a sport-saving cash transfusion in a time of crisis. Just as France turned to a bootlegger to save the sport two decades before, a bootlegger had stepped in to save it again. But Junior didn't just resuscitate racing, he also had a knack for increasing sponsors' confidence in the sport's national potential.

"I met President Reagan in Daytona beach," he said. "I worked for a company called Holly Farms, a poultry company. I drove for them for a while. He came to Daytona beach and I sat across from him and his wife and he'd been out in the sun a long time and his forehead was sunburned and I said, 'Mr. President you need a cap,' and he said 'I sure do.' I had a Holly Farms cap on and I pulled it off and gave it to him and I said 'here, take my cap—I'll get another one.' And he put it on and somebody took his picture with that cap on and it was on *Good Morning America* the next morning."[34]

Years later they met again at the Oval Office when President Reagan pardoned him for his moonshining conviction. They chatted about that day in Daytona and about racing in general. It was a long way from Wilkes County to the White House and it was testament, not just to Junior, but to how far the sport itself had come.

NASCAR Becomes All-American

When the clouds finally cleared that Sunday afternoon in 1979, sixty years of racing history culminated in NASCAR's most transformative moment. CBS rolled up with their cameras to capture Cale Yarborough, Bobby and Donnie Allison, and Richard Petty prowling to the starting line. For the first time a TV network decided to cover the race live in its entirety. Sponsors' names were splashed across the hood of every car giving them five hundred miles of national exposure. Families had turned out in force, buying up merchandise and packing into the stands. Even the snowstorm worked to NASCAR's advantage by keeping the entire Northern population housebound and forced to watch its first fully televised race.

The aging Bill France had long since passed on the NASCAR presidency to his son, but he watched the culmination of a lifetime's work from his usual perch in the control tower. Down below, Raymond and Violet Parks were seated with all the other paying spectators in the grandstands. The two men didn't speak that day, but a decade later when France was suffering with Alzheimer's, he called Parks every day. Despite their checkered past, the bond the men formed during the early days of racing was unbroken. Parks was the only person France could talk to in the end.

"He was all right," the old man said quietly many years after France was gone.[35]

France may have become nostalgic in his twilight hours, but he would feel vindicated after he was gone knowing that the $65,000 first-prize purse in 1979 was chump change compared to the billions that would later flood into the sport and the family coffers. He would be happy to see there were no bootleggers at the starting line, and the sport had finally been ripped from the colorful cast of outlaws in whose ungovernable hands it had evolved. In the hands of his heirs, racing would eventually become the family entertainment he always wanted.

It didn't matter that Junior made a million-dollar sponsorship deal with Budweiser, or that Kyle Petty—the third-generation driver of the teetotaling Petty dynasty—would drive for Coors. It wouldn't have mattered that cars would later be emblazoned with the decals of alcoholic beverages or that big tobacco sponsored his championship. France always hated the moonshine haulers and their whiskey money, but tobacco and beer money was different. They would take his all-American, respectable family sport to new heights. He may not have allowed the cars to be modified, but he always knew how to modify the rules.

To his credit, France turned an outlaw hobby into a lucrative sport. He dragged it from dirt roads to super-speedways and hosed it down along the way. But as Junior stepped into his pit on that wet and windy Daytona afternoon, he knew that none of it would have happened without the bootleggers' feistiness and competitive spirit.

He put on his headset to talk to his driver, Cale Yarborough—he wouldn't be surprised if that day would end with a fistfight. It wouldn't matter who started it or who won. The fight would prove what the "Last American Hero" always maintained—that NASCAR was driven by the whiskey-tripping principle: "Beat your hind end on the track and beat your hind end on the ground."[36]

And with that time-honored tradition, a new generation of Southern boys ran five hundred miles to take this Scots-Irish, whiskey-tripping legacy to the nation.

CHAPTER 9

AMERICAN FAIRY TALE

O nce upon a time there was a beautiful young woman who lived in a village in the mountains of east Tennessee. She fell in love with a strong, handsome man who had shoulder-length hair and piercing blue eyes; he was just as strong as she was beautiful, and he was as good a hunter as she was a homemaker.

On their wedding day there was much laughter, music, and lemonade as the whole community came together to celebrate. When night fell the young couple went off to their newly built cabin in the deep, dark woods. The sound of the revelry faded in the distance and was replaced with the soft, peaceful sounds of crickets, birds, and a small, rushing brook. The happy couple was alone at last, picking their way through the brush unaware that a large sinister creature with vicious yellow eyes was watching them.

The next morning the husband decided it was time to go hunting, but his wife had a bad feeling. She begged him to stay and wait for a hunting party.

"You know that old creature will get you," she cried. "The Ewah will make you crazy if it catches you by yourself."

The Ewah! Ever since the first settlers arrived in those parts, they heard the Cherokee tell of a demon that lurked in the deep, dark forests and terrorized their villages. They said it was the spirit of a Cherokee woman who had disguised herself in the skins of a mountain lion to eavesdrop on the men of the tribe telling sacred stories. The medicine man punished her by transforming her into a demonic wildcat. Anyone who saw her was driven insane.

The brave young man was unafraid and set off for a day's hunting. His dutiful wife was deathly worried about him alone out there in the dark woods. She tried to wash clothes but they wouldn't dry; she tried to bake bread but it wouldn't rise. She paced back and forth from kitchen to porch all day. Then, as the sun was sinking below the rocky cliffs and shadow encroached upon the land, she heard a blood-curdling wail from the forest. She ran inside, fumbled for a rifle, and rushed back onto the porch in time to see a creature crashing out of the woods. Trying to steady the rifle in her trembling hands she took aim, then paused. She looked more closely and realized to her horror that it was indeed her husband. His long, beautiful, blond hair was matted with his own blood, his clothes were torn and ripped to shreds, and his eyes darted back and forth like a caged animal. When she called out to him, he charged back into the brush.

She fell to the ground in a state of inconsolable grief. Her greatest fear was realized—her beautiful, adoring husband had seen the Ewah and was lost to her forever.

Just before daybreak, she rose and walked into the canyon, the one with walls so steep and dark that the sun only hits the floor for fifteen minutes a day at high noon. She had never been to this place, but as a child her grandmother told her stories about an old woman who lived there. They said she was a mad old witch; others said she was an Indian, the last of her people. Could she still be alive?

The bride finally found the old one-room cabin. It had no windows, just a chimney, no porch, and three moss-covered steps. When she placed her foot on the first step, the door creaked open. She cautiously stepped across the threshold into blackness.

"Come in, I've been expecting you!" a shrill voice sounded from the darkness.

As the young wife's eyes adjusted, a figure emerged from back by the stove. She had long hair down to her waist, matted and tangled and covered in leaves like she'd been sleeping on the forest floor. Something skittered across her scalp into her hair.

"You think I can help your husband don't you?" the hag squawked.

The bride pleaded with her to help; she would do anything to save her husband.

"Anything?" the hag cackled carrying a wooden box that she dropped on a dirty old table with a thud.

"You want to scare it first. That's the key, isn't it?" the hag heckled as she creaked open the boxes and pulled out the contents. "My people called this the Wampas Mask. To get rid of the Ewah, you must wear this and look into his eyes before it looks into yours."

She slammed the box shut, thrust it on the young bride, and pushed her outside. The door banged shut, and the old woman's howling laughter faded away.

Back home the young woman opened the box and held the mask up to the firelight. It had long, wispy black hair and demonic yellow eyes that would cleave a person's soul. She put the mask on, tied the leather strings firmly, and stumbled out into the forest. She could barely see through the yellow eyelets as she tripped and bumped into trees. She was terrified; she'd no idea how to scare this fearsome creature, but she had to try. All she could hear were the night owls and crickets and the rushing stream, but as she pushed further into the forest, she heard an unnatural sound coming from the brook. She crept closer, her hands clammy, her heart pounding.

Then she saw it. It was stooping over the water, a long and slender man about seven feet tall. Only this wasn't a man, it was like nothing from the Old World. He was hairy from head to foot; his hands were like claws, with long, curved nails; saliva dripped from his fangs. The bride's courage left her, and she started backing away. She snapped a twig. The creature spun around. She let out an ear-piercing scream, it howled in response, she collapsed to the ground; it leapt to the other side of the river, scraping, slipping, clawing to get up the muddy bank, then disappeared into the woods.

It was gone.

Hours later she came round, rose rather unsteadily, and made her way back home. Had she scared the creature? Was her husband now restored to sanity? She walked along deep in thought, unaware of how well she could see. At the edge of the woods she saw her husband on the front porch of their little cabin. His clothes were fresh, his hair clean, and he looked even more handsome than before. Her heart swelled with love. She called out to him, but when he saw her his brow furrowed. He picked up his rifle and aimed.

"Of course, he sees the mask!" she realized. "My voice must have been muffled. He neither sees nor hears his bride."

She reached back to grab the strings of the mask, fumbling through her long dark hair, but she couldn't find them. She grew more frantic, trying to scratch the mask from her face but it wouldn't budge, as though the thick black whiskers and evil yellow eyes had become her face. Then, to her horror she noticed her hands were covered in fur and her nails had become claws. As her husband squeezed the trigger, she let out a scream—a scream that was too wild to be human, but too soulful to be an animal. Her husband's bullet whizzed past her head and rattled her brain. She fell down on all four paws and ran back into the woods.

To this day they say if you go into those wooded mountains, you might spot the creature that walks on its hind legs in the woods near the cabin of a broken old man, who, a long time ago, lost his beautiful young wife to the demon Ewah.[1]

New Land, New Lore

On reaching the mountaintop, the settlers found themselves gazing down on the stuff of Eden—lush landscapes, strange civilizations, impassible terrains full with utopian hopes and wonder. This was the promise of a different life; princes were left behind, there were no castles on the hill, no overlords or kings or knights who fought heroic battles and saved damsels from some state of wretchedness. Woeful Irish fairies were also left behind—except for one bunch that stowed aboard and ended up in a tavern in New Hampshire. The inn was run by "a spiteful little man" and his "slattern and a tipper" of a wife who drove even the thirstiest customer away. Luckily, trade took a turn for the better when the Irish fairies moved in and began holding conversations in the parlor.

By and large, the Scots-Irish gave the fairies the slip before heading to the frontier, but they still brought their belief in demons and ghouls in the night. The frontier was replete with danger, hardship, and lawlessness; it was fertile ground to spew up extravagant, exaggerated, and death-defying lore. There were ghosts and madmen aplenty, along with "murdering injuns," haunted houses, and wicked witches.

A tradition of storytelling had developed in the mountains where the Scots-Irish, living in a hostile environment, used their fertile imagination to explain the peculiar and frightening happenings around them. The Indian lurked in every shadow, as did evil spirits who roamed the land since time began. Some Indians were tricksters who described horrendous inland dangers to deter settlers from exploring farther. The Mississippi was full of monsters and serpents, and even if a settler's craft survived, it would be drawn "into a horrid whirlpool that swallows up everything that comes near it, in that hideous and bottomless gulf."[2]

Edgar Allan Poe, the Scots-Irishman who emerged as the father of American Gothic literature, merged the demonology of the Old World with the landscape of the New and subjected his heroes to a whole host of fresh terrors.

> To the right and left, as far as the eye could reach, there lay outstretched, like ramparts of the world, lines of horridly black and beetling cliff, whose character of gloom was but the more forcibly illustrated by the surf which reared high up against its white and ghastly crest, howling and shrieking forever. . . . [3]

In addition to the nightmare of an inhospitable terrain, the emerging culture was replete with its own terrors. With no lawmen, it became the responsibility of the corpse to out his murderer. In one tale, two young men quarreled; one killed the other and buried him in the sand. Years later the sand eroded and a bone appeared. When an old white-headed man touched it, it started gushing blood and the murderer was forced to confess the crime. The horror of a bleeding corpse was a dead man's only hope for justice on the lawless frontier.

Meanwhile speculators were running amok in Georgia and along the coast in search of Cherokee pirate-treasure booty. Poe sent an impoverished Southern aristocrat down to the Carolina coast to locate Captain Kidd's swag in *The Gold Bug*, and another American fictional hero, Tom Sawyer, was sent into a cave to unearth a treasure trove stashed by a "murdering Injun." The Southern scribe's pen proved to be mightier than any X that marked the spot.

In the isolated pockets of the mountains, poor, uneducated settlers developed a rich oral tradition full of legends, tall tales, superstition, and their own brand of hero, particularly when a ragamuffin bunch trounced the British at the Battle of Kings Mountain. Foreigners still described them as a rabid pack of hillbillies but mountain folk took pride in their culture—instead of lamenting their calamities, they inflated their poverty. One told a visitor that his coon dogs were so weak they had to lean against a stump to bark; another claimed the summer had been so dry the trees followed the dogs around. A whole community insisted there were pond frogs in the country "as big as a child a year old," and if the traveler didn't believe

Edgar Allan Poe portrait. Graham's magazine, *1845, printed a few months after publication of* The Raven. *From the Harry Lee Poe Collection.*

them he could go ask an Indian. The Indian always managed to heighten the mystique of a tall tale. Off went the travelers thinking they had truly beheld strange savages, beasts, and landscapes, giving the "hillbilly" the last laugh.

When the Jacksonian era dawned, stuffy papers full of foreign news for the haughty elite were replaced with lowbrow newspapers for the local community, packed with tales of pirates, cannibals, animals, freaks of nature, and weird phenomena. The backcountry poured forth the everlasting image of the American hero—epitomized by none other than the self-reliant, individualistic, spitting, bragging, brawling, patriotic, and rebellious Davy Crockett. Crockett was the brash voice of Jacksonian America, who, rather than kneel before the Haitian emperor, allegedly demolished his entire army with two sun-dried sugarcanes. He was the poster child for brawny American culture—the forerunner for the American superhero who rose from the ranks of the common man.

By the late eighteenth century the heroes and anti-heroes of the Scots-Irish imagination scrawled their way into a national storytelling tradition of fantasy, myth, and horror. They gave America the haunted house, buried treasure, an ensemble of depraved characters, and nightmarish worlds wherein the sweetest fairy tale became a pantomime of horror.

Unparalleled Adventures

While England was overrun with mad scientists who dabbled in the netherworld between life and death to bring forth Frankensteins and Draculas, the South was spawning a Gothic tradition of its own that wasn't as concerned with supernatural horror as it was with mad narrators experiencing terror of the soul in a rapidly expanding nation.

They said the conjuror of the macabre Southern mythology was a sexual deviant, drug addict, and raving lunatic who "walked the streets, in madness or melancholy, with lips moving in indistinct curses . . . he would speak as if to spirits."[4] He had a particular talent for transporting aristocratic madmen, tormented murderers, necrophiliacs, and other deviants to dark exotic places as easily as he could write a treatise on physics, send a man to the moon, or investigate bizarre crimes.

In the beginning, Edgar Allan Poe was a happy young man of captivating Southern charm and optimism. His ancestors set sail for Pennsylvania from County Cavan in Ireland in 1742. David Poe, a toddler at the time of their departure, grew up to be an ardent patriot known as "the General" whose particular delight was in terrorizing the Tories during the Revolutionary War. The destiny of his son David Jr., however, was far from battlefield glory. He married a blue-blooded thespian, Elizabeth Arnold, and the pair became well-known but impoverished itinerant players in the theaters of Boston. Three children and four years of living in his wife's shadow later, David Jr. took his fiery temper and fondness for the bottle and absconded. He was never heard of again.

The shy, three-year-old Edgar with his sad, hazel-gray eyes, spent months watching his mother cough blood and eventually suffocate from tuberculosis in their dingy, cold, rented rooms during a Massachusetts winter. Her body was barely cold when Edgar Poe was whisked away by Frances and John Allan, never to see his sister again.

Allan was the epitome of the self-made merchant, successful, hardworking, unimaginative, and unaffectionate. He sent Poe off to an English boarding school for six years, the best part of which was the voyage home with a captain who told him fantastic tales of hurricanes, mutinies, pirates, and monsters of the deep.

At seventeen Poe attended the University of Virginia where he learned to gamble, drink, and run up debts. Mostly he sat alone in his room reading the poetic English Romanticism of the "mad, bad and dangerous to know" Lord Byron, whose infamy derived not only from his poetry about brooding, uncontrollable heroes, but from his own aristocratic excesses, huge debts, numerous love affairs, and self-imposed exile.

Eventually John Allan accused his "wastrel" heir of "eating the bread of idleness"[5] and promptly disowned him. Poe was forced by poverty and hunger to join the United States Army where he published a little collection of poems. Eventually realizing that no amount of diligent, military service would reconcile him to the Allan fold, the penniless poet disobeyed orders until he was court-martialed and dismissed. He fled to his grandmother's house in Baltimore, scribbled furiously in her little attic, and soon won fifty dollars in a short-story contest.

Life was good until 1835 when his grandmother's death left him the sole breadwinner for his Aunt Clemm and his thirteen-year-old cousin Virginia. He secured a job as assistant editor of the *Southern Literary Messenger*, a magazine full of ghost stories and people in impossible predicaments. His "nose for news" and flair for the macabre had audiences riveted. They were happy days, especially when he pestered his aunt to allow him to marry his beloved cousin. Virginia brought him moments of real happiness, quelled his intrinsic loneliness, comforted his darkest days, and was his sweet friend and poetic muse. The trio lived in Richmond, and Poe immersed himself in work.

Almost immediately, the hazards of the expanding nation had him sending all-American pioneering heroes off on grand adventures. In *The Unparalleled Adventure of One Hans Phall*, the hero was forced to soar to the moon to escape his debts and his wife. Poe invented all sorts of plausible facts and real science along with dangers and difficulties, like volcanic fragments, atmospheric pressure, and thunderclouds with which to terrorize his hero. Finally nineteen days after the "balloon arose like a lark, and, soaring far away above the city," Phall landed on the moon and somehow wrote to the States' College of Astronomers that "after a series of great anxieties, unheard of dangers, and unparalleled escapes, I . . . arrived in safety at the conclusion of a voyage undoubtedly the most extraordinary, and the most momentous, ever accomplished." [6] He then went on to request a pardon for his guilt in the death of the creditors.

Hans Phall was the first hero in a fledgling science-fiction genre that, over a hundred years later, would become the mythology of a generation in the hands of another man with Scots-Irish blood trickling in his veins. Poe's fascination with scientific discoveries would culminate in his big-bang theory of the origin of the universe in his treatise *Eureka* in 1848. He should have been the father of science fiction—Jules Verne bestowed on him that accolade—unfortunately *Eureka* was discarded as the product of Poe's deranged mind.

Poe's infamous descent into darkness began after the Panic of 1837 when he couldn't support his family. He started to drink again and was promptly fired. His heroes suddenly became anti-heroes: mad characters that haunted wastelands, ruined battlements, and brooded away in the twilight of some "dim, decaying city." Unlike Gothic literature from the Old World, Poe let his lunatics narrate so his readers could hear them revel in their own insanity.

In 1839 he launched the most deranged of all siblings into American society, in *The Fall of the House of Usher*. Roderick Usher, an anxiety-ridden hypochondriac lives with his cataleptic sister Madeline in what he believes is a sentient house with "vacant and eye-like windows." Roderick eventually entombs his sister, but one night while entertaining a visitor in the midst of a sudden storm, cracking, ripping, and shrieks are heard throughout the house. Roderick gets hysterical, insisting its Madeline, that he has "put her living in the tomb!" Suddenly the doors are thrown open and there stood "the lofty and enshrouded figure of the lady Madeline of Usher," trembling and covered in blood.[7] With a low moan she fell on her brother who collapsed in death from terror, followed by a tumultuous shout from the house as it crumbled into the surrounding lake.

Thus began a series of stories that emerged from the Southern psyche about lunatics, narcissists, premature burials, and dying women that continued for generations, reaching a triumphant flourish in the possessed villainy of Jack Torrence, a character created by Poe's literary heir and member of his Scots-Irish bloodline, Stephen King.

In 1843, Poe, Virginia, and Aunt Clemm set off for new adventures in the chaotic city of New York, with its narrow, muddy streets overrun with down-and-outs and general mayhem. He loved to stroll with Virginia around the Battery. He took to reading newspapers that were packed with news of shipwrecks, collisions, fires, and other catastrophes. Something was always sinking or burning to the ground; it was a grand atmosphere of morbidity and macabre splendor.

Virginia however was very ill. He loved her voice, and while she was singing to him one-day, blood suddenly streamed from her throat. Poe ran for the doctor and for the next two weeks frantically paced the house or watched nervously by her bedside.

"My dear little wife has been dangerously ill," he wrote to a friend. "About a fortnight since, in singing, she ruptured a blood-vessel, and it was only on yesterday that the physicians gave me any hope of her recovery."[8]

But there was no hope. Virginia had tuberculosis. For the next five years he watched her die as his own young life twisted its way into a landscape more ghastly than anything borne of his imagination. Virginia's slow, agonizing death kept him undulating between despair and hope, scarring him so deeply that his only comfort was compulsive drinking to ease the sorrow. In 1846 he moved Virginia and her mother to a cottage in the Bronx, New York, in an effort to find a healthier environment. Unfortunately, it was no help. In their symbiotic relationship, much like Roderick and Madeline's, as she worsened so did he.

"She recovered partially and again I hoped. Each time I felt all the agonies of her death—and at each occasion of the disorder I loved her more dearly and clung to her life with more desperate pertinacity," he wrote to a friend. "But I am constitutionally sensitive—nervous in a very unusual degree. I became insane, with long intervals of horrible sanity. During these fits of absolute unconsciousness I drank, God only knows how often or how much."[9]

Between midnight and morning his sleep was littered with "demons [that] take advantage of the night to mislead the unwary."[10] He poured their terrible visions into his most horrifying stories, where the all-American, visionary, self-reliant hero was replaced with increasingly depraved anti-heroes. In 1844, he sent Cornelius Wyatt across the sea with his deceased wife in *The Oblong Box*, but when the ship sank, the hero drowned, clinging to the coffin. In 1846 a homicidal maniac called Montresor took his revenge on his friend Fortunato with whom he was angry about some insult. He plotted the murder during Carnival when the man is drunk, dizzy, and dressed as a jester. Montresor lured the unfortunate victim into a cellar with the promise of a rare and valuable sherry wine, then slapped him in chains and walled him up. In Poe's nightmare, justice was no longer meted out to madmen. As Virginia wasted away in the same agony he had witnessed with this mother, stories kept pouring out full of death, madness, and disintegration. The frontier was never so dark.

In January 1845 he wrote *The Raven*, a prophetic poem about a man grieving for his deceased love who is visited by a bird that repeats one word: "Nevermore." The distraught narrator believes the bird is a prophet bringing news that the lovers won't be reunited in the afterlife. Tortured with these imaginings, he cries out, "Take thy beak from out my heart, and take thy form from off my door!" But the Raven responded: "Nevermore."

Virginia was buried in fine linen sheets supplied by her mother's friend. As she lay in her coffin that day in January 1847, someone remembered that there was no picture of her in existence, so one of the ladies made a watercolor of her porcelain skin and delicate features. Virginia's only likeness was her death mask.

After the funeral Poe returned to their cottage and collapsed. Each night in the midnight hours, he slipped out of the house and was found hysterically weeping by Virginia's tomb. For the next two years, he was miserable, anxious, unproductive, isolated, and sick, usually suffering brain fever or congestion.

On October 3, 1949, a worker from the *Baltimore Sun* passed a man lying in the street dressed in a torn black coat and ill-fitting gray trousers, with a battered hat and a cane beside him. It was a normal sight on election day when city derelicts were rounded up, plied with alcohol, and sent to the polls to vote multiple times, until they were too inebriated to make their mark. They were then discarded to sleep it off in the streets.

On close inspection of the cane, the *Sun* worker recognized the figure as Poe lying there semiconscious, dressed in cheap, ill-fitting clothes that were not his own. The delirious, groaning writer was admitted to a Baltimore hospital. In the early morning hours of October 7, the forty-year-old exhaled the words "Lord, help my poor soul." He expired like a tortured anti-hero of his own literary invention. He never roused to tell the mystery of his final hours. No autopsy was performed to determine the cause of death.

The next day a black-plumed hearse and one carriage passed through the streets of Baltimore to the Presbyterian Cemetery at Fayette and Green streets. There were four mourners, no display, and no ceremony. The *New York Journal of Commerce* wrote the simple epitaph: "We hope he has found rest, for he needed it."

The Phunny Fellow

The American anti-hero's flights of macabre fancy to exotic landscapes and fantastic worlds came to an end that day on Fayette and Green streets, but twenty years later the homicidal lunatics and crumbling big houses of his imagination reinvigorated Southern scribes. The Civil War had left the South with "enough woe and want and ruin and ravage . . . to satisfy the most insatiate heart . . . enough of sore humiliation and bitter over-throw . . . to appease the desire of the most vengeful spirit."[11] Southerners saw their culture torn asunder and their stories tramped underfoot by a rising tide of nationalism emanating from the North.

"I hate the Yankees more and more every time I look at one of their horrid newspapers and read the lies they tell about us," wrote a Georgia girl in her diary. "While we have our mouths closed and padlocked. The world will not hear our story and we must figure just as our enemies chose to paint us."[12]

A new hero emerged from the blood-soaked land, penned by a humorist who became a chronicler of vanities, hypocrisies, and the murderous acts of mankind after seeing the South "gutted by the buzzards" during the post–Civil War Reconstruction era.

The family of Samuel Langhorne Clemens, more popularly known by his pen name Mark Twain, came from the small town of Ballyclare in northern Ireland, where their oldest known Presbyterian ancestor has occupied a local grave since 1628. Twain screamed his way into the Missouri backcountry in 1835 as Halley's Comet streaked overhead. Shortly afterward the family of nine squeezed through the door of their tiny rough-hewn shack and headed for the lawless Mississippi depot town of Hannibal, where there were killings on the streets, a drunken Injun Joe at large, and an unusual number of bodies washing up with some regularity on the river's edge.

Mrs. Clemens was a beautiful, vivacious woman, an expert horsewoman, witty, genteel, a fabulous storyteller, and devout Presbyterian. Mr. Clemens was a cold, dignified, austere local judge with social ambitions above his income. He left his family in abject poverty when he died after catching pneumonia on his first day in court. The eleven-year-old rambunctious Twain was so grief-stricken, he promised his mother he'd turn over a new leaf if he didn't have to go to school again. The bargain was struck and from that day forward, Twain looked forward to realizing his ambitions to be a clown or an end man in a minstrel show. Unfortunately he was apprenticed to a typesetter to help support the family, but this rather dull job exposed him to a whole world of political news and to the literature of Edgar Allan Poe.

In 1857, at eighteen years of age, Twain gave up typesetting and went tramping about in a proud and rapidly expanding country. His initial plan to explore the Amazon was aborted in favor of a Mississippi River–pilot apprenticeship. For a few years he led a glorious life transporting people and goods on steamboats up and down the thronging river, but it came to a sad end with the outbreak of the Civil War in 1861.

Twain's home state of Missouri stayed with the Union, but the wandering typesetter, along with some old schoolmates from his boyhood gang, joined one of the loose companies of Confederate militia being organized in Hannibal. He was given a mule and an extra pair of cowhide boots, two blankets, a frying pan, an overcoat, and an old Kentucky rifle, and told to report for duty in Florida. The Sunshine State harbored no enemies, and so with little demand for heroics, they sat around firing volleys at the weeds. Twain was assigned to picket duty. He went out and had a nap. A few weeks later, he decided to resume his search for grand adventures and a heroic life in the new American frontier terrain. He deserted and went to Nevada in search of treasure.

"This country is fabulously rich in gold, silver, copper, lead, coal, iron, thieves, murderers, desperadoes, ladies, children, lawyers, Christians, Indians, Chinamen, Spaniards, gamblers, sharpers, poets, preachers," he wrote his mother. "It is the damnedest country under the sun."[13]

He had pitiful mining skills but discovered he was a brilliant satirist and teller of tall tales. He gave up mining and became a widely known traveling journalist and social satirist for the next five years. In 1865 he dragged a famous folktale out of the mountains and dusted it off as "The Notorious Jumping Frog of Calaveras County." He dubbed it a "villainous backwoods sketch," but critics called it "the finest piece of humorous writing yet produced in America." He was unexpectedly catapulted to fame.

His all-American common man frontier hero, Jim Smiley, was a gambling addict who would follow a bug all the way to Mexico to win a bet. Smiley showed up at a mining camp with an array of animals anthropomorphized into American political figures. His bullpup, Andrew Jackson, fought by grabbing the hind leg of his opponent and hanging on

Mark Twain, America's Best Humorist *by J. Keppler (1838–1894)*.
Courtesy of the Library of Congress.

until the other dog gave up. Smiley's dog won every fight until the day he had to fight a dog "didn't have no hind legs, because they'd been sawed off in a circular saw." Smiley consoled himself by educating a frog to out-jump any frog in Calaveras County. He named him Daniel Webster after the senator who made three failed bids for the presidency.

"I don't see no p'ints about that frog that's any better'n any other frog," a stranger said, delivering the line that became the motto for democracy in America.[14] On the frontier where the American character was being forged, no one was any better than anyone else.

The stranger agreed to bet against the frog, so Smiley left Daniel Webster with the stranger and went to the swamp to look for a competitor frog. The stranger filled Daniel Webster's mouth with quail shot. During the competition he was bolted to the ground while the swamp frog leapt off to win the day. American frontier democracy, it seemed, was besieged by corruption.

Twain decided that had the devil been forced to live in Nevada, he'd have gone back to hell. Twain went back to St. Louis. In 1870, he was famous enough to marry Olivia Langdon, daughter of a lumber and coal magnate. Her new husband was a social challenge; he was fond of cigars, addicted to profanity, and prone to social gaffes. At one dinner he spat hot soup on his plate, glared at the woman across from him, and burst out, "Some damn fools would have swallowed that."

Everything was about to change.

Back in Missouri, Twain grasped the extent of the war's annihilation of the South. Out west the Civil War had seemed like an interruption in westward expansion.

"The eight years from 1860 to 1868 uprooted institutions that were centuries old," read a passage from *The Gilded Age: A Tale of Today*, a novel he coauthored. "Changed the politics of a people, transformed the social life of half the country, and wrought so profoundly upon the entire national character that the influence cannot be measured short of two or three generations."[15]

Jumping frogs seemed trivial; the "Phunny Fellow," as he'd become known, was silenced by bloodshed and a scorched earth. He watched the country itching to get rich and everything tainted by greed, money, and merchandising. The "slavocracy" was replaced by criminal mobs; the press was feeding bizarre murders, freakish stories, and scandals to the masses. He tried to address inhumanity, calling for justice and freedom for all people, especially blacks, who were being crushed by racial prejudice. The distress of the nation had driven Poe's heroes to madness and was about to turn Twain's to violence.

Twain went deep into the mountains to recover the familiar folktales of his youth. He returned with a story of a half-wild countryside, replete with violence, terror, and death that lurked at the edge of every village. The new all-American hero, Tom Sawyer, was an imaginative, mischievous twelve-year-old boy living in a town inspired by Twain's very own depraved home of Hannibal. In 1876 *The Adventures of Tom Sawyer* emerged as a tale of childhood innocence, trickery, truancy, bad behavior, piracy, and digging for treasure. It was a Gothic novel full of murdering Injuns, superstition, and grave robbing, masquerading as a children's story.

For thirty-six chapters, Sawyer bungled along with his best friend Huckleberry Finn. Finn was the unsupervised, undisciplined, and unfettered son of the town drunk, who therefore became the "the juvenile pariah of the village." No sooner had Huck sauntered into literary immortality swinging a dead cat, than the story descended into superstition and villainy at the hands of the nefarious Injun Joe—a protagonist comparable to Poe's darkest anti-heroes, in a landscape not dissimilar to Roderick Usher's possessed mansion.

Cornered by Injun Joe while searching for treasure, the boys became trapped inside what became an icon of Southern literature in the post–Civil War land of withering plantations: the decaying, haunted house with "a weed-grown, floorless room, unplastered, an ancient fireplace, vacant windows, a ruinous staircase; and here, there, and everywhere hung ragged and abandoned cobwebs."[16]

Trapped in the house, the terrified boys watch as the villains find $1,000 in gold coins and abscond and bury it in a local cave. There Injun Joe meets his Maker in a Poesque entombment when some locals inadvertently barricaded the cave to prevent the children from wandering in and getting lost. Joe was eventually found "stretched upon the ground, dead, with his face close to the crack of the door, as if his longing eyes had been fixed, to the latest moment, upon the light and the cheer of the free world outside."[17] His bowie knife cleft in two from his desperate scratching on the door that sealed the entrance, and the remains of the bats he'd caught and eaten in his tomb.

As Twain aged he grew even darker, he became disillusioned with life and angered by the human race. He was almost bankrupt.

"I came in with Halley's Comet in 1835," he said. "It is coming again next year, and I expect to go out with it. The Almighty has said, no doubt: 'Now here are these two unaccountable freaks; they came in together, they must go out together.'"[18]

On April 20, 1910, the day after the comet came closest to the earth, they did.

The freakish landscapes and the everyday hero of the post–Civil War South that Twain left behind heralded a new tradition of horror. They would build on the distinctive mythology of the American South and inspire a new kind of all-American hero.

American Fairy Tale

"One thing I never liked . . . was the introduction of witches and goblins into the story," said the shy storyteller Lyman Frank Baum. "I didn't like the little dwarfs in the woods bobbing up with their horrors."[19]

With those words, "the horrible and blood-curdling incidents" of dead cats, murderous Injuns, goblins, and fairies were banished. Baum took the ancient themes whispered in mountain lore and populated his world with a resolute, pragmatic heroine who faced adversity with a pioneering spirit. She had to dig deep within to find inner resources like independence, strength, and courage. It was a land full of hope over the rainbow that oddly also included murdering wizards, wicked witches, winged monkeys, and nightmarish insects.

It was, in short, an American fairy tale.

Baum's parents had met in the hardy community of New Woodstock, upstate New York, that was full of relocated Revolutionary War veterans and Scots-Irish families that had arrived fifty years before. The Baum's seventh child would never be as robust as the rebellious locals. Timid and too weak to play, he relied on his imagination for places and playmates. He read British fairy tales since there weren't any American tales at the time, but they just gave him nightmares.

His father Benjamin, a one-time barrel maker who struck it rich in the oil business, sent his whimsical son to military school hoping to toughen him up. Instead the young Baum, suffering either a heart attack or a nervous breakdown, had to be brought home where his parents nurtured his creative talent with the gift of a small printing press. By fifteen he was writing and publishing his own small newspaper called *The Rose Lawn Home Journal* with his younger brother Harry. The paper was a local success with its articles, editorials, fiction, poetry, and word games. Some local stores even bought advertising space from the boys.

As he got older he added acting to his repertoire and married Maud Gage, the strong-minded daughter of a nationally known suffragist and abolitionist. With the birth of their first child, Baum gave up acting and settled down in Syracuse to work as a salesman in the family business. Unfortunately it put a great strain on his health, which had already been weakened by a heart attack in his early twenties. When his father died, a clerk managed the business by gambling away the family fortune. Baum returned from a sales trip one day, walked into the office, and found the clerk's body sprawled across the desk, with his revolver still in his hand. Maud decided it was time to head west.

Settling in the Dakota territories in 1888, Baum opened a general store that he named "Baum's Bazaar." The store was always crowded with children who bought a penny's worth of candy just to hear him tell stories of faraway places and enchanted lands. But two years later a drought pushed the area's settlers into dire poverty, and unable to deny them credit for necessities, Baum's Bizarre went bankrupt.

As he walked the streets of their little town, children still stopped him and asked for a story. He sat down on the edge of the sidewalk and spun tales of magic countries, told fairy tales about a land called Oz, and recited the Mother Goose rhymes. Although she was never particularly impressed by her whimsical son-in-law, Maud's mother overheard his stories and suggested he publish them. He started writing all his ideas down, and in 1897 his collection called *Mother Goose in Prose* was published.

The family moved to a cottage on Lake Michigan where Baum, who was recovering from an attack of facial paralysis, took up woodworking and made furniture by hand, stenciled with geese, while writing a story he used to tell neighborhood children—the first true American fairy tale called *The Wonderful Wizard of Oz*.

In any good Old World fairy tale the mythological hero sets forth from his castle on a noble quest. In American mythology Dorothy, the everyday, all-American heroine, was involuntarily whisked away in the family cabin from the scorched Kansas wasteland by a cyclone. Her quest started when she flattened the Wicked Witch of the East under her cabin

when it landed in Oz. Oz is uncivilized terrain, overrun with witches and sorcerers, filled with murderous schemes of the Wizard, cruelty of the Wicked Witch, and attacks by hideous creatures. In essence, it wasn't the land of gallant European princes and castles on hills—it was the lawless, hardy, self-reliant American frontier.

On her quest to find the Wizard of Oz to ask him to send her home, Dorothy meets characters typical of the frontier landscape: a woodman turned into a Tin Man without a heart, a mountain lion turned Cowardly Lion without courage, and an everyday field scarecrow without a brain. In her conversations, Dorothy begins to emerge as a distinct American heroine full of plucky American pragmatism—the antithesis of her passive English cousin in *Alice in Wonderland*.

> "Do you think" asked [the scarecrow], "if I go to the Emerald City with you, that the great Oz would give me some brains?"
>
> "I cannot tell," [Dorothy] returned; "but you may come with me, if you like. If Oz will not give you any brains, you will be no worse off than you are now."[20]

The characters are propelled along on their journey to find the Wizard of Oz, whom they hope can grant them the highly regarded frontier qualities of courage, independent thinking, a stalwart heart, and self-reliance. As expected in any self-respecting American fairy tale, there is no benevolent king or welfare state; they are forced to develop these qualities in themselves when the Wizard turns out to be little more than a frontier trickster villain.

> "You have no right to expect me to send you back to Kansas unless you do something for me in return," [said the Wizard]. "In this country everyone must pay for everything he gets. If you wish me to use my magic power to send you home again you must do something for me first. Help me and I will help you."
>
> "What must I do?" asked the girl.
>
> "Kill the Wicked Witch of the West," answered Oz.[21]

This new desolate frontier is populated by winged monkeys that are controlled by the witch. No sooner do the heroes arrive than they are set upon by the Winkies and brought to the witch, who forces Dorothy into a Cinderella role as punishment for refusing to relinquish her magic slippers. But Dorothy was no more fit to play Cinderella than she was to play Alice. Like any self-respecting American heroine, she follows the example of her ancestors—she revolts.

> This made Dorothy so very angry that she picked up the bucket of water that stood near and dashed it over the Witch.
>
> Witch began to shrink into a putrid pile on the ground.
>
> "See what you have done!" she screamed. "In a minute, I shall melt away . . .[22]

In the end of course, the Wizard of Oz did nothing. The age-old struggle between good and evil, courage and cowardice, democracy and autocracy was won by the heroes on their own merits. In true frontier-inspired style, they were forced to rely on themselves: the Cowardly Lion finds the courage to lop the head off a giant spider that was menacing the forest, the Tin Man earns his heart, the Scarecrow finds his brain, and Dorothy returns to a more colorful-looking Kansas.

Baum continued to write Oz-related adventures for the rest of his life. Ten years and five sequels after its first publication, the Baums moved to California hoping it would be better for his fragile health. He fell into an easy routine of gardening in the morning, writing in the afternoons, and answering letters from devoted fans. Unfortunately the California sunshine wasn't the magic elixir he hoped it would be, and before long he was bedridden and in constant pain from angina and seizures. Propped up with pillows, he continued to write another twelve sequels to his original fairy tale. Tears often streamed down his face onto the wet paper, yet he never lost his sense of wonder or his optimism.

"I have lived long enough to learn that in life nothing adverse lasts very long," he wrote his son who was fighting in World War I. "And it is true that as years pass, and we look back on something which, at that time, seemed unbelievably discouraging and unfair. The eventual outcome was, we discover, by far the best solution for us."[23]

On May 6, 1919, Baum, in a semi-comatose state whispered to Maud, "Now we can cross the Shifting Sands" and slipped out of this world, leaving behind the first real American fairy tale.

An Assault on the Nerves

The plucky American hero was about be hurled back into nightmarish scenes that had once unfolded in Poe's exotic but macabre landscapes. There would be no cyclone to whisk the hero off to a magical land. In the hands of a self-mythologizing, literary giant of a Scots-Irishman, the new American hero was a decaying remnant of a desolate world.

The first Mississippi Falkner walked into a den of Scots-Irish renegades thirty miles east of Oxford, Mississippi, in 1838 at the age of thirteen. William C. Falkner, penniless and on the run from his own family after half-scalping his brother, arrived in search of an uncle who was in a local jailhouse awaiting trial for murder. The uncle was acquitted and later prospered as a lawyer. He reared his wandering nephew until the youngster became a local legend in his own right, when he helped to capture an ax murderer and averted his own lynching. His exploits skirmishing with *guerillios* in the Mexican War added to the myth of William C. Falkner, as did his marriage to an heiress upon his return. During the Civil War, while Twain was napping on guard duty, William C. was forming his own regiment and was elected colonel, only to be demoted later for arrogance.

Colonel William C. Falkner returned from the war to find the land ravaged, railroads and bridges destroyed, and whole cities virtually razed to the ground. Confederate money and bonds were worthless, and the majority of slaveholders didn't have the capital to turn their plantations into working farms. Defeat, poverty, and postwar industrialization were relegating the South to a sort of Northern colony, devoid of political power and subject to unfair taxation. Twain predicted it would take three generations before the South realized the full effect of what had been wreaked on its character and terrain, and that realization fell to the third generation of Falkners.

In 1897 the colonel's grandson, William Faulkner (he added the "u") of Oxford, Mississippi, followed in the ancestral footsteps to do the family's notoriety proud. Barefoot and in overalls, with a mule and a fishing rod, he looked more like a boy from Tom Sawyer's gang than his wayward forebears. He was his mother's favorite, poetic and artistic; he had lots of friends and was really only interested in fishing and fun.

Mississippi however was no more an idyll than Twain's Hannibal. Faulkner was surrounded by the white man's lingering fear that black people were becoming bestial. Faulkner was only eleven when he first heard the whooping cheers and the piteous pleas of a lynching not far from his house, and then the days of creaking silence as the corpse swayed from the tree in the Southern wasteland.

The hard-drinking, hard-living Faulkner, who stood just less than five and a half feet, was rejected by the U.S. Air Force during the First World War. Refusing to have his personal hero myth stymied, he turned up at the Royal Canadian Air Force with a couple of forged letters of recommendation and a fake British accent. A clerical typo apparently added the "u" to his name. The war ended before he saw any action, but that didn't stop him from limping home with a mythical plate in his head having been shot down in France. It was the first of many tall tales he told to create a Faulkner mystique.

"Hell," said his uncle, a local judge upon his wayward nephew's return. "He ain't ever going to amount to a damn—not a damn."[24]

And so Faulkner set about proving his uncle right. He got a job in the local post office. The mail came and went, usually slowly and sometimes not at all. When he wasn't writing his own masterpieces, he was holding card games. He failed to deliver holiday hams; he kept magazines until he'd read them; and he closed down early to play golf. One friend described him as "the damnedest postmaster the world has ever seen."

In the summer of 1922, he sent a manuscript to a publisher in Boston. Ironically the rejection letter took six months to make its way through the Mississippi mail.

"Dammit," he said when it finally arrived. "I'll write a book they'll read. If they want a book to remember, by God I'll write it."[25]

In 1929 true to his word, he published "the most horrific tale I could imagine." *Sanctuary* was a crime thriller that dragged all the skeletons out of the Southern closet: the family secrets, violence, sexual depravity, psychopathic bootleggers, corrupt officials, lynch mobs, and the fall of an heiress from grace. Appealing to the national penchant for the horrors perpetrated by the average man, and by stirring the genetic memories of frontier atrocities, it became a bestseller known by critics as "a cold-blooded assault on the nerve-ends." [26]

That same year he had convinced Estelle Oldham—the unrequited love of his high-school days—to be his wife. She tried to drown herself on their wedding night. Then things got worse.

Faulkner spawned the New American Gothic—a literary tradition that personified a defeated society turning to the myth of the past. He created a mythical land called Yoknapatawpha County, some place in Mississippi, and populated it with a cast of confused, dysfunctional characters caught in the crosshairs of history not knowing how to move forward and unable to go back. It was a grand tumultuous world, using bizarre, grotesque, and violent imagery along with corrupt and decaying characters, all wrapped up in an unforgiving Gothic atmosphere burdened with history. This was the South where he said "the past is not dead, it is not even the past."

At its center was the grand symbol of the Southern myth, the plantation house set in "the blood-heat of a long hot summer against miasmal swamps, live oak, Spanish moss."[27] Into this horrifying, degenerate world, he moved himself and Estelle in the spring of 1930. He bought a dilapidated house, one of the many carcasses of former plantation homes that had become symbolic of Southern ruin. The roof leaked, the supporting timbers were rotten; there was no electricity or plumbing. Estelle, who was used to a life of affluence, sat down on the front porch and cried.

A few months later, his novella *As I Lay Dying* was published. It received critical acclaim and was respectfully donned a "twenty-one-gun salute to the absurd,"[28] in which the new American hero entered the story already dead. The recently deceased heroine Addie Bundren takes revenge on her family—particularly her husband, whom she believed tricked her into marriage long ago—by instructing them to bury her with her own kin forty miles away, not with his kin four miles down the road.

Like with Poe's mad hero Cornelius Wyatt, who went to his watery death clinging to his wife's coffin, the Bundrens undertake a ten-day odyssey that includes dangerous river crossings in which two sons almost drown. Another son later sets fire to a barn where Addie's body is being stored, while yet another risks his life to save her from the flames. He would be a hero in any other myth except this one, since the victim is already dead. The stench of her corpse attracts a flock of buzzards that follow them all the way to her grave. In the end, she is buried in her requested resting place. Her husband buys a new set of teeth and gets a new wife; the arsonist son is escorted to an asylum; and the rest of the family sits around eating bananas like monkeys.

After the publication of *As I Lay Dying*, Faulkner was invited into the New York literary scene, where he said he was received like "some strange and valuable beast." At a dinner party when a polite man pulled a dining chair out to seat one of the women, she unwittingly fell to the floor where she stayed in a state of morbid humiliation. Faulkner sat down on the floor beside her and the party went on.

For all his charm, Faulkner was unsettled. The violent tendencies of his bloodline progressively manifested in his writings, and he turned to alcohol for reprieve from his own demons. When Tennessee Williams saw him soon after his descent began, the playwright was startled.

"He looked slowly up, and his eyes were so incredibly sad that I, being a somewhat emotional person, began to cry uncontrollably,"[29] Williams said. "I have never seen such sad eyes on a human face."[30]

By thirty-eight, Faulkner's drinking was excessive. He was worried about money. Estelle lived extravagantly, he was also supporting his three insolvent brothers, who all together spent more than he could earn. He started having an affair. Estelle came after him with a mallet, but his drinking and philandering just escalated.

His descent into darkness reached its nadir in 1936, when he wrote his Gothic masterpiece that exploded the Southern myth of gentility and old-order stability, exposing instead the horrors of miscegenation, incest, fratricide, murder, and oppression. *Absalom, Absalom!* was partly inspired by the guilt of the Faulkner family's temporary slave ownership, and the protagonist is loosely based on his legendary ancestor, the "Old Colonel." Told by four narrators, none of whom have all the facts, the storytelling reflects the incertitude of a society trapped by its own history.

"This is damned confusing," noted his editor on the first chapter.

The hero of the saga, Thomas Supten, son of an itinerant alcoholic sharecropper who is patronized by members of the "slavocracy" in his youth, devises a plan to join them. He marries a plantation heiress in the West Indies, but abandons her and his son when he discovered she has black blood. He arrives in Mississippi with a gang of Haitian slaves, a French architect, and his wife's money to build a monstrous plantation. He marries into a respectable family in Yoknapatawpha County and has two children. His dream of a perfect order is realized. However, having built this perfect order on a damaging footprint in history, his life soon begins to crumble, and his offspring become murderous, incestuous, and estranged.

Supten returns from the Civil War to find his wife dead, his estate overgrown, his son estranged, his buildings in shambles, and his slaves gone. His life becomes an American nightmare. His white offspring produce no heirs, and his black descendents produce a hulking simpleton called Jim Bond and an illegitimate black daughter who burns down the plantation with everyone in it, save the idiot Jim Bond who runs howling into the forest. In Faulkner's mythology, the South, just like Supten, was destined to destroy itself.

In the summer of 1952, at the age of fifty-five, Faulkner was also destroying himself. He was bored, fed up, and beginning to bitterly resent "seeing what remains of life going to support parasites who do not even have the grace to be sycophants."[31] His editor eventually came to Rowan Oak to see whether the crisis was real or whether it was more a figment of Faulkner's self-mythologizing, melodramatic imagination.

"I found Bill completely deteriorated in mind and body," he wrote to his wife in shock. "He mumbles incoherently . . . He pleads piteously for beer all the time and mumbles deliriously. . . . This is more than a case of acute alcoholism. It is a complete disintegration of a man."[32]

Faulkner wasn't alone in his deterioration. Rowan Oak, the house he had hoped to pluck from the annals of decrepit history, had returned to its state of crumbling decay. He was rattling around in empty rooms like his depraved heroes Roderick Usher and Henry Supten.

In the summer of 1962, while staying in a sanitarium, he sat up on the side of his bed, groaned, and fell over dead from a heart attack. Estelle and his nephew squabbled over the funeral arrangements. In an ironic parallel with Addie Bundren that he probably would have enjoyed, Faulkner was traipsed across the town square to the undertaker and back to the house a couple of times. Eventually the matter was settled, and the hearse rolled slowly away from his decaying mansion, passed the courthouse where his grandfather defended criminals, and was finally laid to rest at St. Peter's Cemetery, Oxford, Mississippi.

A new generation of heroes, bred from the imagination of Scots-Irish scribes and born of the ever-changing American terrain, were about to take the helm.

Horror and the Atomic Age

"We were fertile ground for the seeds of terror, we war babies; we had been raised in a strange circus atmosphere of paranoia, patriotism, and national hubris," the heir apparent to Scots-Irish tales of horror wrote in the early 1980s.[33]

Stephen King was only two years old when, in 1949 his father walked out of their home in Portland, Maine, for a pack of cigarettes and never came back. For the next nine years his mother, who was a talented pianist with an eccentric sense of humor, tramped the family around the country, shacking up with relatives, taking on a few jobs at a time, but she could never rise above the poverty line.

They eventually settled in Maine with her parents not far from where the Rev. McGregor settled with his weary Scots-Irish flock in 1719. There King stumbled upon boxes of his father's old books that included an H. P. Lovecraft anthology of horror stories. After reading Poe's haunted landscapes and a few editions of *Ripley's Believe It or Not!* King discovered how fine was the line between the fabulous and the humdrum.

"That [Lovecraft] book, courtesy of my departed father," he said, "was my first taste of a world that went deeper than the B-pictures which played at the movies on Saturday afternoon."[34]

With that, the twelve-year-old kid from Small Town, USA, who felt he'd been born an outcast, began churning out thrillers that scared him half to death and started mailing them off to magazines. In high school, he was making copies of his stories on his brother's old printing press and selling them at school until the principal put a stop to it.

"Inside, I felt different and unhappy a lot of times. I felt violent a lot of times," he said. "But not a whole lot of that came out, because in the family I came from, there was a high premium on keeping yourself to yourself . . . and using your handkerchief even if you're on the Titanic and it's going down."[35]

In the mid-1960s at the University of Maine, the strict Republican from a Methodist home became a long-haired radical. Like the character in one of his early stories, he arrived at university with a Goldwater sticker on his car and left with "Richard Nixon Is a War Criminal" stuck to his backpack. After the failure of the Vietnam War, the covertness of the Cold War, and the liberal, radical, excessive, and flamboyant sixties, King began quietly observing the dark side of American life—it surfaced two decades later in a resurrection myth: *Pet Sematary*.

King's heroes turned out to be plagued by the psychological horror that drove Poe and Faulkner's heroes to madness, but to help them tip into insanity a little quicker, King introduced a supernatural element to the story. He let them dabble in evil and tinker with the natural order, but he wouldn't let them wander off into Poe's exotic lands or be propelled over the rainbow by tornados. Like for Faulkner's depraved Southerners, King's evil was underfoot in every small town in America.

Harking back to old Indian Wampas–type myths of the frontier, the protagonist of *Pet Sematary*, Louis Creed, his wife Rachel, and son Gage move to a house near a sacred Micmac Indian burial ground that brings corpses back from the dead. When their cat is run over by a car, Creed tests the myth by burying the feline in the cemetery only to find it wandering home, sullen, irritable, smelly, and controlled by the Wendigo—the malevolent cannibalistic spirit from Algonquin mythology that controlled the cemetery. Shortly afterward, Creed's two-year-old son Cage is run over by a truck, so he buries the toddler in the ground. The next day, possessed by the Wendigo, the child comes fresh from his grave with his burial suit covered in moss and his hair caked in dirt to visit their neighbor. With one eye on the poor man and the other looking to the wall.

"Hello, Jud," Gage piped in a babyish but perfectly understandable voice. "I've come to send your rotten, stinking old soul straight to hell."[36]

King, the new custodian of the American Gothic that started in the mountain South, was developing the tradition on scraps of paper he found strewn around the library where he worked to support himself at college. There he met his future wife, Tabitha, who described his poverty in a way only his mountain ancestors could truly understand.

"Talk about going to college poor . . . " Tabitha recalled. "This guy was going to college the way people did in the twenties and thirties. He had nothing to eat, he had no money, he had no clothes; it was just incredible that anybody was going to school under those circumstances, and even more incredible that he didn't care."[37]

They were married in the winter of 1971 and started out on a life together in a trailer on the top of a snow-covered hill in Hermon, Maine. He sold an occasional story, but none of his novels were being published, and he couldn't earn enough to pay the bills. Then their old Buick gave out in the middle of winter. To his wife's chagrin, he took refuge in alcohol. Finally they had to call the phone company to remove the phone.

"If anyone should ever ask you, Hermon, Maine . . . if it is not the pits, it is very close," he said. "Having the phone taken out was our one pitiful act of defiance that year. It was quitting before the Credit Department fired us."[38]

In the winter of 1973 with his wife's encouragement, he told a modern Cinderella story about the shy daughter of an alcoholic mother who was teased mercilessly in school. Instead of her being the long-suffering heroine of fairy tales, King created an outcast who used her newly discovered telekinetic powers to kill her mother and burn down the school with everyone in it for causing her torment. *Carrie* was published in 1974, and a film version was released in 1976. King was hurled into literary stardom, the rags-to-riches embodiment of the American dream.

"I live in Bangor, Maine, which is not a town calculated to make anybody feel famous," he said. "The only claim to fame is a big plastic statue of Paul Bunyan."[39]

It's appropriate that his hometown stands in the shadow of the mythological lumberjack of folklore. Bangor, situated on land rich in

Indian lore, is covered in the same scrappy mountain soil that spawned a culture obsessed with horror, suspense, science fiction, and fantasy. King himself was battling demons in the terrifying isolation of rural Maine where nature seemed to be at odds with God. He'd been drinking heavily long before he acknowledged his alcoholism in 1975. Tabitha organized an intervention, so he quit the booze and was spared the fate of Poe and Faulkner. King decided to channel his fatal flaw into the protagonist of his most widely acclaimed novel—the caretaker of a haunted hotel who is driven insane by demons.

At the center of *The Shining* is a return to the big house—or in this case an off-season hotel—the domain of the Gothic nightmare that swallowed Roderick Usher and burned all Henry Supten's descendents save the simpleton. As the literary history of the Scots-Irish scribe teaches—where the decaying house presides, there is usually a depraved mind or depraved morals that is easily manipulated by the malevolent forces from without. In the Overlook Hotel it was the alcoholic, disgraced teacher and aspiring writer Jack Torrance, who had taken the job of the hotel's winter caretaker and moved in with his wife Wendy and his psychic son Danny.

The hotel stifles Jack's creative flow, amplifies his violent tendencies, drives him to the brink of madness, and gets him drunk on supernatural liquor. His wife temporarily halts his murdering rampage by locking him up in a storage room, but unlike the hasty interment of Madeline Usher, there was nothing poetic about Torrance's confinement.

"Let me out of here!" Jack raged. . . .

"You mind your daddy, Danny! You do what I say! You do it or I'll give you a hiding you'll never forget. *Open this door or I'll bash your fucking brains in!*"[40]

In the atomic age, there were no ethereal swoons or death by terror: Jack battered his wife with a mallet; she stabbed him in the back. After Wendy and Danny escape, the Overlook explodes with Jack inside, crumbling with the same macabre drama as the houses of Supten and Usher.

The New American Mythology

"Once the atomic bomb came, everybody got into monsters and science ... they forgot the fairy tales," lamented George Lucas in the mid-1970s.[41] "There was no modern mythology to give kids a sense of values, to give them a strong mythological fantasy life."[42]

George Lucas—the all-American progeny of mainly Scots-Irish, English and German bloodlines—set out to remedy the deficiency by creating a mythology for a new millennium. As Baum had created a fairy tale devoid of the horrors of goblins in 1900, Lucas created a modern fairy tale based on age-old themes that have their roots deep in American popular culture: a mythic hero, a warrior-wizard, a brave princess, and a monstrous villain. He created the new generation's *Wizard of Oz*.

He was born with dark hair and big ears in a small farming town just outside San Francisco that clung to the Scots-Irish values of duty, morality, hard work, fairness, honesty, and faith in God. His father ran the family's store that sold office supplies and toys. His mother managed the household and her four children. The housekeeper, Till, read him children's stories and played records for him until he was about four. By six, he was still small for his age and bullied at school.

"My strongest impression was that I was always on the lookout for the evil monster that lurked around the corner," he recalled.[43]

He shared toys from the shelves of his father's shop like water pistols and trains with his friends. They put together backyard carnivals with the neighborhood pets and created far-off worlds complete with miniature cities and farms and houses. He read "Huck Finn sorts of things," watched westerns, and loved historical stories about real people who changed the world. Then at six he had a mystical experience when he went to a German Lutheran church with Till, and for the first time he asked: what is God?

As a teenager he let his hair grow, cruised around town in his tiny Fiat, looked for drag races, hung out with his "greaser" friends, and racked up a stack of speeding tickets. His older sister called him a "total loss," but that changed in 1962 when a Chevy Impala barreled into him at an intersection. His Fiat rolled several times; his seatbelt snapped, and he was thrown from the car. He was bleeding profusely from a gash in his head, his heartbeat was faint, and he was turning blue by the time the ambulance arrived.

The accident changed his life.

"It made me apply myself more, because I realized more than anything else what a thin thread we hang on in life, and I really wanted to make something out of my life."[44]

When his father gave him an 8-mm-film camera, he sparked a passion that led Lucas to the University of Southern California film program. George Sr. wasn't happy, but his son declared he would never go into the family office supply business and stormed off to film school.

He graduated in 1966 in the shadow of the Vietnam War with little going for him except for his love of storytelling and a determination to break into the movie business. Describing himself and his friends as "beggars and scroungers," they decided to form a collective to help each other make it and survive.

His was a belief in a throwback to the frontier sense of community—survival by unity in a common purpose—that was antithetical to the self-aggrandizement that seemed to have emerged during the space race and Cold War era. Unfortunately, there was no frontier legend like Davy Crockett, or swashbuckler like Errol Flynn; there wasn't even a Dorothy. Movies pointed out the terrible mess the country had made and how Vietnam was wrong. He saw kids without a sense of myth or magic and watched the westerns and pirate movies die. Someone needed to renew the country's sense of wonder, its time-honored love of adventure and adventurers. In 1977 Lucas responded with an old-fashioned coming-of-age fairy tale updated for the new frontier of the space age. "Once upon a time . . ." became "A long time ago in a galaxy far, far away . . ."

In that galaxy, Lucas introduced pioneering special effects technology and reconstructed a fairy-tale future out of the usable pieces of the past. Dorothy became another orphan in a desert wasteland with dreams of going "over the rainbow." The crystal ball became a holographic message, and the transporting tornado, a spaceship. A Jedi knight replaced the Good Witch of the North as the hero's protector, the witch's castle became a planet-destroying Death Star. Friends like the Tin Man, Scarecrow, and Cowardly Lion were replaced with a pair of robots and an alien called Chewbacca. A plucky princess and a character inspired by westerns—a gun-toting, rebellious Han Solo—rounded out the hero's companions.

Like Dorothy, the hero Luke Skywalker, is a farm boy from an arid desert planet who finds himself thrust into the middle of a galactic war. With his newfound friends, he faces off against the dark side of the force:

Darth Vader, the evil emperor, and an army of storm troopers who operate out of the all-powerful Death Star. The struggle between the courage and cowardice, good and evil of frontier lore was now fought on an intergalactic scale. The entire universe is menaced, and the characters must call on their own latent strengths in its defense.

The new all-American hero begins as an ordinary person who undergoes great challenges and eventually masters the skills needed to confront aliens and dark creatures. Age-old American values like courage, loyalty, and honor are essential to survival. Although he has help from allies and teachers, Luke like any self-respecting frontier hero must ultimately rely on himself to find the resources needed to fulfill his destiny.

The galactic battle is paralleled by a psychological struggle that culminates in a duel between Luke, and his father Darth Vader, the good knight gone to the dark side. Unlike Dorothy who melts her nemesis, Luke refuses to surrender to anger and vengeance that would lead him irrevocably to the dark side. Luke destroys evil—at least for the moment; the rebels destroy the Death Star, and peace is restored to the universe.

"One of the basic motifs in fairy tales is that you find the poor and unfortunate along the side of the road, and when they beg for help, if you give it to them, you end up succeeding," Lucas said of themes of good and evil, reward and retribution, that have echoed down the mountains since the first Scots-Irish rambled down the Great Wagon Road. "If you don't give it to them, you end up being turned into a frog or something. It's something that's been around for thousands of years. . . . It is even more necessary today." [45]

CHAPTER 10

THE NEW FRONTIER

Bob Socks was bursting with patriotic pride. At three a.m., he pushed through the crowds to his new orange juice stand in Titusville, Florida, across the bay from Cape Canaveral. Hordes of eyewitness hopefuls had besieged this little town three full days before liftoff. A million people packed into every conceivable spot where a car could park or a tent could be pitched. They rented bits of land from enterprising farmers who capitalized on the most extraordinary event in the history of mankind.

Socks was a teenager working for a New York newspaper when the story broke that the Russians launched the first satellite into space. For years he watched the Soviets inflicting one humiliating defeat after the other in the race to the moon. America needed some good news.

At five a.m., it already promised to be a blistering hot day. Socks was besieged by throngs of hot, thirsty customers retreating into the air-conditioned mall to get a drink and cool down. Outside, the Florida swamplands were swarming with hungry mosquitoes. People set up chairs in the cool, watery inlets, unaware that alligators were slithering around nearby. The party had already started; the cacophony of radio stations and the buzzing of helicopters amplified the excitement of the morning. People set up umbrellas, picnic hampers, ice chests, and telescopes. Everyone clustered around the cars that had a working radio, to listen in on the running commentary as events unfolded inside the Kennedy Space Center. A few boys climbed on top of the portable toilets; an old woman inside yelled at them to get off, but no one paid any attention.

Dr. Ralph Abernathy—successor to the late Dr. Martin Luther King— arrived with a hundred people and a mule to protest the poverty that racked the nation, especially the black communities, while billions were being poured into the space race.

"We are here to say that what we do for space we must do for the starving poor people" he told Tom Paine, the NASA administrator who responded by giving him forty VIP badges. "We may be black, but we're somebody, we feel we're VIPs too."[1]

Across the heartland, farmers stopped working, fishermen waited on wharfs. In Wapakoneta, Ohio, hometown of mission commander Neil Armstrong, the streets were empty; everyone was glued to their TV sets. In the small town of Enniskillen in the north of Ireland, where some of the Armstrong clan's most notorious ancestors lived in the 1600s, neighbors thronged into each other's houses to listen to the radio. Everyone had gone Neil mad. Even the French, who gloated when Soviet space technology humiliated America, wrote that this day "was the greatest adventure in the history of humanity."

At T minus 17, Socks closed his orange juice stand and ran outside where people clustered around radios were counting down in a million-man chorus.

"Twelve, eleven, ten, nine, ignition sequence starts . . . ," they heard Jack King, NASA's public affairs officer broadcast.

"You could feel the excitement," said Socks like a kid who could hardly contain his delight. "The first people to leave earth to actually go to the moon. I mean you can't even imagine how exciting it is. It's incredible! And the Saturn V rocket? The biggest rocket ever!"

" . . . two, one, zero, all engine running," crackled King from the Cape.

No one had any idea how spectacular the Saturn V launch would be: how the thundering F-1 engines would erupt into massive orange flames and black smoke that billowed three-hundred feet high and swirled out across the Cape, or how the ground would shake for almost three miles. The tip of the rocket emerged from the smoke cloud and cleared the launchpad before the crowds even realized Jack King had said:

"We have a liftoff, 32 minutes past the hour. Liftoff on *Apollo 11*."

Everyone burst into cheers.

"People were crying, people from all over the world," Socks choked. "People singing the Star Spangled Banner, it was very emotional."

Inside the capsule, millions of events were happening, switches, buttons, valves had to work to bring this command module and the astronauts back home to the Earth safely. Outside, the whole country was bursting with pride.

"We needed Apollo to be successful," said Socks, remembering the litany of assassinations at home and disastrous news from Vietnam that reverberated through the country the year before. "We needed the success."[2]

Across the bay, people in the VIP bleachers—the politicians, science community, and NASA foot soldiers—chattered and congratulated each other. One man hovered in the shadowy background. He had built America's space empire; he was the power behind Apollo; he rallied a discouraged nation during the worst of times and moved it to a new frontier. He was one of the greatest Americans ever, yet almost no one knew his name.

With his mission accomplished, James E. Webb left the Cape and went home.

Igniting the Space Race

It started with an innocuous little beep. Behind high fortress walls, stuck in the middle of a dilapidated complex of hangars and factories, a handsome fifty-year-old man was working in his sparse, freezing office. He put on his lucky suit, walked into a small control room, and launched an R-7 intercontinental ballistic missile with a little satellite on top. The R-7 took off; the engines suffered a whole host of malfunctions and then flew out of communication range, but four thousand miles away radio operators picked up its beep-beep-beep high above the earth.

The phone rang in President Nikita Khrushchev's office.

"The Soviet Union," the man in the lucky suit told him, "has just put the world's first artificial satellite into space around the earth."[3]

Initially no one grasped the magnitude of his accomplishment. There was no hype or excitement or press coverage. The Soviet news agency put out a simple understatement:

"As a result of very intensive work by scientific research institutes and design bureaus, the first artificial satellite in the world has been created. On October 4, 1957, this first satellite was successfully launched by the USSR."[4]

It didn't even have a name; it was just called "simple satellite," or *Sputnik*.

Word buzzed around the world. In the United States, scientists were dumbstruck and political leaders shaken. Moscow milked the propaganda for everything it was worth.

"Our sputniks are circling the world," Khrushchev gloated. "America sleeps under a Soviet moon."

It was the height of the Cold War, and everyone believed that control of space meant control of the world. Khrushchev blustered that Soviet missiles could be fitted with atomic and hydrogen warheads. He told small countries that America could no longer protect them and perhaps it was time to reevaluate their loyalties. A duped British press bolstered the propaganda by writing that the Soviets could hit any target with ballistic missiles—and as if having *Sputnik's* impudent beeps raining down on the United States wasn't enough—the French reminded the world that the Americans "have little experience with humiliation in the technical domain."

In the United States, President Dwight D. Eisenhower made hollow assurances to diffuse national anxiety, saying that while *Sputnik* represented "an achievement of the first importance . . . the all-over military strength of the Free World is strictly greater than that of the Communist countries."[5]

The Soviet space czar, known only as the Chief Designer, watched the condescension, gloating, and paranoia peddling from the shadows. He had been relegated to remote and deplorable conditions at a makeshift launch facility in Siberia for fear he'd be appropriated or assassinated by the Americans. The Chief Designer kept working with his team to trump his first victory by sending a dog up in a satellite six times the size of the first. The phrase "missile gap" began to appear with the Americans on the losing end.

Unlike the Soviets, no one was driving the U.S. space effort. The armed forces were squabbling over their satellite programs. After World War II, the army had appropriated Werner Von Braun, the thirty-four-year-old German rocket scientist who had terrorized the south of England with flying bombs he invented for Hitler. Von Braun had muscled ahead with the development of a Jupiter intercontinental ballistic missile rocket. Eisenhower was loath to look like a warmonger and chose the navy's scientific rocket, the Vanguard, as America's first space launch.

The navy was horrified—they were nowhere near ready for the glare of the international press. In December 1957, reporters and TV cameras clamored to witness their momentous launch. The navy tried to play the event down as a test, but no one paid them any attention. The Vanguard and its little payload sat out on a lonely pad. The countdown was smooth; the rocket ignited, lifted off, faltered, fell back onto the pad in a crumple, then exploded into a brilliant orange ball of fire and smoke. Its little satellite rolled away and could be heard beeping somewhere off in the distance.

"Oh what a flopnik," the headlines read. The British called it a "Kaputnik." At the United Nations, Russian delegates glibly suggested the Americans take advantage of a Soviet program offering technical assistance to backward nations. It was a national disaster.

On St. Patrick's Day in 1958—after a series of crumples and half-cocked blastoffs—a Vanguard made it into orbit and sent back blurry distorted pictures of the Earth. It was a resounding first for America. The Russians, cut the celebrations short with the launch of *Sputnik 3*, an automatic scientific laboratory that transmitted data back like a workhorse, putting the Vanguard's fuzzy pictures to shame.

Eisenhower had had enough. He created a full-fledged civilian space agency out of the remnants of an old aviation committee, several satellite programs, a few labs, lunar probes, and Defense Department rocket engines. Von Braun was wrestled away from the army, and the new National Aeronautics and Space Administration or NASA was born.

For the next three years, however, NASA was battered by the Soviet space czar. Then one man came along to transform NASA from a vulnerable agency into a space empire, capable of vanquishing the Russian technological onslaught. He was one of the most dynamic, visionary, and mysterious political operators America had ever known.

The Fastest Mouth in the South

Little is known about how the Webb patriarch got out of Ireland, and no one really knew exactly how all the disparate branches of the Webb family in North Carolina were related. Some say the patriarch landed in the wilderness of Chuckatuck, Virginia, after sailing out of England sometime before 1667. What is known is that by the mid-1800s, Webbs were living in the Scots-Irish bulwark of Tally Ho, North Carolina—a stop on the road to the state capital at Hillsborough where stagecoaches changed and watered their horses. At the outbreak of the Civil War, four Webbs, including First Lieutenant Thomas Shappard Webb, entered Confederate service. Two were killed; Thomas was taken prisoner at the Battle of Corinth and sent to Johnson's Island prison on the coast of Lake

Erie. He was exchanged after the surrender and went on to become a frontier lawman.

In 1906, when James E. Webb was born, Tally Ho had burgeoned into a neighborhood of three houses. His uncle ran the family farm. His father was a scholar and an ideas man who carried little cards around in his pocket with quotes from Greek or Roman intellectuals or from his favorite philosopher-poet Ralph Waldo Emerson. He gave them out at the post office or to people he met on his travels. This obsession with education and organization developed as a child when he went to the Webb School in Tennessee, a school run by the distant relative, and famous disciplinarian, Old Sawney Webb. If boys tried to run away, Old Sawney could chase them down and whip them in the fields. By the time Webb Sr. graduated, he had Latin, Greek, and English whipped into his head and was a staunch advocate for education reform.

The Webbs may have been better educated than the other Scots-Irish families in the rural backcountry, but they were still a normal, rural Presbyterian family: churchgoing, neighborly, hard-working, and doggedly self-reliant. Young Webb spent his childhood delivering papers, selling magazines, and odd-jobbing around farms, nickel-and-dime stores, and construction sites trying to help the family make ends meet. He was a sociable child, always eager to please, full of energy and volubility, and confident enough even as a ten-year-old to chat with his customers on his paper round because it was good business.

Webb's father was a progressive thinker who, as superintendent of schools, worked hard to improve society through education. His uncle instilled in the boy a keen sense of competitiveness and inspired him with a desire to live a "large life" in which he could devote himself to something greater than himself. Webb came to believe he was destined to make America better through education. Growing up to be a sturdy youth with dark hair and a big smile, he scraped up enough money to go to the University of North Carolina where he studied like a man obsessed.

Unfortunately, his dreams were cut short by the Crash of 1929 that devastated their little town. Farms and businesses collapsed, unemployment was rampant, and the South looked at a bleak future of hunger and hopelessness. Webb saw an advertisement for jobs with a reserve force of aviators in the Marine Corps in New York. He knew nothing about the marines or aviation, but he applied, and to his surprise was accepted.

So at twenty-three with his destiny to become education czar thwarted by economic desperation, he set off for a new adventure.

Right away and perhaps for the first time in his life, the charming, verbose Webb felt inadequate. He was a rough-hewn Scots-Irish kid from a backcountry of farmers and outlaws now surrounded by athletic Ivy Leaguers. His Southern charm and outgoing personality eventually prevailed as he discovered that despite his down-home accent and country ways, he had a knack for blending into any situation and excelling. He thrived in the Marine Corps. He discovered he loved flying and the sense of common purpose. At twenty-four he was no longer the poor kid driving construction trucks and slopping hogs; he was a smartly dressed, educated pilot on active duty.

"That was the first place, I think, that I realized I could compete with the wealthy fellows from Harvard and Princeton and so forth," he said. "I started at the very bottom, just getting by."[6]

Two years later, as if by cosmic design, the sequence of events that would lead to a large life began to unfold rapidly; he went to study law in Washington where a chance meeting landed him a job as secretary to a powerful North Carolina congressman. In his new job he absorbed everything he could about the nuts and bolts of political deal making and was inspired to see President Roosevelt's New Deal transform a nation.

In 1939 in his early thirties, he joined Sperry Corporation, a demanding, high-tech company that mobilized for the war effort. There he discovered his real talent for leading, managing, and motivating—leading the company through a massive expansion from eight hundred to thirty thousand workers.

"[He] seemed to have his finger on everything," said his assistant. "A very impressive man, he was youthful, confident, and vigorous. He imbued others with confidence."[7]

After the war the poor Southern boy blazed a trail through Washington, first as Under Secretary of the Treasury, then as director of the Bureau of the Budget, and eventually as Under Secretary of State.

"Instead of Harvard and wire-rimmed glasses, clipped accents and dry wit," wrote one political correspondent, "he was of the University of North Carolina and rumpled collars, corn-pone accent and down-home homilies, a good ol' boy with a law degree."[8]

Webb's days of feeling inadequate around better-educated sophisticates were long gone. Now he exploited his rural background, combining his disarming Southern drawl with an avalanche of words that could intimidate or confuse the smartest, strongest, most condescending of them and leave them reeling in a state of bewilderment.

"He'd play that good ol' southern boy 'I just fell off the turnip truck' routine and he was a master at it," said one colleague. "By the time you were finished talking to him, you had agreed to all kinds of things that you'd never conceive of before."[9]

No one knew how he did it, but everyone invariably marched to the beat of his drum. He combined the genteel with intensity and energy. He added, "Do you follow me?" to every other sentence like a nervous twitch. One person said having a conversation with him was "like trying to get information out of a fire hydrant."[10] No one could outtalk or outcajole "the fastest mouth in the south." The poor country kid was one of the most skilled political operators in Washington—nothing could stop him.

Then he got the call he didn't want.

Commanding the American Space Empire

President John F. Kennedy was getting annoyed. Since his inauguration in January 1961, he had every intention of maintaining his dynamic public image, but the brain behind the Russian space program was making him look like a half-wit. Someone had to take the helm, but nobody would accept NASA's top-dog job. Everyone knew that whoever took that job would be riddled with conflicts. They'd report directly to Vice President Lyndon B. Johnson but would essentially have no real political support. Kennedy wanted Webb, but the Scots-Irishman didn't want the job, and there wasn't a man in town that could get him out of this predicament.

The American space empire was a mess. For three years America and Soviets had been lobbing lunar probes into space. The first three American probes didn't get off the pad. A Russian probe came within thirty-seven hundred miles of the moon; America's fourth probe came within a pitiful thirty-seven thousand. The Soviets sent another probe that photographed the dark side of the moon, processed the photos, and sent them back to Earth. It was a technical coup that splashed its way across the international press. The Chief Designer followed up with a Mars fly-by, a Venus impact, and in 1960, he sent two dogs into space and brought them back alive—the first time a living entity left the Earth and returned safely.

Meanwhile, the United States had traumatized a monkey. Ham took off in January 1961; his rocket went off course, a valve opened and let most of the pressurized oxygen out of the capsule, and he was subjected to almost double the expected G-force and weightlessness. He splashed down a hundred miles past the target point and was sinking by the time the navy pulled him to safety. The Science Committee recommended fifty more monkey test flights before letting a human launch.

Monkey cartoons appeared in the papers. In one, a pair of apes landed their capsule and strolled away saying, "I think we're behind the Russians but slightly ahead of the Americans."[11]

That was it! Kennedy decided Webb was the man to take over NASA, and there was nothing more to be said.

"You need a scientist or a engineer," Webb pleaded with the president.

"No, I need somebody who understands policy," Kennedy responded. "You've been Under Secretary of State and Director of the Budget. This program involves great issues of national and international policy, and that's why I want you to do it."[12]

Even the fastest mouth in the South couldn't outmaneuver Kennedy; besides refusing the president was abhorrent to the strong patriotic streak encoded to his bloodline. After assuring him that it wasn't a paper-pushing monkey job and proposing the Southerner present a new space policy, Webb relented. Kennedy's problem was solved—he lit a fat cigar, told an aide to "call in the press," and slipped out the side door.

It was downhill from here. Affairs were much worse than Webb anticipated. Not only had the United States been humiliated by NASA's ineptitude for three years, the Air Force was waiting for a chance to scoop them as the nation's primary space agency. The intelligence community's flow of information was so pitiful they usually found out what the Soviets were up to only when they saw their missiles flying overhead. Then there was the Department of Defense—even Webb's enigmatic charm was lost on the omnipotent Secretary of Defense Robert McNamara, whose negotiating style he said was to "knock you down on the floor with a sledge-hammer, and then, while you're down, ask you to sign off on a particular decision."[13]

Webb needed to imbue the agency with a vision. Something bold was needed to make it appear competent and strong. He buried himself in research, talking to deputies and scientists, reading technical and intelligence reports.

His imagination was teeming with huge ideas while his intellect was assessing the methodology. He wanted to take the Mercury program—NASA's manned space flight program—to the next level. He needed money to build a big booster if they were going to compete with the Soviets. Unfortunately the president wasn't too keen on the price tag. Webb took his bag of dreams and dragged himself back to the office. It was not an auspicious start for the new plan for outer space.

The one area where Webb could exercise his authority was to stop the monkey fight. With his inimitable charm, he convinced the Space Committee and medics that putting a man in a rocket to make a suborbital hop was no more dangerous than putting him in the experimental aircraft he'd flown as a test pilot. They acquiesced and cleared Alan Shepard—one of the seven NASA astronauts trained in 1959—to launch in May. Preflight training jumped into high gear, and America prepared to put the first man in space.

CIA reports showed the Chief Designer might be preparing to launch his own manned capsule. This would leave Webb's new agency in that

NASA Administrator James E. Webb seated in the Gemini rendezvous and docking simulator during an August 7, 1965, visit to the Manned Spacecraft Center. Courtesy of NASA.

intolerable second-place position again. Webb had to find a way to get support fully behind funding a manned space program. But as he mulled over a strategy, he couldn't help but wonder, who was this mysterious Russian, and was he really about to put a man on the moon?

The Chief Designer

He was everyone's favorite, his mother crooned, "this little fellow with long golden locks and dark big eyes."[14] She used to take him on great flights of fantasy on a magic carpet where they imagined all sorts of mystical creatures below; that was before she told him his father was dead, dropped him at his grandparents, and went back to school.

Sergei Pavlovich Korolev's grandparents dressed him neatly and fed him well, which was unusual for a poor child born in a small town in the Ukraine in 1907. He was always lonely and nearly always sad. He spent hours looking up at the silvery moon that peeked out from the small clouds over Odessa. One of his few good memories was of an air show he went to at the age of six that imbued him with a passion for aviation.

In his teens a military seaplane detachment moved into Odessa to protect the coast. After watching them fly overhead, he jumped into the water, swam a considerable distance to the jetty, and hung onto the barbed wire for hours mesmerized by the bustle of work, the sweat and grease and purpose.

"Well what are you hanging around for?"

A mechanic who saw him spying on the detachment broke his trance. The boy shrank back.

"Why don't you give me a hand?" the mechanic yelled. "Can't you see I'm having trouble with this motor?"[15]

Korolev didn't need to be asked twice. He crawled under the wire and got to work. He soon became a regular face around the base. From there he went to technical schools to study aeronautics and, in 1923, found his way into an aircraft design bureau where he started playing with the idea of liquid-fueled rockets. By twenty-five, despite having broken two ribs flying his own experimental glider, he was made chief of one of the earliest state-sponsored centers for rocket development. He was a great designer who also had strong organizational and strategic planning skills. Korolev was on a trajectory toward greatness.

Then along came Stalin's Great Purge to kill his dreams. The government had discovered a correlation between natural science and revolutionary tendencies, and Korolev was accused of collaborating with an anti-soviet organization in Germany. He was tortured to extract a confession and sentenced to ten years' imprisonment in a Siberian gulag.

After five freezing winter months of hard labor, he was recalled to Moscow for a reinvestigation of his case. His fellow inmates collected some clothing for him. He took one last look at their forlorn, blackened faces and set off on foot through the snow to the nearest port where he would take a ship to the mainland. Anyone else in his half-starved state probably wouldn't have survived the trip. A truck finally passed him on the long desolate road. The driver agreed to take him to the port in exchange for his sweater, but when he got there the last ship of the season had left. He had no food or winter clothing. A few days later, however, that ship sank, killing all passengers on board. Korolev was luckier than he knew.

The designer pressed on through the snow until he found a barracks in which to seek shelter. He was discovered and thrown out onto the roadway, exhausted, freezing, and on the point of collapse. Staggering along the path, he came upon a warm loaf of bread sitting in the middle of the remote road. He ate till he got hiccups, then snuck back to the barracks and hid under a bed. For the rest of his life he would wonder from where that loaf magically appeared.

When the spring rolled in, Korolev set sail for the mainland but was thrown off the train to Moscow when they discovered he had scurvy. He could take no more. He lay on the ground depleted, his body was swollen, his gums bleeding, and his teeth were falling out. He was near death when an old man came along and propped him up under a tree facing the sun before disappearing again.

"When I opened my eyes," Korolev said, "I could see something fluttering. It was a butterfly, something on this earth still alive and beautiful. I was alive!"[16]

The old man returned with some herbs to massage his bleeding gums and within a week the designer was well enough to get back on the train to Moscow.

After his harrowing journey, his sentence was only reduced from ten years to eight. He was, however, allowed to serve the next seven and a half years in a prison where he was ordered to work with scientists and engineers on projects assigned by the Communist Party leadership. His new prison was sheer luxury—they had beds in their dormitory, were fed three times a day, and finished work at six so they could go into the yard and see the sky.

When Hitler approached Moscow in 1941, they were shipped back to a bare-bones industrial compound in Siberia where they lived in tents through the freezing winter and the blistering summer. When the war ended, they were all freed, but Korolev stayed in the Siberian compound to continue his rocketry research. But he was no longer the imaginative child who rode magic carpets or the youth who built experimental gliders. He was thirty-eight years old, but life had worn on him heavily. His jaws had set improperly after years of torture and most of his rotten teeth had fallen out. Worst of all, he had become volatile and quick to rage.

He was a "brilliant engineer and organizer and a colorful personality" who dreamed of the cosmos, according to his colleagues, but he was

Artillery Colonel Georgiy Tyulin (left) and Sergey Korolev in Germany in 1946 during the A-4 missile recovery operations. Image from the files of Peter Gorin. Courtesy of NASA.

cunning, ruthless, and cynical. His team was terrified of him, but they all agreed he had an extraordinary aura and an ability to inspire large numbers of people.

Despite their incomparable backgrounds, the lives of Webb and Korolev were remarkably similar. Both were building space empires; both had an ability to mobilize, inspire, and manipulate people. Webb expanded into private contractors, universities, and the halls of Congress. Korolev also acquired institutions, factories, labs, and subcontractors who didn't even know they worked for him. Their dominions reached everywhere, amassing millions of employees. They shared a passion for flying, were intensely competitive, pushed themselves mercilessly, believed they had a special destiny, and neither would ever accept second place.

It was going to be a bitter fight to the moon.

"He would tell us that the 'Americans are at our heels . . . '" said one of Korolev's team. "He wouldn't use the word '*Amerikansi*' but '*American-ye*' as if these weren't just American residents but the entire American culture we were competing with."[17]

After NASA transformed seven men into astronauts, Korolev decided to get some spacemen of his own. His mythological standing brought hordes of well-conditioned, tough fighter pilots clamoring to his door.

"Sit down my little falcons," Korolev said to twenty applicants.

They were on tenterhooks, afraid of making a wrong move and invoking the legend's wrath. He did a roll call and looked them over. Yuri Gagarin had blue eyes, a nice, bright smile, and a relaxed way of talking. Korolev clearly liked him.

"Patriotism, courage, modesty, iron will, knowledge and love of people—cosmonauts must have those qualities," Korolev told them.[18]

He didn't include love of the "party." When he left the room, the pilots gathered round Gagarin knowing he was the space czar's choice. They were right. Neither country had the technology to achieve escape velocity, but they could make a suborbital flight. Gagarin's first orders were to beat Shepard to become the first man in space.

Shepard readied to roll out onto the launch pad in April 1961 for a quick fifteen-minute sub-orbital ballistic hop. As if Korolev could read Webb's mind, he pushed Gagarin into a *Vostok* capsule eleven days earlier and prepared him for an Earth orbit. Korolev hid his illness that day better than he hid his jitters. Fearing a jinx, he banned an associate who'd witnessed a number of rocket explosions from the launch and showed up in his usually lucky suit. Gagarin was ready. He smiled and waved: "Let's go!"

On April 12, 1961, at 1:07a.m. EST, NATO radar stations recorded the launch of a large R-7 Soviet rocket. Fifteen minutes later dialogue was heard. The Russians had put the first man in space just hours before the medics cleared Shepard to fly. If only Webb had joined NASA earlier, the monkey fight wouldn't have delayed manned flight.

"We had 'em by the short hairs and we just gave it away," snapped Shepard.[19]

Gagarin meanwhile was jolted around and plunged through the atmosphere. The hatch blew off, his seat ejected, and his parachute deployed. He landed in the fields along the Volga River, where he saw a woman and a little girl.

"I'm Soviet," he said to their surprise, "I've come from outer space."

Helicopters swooped in to recover him. Radio Moscow was broadcasting nonstop about his historic mission. Yuri Gagarin was paraded through Red Square before thousands of ebullient Russians. Korolev was shunted to background obscurity. His daughter, who was one of the thousands thronging into the square, couldn't see him.

"I would love to know who was this Chief Designer who launched Gagarin," said her friend.[20]

She was desperate to give her father his due credit, but she had been told never, under any circumstances, to reveal his name. He was the property of the state.

The Surrealist Adventure

Kennedy was furious. He wondered what they could do to catch up. Webb braced for an onslaught of unbridled desperation. Khrushchev was rubbing Kennedy's capitalist nose in the "genius of the Soviet people and the powerful force of socialism." The Soviets were indeed too far ahead to catch. A new game was needed, a new set of rules to level the playing field, something so difficult that both the Russian and American engineers would have to start from scratch. What Webb and NASA needed was the political support to go to the moon.

Lunar missions would require a dramatic and widespread mobilization of the nation. He wanted to develop a Sustaining University program that would involve academia across the country in research and development. The Apollo program would be so massive it would strengthen the United States educationally and economically, make the country preeminent in space, and usher in a new "space-age America." Webb channeled a lifetime's experience as if every decision he ever made was converging on this moment in a harmonized, grand, transformative vision. He proposed that a lunar landing should be NASA's major mission, "the first project we could assure the president that we could do and do ahead of the Russians or at least had a reasonable chance to do."

Vice President Johnson sought the advice of Webb's colleague, Senator Kerr.

"If Jim Webb says we can land a man on the moon and bring him safely home," Kerr replied. "Then it can be done."[21]

So Webb laid out his demands: a big rocket, a docking station in space, a substantial commitment of funding, and a guarantee that there would be political support for at least ten years. He was never more determined, patriotic, or audacious than now. NASA had failed more than it succeeded, but he was sticking by his brazen assertion. Kennedy made a bold address to a Joint Session of Congress on May 25, 1961.

"I believe that this nation should commit itself to achieving the goal, before this decade is out of landing a man on the Moon and returning him safely to the Earth," he declared, "for while we cannot guarantee that we shall one day be first, we can guarantee that any failure to make this effort will make us last."[22]

Kennedy publicly vowed never to see the moon governed by a hostile flag of conquest. This rid NASA of Washington's penny-pinching caution and allowed it to transform. Within three months of taking over, Webb was in charge of the largest, costliest, and most ambitious engineering project in human history. All resources were poured into developing the hugely complex Apollo capsule and a Saturn V booster. A giant space control facility was built in Texas; research and technology contracts were awarded across the country. It was the biggest national mobilization since World War II, this time for preeminence in space and renewed national prestige.

Webb began making decisions and making things happen at unprecedented speeds. NASA went from six thousand employees to more than forty thousand. Everything was handled with his characteristic doggedness and volubility.

"If you ask him a question," a top executive said, "you'll get fifty facts when two or three would do, but he has the knack of getting large numbers of people moving. I'm damned if I can understand how he does it."[23]

New technology had to be developed and quickly; a new and radically different understanding of space had to be acquired. The notion of rocketing a capsule off, landing on the moon, doing a U-turn, and heading back was abandoned. They would never get a rocket off the moon without a ground crew or a refueling station. Besides, there wasn't a rocket big enough.

They decided they needed to be able to rendezvous in space so a small lunar module could separate from a command module, land on the moon, blast off on a little tank of fuel, dock with the command and service module (CSM), and power back to Earth. That required developing sophisticated navigational controls. Webb trimmed here and there, reallocated money, and kept resources pouring into Apollo. No matter how much wheeling and dealing he had to do, or how often he had to rob Peter to pay Paul, nothing would get in his way.

"A giant government bureaucracy had committed itself to a surrealist adventure," Norman Mailer wrote. "Its purpose was clear; but its logic was utterly mysterious."[24]

Korolev understood the purpose—the lunar landing would be a victory in the Cold War, a humiliating defeat of the Soviets, and the return of American technological superiority. The Kremlin loosened its purse strings to allow Korolev to rise to the challenge of the race. Kennedy, not Khrushchev, made it possible for the chief designer to pursue his lifelong dream to reach the moon.

Korolev pushed his team at a frenzied pace to develop new engines, new technology, and new facilities. He needed everything: instruments, environmental chambers, power supplies, navigation controls. He kept popping hydrogen bombs onto his rockets to get additional military funding flowing his way. He was doing anything to get his man on the moon first. For all the pain he still endured from the physical abuse of the gulag, he worked like a man possessed—cursing and yelling and riding everyone mercilessly.

On February 20, 1962, fifty thousand people lined the beach and blocked the roads into Cape Canaveral to see astronaut John Glenn blast off from the Kennedy Space Center. They cheered as they watched him disappear into the clouds. He set off to orbit the earth and took color pictures with a camera he bought in a convenience store. In Perth, the Australians turned on all their lights in the middle of the night to illuminate their city so he could see them, and to their delight—he did. By the time Glenn splashed down again, he was welcomed by an exhilarated nation.

Korolev needed something quickly and settled on the idea of conducting the first rendezvous in space. He sent up two men on Vostoks a day apart. They came within almost three miles of each other until they could see each other out their windows. There was no new technology involved, and three miles hardly constituted a rendezvous, but Radio Moscow broadcast it as such, and the British ran headlines "Two Upsmanship."

"I think that the Russians are so far ahead in the technique of rocketry," Korolev told a reporter under a pseudonym, "that the possibility of America catching up in the next decade is remote."[25] It was bluster: he knew it, so did Webb. Nevertheless NASA kept its head down and its eye on the new Saturn V rockets.

Korolev kept up the pressure by launching the first woman into space, but his health was failing. At one point in the race, a friend said he had an "awful night attack of gastric and intestinal pains and an ambulance had taken him to hospital." The strain of his schedule kept mounting, but he kept rallying.

Then Webb was dealt a devastating blow. President Kennedy—his staunchest ally and the country's dynamic leader—was assassinated in Dallas. Webb kept up the fight; he had made the president a promise and he intended to keep it. But the new president, Lyndon B. Johnson, was more interested in his Great Society policies like the War on Poverty and the fighting in Vietnam than in his predecessor's cosmic vision.

In the spring of 1963, American spy satellites photographed a massive construction project in Tyuratam in Kazakhstan. The launch facility had huge flame trenches that looked like it was intended for launching a new rocket. It appeared that the Soviets were preparing for a lunar launch. The sense of urgency was mounting.

Like *Apollo*, Korolev's multi-manned spacecraft, *Soyuz*, was still in development, so he made his team work through the winter to convert a one-man *Vostok* capsule into a three-man called *Voskhod*. The cosmonauts climbed into the cramped tin can with their faces squashed up against the window. They had one mission objective—upstage NASA. They took off on a twenty-four-hour ride, landed with a thud, and pried themselves out, stiff and knocked around but otherwise without problems. Korolev sent them back up with a pressurized backpack. Once in orbit, one was pushed out of the airlock to become the first man to walk in space. Korolev was playing with smoke and mirrors but the world believed the Soviets had a new multi-manned ship.

The scientists all knew that whoever managed a real docking in space would be the closest to reaching the moon. In December 1965, NASA sent up two capsules from its two-man Gemini program: *Gemini VII* and *VI*. *Gemini VII* waited in space for *Gemini VI* to rendezvous. After stopping, thrusting, scanning, stopping again, they saw each other. *Gemini VI* fired its jets, stopped, and coasted nose to nose with *Gemini VII*. It was a real, controlled rendezvous, not the fly-by waving stunt of the Russians.

Korolev was furious that the Americans had a legitimate reason to be elated. He was plagued by respiratory diseases, abdominal pain, and headaches, but he kept on with the same relentless determination as his nemesis. Whatever the cost to his health or his budget, he was determined to upstage Webb and what he considered his Florida holiday-resort program. Unfortunately for Korolev, a new dogged, rational, and brilliant daredevil was about to revolutionize the race. He was molded from the same clay as his infamous ancestors who crossed the seas and settled in the densely Scots-Irish counties of Pennsylvania before braving the old frontier as trappers, hunters, explorers, and war heroes.

The Ice Commander

"Stand there like a man," Viola Armstrong told her shy son,[26] much like Elizabeth Jackson had once admonished her legendary offspring. Neil Armstrong, a sandy-haired, quiet boy, made up for what his brother called a lack of "outer fire" with a lion's heart and a passion for flying.

Almost from the time he was born in Wapakoneta, Ohio, in 1930, he was obsessed with flight. His bedroom was filled with aviation magazines and model airplanes. He ran down the stairs, out the door, and set them off in flight, having marked a hopeful landing site with sticks. While his sister's friends complained that he wouldn't notice them unless they were talking about planes, he was concerned about having missed the most important period in the history of aviation—the Lindbergh era.

"I was disappointed by the wrinkle in history that had brought me along one generation late," he lamented. "I had missed all the great times and adventures in flight."[27]

Despite feeling lost to history, he saved up enough money from his job at a drugstore to pay for flying lessons; he had to work twenty hours to afford one lesson. By fifteen he had his student pilot license in his hot little hand and could be found every Saturday riding his bicycle to the local airfield where he persuaded them to let him work as a grease monkey in exchange for flying lessons.

It was a characteristic move for an intense, aloof, self-willed boy who—like the long line of competitive, intrepid rebels from whom he descended—thrived on danger. His mother told him a colorful story about how the clan used to be called Fairbairn until one day in battle one of his ancestors remounted the king of Scotland after his horse had been shot out from under him. In gratitude, the king granted Fairbairn acres of land and honored him with the new name "Strong of Arm" or Armstrong.

The Armstrongs became a twelve-thousand-strong clan of marauding rebels that terrorized the English along the Scottish border, as their Irish and Pictish ancestors had once terrorized the Roman Empire. It was said they were "able men, somewhat unruly, and very ill to tame." It was certainly true of the notorious Johnnie "Black Jock" Armstrong—a passionate man full of fiery determination and disdain for authority. When the Armstrongs burned down fifty-two Scottish churches in the early 1500s, King James V of Scotland mustered eight thousand soldiers to quell them. Knowing he'd need more than muscle to crush Johnnie Armstrong, James resorted to some nefarious tactics—he requested a meeting with the rebel with a promise of safe passage. When Black Jock arrived at court, James hung him from the nearest tree.

He didn't plea for mercy in his final moments or try to negotiate a deal, he simply said. "If I knew you were going to do this I never would have come." In life and in death, the rebel and his descendents who inherited his feisty sense of adventure were mythologized in ballads and immortalized in epic poems.

In the early 1600s, hundreds of Armstrongs migrated to northern Ireland, mainly to County Fermanagh. In the early 1700s after losing their tenancies, many boarded the brigantines in Larne and Belfast harbors and set sail for America. One of the first stalwarts was John Armstrong who, after the horrendous voyage of 1717, persevered in the face of hostiles to found Portland, Maine. Other Armstrongs tumbled into Cumberland County in Pennsylvania, a bastion of Scots-Irish settlers, bringing Black Jock's passion, courage, defiance, and determination.

More than two centuries later, Neil Armstrong went to the naval aviation college of Purdue University on a four-year scholarship with a three-year commitment to naval service. Before he graduated, the specter of the Korean War fell over the school, and he was called to duty. He reported to Fighter Squadron 51; the legendary Screaming Eagles boarded the *USS Essex* and set off for Korea.

It was a bloodbath from day one. Planes were shot out of the air, exploding and crashing, killing pilots and radiomen on a daily basis. Armstrong was bridge-busting behind enemy lines in 1951 when he spotted a truck convoy and swept in low over enemy fire. A wire set up to trap low-flying bombers clipped his wing. It tore away chunks of his Panther's wing and tail section, but he nursed the plane back to altitude, flew a hundred miles till he was near friendly territory, and ejected.

He was called "Mighty Mouse" because he was five-foot-four and fearless. He had rapid reflexes and the ability to coolly analyze and act under pressure. No one however could really figure him out. He was more apt to say "Roger" than "Hooah!" He was enigmatic, aloof, yet intensely competitive. Even the astute journalist Norman Mailer was baffled. He's "apparently in communion with some string in the universe others did not think to play," he wrote. "Simply not like other men."[28]

After the war, Armstrong graduated from Purdue, joined the navy reserves, and headed off to Edwards Air Force Base to fly experimental, rocket-powered X-planes that set speed and altitude records on the edge of outer space.

Then in 1962, he encountered James Webb and Lieutenant Colonel John Glenn speaking about scientific exploration at the Seattle World's Fair. Webb's vision, energy, and intensity could motivate almost anyone, but for Armstrong it was an epiphany: he should be flying in space. He applied and was accepted to NASA.

"He was so far and away the best qualified, more than any other, certainly as compared to the first group of astronauts," said a NASA worker. "We wanted him in."[30]

While Armstrong was undergoing a grueling training regimen, Korolev was reeling from the American rendezvous in space that outclassed his own. In early 1966, he sent up a new *Luna 9* spacecraft that made the first soft, or survivable, landing on the moon. The capsule opened out like four petals, and a rotating TV camera emerged to photograph the moon's surface. This wasn't smoke and mirrors; this was the first successful lunar landing complete with a whole host of new technology.

The gloves were off. It was time to end eight years of national humiliation and put America genuinely ahead in the race. Webb positioned NASA to punch through the last barrier to a lunar mission with a successful rendezvous and docking in space.

The job was assigned to Armstrong. He was under a colossal amount of pressure and loved every minute. Twenty of the sixty simulations he'd done with copilot Dave Scott had some sort of emergency, but he was confident they needed to go. As President Kennedy said, the country must be "bold and daring and unflinching." There was no better man for the job than this young Armstrong.

In March 1966, he launched with copilot David Scott in *Gemini VIII* to rendezvous with an Atlas-Agena vehicle already in space. Mission control was filled with overwrought nerves.

"Ok we're sitting about two feet out," said Armstrong calmly.

"Go ahead," said Capcom.

"We'll go ahead and dock," Armstrong replied.

"Roger. Stand by for a couple minutes here," Capcom paused. "Ok, Gemini VIII. It looks good here from the ground. We're showing CONE RIGID everything looks fine for the docking."

"Flight, we are docked! Yes it's really a smoothie," said Armstrong.[31]

Mission control erupted in cheers. Webb was in Washington from where he monitored launches in case something malfunctioned and he had to do some political damage control. This was a very significant first for America. His fledgling agency was coming of age. Suddenly there was a crackled transmission from Scott in the capsule.

"We have serious problems here. We're tumbling end over end up here. We're disengaged from the Agena."

They started spinning dangerously out of control, tumbling faster and faster; their vision was blurring, and they were getting dizzy. Before they passed out, Armstrong fired the reentry control system and stabilized the capsule but that used most of their fuel. They had to abort secondary objectives and make an emergency landing at a backup site in the Pacific. It was still a magnificent triumph, but Armstrong the perfectionist felt he'd let everyone down. It was ironic that while he berated himself, he had provided mission control with the confidence they needed in an astronaut's ability to shift into emergency mode and salvage a mission independently from space.

It was nine years since *Sputnik* beeped, but now they had finally trumped the Russians. Webb waited for his nemesis's response. What spectacular humiliating coup was in the offing? Weeks passed but everything was strangely quiet on the Soviet front.

Fall of the Soviet Space Empire

"They'll shoot us without an obituary," Korolev joked with his colleagues. He acquired this dark sense of humor during his wretched years in the gulag. He also picked up some serious ailments from disease, starvation, and physical punishment. Pride prevented him from revealing this to anyone, but by 1963 he could hide it no longer.

"What do you think if I go home and lie down?" Korolev whispered to a party worker at a membership meeting just after his tandem launch. Beads of sweat dripped from his forehead. "I'm not feeling well. I can barely sit up."[32]

The party worker was startled. Korolev was a robust man, but tonight he was in really bad shape, as sweat was pouring down his face. It was the beginning of an accelerated decline. Korolev was doubled up in pain after many launches, but on the pad he was a general showing up in his lucky suit, marshalling his troops like a man shaking his fist at the devil.

"I'll just reach sixty, and that's all," he started joking with his staff. "I'll not stay here a day longer. I'll go out and plant flowers."[33]

His colleagues were bewildered. Their Chief Designer swore he'd die at his desk; these words were not in his lexicon. As 1965 drew to a close, his compounded successes in space and the relentless humiliations he inflicted on the capitalist enemy had made him a mysterious, celebrated hero, yet he was growing despondent.

"I am somehow unusually deeply tired. . . ." he wrote to his wife. "In the days of our troubles, it is especially heavy and hard, sometimes the little heart aches a bit and I . . . receive large . . . doses of Validol."[34]

He had been sad since childhood, but now his heart didn't just ache, it was dangerously weak. In December he was preparing to fly a new Zond capsule, planning to squeeze one astronaut inside and propel him to the moon. During preparations he frequently disappeared to the hospital for tests, leaving his deputy Vasily Mishin in charge. But even his short absences showed the extent to which he deflected political meddling and manipulated bureaucratic restrictions. Now without the pit-bull space czar to protect the empire, Mishin felt its overwhelming force. After a minister relentlessly harassed him and severely reprimanded him for alleged failures, he sat at his desk writing his resignation. His colleague phoned Korolev at the hospital.

"What are you doing?" Korolev asked Mishin on the phone.

"Writing the report," replied Mishin. "It's hard enough to work with you, but with him there is no way."

"Tear up that report," said Korolev, "ministers come and ministers go but we stay in our own business."[35]

Unfortunately, his political theory was no longer prescient. The days of unfettered technical development and unhindered cash flow were ending. So was Korolev's life. The medical analysis showed he had bleeding polyps in his intestine. He was scheduled to have them removed endoscopically the following month. With characteristic practicality, he moved his appointments to the end of January and, since the procedure was minor, he scheduled another for the same day. The night before his surgery he worked late and the next morning took himself to the hospital.

On January 14, 1966, he hemorrhaged on the operating table. When the doctor cut him open to stop the bleeding, he found a malignant tumor. For the next eight hours, Korolev remained under anesthesia as the doctor tried to cut out the cancer. Meanwhile Mishin was driving the engineers to convert the Zond capsule for manned space flight as the Chief Designer ordered. He wanted to have progress to report upon his mentor's return.

Korolev didn't return. The doctor finished the operation, but Korolev never regained consciousness; his heart was too weak for the surgery.

News of his death spread quickly. Khrushchev mourned his passing like the loss of his commander-in-chief in the middle of an offensive.

"[It was] like an avalanche this terrible misfortune came down upon us rapidly and unexpectedly," wrote one Red Army general. "The country had lost one of its most outstanding sons and our cosmonautics had been orphaned. He was the main author and organizer of all our space successes."[36]

On January 16, *Pravda* ran an obituary for a man called Sergei P. Korolev along with a photograph of him wearing his medals. A whisper rustled through the Soviet republics—for the first time they heard the name of the man who had brought them victory. The whisper became a mournful cry when his coffin appeared covered in a red drape and wreaths. His remains were led in a solemn state funeral procession to Red Square—the same place where five years earlier, he had been shunted to the back as the celebrated Yuri Gagarin became the face of the space race. This day thousands of people thronged the square to say farewell to their unsung hero. For hours they filed up to his coffin to pay their teary respects. Last came the cosmonauts.

"It was very touching that so many people came on those cold, January days," said his daughter, proud she could finally proclaim her father's name. "In an ironic twist of fate, he received the recognition he'd craved only after his death."[37]

The hours and months after the brilliant mind behind the Soviet space empire was gone, his legacy became a shambles, marred by bitter infighting. A year later, Mishin his deputy and protégé finally wrestled control of the program. But they were way behind, probably too far to catch up; Mishin however was determined to realize his mentor's dreams.

The Undoing of James E. Webb

"We've got a fire in the cockpit," cried Gus Grissom.[38]

Mission control heard the crackle of the astronauts' voices before fire flared inside the command module and exploded through the pressure hull, belching black smoke all over the pad crew who were desperately trying to throw open the hatch. It took four minutes. When it was released, the three astronauts were dead.

Webb stopped in his tracks; how did this happen? It wasn't even a mission. The Saturn V rocket's hydrogen-fueled system had been problematic, but Gus Grissom, Ed White, and Roger Chaffee climbed into the *Apollo 1* command module in January1967 to conduct a routine checkout, not to launch. The engines weren't even fueled.

The entire nation went into shock. Webb was sad and angry. He doubted himself: did someone fail the system or did his system fail Grissom, White, and Chaffee?

"The fire came as a terrible blow to him," said his associate administrator. "Before the accident, he and his program were riding high . . . getting acclaim from many, many quarters and deserving it . . . now his house of cards was down. . . . who had destroyed his dream? He wanted to know what individuals had failed him. He felt personally betrayed."[39]

Webb remained very cool in the days after the fire, like a commander standing by his troops and ready to protect his domain. *Aviation Week* magazine described him as "a combative bureaucrat who guarded his turf with canine ferocity." He was besieged with questions about competence, pushing too hard, moving too fast. He needed to find out what happened and fix it quickly. He needed to save NASA.

"I suppose you're much . . . more likely to accept loss of a friend in flight, but it really hurt . . . to lose them in a ground test," Armstrong said, berating himself with the same painful thought as Webb—that they had somehow let the astronauts down. "That's doubly, doubly traumatic."[40]

Webb established the Apollo 204 Review Board and distanced himself from the investigation, lest he be accused of manipulating the findings. Astronaut Frank Borman was a member of the board.

"Remember to tell the whole truth," Webb told him.[41]

Then the onslaught started. It didn't matter that NASA had previously completed sixteen manned missions without losing any crewmen, or that the U.S. military lost more than fifty thousand men in Vietnam, or that only a month before, Grissom told a reporter that if they die people should accept it and not delay the program because "the conquest of space is worth the risk of life." The witch hunt was executed without mercy. NASA was plagued by leaks to the media suggesting the pressure to meet schedules had encouraged shortcuts and that safety recommendations had been ignored.

"Jim took all this personally. He became terribly tense," said one of his associates. "Migraine headaches, which he tended to have anyway, were exacerbated. I had the feeling I was dealing with somebody who could explode at any moment."[42]

Then the villain of the piece appeared brandishing a report Webb had never seen.

Junior Senator Walter F. Mondale from Minnesota, who had till now been more concerned with poverty and social issues, turned to the high-profile NASA investigation in an effort to propel himself onto the national stage.

On the first day of Senate hearings, Mondale was in possession of a 1965 report by General Samuel C. Phillips who—at the request of a NASA associate administrator—investigated why a contractor was behind schedule and over budget on the Apollo spacecraft. Phillips determined that the contractor was guilty of substandard workmanship, engineering, and quality control. The report was never brought to Webb's attention but was leaked to Mondale and to the media ahead of the hearings. Webb was being ambushed.

"Mondale tore around the Hill saying to anyone who'd listen, 'Webb's lying. He's a liar, and I'm gonna get him,'" said Webb's counsel Paul Dembling. "I don't know why, but he really had it in for us."[43]

Denying he knew of the report's existence made Webb look shifty, evasive, and guilty of a cover-up, which shattered his credibility with Congress. He defended the Apollo managers publicly, but privately he felt let down by his colleagues who hadn't reported safety issues to him, and he felt betrayed by whomever leaked the report. Past decisions were dredged up and used against him, like his decision in 1964 to reallocate $400 million earmarked for a defunct Nova rocket to the Apollo program.

"The law gave me the authority and I transferred [it] to the right place," he said in his own defense,[44] but the Senate Space Committee decided to eliminate his fiscal authority. Webb was relegated to the paper-pushing monkey the late President Kennedy promised he would never be. His old allies were gone; no one could prevent the unknown hero who restored the nation's prestige from becoming a man who could do no right.

In April 1967, the three-thousand-page report of the Apollo 204 Review Board presented their findings. Among many assessments, they concluded the risk of fire was greater than they recognized, that flammable items such as Velcro in the cockpit and soldered joints in piping melted away, resulting in leakage that accelerated the fire. Borman added that there were hazards present that were beyond the understanding of the engineers or astronauts. The report nevertheless concluded that the deaths were the result of human error, and Congress prepared to shut Apollo down for five years.

"If any man wants to ask for whom the Apollo bell tolls, I can tell him," Webb said in an impassioned plea for fairness. "It tolls for him and for me as well as for Grissom, White and Chaffee . . . It tolls for every astronaut-scientist who will lose his life on some lonely hill on the moon or Mars . . . [We] have a grave responsibility to work together to purge what is bad in the system [and] to preserve what is good, and what represents still, at this hour, a high point in all mankind's vision."[45]

The committee was unmoved. Borman saved the day by testifying that all the astronauts had confidence in the spacecraft, their training, and their leaders. The program was allowed to continue, but the man that had once "politicked, coaxed, cajoled, and maneuvered" for NASA in Washington had lost his political credibility. He could no longer muster the funding he needed. He had to abandon his hopes for national education programs, space stations, preeminence in space, and his dream of transforming the nation into a "Space Age America." The vision of a brilliant administrator, and the space empire he had worked so hard to build, began to die; if there was any chance of recovery there had to be one large, visible goal. He had to put a man on the moon and that meant getting an Apollo–Saturn V spacecraft off the pad.

"I know now why Jim was an old marine and a good one," President Johnson remarked to his wife. "He's got the courage. He goes through a disaster like this and he says 'we just got to go on and do what we know is right.'"[46]

Unfortunately, the fire and the hearings had taken a huge physical and emotional toll on Webb. He wasn't the same defiant man who told the president he would tolerate no interference in NASA's decisions and argued that the lunar landing should only be one element in the much larger vision for America. The James E. Webb that woke up in 1968 was much diminished.

In January, the monstrous Saturn V rocket was on the pad, the press was moved three miles back, and steel shutters were installed on the control room—so great was the expected power from its engines. They spluttered and failed. Another test in April ended with the rocket tumbling out of control after takeoff.

In Russia, Mishin was still struggling to get Korolev's program on track, particularly the Soyuz lunar program. He tried unsuccessfully to dock two unmanned capsules, but later that year, he successfully sent biological specimens into lunar orbit and brought them back safely. He was building momentum and hatching greater plans.

CIA surveillance detected a giant rocket and concluded that the Soviets were attempting a lunar landing. Webb brought the discovery to White House attention. The press derisively dubbed the rocket "Webb's Giant"; others called it "the James E. Webb Memorial Rocket." There was no hard evidence of its existence, so they believed it was a figment of his overactive imagination. The visionary giant was becoming an object of ridicule. When Johnson decided not to run for reelection, Webb grew concerned that the next president would replace him with his own man at NASA. He wasn't as worried about his job as he was about his vision and legacy. He needed a successor who could give Apollo a chance to succeed, someone who could stay above the political fray.

Webb decided Thomas Paine, his deputy administrator and an apolitical technocrat, could probably survive President Richard Nixon's purge, especially if he had a chance to rack up some credibility with successful launches before the transition of power. This meant Webb had to make some very hard professional decisions; he had to sacrifice his dream. In eight years he had transformed NASA from a vulnerable agency to a powerhouse of an organization, but now in order to save it he had to give it up.

In September 1968, he announced his resignation and prepared deputy administrator Tom Paine to take over. Paine was amazed to see how efficient the NASA machine really was, how seamlessly it integrated government, industry, and universities.

"Remember you report to the President," Webb counseled. "Never forget it."[47]

With those words he handed over the reins and left.

The New Frontier

Before Paine could get anything off the pad, Mishin began 1969 with a spectacular coup. He got Korolev's Soyuz rendezvous capsules to fly with four cosmonauts in two vehicles. They docked, space-walked from one capsule to another, orbited the Earth multiple times, and came home safely. It was proclaimed "the world's first orbiting space station."

Paine followed by blasting an *Apollo 8* capsule to the moon on a Saturn V rocket—the first manned spacecraft to penetrate that deeply into space. He followed up by sending three astronauts within nine miles of the moon on a dry run for *Apollo 11*.

In July, the Soviet rocket that had been the cause of Webb's ridicule rolled out onto the pad at the enormous Tyuratam launch facility for final testing. It was the massive N-1 rocket with the thrust of thirty engines that Korolev began designing in 1961 with one single-minded purpose—to take a man to the moon. American spy satellites saw it sitting on the launch pad. The countdown was smooth; the engines ignited successfully. Suddenly a fuel pump failed when it ingested a loose bolt. The automatic control shut off the other twenty-nine engines. Twenty-three seconds later the rocket exploded with the power of a small nuclear bomb. It rained fuel and flaming debris and smashed windows for thirty miles. One moment surveillance images showed the rocket and complex, the next there was just charred and smoking devastation. Mishin's career was effectively over, but the incident was hushed up for twenty years.

Two weeks later NASA had *Apollo 11* on the pad. It was to be commanded by Neil Armstrong with Buzz Aldrin in the lunar module (LM) they nicknamed "Eagle," and Mike Collins in the command module he nicknamed "Columbia." The plan was that Armstrong and Aldrin would siesta on the moon, then blast off in the lunar module, dock with the command module that Collins said would be "whizzing around the Earth," and they'd all go home.

Collins was a lighthearted guy of Irish descent whose namesake was Ireland's most beloved rebel. He was a well-traveled army brat with a lust for life. Edwin Aldrin inherited a love of planes from his father who was an army pilot. He was well educated and a very determined man. For all of them, the preparation was grueling. They logged sixty hours a week of training and study. They did hundreds of simulations. In one, Armstrong enraged Aldrin by crashing the landing module. Aldrin complained to Collins.

"As the scotch bottle emptied and his complaints became louder and more specific," recalled Collins. "Neil suddenly appeared in his pajamas, tousle-haired and coldly indignant, and joined the fray."[48]

Collins snuck off to bed to avoid the clash of self-willed personalities. Armstrong and Aldrin stayed up half the night, till they reached some sort of peace agreement.

Two weeks before the flight, they were put into strict quarantine so doctors could conduct a baseline comparison after splashdown to determine if they were carrying hostile alien organisms. On July 6, the embarrassed trio held a press conference in gas masks and a three-sided plastic box to keep the journalists' germs away. After the jokes subsided, the controversy started. A government committee decided they were to bring a plaque saying they came in peace for all mankind, a disk with letters from world leaders, and an American flag. People bickered about the flag: some thought it should be a UN flag, and others thought flags from lots of nations should be flown. Armstrong simply said it was his job to get the flag there, not decide which flag to bring. When asked what he would like to bring to the moon, he answered with characteristic hyper-rationalism, "If I had a choice, I would take more fuel."

However he did give one surprisingly philosophical answer to the question of why go to the moon at all.

"I think we're going to the moon, because it's in the nature of the human beings to face challenges," he answered as though he carried a genetic memory of all the Armstrongs who had braved the seas and hostile conditions to settle the old frontier. "It's by the nature of his deep inner soul."[49]

On July 16, 1969, the trio were strapped into the Apollo capsule by 7 a.m. At 9:32 a.m., Saturn's first-stage engines ignited in a blinding explosion of orange flame and black smoke. The rocket shook the ground for three miles as it began to rise. It cleared the launch tower and thundered into the sky, drowning out the cheers and tears of the million people in Titusville. The young Vietnam veteran, Bob Socks, who had suffered at the hands of the national shame that surrounded the war, felt redeemed at last.

James Webb sat in the bleachers on the sidelines, careful not to detract attention away from Paine. In the end, his life had taken a strange turn that paralleled that of his nemesis. He was at the back, given and claiming no credit for this momentous achievement. When *Apollo* disappeared into the skies he quietly slipped away.

Four days later as the three astronauts approached the moon, the decade of combative sparring with the Russians suddenly seemed unimportant. Collins saw the whole beautiful blue ball—he could see the whole world in his window he said. Aldrin was unable to reconcile the idea of the endless wars being fought below with the "benign quality" the earth seemed to exude from space. Even Armstrong was moved to poetic musings.

"Compared with all the other celestial objects, which in many cases are much more massive and more terrifying, it just looks like it couldn't put up a very good defense against a celestial onslaught."[50]

On July 20, in lunar orbit, Collins threw the switch to release the LM.

"Now you're looking good," he said with his face pressed up against the window.

"Roger. Eagle's undocked," replied Armstrong. "The Eagle has her wings."[51]

After a few screeching false alarm bells, they drifted over boulders and craters looking for a spot to land. The fuel alarm sounded—they had only fifty seconds to land or abort. Across the world people were glued to their TV sets. CBS News anchorman Walter Cronkite could barely handle the strain: "I don't know whether we could take the tension if they decided to go around again."[52]

Webb was watching at home on his TV. They were seconds away from that moment about which he and McNamara had sparred a decade earlier. When Webb maintained that "large national projects on which success or failure will determine our destiny," McNamara wholeheartedly disagreed.[53] Yet this was the moment of destiny—the giant national effort that would show people, despite the tragedy of the sixties, that the country could still accomplish great deeds.

Webb couldn't see past this moment to the awards he would later receive for outstanding achievement and the epithet he'd earn as "a Washington legend." Neither could he see the Parkinson's disease that would eventually diminish his intellect or, like Korolev, the weak heart that would eventually kill him. Webb stepped into the shadows that day, but a former member of the president's Science Advisory Committee in Washington wasn't prepared to let him go silently.

"As we celebrate the successful accomplishment of our great lunar adventure and feel pride in our technical achievement," Jerome Wiesner started writing in a letter to the *New York Times*, "we should give proper credit to James Webb, whose organization skill, vision and drive played a major part in its success. . . . We should honor the man who directed its accomplishment."[54]

Twenty-five seconds before having to abort, Armstrong finally navigated through the boulders and craters to a clearing.

"Twenty feet, down a half," said Aldrin. "Drifting forward just a little bit."

When Armstrong put the lunar module down on its spindly legs it kicked up a huge dust storm that covered them like a blanket. He couldn't tell if he had contact.

"Ok. Contact light," Aldrin confirmed.

"Shutdown," Armstrong said.

"Ok engine stop," responded Aldrin.

"Copy you down, Eagle," said Houston.

"Houston. Tranquility Base here," said Armstrong. "The Eagle has landed."[55]

For Webb there came at last a deep, sublime sense of relief. The unassuming Scots-Irishman had kept the promise he made to a great president years before.

America reached the new frontier.

ACKNOWLEDGMENTS

While I was fortunate to spend time with the people mentioned below who shared many of their stories and family histories with me during our long interviews, I owe considerable thanks to the many rich and colorful characters quietly living in the Appalachian Mountains who are not mentioned, but whose hospitality and talent for storytelling allowed me understand the remarkable history of the Scots-Irish in America.

I owe a special thanks to two great research assistants, Rachel Hildebrandt and Michael Birmingham, for their hard work and resourcefulness, to Brandon Reed for his seemingly limitless knowledge of Southern racing history, to Colm Maguire for use of his "eminently quotable" brain, to Kurt Przybilla for his feedback throughout, and to Susanna Murphy who pitched in when the reading list kept growing.

To my agent Ryan Fischer-Harbage and to Nicole Robson for their faith in the book, to Laura Swerdloff at Sterling for her advice and great editing, and to my mentor Sue Shapiro, whose indefatigable energy started it all.

To my parents and my brother for their inexhaustible encouragement from the beginning, and to Adrian and Tommy who passed on to new adventures before the end.

Selected Bibliography

General References

Harkins, Anthony. *Hillbilly: A Cultural History of an American Icon*. New York: Oxford University Press, 2004.

Herman, Arthur. *The Scottish Enlightenment—The Scots Invention of the Modern World*. New York: Three Rivers Press, 2002.

Jackson, Carlton. *A Social History of Scotch Irish*. Lantham, Maryland: Madison Books, 1993.

Johnson, Paul. *A History of the American People*. 1st ed. New York: Harper Perennial, 1999.

Remni, Robert V. *A Short History of the United States*. New York: HarperCollins, 2008.

Scott, Walter, Esq. *The Works of Jonathan Swift, D.D. Volume VII*. Printed by George Ramsey and Company, 1814.

Webb, James. *Born Fighting: How the Scots-Irish Shaped America*. 1st ed. New York: Broadway Books, 2005.

Chapter 1: Invasion of the Other Irish
Bibliography

Bolton, Charles Knowles. *Scotch-Irish Pioneers in Ulster and America*. Boston: Bacon and Brown, 1919.

Derry City Council. *Siege of Derry*. Irish Heritage Series 65. Dublin: Eason & Sons Ltd., 1989.

Ford, Henry Jones. *The Scotch-Irish in America*. New York: Arno Press, 1969.

Green, E. R. R., editor. *Essays in Scotch-Irish History*. London: Routledge & Kegan Paul, 1969.

Hume Brown, Peter. *John Knox: A Biography, Volume 2*. Adam and Charles Black, London, 1895.

Jackson, Carlton. *A Social History of Scotch Irish*. Lantham, Maryland: Madison Books, 1993.

Keating, Geoffrey. *The History of Ireland*. Cork, Ireland: University College, 1640. Distributed by CELT, http://www.ucc.ie/celt/online/T100054/.

Leyburn, James G. *The Scotch-Irish: A Social History*. Chapel Hill: University of North Carolina Press, 1962.

Marshall, Rosalind K. *John Knox*. Edinburgh: Birlinn, 2000.

Miller, Kerby A. *Ireland and Irish America*. Notre Dame, Indiana: Field Day in association with the Keough-Naughton Institute for Irish Studies at the University of Notre Dame, 2008.

Stewart, Rev. Eric V. *A Short History of First Larne Presbyterian Church 1715–1965*. Larne, Ireland: McGowan & Ingram, Belfast, 1910.

William of Malmesbury. *Gesta Regum Anglorum: The History of the English Kings. Volume: 2*. R. M. Thomson, M. Winterbottom (eds). Oxford, England: Clarendon Press, 1998.

Wilson, David A., and Mark G. Spencer. *Ulster Presbyterians in the Atlantic World*. Dublin, Ireland: Four Courts Press, 2006.

Woods, Arthur. *From the Shankill to the Shenandoah: A Personal View*. Glasgow, Scotland: The Grimsay Press, 2007.

CHAPTER 2: THREE FRONTIERSMEN AND THEIR GUNS

INTERVIEWS

David Crockett interview with Karen McCarthy, Chattanooga, Tennessee, February 13, 2010.

BIBLIOGRAPHY

Bryan, George S. *Sam Houston*. New York: The Macmillan Company, 1917.

Campbell, Randolph. *Gone to Texas: A History of the Lone Star State*. New York: Oxford University Press, 2003.

Cramer, Clayton E. *Armed America: The Story of How Guns Became as American as Apple Pie*. Nashville, Tennessee: Nelson Current, 2006.

Crockett, David. *The Narrative of the Life of David Crockett of the State of Tennessee*. Baltimore, Maryland: Cary Hart & Co., 1834.

"Davy Crockett's Opinion of Andrew Jackson." *New York Times*. March 12, 1876.

Groneman, William III. *David Crockett: Hero of the Common Man*. New York: Forge Books, 2007.

Hansen, Todd. *The Alamo Reader: A Study in History*. Mechanicsburg, Pennsylvania: Stackpole Books, 2003.

James, Marquis. *The Raven: A Biography of Sam Houston.* Austin: University of Texas Press, 1988.

Kennedy, Billy. *Three Men of Destiny.* Greenville, South Carolina: Ambassador International, 2008.

Ogg, Frederic Austin. *The Reign of Andrew Jackson: A Chronicle of the Frontier in Politics.* New Haven: Yale University Press, 1919.

"People & Events: Indian Removal 1814–1858." *Africans in America.* http://www.pbs. org/wgbh/aia/part4/4p2959.html.

Roberts, Madge Thornall. *Star of Destiny: The Private Life of Sam and Margaret Houston.* Denton: University of North Texas Press, 1993.

Sanders, Daniel Clarke. *A History of the Indian Wars.* Rochester, New York: Wright and Sibley, 1812.

CHAPTER 3: THEM THAT BELIEVE
INTERVIEWS

Pastor Jimmy Morrow. Edwina Church of God in Jesus Christ's Name interview with Karen McCarthy, Del Rio, Tennessee, May 22, 2010.

Ralph Hood PhD, Professor of Psychology. University of Tennessee at Chattanooga, phone interview with Karen McCarthy, May 20, 2010.

BIBLIOGRAPHY

Beard, Richard. *Brief Biographical Sketches of Some of the Early Ministers of the Cumberland Presbyterian Church.* Nashville, Tennessee: Southern Methodist Publishing House, 1867, pages 7-17, archived at www.cumberland.org/hfcpc/McGready.htm.

de Tocqueville, Alexis. *Democracy in America.* Harry Reeve (translation). New York: George Dearborn and Company, 1838.

Dixon, A. C. (editor). *The Fundamentals: A Testimony to the Truth.* Bible Institute of Los Angeles, 1910 to 1915. www.xmission.com/~fidelis/volume1/volume1.php.

"First 100 Years." *New Castle Presbytery History.* www.ncpresbytery.org/history.htm.

Grantham, Dewey W. *The South in Modern America: A Region at Odds.* Fayetteville, Arkansas: University of Arkansas Press, 2001.

Hedges, Chris. *American Fascists: The Christian Right and the War on America.* London: Jonathan Cape, 2007.

Hill, Roger B., PhD. *History of Work Ethic.* College of Education, University of Georgia, Athens, Georgia, 1999, www.coe.uga.edu/~rhill/workethic/hist.htm.

Hood, Ralph, Ph.D. *Them That Believe: The Power and Meaning of the Christian Serpent-Handling Tradition.* 1st ed. Berkeley, Los Angeles, London: University of California Press, 2008.

Hudson, Winthrop S. *Religion in America.* New York: Charles Scribner's Sons, 1965.

Jackson First Presbyterian Church. *An Introduction to Southern Presbyterian History (1611-2001).* 2005. www.fpcjackson.org.

"Jerry Falwell." *Encyclopædia Britannica.* www.britannica.com.

Larson, Edward J. *Summer for the Gods: The Scopes Trial and America's Continuing Debate over Science and Religion.* New York: Basic Books, 1997.

Livingstone, David N. *Ulster-American Religion: Episodes in the History of a Cultural Connection.* Notre Dame, Indiana: University of Notre Dame Press, 1999.

McMullan, Harry III. *Understanding Christian Fundamentalism.* The Urantia Book Fellowship. Broomfield, Colorado, 1999. www.urantiabook.org.

Micklethwait, John, and Adrian Wooldridge. *The Right Nation: Why America Is Different.* London: Allen Lane, an imprint of Penguin Books, 2004.

Moody, Andrew. *Francis Makemie: The Father of American Presbyterianism.* www.francismakemie.com/Francis_Makemie.htm.

Tennent, Rev. Gilbert. "The Danger of an Unconverted Ministry." From the *Soli Deo Gloria* title *Sermons of the Log College.* www.sounddoctrine.net.

Sweet, William Warren. *Religion and the Development of American Culture 1765–1840.* New York: Charles Scribner's Sons, 1952.

Sweet, William Warren. *Revivalism in America.* New York: Charles Scribner's Sons, 1944.

Tracy, Joseph. *The Great Awakening.* Boston: Tappan and Dennet, 1842.

Weisberger, Bernard A. *They Gathered at the River.* Chicago: Quadrangle Paperbacks, 1958.

CHAPTER 4: AMERICAN SOLDIER

INTERVIEWS

Colonel Fred Johnson, U.S. Army, interview with Karen McCarthy, Fort Knox, Kentucky, February 19, 2010.

General David Petraeus, U.S Army, phone interview with Karen McCarthy, March 5, 2010.

Colonel Avanulas Smiley, U.S. Army, phone interview with Karen McCarthy, February 22, 2010.

Lieutenant Colin Layne, U.S. Army, phone interview with Karen McCarthy, February 22, 2010.

Lieutenant David Stroud U.S. Army, phone interview with Karen McCarthy, February 22, 2010.

Wayne Musick, Vietnam War veteran, interview with Karen McCarthy, Bristol, Tennessee, February 25, 2010.

Leo J. Daugherty III, PhD, Command Historian for the United States Army Accessions Command at Fort Knox, interview with Karen McCarthy, Fort Knox, Kentucky, February 18, 2010.

BIBLIOGRAPHY

Alderman, Pat. *The Overmountain Men*. 2nd ed. Johnson City, Tennessee: Overmountain Press, 1986.

Appy, Christian G. *Working-Class War: American Combat Soldiers and Vietnam*. Chapel Hill: University of North Carolina Press, 1993.

Bailey, Beth. *America's Army: Making the All-Volunteer Force*. 1st ed. Cambridge, Massachusetts: Belknap Press of Harvard University Press, 2009.

Basler, Roy P. *A Short History of the American Civil War*. New York: Basic Books, 1967.

"British Surrender at Yorktown, 1781, The." *EyeWitness to History*. www.eyewitnesstohistory.com (2002).

Coburn, Frank Warren. *The Battle of April 19, 1775, in Lexington, Concord, Lincoln, Arlington, Cambridge, Somerville, and Charlestown, Massachusetts*. Port Washington, New York: Kennikat, 1970.

Dawson, Joseph G., ed. *The Texas Military Experience: From the Texas Revolution through World War II*. 1st ed. College Station: Texas A&M University Press, 1995.

D'Este, Carlo. *Patton: A Genius for War*. New York: HarperCollins Publishers, 1996.

de Tocqueville, Alexis. *Democracy in America*, Harry Reeve (translation). New York: George Dearborn and Company, 1838.

Donaldson, Gary A. *America at War since 1945: Politics and Diplomacy in Korea, Vietnam, and the Gulf War*. Westport, Connecticut: Greenwood Press, 1996.

Drake, F. S. *Dictionary of American Biography*. Boston: Houghton, Osgood & Co., 1879.

Essame, H. *Patton: As Military Commander*. Conshohocken, Pennsylvania: Combined Publishing, 1973.

"The Final Report of Gen. John J. Pershing" (Washington, D.C.: Government Printing Office, 1919), pp. 38-43, excerpt reprinted online at Sam Houston State University, Huntsville, Texas, http://www.shsu.edu/~his_ncp/Pershing.html.

"First Battle of Bull Run, 1861, The." *EyeWitness to History*. www.eyewitnesstohistory.com, 2004.

"First Shot of the Civil War: The Surrender of Fort Sumter, 1861, The" *EyeWitness to History*, www.eyewitnesstohistory.com, 2006.

Hallas, James H. *Doughboy War: The American Expeditionary Force in World War I*. Boulder, Colorado: Lynne Rienner, 2000.

Heiskell, Samuel Gordon. *Andrew Jackson and Early Tennessee History*. Nashville, Tennessee: Ambrose Printing Company, 1918.

Henderson, George Francis Robert. *Stonewall Jackson and the American Civil War, Volume 1*. London: Longmans Green & Co., 1900.

Hoffman, George. *Vietnam in Perspective*. www.vietvet.org, 1994.

Imboden, John D., Brigadier General, C.S.A. "Stonewall Jackson in the Shenandoah." *Home of the American Civil War*. www.civilwarhome.com/.

Mason, Emily V. (ed). *The Southern Poems of the War*. Baltimore, Maryland: John Murphy and Co., Publishers, 1867.

Long, A. L. *Memoirs of Robert E. Lee*. New York: J. M. Stoddard & Co., 1886.

McPherson, James M., *What They Fought For 1861–1865*. Baton Rouge: Louisiana State University Press, 1994.

"The Origin of the Regulation in North Carolina." Journal article by Alan D. Watson; *The Mississippi Quarterly*, Mississippi State, Vol. 47.

Patton, George S., and Martin Blumenson. *The Patton Papers: 1940–1945*. New York: Da Capo Press, 1973.

Pershing, John J. *Final Report of Gen. John J. Pershing*. Washington, DC: Government Printing Office, 1919, pp. 38–43. www.shsu.edu/~his_ncp/Pershing.html

"President Harry S. Truman's Annual Message to the Congress on the State of the Union," January 6, 1947. Archived at C-Span.org http://legacy.c-span.org/Transcripts/SOTU-1947.aspx.

Province, Charles. *Patton's One-Minute Messages: Tactical Leadership Skills of Business Managers*. New York: Ballantine Books, 1995.

Province, Charles M. *Patton's Third Army: A Chronology of the Third Army Advance, August, 1944 to May, 1945*. First Ed., First Printing. New York: Hippocrene Books Inc., 1992.

Raphael, Ray. *The American Revolution: A People's History*. London: Profile Books, 2001.

Remini, Robert Vincent. *The Battle of New Orleans*. New York: Penguin, 1999.

———. *A Short History of the United States*. New York: HarperCollins, 2008.

Robertson, James I., *Stonewall Jackson the Man, the Soldier, the Legend*. New York: Macmillan, 1997.

Roosevelt, Theodore. *The Winning of the West*. University of Michigan Library, 2010.

Royster, Charles. *A Revolutionary People at War: The Continental Army and American Character*. Chapel Hill: University of North Carolina Press, 1979.

Sears, Stephen W. *Chancellorsville*. New York: Houghton Mifflin Company, 1996.

Simmons, Lewis M. "Free Fire Zones," *Crimes of War: What the Public Should Know*. New York: W. W. Norton & Company, 1999.

Timburg, Robert. *The Nightingale's Song*. New York: Touchstone ed. Free Press, 1996.

"Vietnam Statistics." *VFW Magazine* and the Public Information Office, HQ CP Forward Observer -1st Recon, 1997. http://history-world.org/vietnam_war_statistics.htm.

Ward, Laura, and Robert Allen. *Famous Last Words: The Ultimate Collection of Finales and Farewells*. London: PRC Publishing, 2004.

Watson, Alan D. "The Origin of the Regulation in North Carolina." *The Mississippi Quarterly*, Vol. 47, 1994.

Williams, R.G., Jr. *Stonewall Jackson, Champion of Black Literacy*. LewRockwell.com, 2002.

Wilson, Joe W. *The 761st "Black Panther" Tank Battalion in World War II."* Jefferson, North Carolina: McFarland & Company, 1999.

Wilson, Woodrow. *The State: Elements of Historical and Practical Politics*. Boston: D. C. Heath & Co. Publishers, 1889.

CHAPTER 5: GOVERNMENT OF, BY AND FOR THE LITTLE GUY
INTERVIEWS

David "Mudcat" Saunders, Political Strategist, interview with Karen McCarthy, Roanoke, Virginia, February 26, 2010.

Ed Harlow, interview with Karen McCarthy, Bristol, Tennessee, May 22, 2010.

Marvin Harlow, interview with Karen McCarthy, Copper Hill, Virginia, May 22, 2010.

Catherine Brillhart, interview with Karen McCarthy, Bristol, Tennessee, February 24, 2010.

BIBLIOGRAPHY

Agatino, Daniel, PhD. *The Tao of Reagan: Common Sense from an Uncommon Man*. Parsippany New Jersey: Vinci-Agatino Enterprises, 2004

Bass, Jack, and Walter Devries. *The Transformation of Southern Politics: Social Change and Political Consequence since 1945*. New York: Basic Books, 1976.

———, and Marilyn W. Thompson. "Strom: The Complicated Personal and Political Life of Strom Thurmond." New York: *Public Affairs*, 2005.

Bell, H.C.F. *Woodrow Wilson and the People*. Garden City, New York: Doubleday, 1945.

Brokaw, Tom. *Boom!: Talking about the Sixties: What Happened, How It Shaped Today, Lessons for Tomorrow*. New York: Random House Trade Paperbacks, 2008.

Byrd, Robert C., and Mary Sharon Hall. *The Senate, 1789–1989*. Washington D.C.: U.S. Government Printing Office, 1988.

Domke, David, and Kevin Coe. *The God Strategy: How Religion Became a Political Weapon in America*. New York: Oxford University Press, 2008. 3.

"The Fair Deal." *United States History*. Washington D.C.: U.S. Department of State. countrystudies.us/united-states/history-115.htm.

Gardner, Michael R. *Harry Truman and Civil Rights: Moral Courage and Political Risks*. Carbondale, Illinois: Southern Illinois University Press, 2002.

Heckscher, August. *Woodrow Wilson: A Biography*. New York: American Political Biography Press, 2001.

Jarding, Steve, and Dave Saunders. *Foxes in the Henhouse: How the Republicans Stole the South and the Heartland and What the Democrats Must Do to Run 'em Out*. New York: Touchstone, 2006.

Labash, Matt. "Hunting Bubba." *Weekly Standard*. No. 38, Vol. 10, June 20, 2005.

Lynn, Kenneth S. "The Hidden Agony of Woodrow Wilson." *Wilson Quarterly*. Vol. 28, Winter, 2004.McCullough, David. *Truman*. New York: Simon & Schuster, 1992.

McElvaine, Robert S. *Grand Theft Jesus: The Hijacking of Religion in America*, 1st reprint ed. New York: Three Rivers Press, 2009.

Meacham, Jon. *American Lion: Andrew Jackson in the White House*. Reprint ed. New York: Random House Trade Paperbacks, 2009.

Muller, Jules, ed. *Presidential Messages and State Papers: Volume 10*. New York: The Review of Reviews Company, 1910.

"Q&A: James Webb; Former Secretary of the Navy." *San Diego Union-Tribune.* October 30, 2005. http://www.signonsandiego.com/uniontrib/20051030/news_mz1e30webb.html.

Remini, Robert Vincent. *Andrew Jackson: The Course of American Democracy, 1833–1845*. New York: Harper & Row, 1984.

"Secret GOP Weapon: The Scots-Irish Vote." *Wall Street Journal.* Oct 19, 2004., reprinted at http://www.jameswebb.com/articles/wsj-scotsirishvote.html.

Sharlet, Jeff. "Virginia Senator James Webb: Washington's Most Unlikely Revolutionary." *Rolling Stone Magazine.* June 14, 2007.

Shear, Michael D. "In Following His Own Script, Webb May Test Senate's Limits." *Washington Post.* Metro Section November 29, 2006. http://www.washingtonpost.com/wp-dyn/content/article/2006/11/28/AR2006112801582.html.

Steigerwald, David. *Wilsonian Idealism in America*. Ithaca, New York: Cornell University Press, 1994.

"Text of the Platform Adopted by Democratic Convention." *Associated Press.* July 14, 1948.

Truman, Harry. *Memoirs, Volume 2*. New York: Doubleday, 1955.

Underhill, Robert. *FDR and Harry: Unparalleled Lives*. Westport, Connecticut:: Praeger Publishers, 1996.

"Wanted 'Dixie' Pro, Con, But Walked Out Without It." *New York Times.* Section A, Page 8, July 15, 1948.

Watson, Alan D. "The Origin of the Regulation in North Carolina." *Mississippi Quarterly.* Vol. 47, 1994.

Webb, Jim. *A Time to Fight: Reclaiming a Fair and Just America*. New York: Broadway Books, 2008.

White, William Allen. *Woodrow Wilson: The Man, His Times and His Task*. Boston: Houghton Mifflin Co., 1924. Kormendi Press, 2007.

CHAPTER 6: THE ABOLITIONIST AND THE ARISTOCRAT

INTERVIEWS

Bill Emmett, interview with Karen McCarthy, Sand Mountain, September 2010.

Willie Haslerig, interview with Karen McCarthy, Lafayette, Georgia, February 10, 2010.

BIBLIOGRAPHY

Adams, John Quincy. *Memoirs of John Quincy Adams: Volume 8*. Elibron Classics ed. Philadelphia: J. B. Lippincott & Co., 1876.

Bayor, Ronald H., ed. *Race and Ethnicity in America: A Concise History*. New York: Columbia University Press, 2003.

Brundage, W. Fitzhugh, ed. *Under Sentence of Death: Lynching in the South*. Chapel Hill: University of North Carolina Press, 1997.

Calhoun, John C. *Slavery a Positive Good*. February 6, 1837. Reprinted at http:// teachingamericanhistory.org/library/index.asp?document=71.

Coit, Margaret L. *John C. Calhoun: American Portrait*. Cambridge, Massachusetts: The Riverside Press; Boston: Houghton Mifflin Company, 1950.

Covington, Dennis. *Salvation on Sand Mountain: Snake Handling and Redemption in Southern Appalachia*. Reading, MA: Addison-Wesley, 1995.

Cralle, Richard K., ed. *The Works of John C. Calhoun, Vol. II: Speeches of John C. Calhoun Delivered in the U.S. House of Representatives, and the Senate of the United States*. New York: D. Appelton and Company, 1888.

Dunaway, Wilma. *Slavery in the American Mountain South*. Cambridge, United Kingdom: Cambridge University Press, 2005.

Hagedorn, Ann. *Beyond the River*. New York: Simon & Schuster Paperbacks, 2002.

Inscoe, John C. *Appalachians and Race: The Mountain South from Slavery to Segregation*. Lexington, Kentucky: University Press of Kentucky, 2005.

Lincoln, Abraham. *Letters and Addresses of Abe Lincoln*. New York: Howard Wilford Bell, 1903.

Loury, Glen C. "An American Tragedy: The Legacy of Slavery Lingers in Our Cities' Ghettos." *Brookings Review*, Spring 1998: 38ff.

McPherson, James M. *What They Fought For 1861–1865*. Baton Rouge: Louisiana State University Press, 1994.

Olmsted, Frederick Law. *A Journey in the Back Country*. New York: Mason Brothers, 1861.

Provosty, Laura, and Douglas Donovan. "White Trash: Transit of an American Icon." *American Studies at the University of Virginia*. Charlottesville, Virginia: University of Virginia, 2009.

Pudup, Mary Beth, Dwight B. Billings, and Altina L. Waller, eds. *Appalachia in the Making: The Mountain South in the Nineteenth Century*. Chapel Hill: University of North Carolina Press, 1995.

Rankin, John, Rev. *Life of Rev. John Rankin*. From the manuscript collection of Lobena & Charles Frost.

Stampp, Kenneth M. *The Era of Reconstruction, 1865–1877*. New York: Vintage Books, 1965.

Starobin, Robert S. *Industrial Slavery in the Old South*. New York: Oxford University Press, 1971.

CHAPTER 7: MAYBELLE AND THE MOUNTAIN
INTERVIEWS

John Carter Cash, phone interview with Karen McCarthy, March 30, 2010l.

Rodney Crowell, interview with Karen McCarthy, Nashville, Tennessee, February 16, 2010.

Ralph Stanley, interview with Karen McCarthy, Clintwood, Virginia, February 23, 2010.

BIBLIOGRAPHY

Bufwack, Mary A., and Robert K. Oermann. *Finding Her Voice*. Nashville, Tennessee: The Country Music Foundation & Vanderbilt University Press, 2003.

Cash, John Carter. *Anchored in Love*. Nashville, Tennessee: Thomas Neilson, 2007.

Cash, Johnny, with Patrick Carr. *Cash: The Autobiography*. New York: Harper Collins, 1997.

Davidoff, Nicholas. *In the Country of Country*. London: Faber & Faber, 1997.

Dundy, Elaine. *Elvis and Gladys*. Jackson, Mississippi: University Press of Mississippi, 2004.

Eder, Bruce. "The Nitty Gritty Dirt Band." *Allmusic.com*. 2010. http://allmusic.com/artist/the-nitty-gritty-dirt-band-p1747/biography.

Escott, Colin, and Kira Florita. *Hank Williams: Snapshots from the Lost Highway*. Cambridge, Massachusetts: Da Capo Press, 2001.

———, George Merritt, and William MacEwen. *Hank Williams: The Biography*. Boston: Back Bay Books, 2004.

Ewing, Tom. *The Bill Monroe Reader*. Champaign, Illinois: University of Illinois Press, 2006.

Laird, Tracey E. W. *Louisiana Hayride: Radio and Roots Music along the Red River*. New York: Oxford University Press, 2005.

Langman, Larry, and David Ebner. *Hollywood's Image of the South: a Century of Southern Films*. Westport, Connecticut: Greenwood Press, 2001.

Lewis, George H., ed. *All That Glitters: Country Music in America*. Bowling Green, Ohio: Bowling Green State University Popular Press, 1993.

Malone, Bill C., and Judith McCulloh. *Stars of Country Music: Uncle Dave Macon to Johnny Rodriguez*. Cambridge, Massachusetts: Da Capo Press, 1991.

———. *Country Music USA*. Austin, Texas: University of Texas Press, 2002.

Porterfield, Nolan. *Jimmie Rodgers: the Life and Times of America's Blue Yodeler*. Jackson, Mississippi: University Press of Mississippi, 2007.

Rooney, James. *Bossmen: Bill Monroe and Muddy Water*s. Cambridge, Massachusetts: Da Capo Press, 1991.

Schaap, David. "Review: 'O Brother, Where Art Thou?' Nothing More, and Nothing Less." *Mars Hill Review*. www.marshillreview.com/reviews/brother.shtm. August 11, 2007.

Schauffler, Henri. "Traditional American Music Takes Root." *World and I, Vol. 18*. February 2003, reprinted online at http://www.questia.com/PM.qst?a=o&d=5002514315.

Stanley, Ralph. *Man of Constant Sorrow: My Life and Times*. 1st ed. New York: Gotham, 2009.

Wolfe, Charles K. *Classic Country: Legends of Country Music*. New York: Routledge, 2001.

Zwonitzer, Mark, with Charles Hirshberg. *Will You Miss Me When I'm Gone?* New York: Simon & Schuster Paperbacks, 2002.

CHAPTER 8: RACING MOONSHINE
INTERVIEWS

Junior Johnson, interview with Karen McCarthy, Hamptonville, North Carolina, February 24, 2009.

Raymond & Violet Parks, interview with Karen McCarthy, Atlanta, Georgia, February 27, 2009.

Brandon Reed interview with Karen McCarthy, Atlanta, Georgia, February 26, 2009.

Gordon Pirkle, interview with Karen McCarthy, Atlanta, Georgia, February 26, 2009.

Jim Rhyne, interview with Karen McCarthy, Tuskeegee, North Carolian, February 22, 2009.

BIBLIOGRAPHY

"1979 Daytona 500," CBS Sports, February 18, 1979. Released on DVD by Team Marketing, January 27, 2004.

Chapin, Kim. *Fast as White Lightning: The Story of Stock Car Racing*. Rev. ed. New York: Three Rivers Press, 1998.

Edelstein, Robert. *Full Throttle: The Life and Fast Times of NASCAR Legend Curtis Turner*. Woodstock, New York: Overlook Hardcover, 2005.

Golenbock, Peter. *The Last Lap: The Life and Times of NASCAR's Legendary Heroes*. 1st ed. New York: Hungry Minds, Inc., 2001.

Hemphill, Paul. "One Last Lap Around The Speedway." *New York Times* Opinion Seciton. February 24, 2001. http://www.nytimes.com/2001/02/24/opinion/one-last-lap-around-the-speedway.html.

Higgins, Tom, and Steve Waid. *Junior Johnson Brave in Life*. Phoenix, Arizona: David Bull Publishing, 1999.

Hodges, Gerald. "The Godfather of Stock Car Racing." *Racing Reporter*. December 14, 2006.

Menzer, Joe. *The Wildest Ride*. New York: Simon & Schuster, 2001.

Pierce, Dan, PhD. *Richard Petty Oral History*. University of Western North Carolina. October 18, 2005.

Reed, Brandon. "Hall of Fame Racer Recalls Lakewood Speedway." *Georgia Racing History*. February 19, 2010. http://georgiaracinghistory.com/2010/02/19/hall-of-fame-racer-recalls-lakewood-speedway/.

Thompson, Neal. *Driving with the Devil: Southern Moonshine, Detroit Wheels, and the Birth of NASCAR*. New York: Three Rivers Press, 2007.

Wolfe, Tom. "The Last American Hero Is Junior Johnson. Yes!" *Esquire*, March 1965.

CHAPTER 9: AMERICAN FAIRY TALE
INTERVIEWS

Harry Poe, PhD, president of the Edgar Allan Poe Museum of Richmond, Virginia. Interview with Karen McCarthy, Jackson, Tennessee, February 17, 2010.

Jim Pfitzer, storyteller, interview with Karen McCarthy, Chattanooga, Tennessee, February 12, 2010.

BIBLIOGRAPHY

"About George Lucas." *PBS American Masters*. www.pbs.org. January 13, 2004.

Allen, Hervey. *Israfel: The Life and Times of Edgar Allan Poe, Volume 2*. Whitefish, Montana: Kessinger Publishing, 2004.

Baum, L. Frank. *The Wonderful Wizard of Oz*. Chicago: George M. Hill Co., 1900, reprinted by Electronic Text Center, University of Virginia Library.

Bittner, William. *Poe: A Biography*. 1st ed. Boston: Little, Brown, 1962.

Botkin, B. A. *A Treasury of Southern Folklore: Stories, Ballads, Traditions, and Folkways of the People of the South.* New York: Crown Publishers, 1949.

Davis, Jonathan P. *Stephen King's America.* Bowling Green, OH: Bowling Green State University Popular Press, 1994.

Dorson, Richard Mercer. *American Folklore.* Chicago: University of Chicago Press, 1977.

Emerson, Everett. *The Authentic Mark Twain: A Literary Biography of Samuel L. Clemens.* Philadelphia: University of Pennsylvania Press, 1984.

Faulkner, William. *As I Lay Dying: The Corrected Text.* New York: Modern Library Edition, Random House, 2000.

Faulkner, William. *The Portable Faulkner.* Malcolm Cowley, ed. Rev. and exp. ed. New York: Penguin Books, 2003.

"The Force Behind Star Wars" Paul Scanlon, *Rolling Stone*, May 25,1977, archived at http://www.rollingstone.com/news/story/7330268/the_force_behind_star_wars.

George Lucas Interview. *Academy of Achievement.* www.achievement.org, June 19, 1999.

Gordon, Andrew. "Star Wars: A Myth for Our Time." *Literature/Film Quarterly.* Fall, 1978. pp. 314-26.

Gray, Richard. *Writing the South: Ideas of an American Region.* Baton Rouge: Louisiana State University Press, 1998.

Gretlund, Jan Nordby. "The Wild Old Green Man of the Woods: Katherine Anne Porter's Faulkner." *Notes on Mississippi Writers 12.* Hattiesburg: University of Southern Mississippi, 1980.

Hazard, Lucy Lockwood. *The Frontier in American Literature.* New York: Thomas Y. Crowell Company, 1927.

Henneman, John Bell, ed. *The South in the Building of the Nation, History of Southern Fiction Vol 8.* Louisanna: Pelican Publishing Gretna, 1909.

Hoppenstand, Gary, and Ray B. Browne, eds. *The Gothic World of Stephen King: Landscape of Nightmares.* Bowling Green, Ohio: Bowling Green State University Popular Press, 1987.

Inge, M. Thomas. "The Dixie Limited: Writers on Faulkner and His Influence." *The Faulkner Journal of Japan No.1 May 1999.* www.isc.senshu-u.ac.jp/~thb0559/EJNo1.htm.

Kerr, Elizabeth M. *William Faulkner's Gothic Domain.* Port Washington, New York: Kennikat Press, 1979.

King, Stephen. *Stephen King's Danse Macabre.* New York: Berkley Books, 1983.

————. *Pet Sematary*. New York: Doubleday, 1983.

————. *The Shining*. New York: Doubleday, 1977.

Lawrence, John Shelton, and Robert Jewett. *The Myth of the American Superhero*. Grand Rapids, Missouri: Wm. B. Eerdmans Publishing Co., 2002.

Levenger, Larry. "Prophet Faulkner: Ignored for Much of His Own Time and Then Embalmed in Dignity by the Nobel Prize, William Faulkner Spoke to the Violence and Disorder of Our Time." *The Atlantic Monthly*, Vol. 285, June 2000.

Lucas, George, and Sally Kline. *George Lucas: Interviews*. Jackson, Mississippi: University Press of Mississippi, 1999.

"Making of America Project," *Harper's*. Volume 125, 1912. p. 931.

Morena, Gita Dorothy. *The Wisdom of Oz: Reflections of a Jungian Sandplay Therapist*. Berkeley, California: Frog Books, 2001.

Oates, Stephen B. *William Faulkner, the Man and the Artist: A Biography*. New York: HarperCollins, 1987.

Poe, Edgar Allan. *Complete Stories and Poems of Edgar Allan Poe*. New York: Doubleday, 1984.

Poulakis, Peter. *American Folklore*. New York: Charles Scribner's Sons Ltd., 1969.

Richmond, Mary E., and Anzolette D. Ellsworth. *New Woodstock and Vicinity Past and Present*. Cazenovia, New York: J.A. Loyster, 1901. http://www.archive.org/details/newwoodstockvici00ells.

Ruland, Richard, and Malcolm Bradbury. *From Puritanism to Postmodernism: A History of American Literature*. New York: Viking, 1991.

Russell, Sharon A. *Revisiting Stephen King: A Critical Companion*. Westport, Connecticut: Greenwood Press, 2002.

Scanlon, Paul. "The Force Behind Star Wars: George Lucas Talks About Why Robots Need Love and Where Wookies Come From." *Rolling Stone*, May 25, 1977.

Twain, Mark. *The Writings of Mark Twain, Volume 19*. Hartford, Connecticut: The American Publishing Co., 1908.

————. *The Writings of Mark Twain, Volume 10*. Hartford, Connecticut: The American Publishing Co., 1908.

————. *The Adventures of Tom Sawyer*. Syracuse, New York: The American Publishing Company, 1892.

White, Dana. *George Lucas*. Minneapolis: Twenty-First Century Books, 2000.

Williamson, Joel. *William Faulkner and Southern History*. New York: Oxford University Press, 1993.

CHAPTER 10: THE NEW FRONTIER
INTERVIEWS

William H. Lambright, Ph.D., Professor of Public Administration and Political Science at Maxwell School of Syracuse University, phone interview with Karen McCarthy, February 9, 2010.

Bob Socks, interview with Karen McCarthy, Titusville, Florida, February 2, 2010.

BIBLIOGRAPHY

Baker, T. H. "James E. Webb Oral History. Interview I." Lyndon Baines Johnson Library Oral History Collection, 1969.

Bizony, Piers. *The Man Who Ran the Moon*. New York: Thunder Mouth Press, an imprint of Avalon Publishing Group, 2006.

Cadbury, Deborah, *Space Race*. New York: HarperCollins Publishers, 2006.

Hanna, George. "NASA Treats Poor People Like VIPs." *Today Newspaper*, Section A, July 16, 1969.

Hansen, James R. *First Man: The Life of Neil Armstrong*. New York: Simon & Schuster, 2006.

Harford, James. *Korolev: How One Man Masterminded the Soviet Drive to Beat America to the Moon*. New York: John Wiley & Sons, 1997.

Lambright, William Henry. *Powering Apollo: James E. Webb of NASA*. Baltimore, Maryland: Johns Hopkins University Press, 1998.

LaMont, Sanders. "Four-Day Trip to Lunar Site." *Today Newspaper*, Section A, July 17, 1969.

Lewis, Richard S. *Appointment on the Moon—The Inside Story of America's Space Venture*. 1st ed. New York: Viking Press, 1968.

Nelson, Craig. *Rocket Men: The Epic Story of the First Men on the Moon*. New York: Penguin Group, 2009.

Schefter, James. *The Race: The Definitive Story of America's Battle to Beat Russia to the Moon*. London: Century, 1999.

"Secret Soviet Moon Mission." *Red Files* Episode 3. *PBS*. February 5, 1999.

"Video Transcript for Archival Research Catalog (ARC) Identifier 45017," *National Archives and Records Administration*, www.archives.gov/.../transcripts/transcript-eagle-has-landed-1969-45017.pdf.

NOTES

CHAPTER 1: INVASION OF THE OTHER IRISH

1. Carlton Jackson, *A Social History of Scotch Irish* (Lantham, Maryland: Madison Books, 1993), 49.

2. From "Rambles Through Europe," by Mr. L. A. Morrison, cited in Henry Jones Ford, *The Scotch-Irish in America* (New York: Arno Press, 1969), 86.

3. Jackson, *Social History of Scotch Irish*, 49.

4. William of Malmesbury, *Gesta Regum Anglorum: The History of the English Kings. Volume: 2.* R. M. Thomson, M. Winterbottom (eds) (Oxford, England: Clarendon Press, 1998), 157.

5. Alan Orr Anderson (ed.), *Early Sources of Scottish History: AD 500–1286*, 2 vols, (Edinburgh: Nabu Press, 1922), 232–233.

6. James G. Leyburn, *The Scotch-Irish: A Social History* (Chapel Hill: University of North Carolina Press, 1962), 54.

7. "A Letter from a Blacksmith to the Ministers and Elders of the Church of Scotland," 1759, quoted in Robert T. Fitzhugh, *Robert Burns* (Houghton Mifflin, Boston, 1970), 72.

8. Peter Hume Brown, *John Knox: A Biography, Volume 2*, (London: Adam and Charles Black, 1895), 288.

9. Leyburn, *Scotch-Irish*, 119.

10. David A. Wilson and Mark G. Spencer. *Ulster Presbyterians in the Atlantic World* (Dublin, Ireland: Four Courts Press, 2006), 139.

11. Ibid.

12. Walter Scott, Esq., *The Works of Jonathan Swift, D.D.*, Vol. 7 (George Ramsey and Company, 1814), XX.

13. *The Prose Works of Jonathan Swift, D.D.—Historical and Political Tracts—Irish*, cited in Leyburn, *Scotch-Irish*, 171.

14. Kerby A. Miller, *Ireland and Irish America* (Notre Dame, Indiana: Field Day in association with the Keough-Naughton Institute for Irish Studies at the University of Notre Dame, 2008), 127.

15. Leyburn, *Scotch-Irish*, 241.

16. Ibid., 192.

17. Ibid.

18. Ibid., 171.

CHAPTER 2: THREE FRONTIERSMEN AND THEIR GUNS

1. David Crockett in interview with Karen McCarthy, Chattanooga, Tennessee, February 13, 2010.
2. Jackson, *Social History of Scotch Irish*, 106.
3. Henry Jones Ford, *The Scotch-Irish in America* (New York: Arno Press, 1969), 275.
4. Clayton E. Cramer, *Armed America: The Story of How Guns Became as American as Apple Pie* (Nashville, Tennessee: Nelson Current, 2006), 207.
5. Ibid., 76.
6. Ford, *Scotch-Irish in America*, 275.
7. Ibid., 279.
8. Cramer, *Armed America*, 10.
9. Ibid., 230.
10. Davy Crockett, *A Narrative of the Life of David Crockett of the State of Tennessee* (Baltimore: E. Carey, Hart & Co., 1834), 15.
11. Leyburn, *Scotch-Irish*, 227.
12. Crockett, *A Narrative of the Life of David Crockett*, 15.
13. Frederic Austin Ogg, *The Reign of Andrew Jackson: A Chronicle of the Frontier in Politics* (New Haven: Yale University Press, 1919), 6.
14. Jon Meacham, *American Lion: Andrew Jackson in the White House* (repr., New York: Random House Trade Paperbacks, 2009), 11.
15. Cramer, *Armed America*, 230.
16. Ogg, *Reign of Andrew Jackson*, 18.
17. Ibid., 21.
18. William Groneman, III, *David Crockett: Hero of the Common Man* (New York: Forge Books, 2007), 105.
19. Ford, *Scotch-Irish in America*, 239.
20. Crockett, *A Narrative of the Life of David Crockett*, 105.
21. Marquis James, *The Raven: A Biography of Sam Houston* (Blue Ribbon, 1929), 29.
22. Paul Johnson, *A History of the American People*, (New York: Harper Perennial, 1999), 272.
23. "Horseshoe Bend," *National Park Service*, 2007.
24. George S. Bryan, *Sam Houston* (New York: The Macmillan Company, 1917), 16.
25. Johnson, *A History of the American People*, 274.
26. Meacham, *American Lion*, 95.
27. Ibid., 94.
28. Groneman, *David Crockett*, 96.
29. Bryan, *Sam Houston*, 38.
30. Crockett, *A Narrative of the Life of David Crockett*, 110.
31. Groneman, *David Crockett*, 136.
32. Interview with David Crockett, Chattanooga, Tennessee, February 2010.

33. Bryan, *Sam Houston*, 83.

34. Ibid., 79.

35. Ibid., 89.

36. Meacham, *American Lion*, 316.

37. Groneman, *David Crockett*, 148.

38. Hansen, Todd, *The Alamo Reader: A Study in History* (Mechanicsburg, Pennsylvania: Stackpole Books, 2003), 32

39. Groneman, *David Crockett*, 156.

40. Ibid., 149.

41. Ibid., 179.

42. Bryan, *Sam Houston*, 154.

43. Interview with David Crockett, Chattanooga, Tennessee, February 2010.

CHAPTER 3: THEM THAT BELIEVE

1. Pastor Jimmy Morrow in interview with Karen McCarthy at Edwina Church of God in Jesus Christ's Name, Del Rio, Tennessee, February 22, 2010.

2. Ibid.

3. Ibid.

4. Ibid.

5. Ibid.

6. William Warren Sweet, *Revivalism in America* (Charles Scribner's Sons, New York, 1944), 3.

7. Ibid., 6.

8. Ibid., 62.

9. V. Syman, *The Holiness-Pentecostal Movement in the United States* (Grand Rapids, MI: Eerdmans, 1971), 12, cited in Ralph Hood, Ph.D., *Them That Believe: The Power and Meaning of the Christian Serpent-Handling Tradition*, 1st ed. (University of California Press, 2008), 16.

10. Henry Jones Ford, *The Scotch-Irish in America* (New York: Arno Press, 1969), ch. 15.

11. E. R. R. Green, *Essays in Scotch-Irish History* (Routledge & Kegan Paul, 1969), 23.

12. Sweet, *Revivalism in America*, 58.

13. Francis Samuel Drake, *Dictionary of American Biography* (James R. Osgood & Co., 1872), 898.

14. Joseph Tracy, *The Great Awakening* (Boston: Tappan and Dennet, 1842), 24.

15. Green, *Essays in Scotch-Irish History*, 25.

16. Sweet, *Revivalism in America*, 492.

17. Johnson, *A History of the American People*, 116.

18. Sweet, *Revivalism in America*, 192.

19. Bernard Weisberger, *They Gathered at the River* (Chicago: Quadrangle Paperbacks, 1958), 345.

20. Ibid., 24.
21. Alexis de Tocqueville, *Democracy in America*, Harry Reeve (translation) (George Dearborn and Company, New York, 1838), 214.
22. Edward J. Larson, *Summer for the Gods: The Scopes Trial and America's Continuing Debate over Science and Religion* (New York: Basic Books, 1997), 177.
23. Ibid.
24. Ibid., 179.
25. Ibid., 180.
26. Ibid., 189.
27. Grantham, Dewey W., *The South in Modern America: a Region at Odds*, University of Arkansas Press, Fayetteville, Arkansas (May 1, 2001), 112.
28. Larson, *Summer for the Gods*, 199.
29. *New York Times*, National Desk, August 26, 1992.
30. Prof. Ralph Hood in interview with Karen McCarthy, University of Chattanooga, Tennessee, May 2010.
31. Pastor Jimmy Morrow in interview, 2010.

CHAPTER 4: AMERICAN SOLDIER
1. Lieutenant Colin Layne in interview with Karen McCarthy (phone), February 22, 2010.
2. Gen. David Petraeus in interview with Karen McCarthy (phone), March 5, 2010.
3. Colonel Fred Johnson in interview with Karen McCarthy, Fort Knox, Kentucky February 19, 2010.
4. Colonel Avanulus Smiley in interview with Karen McCarthy, Fort Knox, Kentucky February 22, 2010.
5. Lieutenant Colin Layne in interview, 2010.
6. "Lancaster County, Pennsylvania, A History," cited in Carlton Jackson, *A Social History of Scotch Irish* (Lantham, Maryland: Madison Books, 1993), 777.
7. Cramer, *Armed America*, 10.
8. Ray Raphael, *The American Revolution: A People's History* (Profile Books, 2001), 204.
9. Leyburn, *Scotch-Irish*, 308.
10. Ibid., 305.
11. Raphael, *American Revolution*, 265.
12. Pat Alderman, *The Overmountain Men* (Johnson City, Tennessee: Overmountain Press, 1986), 80.
13. Ibid., 83.
14. Raphael, *American Revolution*, 100.
15. Heiskell, Samuel Gordon, *Andrew Jackson and Early Tennessee History* (Nashville, Tennessee: Ambrose Printing Company, 1918), 265.
16. Leyburn, *Scotch-Irish*, 305.

17. Frederic Austin Ogg, *The Reign of Andrew Jackson: A Chronicle of the Frontier in Politics* (Yale University Press, 1919), 24.

18. Johnson, *A History of the American People*, 266.

19. Ibid., 267.

20. Robert Vincent Remini, *The Battle of New Orleans* (New York: Penguin, 1999), 6.

21. Ibid., 146

22. George Francis Robert Henderson, *Stonewall Jackson and the American Civil War, Volume 1* (Longmans Green & Co, 1900), 115.

23. James M. McPherson, *What They Fought For 1861–1865* (Louisiana State University Press, 1994), 47.

24. Ibid., 59.

25. A. L. Long, *Memoirs of Robert E. Lee* (New York: J. M. Stoddard & Co, 1886), 94.

26. McPherson, *What They Fought For*, 455.

27. James I. Robertson, *Stonewall Jackson the Man, the Soldier, the Legend* (Macmillan, 1997), xiii.

28. "The First Battle of Bull Run, 1861," *EyeWitness to History* (www.eyewitnesstohistory.com), 2004.

29. Stephen W. Sears, *Chancellorsville* (New York: Houghton Mifflin Company, 1996), 447.

30. William Rev. Jones, *Southern Historical Papers* (Southern Historical Society, 1886), 162.

31. Robert Alonzo Brock, *Southern Historical Society*, Volume 15 (Virginia Historical Society, 1887), xxi.

32. Laura Ward and Robert Allen, *Famous Last Words: The Ultimate Collection of Finales and Farewells* (London: PRC Publishing, 2004), 169.

33. The Final Report of Gen. John J. Pershing (Washington, D.C.: Government Printing Office, 1919, excerpt reprinted online at Sam Houston State University, http://www.shsu.edu/~his_ncp/Pershing.html), 38–43.

34. Ibid.

35. Carlo D'Este, *Patton: A Genius for War* (New York: Harper Perennial, 1996), 265.

36. George S. Patton, and Martin Blumenson, *The Patton Papers: 1940–1945*, (Cambridge, Massachusetts: Da Capo Press, 1973), 457.

37. Ibid., 457.

38. Joe W. Wilson, *The 761st "Black Panther" Tank Battalion in World War II* (Jefferson, North Carolina: McFarland & Company, 1999), 53.

39. D'Este, *Patton: A Genius for War*, 684.

40. "The Battle of the Bulge: Sixty-Six Years Ago," The United States Army Center of Military History, http://www.army.mil/botb/overview.html.

41. Patton, *Patton Papers*, 698.

42. Robert Timburg, *The Nightingale's Song* (New York: Simon & Schuster, 1995), 152.

43. From Hillstrom, *Vietnam War: Almanac, The American Soldier in Vietnam*,

(Copyright © 2000 Gale, a part of Cengage Learning, Inc.) Reproduced by permission. www.cengage.com/permissions.

44. Tom Brokaw, *Boom!: Talking About the Sixties: What Happened, How It Shaped Today, Lessons for Tomorrow* (New York: Random House, 2007), 63.

45. Herman, *The Scottish Enlightenment*, 236.

46. Wayne Musick in interview with Karen McCarthy, Bristol, Tennessee, February 25, 2010.

47. Hillstrom. *Vietnam War: Almanac.*

48. Timburg, *Nightingale's Song*, 161.

49. D'Este, *Patton: A Genius for War*, 573.

50. Timburg, *Nightingale's Song*, 161.

51. Christian G. Appy, *Working-Class War: American Combat Soldiers and Vietnam*, (Copyright © 1993 by the University of North Carolina Press, www.uncpress. unc.edu). Used by permission of the publisher.

52. "Q&A: James Webb, Former Secretary of the Navy," *San Diego Union-Tribune*, October 30, 2005.

53. Hillstrom. *Vietnam War: Almanac.*

54. Colonel Fred Johnson in interview, 2010.

55. Ibid.

56. Beth Bailey, *America's Army: Making the All-Volunteer Force* (Cambridge, Massachusetts: Belknap Press of Harvard University Press, 1st ed., 2009,) 252.

57. Colonel Fred Johnson in interview, 2010.

CHAPTER 5: GOVERNMENT OF, BY, AND FOR THE LITTLE GUY

1. Ed Harlow in interview with Karen McCarthy, Bristol, Tennessee, February 22, 2010.

2. Marvin Harlow in interview with Karen McCarthy, Copper Hill, Tennessee, February 23, 2010.

3. Alan D. Watson, "The Origin of the Regulation in North Carolina," *The Mississippi Quarterly*, Vol. 47, 1994.

4. Ibid.

5. Meacham, *American Lion*, 238.

6. Frederic Austin Ogg, *The Reign of Andrew Jackson: A Chronicle of the Frontier in Politics* (New Haven: Yale University Press, 1919), 18.

7. Ibid., 20.

8. Ibid., 65.

9. Ibid., 73.

10. Ibid., 78.

11. Ibid., 119.

12. Ibid., 127.

13. Robert Vincent Remini, *A Short History of the United States* (New York: HarperCollins, 2008), 108.

14. Meacham, *American Lion*, 278.

15. Woodrow Wilson, *The State: Elements of Historical and Practical Politics* (Boston: D. C. Heath & Co. Publishers, 1889), 664.

16. Kenneth S. Lynn, "The Hidden Agony of Woodrow Wilson," *The Wilson Quarterly*, Vol. 28, Winter 2004, 59.

17. William Allen White, *Woodrow Wilson: The Man, His Times and His Task* (Boston: Houghton Mifflin Co., 1924; Kormendi Press, 2007), 186.

18. Jules Muller, ed., *Presidential Messages and State Papers: Volume 10* (New York: The Review of Reviews Company, 1910), 8.

19. Ibid., 7.

20. August Heckscher, *Woodrow Wilson: A Biography* (American Political Biography Press, 2001), 318.

21. Ibid., 316.

22. "In a letter to Champ Clark from W.J. Bryan, May 30, 1911," quoted in *The Memoirs of William Jennings Bryan, by Himself and His Wife Mary Baird Bryan* (Chicago: The John C. Winston Company, 1925), 336.

23. "President Woodrow Wilson's Fourteen Points." *Wilson, Woodrow* (January 8, 1918). Yale Law School. http://www.yale.edu/lawweb/avalon/wilson14.htm

24. Lynn, "Hidden Agony of Woodrow Wilson."

25. Robert C. Byrd and Mary Sharon Hall, *The Senate, 1789–1989* (U.S. Government Printing Office), 426.

26. Lynn, "Hidden Agony of Woodrow Wilson."

27. Robert Underhill, *FDR and Harry: Unparalleled Lives* (Westport, Connecticut: Praeger Publishers, 1996), 34.

28. Ibid., 35.

29. David McCullough, *Truman* (New York: Simon & Schuster, 1992), 721.

30. President Harry S. Truman's Annual Message to the Congress on the State of the Union (Archived at C-Span.org http://legacy.c-span.org/Transcripts/SOTU-1947.aspx).

31. Harry Truman, *Memoirs, Volume 2* (New York: Doubleday, 1955), 182.

32. Text of the 1948 Democratic platform, preprinted in the *Associated Press*, July 14, 1948.

33. Jack Bass and Marilyn W. Thompson, *Strom: the Complicated Personal and Political Life of Strom Thurmond* (New York: Public Affairs, 2005), 105.

34. Statement by Senator Strom Thurmond, United States Senate, www.senate.gov.

35. Quote by Henry Ward Beecher; cited in John Micklethwait and Adrian Wooldridge, *The Right Nation: Why America Is Different* (New York: Allen Lane, an imprint of Penguin Books, 2004), 20.

36. Bass, *Complicated Life of Strom Thurmond*, 216.

37. Ryan Frederick, ed., *Ronald Reagan: The Great Communicator* (Diane Pub Co., 2003), 78.

38. Robert S. McElvaine, *Grand Theft Jesus: The Hijacking of Religion in America*, 1st reprint ed. (Three Rivers Press, April 7, 2009), 140.

39. Agatino, Daniel, PhD, *The Tao of Reagan: Common Sense from an Uncommon Man* (Parsippany, New Jersey: Vinci-Agatino Enterprises, 2004), 108.

40. David Domke and Kevin Coe, *The God Strategy: How Religion Became a Political Weapon in America* (New York: Oxford University Press, 2008).

41. Robert Vincent Remini, *Andrew Jackson: The Course of American Democracy, 1833–1845* (New York: Harper & Row, 1984), 428.

42. Steve Jarding and Dave Saunders, *Foxes in the Henhouse: How the Republicans Stole the South and the Heartland and What the Democrats Must Do to Run 'em Out* (Austin, Texas: Touchstone Publishing, 2006), 140.

43. Catherine Brillhart in interview with Karen McCarthy, Bristol, Tennessee, February 24, 2010.

44. Stated in a 2007 interview with *Rolling Stone*, Jeff Sharlet, "Virginia Senator James Webb: Washington's Most Unlikely Revolutionary," *Rolling Stone*, June 14, 2007.

45. Dave "Mudcat" Saunders in interview with Karen McCarthy, February 26, 2010.

46. Michael D. Shear, in "In Following His Own Script, Webb May Test Senate's Limits." *Washington Post*, Metro Section November 29, 2006.

47. Mudcat Saunders in interview, 2010.

CHAPTER 6: THE ABOLITIONIST AND THE ARISTOCRAT

1. Willy Haslerig in interview with Karen McCarthy, Lafayette, Georgia, February 10, 2010.

2. Rev. John Rankin, *Life of Rev. John Rankin*, from the manuscript collection of Lobena and Charles Frost, 3.

3. Ibid., 9.

4. Ibid.

5. Margaret L. Coit, *John C. Calhoun: American Portrait*, (Cambridge, Massachusetts: The Riverside Press, Boston: Houghton Mifflin Company, 1950), 12.

6. Ibid., 26.

7. Ibid., 36.

8. Ibid., 98.

9. Rankin, *Life of Rev. John Rankin*, 39.

10. Ann Hagedorn, *Beyond the River* (New York: Simon & Schuster Paperbacks, 2002), 137.

11. Ibid., 47.

12. Coit, *John C. Calhoun*, 48.

13. Meacham, *American Lion*, 136.

14. Frederic Austin Ogg, *The Reign of Andrew Jackson: A Chronicle of the Frontier in Politics* (New Haven: Yale University Press, 1919), 167.

15. Meacham, *American Lion*, 245.

16. Ibid., 244.

17. Ibid., 185.

18. John C. Calhoun, *Slavery a Positive Good*, February 6, 1837 (reprinted by TeachingAmericanHistory.org).

19. John Quincy Adams, *Memoirs of John Quincy Adams: Volume 8*, Elibron Classics ed. (Philadelphia: J. B. Lippincott & Co., 1876), 441.

20. John C. Inscoe, *Appalachians and Race: The Mountain South from Slavery to Segregation* (Lexington, Kentucky: University Press of Kentucky, 2005), 24.

21. Ibid., 160.

22. Frederick Law Olmsted, *A Journey in the Back Country* (New York: Mason Brothers, 1861), 239

23. Wilma Dunaway, *Slavery in the American Mountain South* (Cambridge, United Kingdom: Cambridge University Press, 2005),158.

24. Laura Provosty and Douglas Donovan, "White Trash: Transit of an American Icon," *American Studies at the University of Virginia*, Charlottesville, Virginia, 2009.

25. Olmsted, Frederick Law, *A Journey in the Back Country: Volume 3* (New York: Mason Brothers, 1860), 228.

26. Ibid., 263.

27. Ibid., 293.

28. Robert S. Starobin, *Industrial Slavery in the Old South* (New York: Oxford University Press, 1971), 141.

29. Inscoe, *Appalachians and Race*, 41.

30. Ibid., 19.

31. Dunaway, *Slavery in the American Mountain South*, 94.

32. Starobin, *Industrial Slavery in the Old South*, 78.

33. Ibid., 81.

34. Hagedorn, *Beyond the River*, 98.

35. Coit, *John C. Calhoun*, 41.

36. Speech on the Senate floor, February 1837, reprinted by Richard K. Cralle, ed., *The Works of John C. Calhoun: Volume II* (New York: D. Appleton and Co., 1860–70), 632.

37. Hagedorn, *Beyond the River*, 131.

38. Ibid., 194.

39. Ibid., 105.

40. Ibid., 262.

41. Coit, *John C. Calhoun*, 48.

42. Hagedorn, *Beyond the River*, 264.

43. Inscoe, *Appalachians and Race*, 157.

44. Coit, *John C. Calhoun*, 478.

45. Abraham Lincoln, *Letters and Addresses of Abe Lincoln*, (New York: Howard Wilford Bell, 1903), 105.

46. James M. McPherson, *What They Fought For 1861-1865* (Baton Rouge, Louisiana: Louisiana State University Press, 1994), 19.

47. Rankin, *Life of Rev. John Rankin*, 41.

48. Hagedorn, *Beyond the River,* 274.

49. Bill Emmett of Sand Mountain in interview with Karen McCarthy, September 2010.

50. Willy Haslerig in interview, 2010.

51. Ibid.

CHAPTER 7: MAYBELLE AND THE MOUNTAIN

1. Rodney Crowell, in interview with Karen McCarthy, Nashville, Tennessee, February 16, 2010.

2. Ibid.

3. Ibid.

4. Ibid.

5. Rodney Crowell, "The Houston Kid" in Burton Clayman, *Telephone Road, Texas* (Sugar Hill, Texas: Baxter Press, 2007).

6. Mark Zwonitzer, with Charles Hirshberg, *Will You Miss Me When I'm Gone?* (New York: Simon & Schuster Paperbacks, 2002), 78.

7. Bill Malone, *Country Music USA* (Austin: University of Texas Press, 2002), 87.

8. Anthony Harkins, *Hillbilly: A Cultural History of an American Icon*, ill. ed. (New York: Oxford University Press, 2005), 78.

9. Zwonitzer, *Will You Miss Me When I'm Gone?*, 101.

10. Ibid., 142.

11. Nolan Porterfield, *Jimmie Rodgers: The Life and Times of America's Blue Yodeler,* (Jackson, Mississippi: University Press of Mississippi, 2007), 4

12. Zwonitzer, *Will You Miss Me When I'm Gone?*, 229.

13. Ibid., 284.

14. James Rooney, *Bossmen: Bill Monroe and Muddy Water*s (Cambridge, Massachusetts: Da Capo Press, 1991), 36.

15. Nicholas Davidoff, *In the Country of Country* (New York: Faber & Faber, 1997), 115.

16. Dr. Ralph Stanley in interview with Karen McCarthy, Clintwood, Virginia, February 23, 2010.

17. Rooney, *Bossmen: Bill Monroe and Muddy Water*s, 46.

18. Ralph Stanley, *Man of Constant Sorrow: My Life and Times*, 1st ed. (New York: Gotham Books, 2009), 111.

19. Stanley, *Man of Constant Sorrow*, 2.

20. Ibid., 123.

21. Dr. Ralph Stanley in interview, 2010.

22. Rooney, *Bossmen: Bill Monroe and Muddy Waters*, 46.

23. Stanley, *Man of Constant Sorrow*, 416.

24. Les Leverett in interview with Karen McCarthy, Nashville, Tennessee, February 2010.

25. Dr. Ralph Stanley in interview, 2010.

26. Stanley, *Man of Constant Sorrow*, 422.

27. Dr. Stanley in interview, 2010.

28. Rodney Crowell in interview, 2010.

29. Dr. Stanley in interview, 2010.

30. Colin Escott, George Merritt, and William MacEwen, *Hank Williams: The Biography* (Boston, Massachusetts: Back Bay Books, 2004), 6.

31. Ibid., 9.

32. Ibid.

33. Davidoff, *In the Country of Country*, 203.

34. Tracey E. W. Laird, *Louisiana Hayride: Radio and Roots Music along the Red River* (New York: Oxford University Press, 2005), 129.

35. Bill C. Malone and Judith McCulloh,. *Stars of Country Music: Uncle Dave Macon to Johnny Rodriguez* (Cambridge, Massachusetts: Da Capo Press, 1991), 246.

36. Escott, *Hank Williams*, 151.

37. Malone, *Country Music USA*, 242.

38. Zwonitzer, *Will You Miss Me When I'm Gone?*, 295.

39. Ibid., 295.

40. Colin Escott and Kira Florita, *Hank Williams: Snapshots from the Lost Highway*, (Cambridge, Massachusetts: Da Capo Press, 2001), 181.

41. Elaine Dundy, *Elvis and Gladys* (University Press of Mississippi, 2004), 163.

42. Neil Strauss, "New Rebel for the 90's: Meet Johnny Cash, 62," *New York Times*, Arts Section, September 14, 1994 (http://www.nytimes.com/1994/09/14/arts/new-rebel-for-the-90-s-meet-johnny-cash-62.html).

43. Zwonitzer, *Will You Miss Me When I'm Gone?*, 6.

44. John Carter Cash, *Anchored in Love* (Nashville, Tennessee: Thomas Neilson, 2007), 155.

45. Zwonitzer, *Will You Miss Me When I'm Gone?*, 366.

46. Ibid., 368.

47. Dr. Stanley in interview, 2010.

48. Mary A. Bufwack and Robert K. Oermann, *Finding Her Voice* (Nashville, Tennessee: The Country Music Foundation & Vanderbilt University Press, 2003), 313.

49. Larry Langman and David Ebner, *Hollywood's Image of the South: a Century of Southern Films* (Westport Connecticut: Greenwood Press, 2001), 205.

50. Davidoff, *In the Country of Country*, 196.

51. John Carter Cash in interview with Karen McCarthy, New York, March 30, 2010.

52. Henri Schauffler, "Traditional American Music Takes Root," *World and I*, Vol. 18, February 2003 (Reprinted online at http://www.questia.com/ PM.qst?a=o&d=5002514315).

53. Stanley, *Man of Constant Sorrow*, 435.

54. John Carter Cash in interview, 2010.

55. Rodney Crowell in interview, 2010.

56. Stanley, *Man of Constant Sorrow*, 445.

CHAPTER 8: RACING MOONSHINE

1. "1979 Daytona 500," CBS Sports, February 18, 1979. (Released on DVD by Team Marketing, January 27, 2004.)

2. Joe Menzer, *The Wildest Ride* (New York: Simon & Schuster, 2001), 231.

3. Junior Johnson in interview with Karen McCarthy, Hamptonville, North Carolina, February 24, 2009.

4. Ibid.

5. Tom Higgins and Steve Waid, *Junior Johnson: Brave in Life* (Phoenix, Arizona: David Bull Publishing, 1999), 19.

6. Ibid., 19.

7. Junior Johnson in interview, 2009.

8. Jim Rhyne, Robbinsville in interview with Karen McCarthy, North Carolina, February 2009.

9. Junior Johnson in interview, 2009.

10. Ibid.

11. Ibid.

12. Ibid.

13. Ibid.

14. Violet Parks in interview with Karen McCarthy, Atlanta, Georgia, February 27, 2009.

15. Raymond and Violet Parks in interview with Karen McCarthy, Atlanta, Georgia, February 27, 2009.

16. Ibid.

17. Paul Hemphill, "One Last Lap Around the Speedway," *New York Times Opinion Section*, February 24, 2001. http://www.nytimes.com/2001/02/24/opinion/one-last-lap-around-the-speedway.html

18. Peter Golenbock, *The Last Lap: The Life and Times of NASCAR's Legendary Heroes*, 1st ed. (New York: Hungry Minds, Inc., 2001), 15.

19. Violet Parks in interview, 2009

20. Junior Johnson in interview, 2009.

21. Brandon Reed, "Hall of Fame Racer Recalls Lakewood Speedway," *Georgia Racing History*, February 2010 (http://georgiaracinghistory.com/2010/02/19/hall-of-fame-racer-recalls-lakewood-speedway/).

22. Neal Thompson, *Driving with the Devil: Southern Moonshine, Detroit Wheels, and the Birth of NASCAR* (New York: Three Rivers Press, 2007), 243.

23. Violet Parks in interview, 2009.

24. Robert Edelstein, *Full Throttle: The Life and Fast Times of NASCAR Legend Curtis Turner* (Woodstock, New York: Overlook, 2005), 15.

25. Ibid., 7.

26. Junior Johnson in interview, 2009.

27. Tom Wolfe, "The Last American Hero Is Junior Johnson. Yes!," *Esquire*, March 1965. 2

28. Junior Johnson in interview, 2009.

29. Higgins, *Junior Johnson: Brave in Life*, 73.

30. Brandon Reed in interview with Karen McCarthy, Dawsonville, Georgia, February 26, 2009.

31. Golenbock, *The Last Lap*, 170.

32. Dan Pierce in interview, "Oral History Collections" (Asheville, North Carolina: D.H. Ramsey Library, Special Collections, University of North Carolina, date unknown), 5.

33. Junior Johnson in interview, 2009.

34. Ibid.

35. Raymond Parks in interview, 2010.

36. Junior Johnson in interview, 2009.

CHAPTER 9: AMERICAN FAIRY TALE

1. Jim Pfitzer in interview with Karen McCarthy, Chattanooga, Tennessee, February 2010.

2. Richard Mercer Dorson, *American Folklore* (Chicago: University of Chicago Press, 1977), 16.

3. Edgar Allan Poe, "Descent into the Maelstrom," *Complete Stories and Poems of Edgar Allen Poe* (New York: Doubleday, 1984), 108.

4. Hervey Allen, *Israfel: The Life and Times of Edgar Allan Poe, Volume 2* (Whitefish, Montana: Kessinger Publishing, 2004), 573.

5. William Bittner, *Poe: A Biography* 1st ed. (Boston: Little, Brown, 1962), 47.

6. Poe, "The Unparalleled Adventure of One Hans Phall," *Complete Stories*, 520.

7. Poe, "The Fall of the House of Usher," *Complete Stories*, 190.

8. Bittner, *Poe: A Biography*, 172.

9. Allen, *Israfel*, 521.

10. Bittner, *Poe: A Biography*, 173.

11. Richard Gray, *Writing the South: Ideas of an American Region* (Baton Rouge, Louisiana: Louisiana State University Press, 1998), 88.

12. Ibid., 75.

13. Everett Emerson, *The Authentic Mark Twain: A Literary Biography of Samuel L. Clemens* (Philadelphia: University of Pennsylvania Press, 1984), 44.

14. Mark Twain, *The Writings of Mark Twain, Volume 19* (Hartford, Connecticut, American Publishing Co., 1908), 32.

15. Mark Twain, *The Writings of Mark Twain, Volume 10* (Hartford, Connecticut: American Publishing Co., 1908), 201.

16. Mark Twain, *The Adventures of Tom Sawyer* (Syracuse, New York: American Publishing Company, 1892), 242.

17. Ibid., 298.

18. "Making of America Project, 1912," *Harper's*, Volume 125, 931.

19. "The Man Behind the Curtain: L. Frank Baum and the Wizard of Oz" in Literary Traveler, LiteraryTraveler.com.

20. L. Frank Baum, *The Wonderful Wizard of Oz* (Chicago: George M. Hill Co., 1900; reprinted by Electronic Text Center, University of Virginia Library), 38.

21. Ibid., 123.

22. Ibid., 150.

23. Gita Dorothy Morena, *The Wisdom of Oz: Reflections of a Jungian Sandplay Therapist* (Berkeley, California: Frog Books, 2001), 20.

24. Stephen B. Oates, *William Faulkner, the Man and the Artist: A Biography* (New York: HarperCollins, 1987), 19.

25. Joel Williamson, *William Faulkner and Southern History* (New York: Oxford University Press, 1993), 41.

26. Jan Nordby Gretlund, "The Wild Old Green Man of the Woods: Katherine Anne Porter's Faulkner," *Notes on Mississippi Writers 12* (Hattiesburg, Mississippi: University of Southern Mississippi, 1980), 22.

27. Elizabeth M. Kerr, *William Faulkner's Gothic Domain* (Port Washington, New York: Kennikat Press, 1979), 28.

28. M. Thomas Inge. "The Dixie Limited: Writers on Faulkner and His Influence," *Faulkner Journal of Japan*, www.isc.senshu-u.ac.jp/~thb0559/EJNo1.htm, 1999.

29. Williamson, *William Faulkner and Southern History*, 234.

30. "Prophet Faulkner: Ignored for Much of His Own Time and Then Embalmed in Dignity by the Nobel Prize, William Faulkner Spoke to the Violence and Disorder of Our Time," (magazine article by Larry Levinger; *The Atlantic Monthly, Vol. 285*, June 2000). 340

31. Williamson, *William Faulkner and Southern History*, 285.

32. Ibid.

33. Stephen King, *Stephen King's Danse Macabre* (New York: Berkley Books, 1983), 10.

34. Ibid., 96.

35. Gary Hoppenstand and Ray B. Browne, eds., *The Gothic World of Stephen King: Landscape of Nightmares* (Bowling Green, Ohio: Bowling Green State University Popular Press, 1987), 2.

36. Stephen King, *Pet Sematary*, (New York: Doubleday, 1983), 233.

37. Sharon A. Russell, *Revisiting Stephen King: A Critical Companion* (Westport, Connecticut: Greenwood Press, 2002), 6.

38. Hoppenstand, *Gothic World of Stephen King*, 3.

39. Russell, *Revisiting Stephen King*, 10.

40. Stephen King, *The Shining* (New York: Doubleday, 1977), 216–17.

41. Noted in *Rolling Stone*, Paul Scanlon, "The Force Behind Star Wars" archived at http://www.rollingstone.com/news/story/7330268/the_force_behind_star_wars, May 25,1977

42. "About George Lucas." *PBS American Masters*. www.pbs.org. January 13, 2004.

43. Dana White, *George Lucas* (Twenty-First Century Books, 2000), 13.

44. George Lucas in interview, *Academy of Achievement*, www.achievement.org, June 19, 1999.

45. Ibid.

CHAPTER 10: THE NEW FRONTIER

1. Hanna, George. "NASA Treats Poor People Like VIPs." *Today*, July 16, 1969. Section A, 4.

2. Bob Socks in interview with Karen McCarthy, Titusville, Florida, February 2, 2010.

3. James Schefter, *The Race: The Definitive Story of America's Battle to Beat Russia to the Moon* (London: Century, 1999), 21.

4. Cited in Schefter, *The Race*, chapter 1.

5. Schefter, *The Race*, 23.

6. Piers Bizony, *The Man Who Ran the Moon* (New York: Thunder Mouth Press, an imprint of Avalon Publishing Group, 2006), 9.

7. William Henry Lambright, *Powering Apollo: James E. Webb of NASA* (Baltimore, Maryland: Johns Hopkins University Press, 1998), 27.

8. Bizony, *The Man Who Ran the Moon*, 18.

9. Ibid.

10. Ibid., 19.

11. Ibid., 24

12. Ibid., 17.

13. Lambright, *Powering Apollo*, 119.

14. James Harford, *Korolev: How One Man Masterminded the Soviet Drive to Beat America to the Moon* (New York: John Wiley & Sons, 1997), 10.

15. Ibid., 22.

16. Ibid., 46.

17. Ibid., 3.

18. Ibid., 153.

19. Schefter, *The Race*, 159.

20. "Secret Soviet Moon Mission," *Red Files* Episode 3, *PBS*. February 5, 1999.

21. Lambright, *Powering Apollo*, 97.

22. Ibid., 101.

23. Ibid., 5.

24. Bizony, *The Man Who Ran the Moon*, 34.

25. Deborah Cadbury, *Space Race* (New York: HarperCollins Publishers, 2006), 266.

26. James R. Hansen, *First Man: The Life of Neil Armstrong* (New York: Simon & Schuster, 2006), 30.

27. Ibid., 53.

28. Ibid., 400.

29. Craig Nelson, *Rocket Men: The Epic Story of the First Men on the Moon* (New York: Penguin Group, 2009), 47.

30. Hansen, *First Man*, 195.

31. Cited in Hansen, *First Man*, 257.

32. Harford, *Korolev*, 277.

33. Ibid., 276.

34. Ibid., 286.

35. Ibid., 288.

36. Ibid., 291.

37. "Secret Soviet Moon Mission," *Red Files* Episode 3, *PBS*. February 5, 1999.

38. Lambright, *Powering Apollo*, 144.

39. Bizony, *The Man Who Ran the Moon*, 128.

40. Hansen, *First Man*, 307.

41. Lambright, *Powering Apollo*, 169.

42. Bizony, *The Man Who Ran the Moon*, 144.

43. Ibid., 121.

44. Ibid., 119.

45. Ibid., 134.

46. Lambright, *Powering Apollo*, 203.

47. Ibid., 206.

48. Hansen, *First Man*, 379.

49. Ibid., 399.

50. Ibid., 417.

51. Ibid., 448.

52. Ibid., 455.

53. Lambright, *Powering Apollo*, 212.

54. Jerome Wiesner, *New York Times*, Letters to the Editor, August 5, 1969) reprinted in Bizony, *The Man Who Ran The Moon*), 181

55. "Video Transcript for Archival Research Catalog (ARC) Identifier 45017," *National Archives and Records Administration* (www.archives.gov/.../transcripts/transcript-eagle-has-landed-1969-45017.pdf).

INDEX

Note: Page numbers in *italics* include illustrations, photographs and captions.